# Small Group
# Decision Making
## Communication and the Group Process

# McGraw-Hill Series In Speech

John J. O'Neill, Consulting Editor in Speech Pathology

**Baird, Knower, and Becker:** Essentials of General Speech Communication
**Fisher:** Small Group Decision Making: Communication and the Group Process
**Gibson:** A Reader in Speech Communication
**Hasling:** The Audience, the Message, the Speaker
**Kaplan:** Anatomy and Physiology of Speech
**Kruger:** Modern Debate
**Reid:** Speaking Well
**Reid:** Teaching Speech
**Robinson and Becker:** Effective Speech for the Teacher
**Tiffany and Carrell:** Phonetics: Theory and Application
**Wells:** Cleft Palate and Its Associated Speech Disorders

# Small Group Decision Making

Communication and the Group Process

**Second Edition**

B. Aubrey Fisher, Ph.D.
*Professor of Communication*
*University of Utah*

**McGraw-Hill Book Company**

New York   St. Louis   San Francisco   Auckland   Bogota   Düsseldorf
Johannesburg   London   Madrid   Mexico   Montreal   New Delhi   Panama
Paris   São Paulo   Singapore   Sydney   Tokyo   Toronto

This book was set in Times Roman by Black Dot, Inc. (ECU). The editors were Richard R. Wright and Susan Gamer; the cover was designed by Saiki & Sprung Design; the production supervisor was Diane Renda.
R. R. Donnelley & Sons Company was printer and binder.

**SMALL GROUP DECISION MAKING**
**Communication and the Group Process**

4 5 6 7 8 9 0   D O D O   8 3 2 1

**Library of Congress Cataloging in Publication Data**

Fisher, B     Aubrey, date
    Small group decision making.

    (McGraw-Hill series in speech)
    Bibliography: p.
    Includes index.
    1. Small groups.   2. Decision-making, Group.
3. Communication.   I. Title.
HM133.F55 1980        301.18'5        79-14472
ISBN 0-07-021091-8

# Contents

# Preface

*Small Group Decision Making: Communication and the Group Process* emphasizes two perspectives within the group context—decision making and communication. While groups serve a multitude of purposes in our society, probably the most typical purpose is some form of decision making. This book considers knowledge gained from studying all facets of group life—including training groups, family groups, and therapy groups—but its principal interest is the group that makes decisions in face-to-face interaction.

"Communication" is often defined as merely the transmitting and receiving of messages. While this purely structural concept of communication is certainly important, this book emphasizes the process of communication. Communication is considered *the* organizing element of the group. Through communication human beings process information, test ideas, exchange opinions, and achieve consensus on decisions. Through communication human beings develop interpersonal relationships and form "groups" from aggregates of individuals. Thus, communication is the crux of the task and social dimensions of all groups.

This book is intended for university students studying group discussion. The students' primary interest may lie in group formation, in task performance, in social systems, in decision making, in social conflict, or in a variety of other areas. The common point of departure, however, is communication which organizes people into an active social system for the purpose of performing some task—notably decision making. Therefore, this book may be used in a variety of courses in a variety of university departments at different levels in an undergraduate curriculum.

No book springs full-blown from a single person's mind. Although I assume full responsibility for my own biases and idiosyncrasies, this book is also the product of many influences, direct and indirect. Unfortunately, any attempt to list them comprehensively in order to express my appreciation will be inevitably incomplete.

In revising this book I must acknowledge the volunteered assistance of a number of friends at Northern Illinois University and Arizona State University. They provided comments from students enrolled in their group decision-making classes. I am extremely thankful and flattered that they should go out of their way to provide this assistance. What they may not realize, however, is that I have also found conversations with them especially helpful: these casual conversations provided me with numerous ideas and suggestions. While I may not have lived up to the expectations of these friends, I remain grateful for their advice.

I am particularly grateful for my association with the department of communication at the University of Utah. My colleagues, both faculty and students, provide intellectual stimulation and healthy argument which can do nothing but make us better teachers, scholars, and friends.

And to Irene—wife, companion, and lover (but no longer my secretary)—who, after twenty years of marriage (has it really been that long?), is still my best friend.

*B. Aubrey Fisher*

# Introduction

I must inform you at the outset that I am well aware of many of the jokes concerning decisions made by groups and the process of group decision making generally. I do not wish to count the times I have been told that the camel is a horse designed by a committee, or that a committee is a group of people that keeps minutes and wastes hours. I have also heard that a committee is a group of people who can do nothing individually but, as a group, can meet and decide that nothing can be done. Group decision making has been defined as the confusion of the loudest talking member multiplied by the number of members present. In regard to the propensity of organizations to appoint committees at every opportunity, it has been said that if several average Americans found themselves on an airplane about to crash, at least one of them would take time to appoint a landing committee.

Occasionally one of the jokes will contain a germ of truth. One of my favorite stories about group decision making involves the "blinder system." As the story goes, a farmer always plowed his field with a single horse hitched to the plow. Nevertheless, the farmer yelled, "Giddyup

Jack! Giddyup Casey! Giddyup Jerry! Giddyup Tom!" Day after day, his neighbor heard the farmer shouting all those names at the lone horse. One day his curiosity and bewilderment proved too much. He went to the farmer and asked why he called his horse by all the different names. "Oh," replied the farmer, "the horse's name is Jack. But, you see, he doesn't know his own strength. So I put blinders on him, and I yell all those other names. Then he works hard, and he pulls the plow mighty fine. All the time, you see, he thinks he's got all those other horses helping him"

The "blinder system" may indeed be less of a joke than it appears. Perhaps the term is simply another name for the "assembly effect." Despite all the witticisms and the alleged limitations of the group process of making decisions, it remains one of the most potent and valuable tools of our society.

The process of decision making in a social setting is vitally important in a democratic society. Nearly every facet of our society—political, legislative, judicial, economic—functions through decisions made by groups. Laws are formulated by large groups of legislators and small groups of legislative committees. National executive decisions come from meetings of the President and the Cabinet or small groups of advisors. The decisions of juries determine the fates of civil and criminal defendants in our courts. Negotiating teams decide the wages and benefits of millions of labor union members. The functioning of every business, educational, and political organization relies on decisions made by management teams. Group decisions ultimately determine what television programs we are able to view, what products are available to purchase, what new automobiles will look like, what taxes we will pay, and so forth. Although we are often unaware of the pervasive influence of group decisions, the effects of those decisions on our lives are inescapable.

The small group has been a very common phenomenon in every society from the beginning of civilization. In our society, probably the most common small group is the family. In many respects, the family is a decision-making group that has, as its principal task, the rearing of children. On the other hand, the family group is little more than a biological accident. Group members do not choose to belong to the family group, nor are they typically free to remove themselves from its confines. Runaway children and deserting mothers and fathers are not condoned by our society. Nevertheless, since families do engage in many decision-making activities, they may be considered examples of decision-making groups and included in our study. (See, for example, Tallman, 1970; Pollay, 1969.)

Certainly many other types of groups exist in our society, but they are not included in the following discussions of group decision making.

The encounter group, the laboratory training group, the consciousness-raising group, the creativity workshop, the awareness group, the assertiveness training group, etc., exist for purposes other than the performance of a group task. Moreover, the groups do not function as bona fide "groups." Rather, they remain collections of individuals, each of whom is pursuing a basically individual goal. The purpose of such groups is to provide individual members with some outcome—perhaps increased sensitivity, increased awareness, increased assertiveness, self-identity, or ventilation of aggressions and feelings. In some respects, these groups are oriented to therapeutic goals. That is, they provide a group context for the behavioral change of individual members.

Our perspective of a group will assume a specific identity of the group in which each individual member experiences a sense of membership or loyalty. The group is not merely a convenient context in which individuals make decisions. Rather, it is a specific process of making decisions socially. Group decision making, as a process, is quite different from decision making performed by individuals.

"Task-oriented group" is a generic term that identifies any one of an enormous variety of groups whose very existence depends on its performing some task. An outside authority often assigns the task to the group although individuals may, of their own volition, form a group by themselves. They may decide to form a group in order to perform some task that either cannot be accomplished by a single person or cannot be accomplished as effectively by persons acting alone. The nature of what constitutes tasks performed by groups varies widely, ranging from an assembly-line work group whose assigned task is to put bolts A, B, and C through holes 1, 2, and 3 to a group of jury members who ponder the evidence presented at a trial and decide on the guilt or innocence of a defendant. Some tasks, such as that of the jury, obviously require verbal and oral interaction. Others such as the assembly-line group, require no oral interaction at all.

The task-oriented group is by far the most prevalent group in our society. Every human organization—business, educational, service, and political—includes numerous task-oriented groups to carry out the various functions of that organization and other task-oriented groups to coordinate the efforts of all other groups. Perhaps the most interesting of these organizational subgroups are the management groups—those groups charged with the task of organizing various organizational groups and subgroups into a unitary, efficiently functioning organization. Management groups may be the most interesting because they deal directly with issues confronting every social system. And much of being a group member is knowing how to work productively with others in a social situation.

Our present focus is narrower than the broad variety of purposes implied by the term "task-oriented group." Specifically, our concern is with one of those purposes, probably the most common group purpose of all—decision making. Decision-making groups make up the bulk of all groups in most human organizations. Groups decide what new products will be manufactured, for example, and how they are to be designed, advertised, and sold. Groups decide which laws will govern a society, how those laws will be enforced, how they are to be interpreted, and even how those who violate the laws will be dealt with. Our entire society functions through the organizations that it comprises. And each organization functions through decisions made by groups within that organization. This type of group—the decision-making group—is the primary concern of this book. As later discussion will illustrate, group decision making differs inherently from individual decision making, both in the process of making decisions and in the nature of the decision-making task. Thus, the *group* is considered a decision-making *system.*

Effective decision making is regarded as a natural consequence of the members' abilities to analyze and understand the process of group decision making. But no one can aquire such an ability without active participation in group decision making. Although some people may argue that one cannot effectively experience any phenomenon without thoroughly studying it from the impartial and objective perspective of the observer, others argue just as vehemently that there is no substitute for experience. Both sides of this hackneyed controversy between the values of education and experience are probably at once both right and wrong. Knowledge of anything without experiencing it is as sterile as experiencing it without any knowledge. Students of group decision making are strongly urged to incorporate their understanding of group decision making, gained from reading this book and others, with actual participation in groups engaged in decision-making tasks. Combining understanding with experience leads to the most fruitful results and maximizes the effectiveness of group decision making.

Too often overlooked in the study of group decision making is the process of communication—the vitally essential ingredient of any social system. Communication is *the* organizing element of a social system. To highlight the study of group communication, the group is defined in a face-to-face setting that absolutely requires verbal and oral communication as the principal mode of interaction.

**WHAT TO EXPECT**

Some expectations have probably been established at this point. The first: that the group will be treated as a "whole." That is, the group is a phenomenon quite distinct from its individual members. In this sense, I am employing the concept of "holism" or "nonsummativity"—a tenet of general systems theory. We shall think of a group as a social system characterized by "wholeness" and inseparability. In this respect, we can say that the group is different from (and sometimes more than) the sum of its members. The many references to the "group" in the ensuing chapters assume a single entity which, in the context of task performance, is more significant than the specific characteristics (for example, personalities, intelligence, and abilities) of the individual persons who constitute the membership.

A second expectation should also be clear. Our focus will be on decision making, a specific task orientation of the group. The title of this book should make that emphasis clear. Every chapter is oriented to this emphasis. Certainly, aspects of groups other than the specific task are also important in understanding how groups develop and how they make decisions. The following chapters will include discussions of such phenomena of groups. Although they are not unique to decision making, they contribute to understanding the group process. For example, "norms" and "roles" exist in all groups, whether they make decisions or not. The book includes discussion of these group concepts because they are characteristics of decision-making groups.

This book is not a how-to-do-it manual for being successful in decision-making groups. You will find no lists of things to do and things not to do. You will find some suggestions for improving the effectiveness of communication and the group process. But you will probably be disappointed that these suggestions are rarely specific enough to qualify as sure-fire principles for ensuring success in group decision making. Some textbooks may make promises to the readers and suggest that if they follow the guidelines in the book, they will know how to "control" or "win" the conference or the group. The present perspective of group decision making, viewing the group as a whole and communication as an interactive process, deemphasizes and even contradicts the possibility of an individual member's controlling other members. Such control is simply not available in most groups. And when it is available (for example, to the "boss" in a group of subordinates), group decision making does not exist. Rather, the "boss" makes the decision and informs the others. The assumption that a group exists is superficial and misleading.

The primary purpose of this textbook is to generate in students an understanding of communication and the group process and, hence, of group decision making. I shall consistently emphasize understanding rather than mere knowledge. Understanding involves experience—not merely *knowing* what to do but *understanding* what is going on and then adapting to that experience.

I advocate in this book that each group member should develop the feeling of being both a participant and an observer of group decision making. In other words, the quality of group decision making improves when members are sensitive to the process of communication and group development and thus experience that process while it is occurring. As a result of observing the group during this process, you will be able to participate in the process more effectively. Being a participant-observer—that is, both a participant and an observer—requires understanding as well as knowledge of group decision making. Knowing group decision making is one thing; understanding it is much more significant. I hope that the distinction between understanding and knowledge will become apparent as you continue your reading.

## CONVENTIONAL WISDOM: BARRIER TO UNDERSTANDING

As a high school instructor some years ago, I engaged in an unresolved difference of opinion with an instructor of instrumental music in that same school. He contended that I "had it easy" teaching students the principles of communication, because high school students were able to benefit from experience. After all, they had spent ten to fifteen years actually communicating every day. But teaching a beginning student how to play the trombone, he maintained, is much more difficult since there is no basis of past experience in trombone playing from which to draw. I maintained that is was precisely for that reason that trombone playing is probably less difficult. Because the students had vast communicative experience, they possessed a large repertoire of alleged "knowledge" gained from that experience—beliefs widely held and tenaciously maintained whether or not they reflected reality. And that knowledge served to inhibit rather than assist the students' understanding of communication principles.

Nonspecialists' beliefs which are widely if carelessly held fall into the genre of "conventional wisdom." Principles from conventional wisdom are considered credible and true, not because they are actually true, but because they are conventional—because many people believe them to be true. The advertising slogan "Fifty million Frenchmen can't be wrong" reflects the simplistic wisdom based on conventionality. If so many people believe it to be true, then it must be true. But if fifty million Frenchmen believed the earth were flat, they would be wrong nonetheless. Conventionality may lead to increased credibility, but it has no direct bearing on reality.

Belief based on conventionality often takes the form of a cliché or an adage believed to possess truth because it is so familiar. We sometimes call such beliefs "folk wisdom" and fall prey to their influence. How and why conventional wisdom gains credibility through familiarity is a matter of some conjecture. The axiom "Early to bed, early to rise" may even be traced to Benjamin Franklin's mother trying to urge her recalcitrant son into bed at the appointed hour. Conventional wisdom is also not necessarily easily identified as conventional wisdom. It is difficult to resist the influence of the familiar antecedent that often precedes a principle from conventional wisdom—"Everyone knows that. . . ." Who wants to be out of step with the rest of the world?

### Dangers of Conventional Wisdom

Because conventional wisdom is conventional, it is not necessarily false. To the contrary, many clichés have some basis in fact. But accepting such "wisdom" at face value is nonetheless dangerous. At its worst, conventional wisdom is blatantly false and leads to greater problems than originally existed. At its best, conventional wisdom oversimplifies the situation and desensitizes us to reality. In the case of group decision making, members either create more social problems for themselves because of false "wisdom" or are led to inefficient and unproductive effort by the demands of irrelevant "wisdom."

Most important, axioms based purely on conventionality masquerade as real knowledge and thwart genuine understanding. In the case of group communication, which abounds with "folk wisdom," conventional wisdom severely inhibits improvement of decisional quality and improvement of group communication. In almost no other area of human endeavor do we rely so heavily and so trustingly on conventional wisdom. Although some persons suffering from arthritis continue to wear copper bracelets on their wrists, we generally seek the expert assistance of a physician when illness strikes. Although we may "starve a cold and stuff a fever" (or is it the other way around?), we don't seriously believe that eating an apple every day will protect us from illness. We generally don't rely on a pain in the foot to predict bad weather or take delight from a red sky in the evening. When we really want to know what weather is in store, we seek out the forecasts made by expert meteorologists. But when it comes to communication and the group process, everyone seems to be an expert, reverting to the oversimplifications of conventional wisdom.

### Conventional Wisdom about Group Decision Making

A representative list of examples of conventional wisdom pertaining to group decision making appears below. Many of these examples may seem sensible and eminently reasonable. You will probably discover that you may believe more than a few of them. The list is by no means complete. It samples but a minute portion of the clichés surrounding group decision making. The examples chosen from various areas of communication and the group process possess only one trait in common. They are all false.

Relying on conventional wisdom is a formidable barrier to the understanding and knowledge of group decision making. By the time you have read the ensuing chapters, you should understand why and how these examples of conventional wisdom are not true. At that time you should also be able to add many other examples to the list. When you are able to do that, you have taken one giant step forward toward a robust understanding of group decision making.

The following are examples of conventional wisdom surrounding group decision making. Without exception each item in the list is untrue.

**1** Discussion differs from debate in that members of a group discussion do not advocate argumentative positions but maintain an open mind and a spirit of free inquiry. *Corollary:* The effective decision-making group exhibits a minimum of argument and interpersonal conflict.

**2** Too much interpersonal criticism leads to communication breakdowns or develops communication barriers.

**3** To be effective, the group should strive for nearly equal participation among group members.

**4** Each member of the group should perform certain duties required of group membership. *Corollary:* The duties of the leader differ from the duties of the other group members.

**5** In the group context, getting the job done—that is, making the decisions—is more important than getting along with other group members. *Correlative opposite:* In the group context, developing close interpersonal relationships is more important than the actual performance of the decision-making task.

**6** The effective decision-making group normally follows an orderly agenda which directs its progress toward its group goal.

**7** Some people are natural-born leaders. *Corollary:* Some people possess the characteristics or quality of leadership.

**8** The personalities of the members exert the most significant effect on the process of group decision making.

**9** In the long run, a group will achieve better results through using democratic methods than through achieving specific results by other means.

**10** Almost any job that can be done by a committee can be done better by having one person responsible for it.

**11** We talk with one another, but we just don't communicate.

**12** Two-way communication is preferable to one-way communication.

**13** Compromise is the most effective strategy for resolving social conflicts.

## AN OVERVIEW OF THE BOOK

The preceding pages have established the primary focus of this book—group decision making. But there are dozens of methods one can use to approach the study of group decision making. The subtitle of this book provides an insight into the perspective employed in the ensuing chapters. Although "communication and group process" may imply two perspectives, the following chapters will attempt to illustrate that communication and group process comprise a single unified perspective.

Chapters 1 and 2 lay out the framework of the group process, and Chapters 3 and 4 describe the nature of the communicative process. While reading these chapters, you will probably note that both "communication" and "group" are defined as a process—in fact, a single process. As a process, communication and group are composed of patterned behaviors or actions that are constantly in a state of change. Neither communication nor a group should be considered as a "thing." Rather, each is a process which is constantly *in process* of continually developing. Both are continually evolving and changing over time. Some theorists have described this concept as "Being is becoming."

Chapter 1, The Group Process, employs the "leaderless group discussion" (LGD) as the prototype for understanding the complete and natural group process. Of course, a "pure" LGD (a group with 100 percent capacity for and freedom of self-regulation) probably does not exist, but every group is to some degree free to control its own functioning and its own destiny. That is, every group is to some extent an LGD. This initial chapter emphasizes how individuals organize themselves into a single entity, a group, and thereby develop the social system that is essential to effective group decision making.

Chapter 2, Dimensions of the Group Process, illustrates the interdependence of the social and task dimensions of group decision making. For group members to be effective as a decision-making system, their interpersonal relationships must also be effective. In fact, effectiveness in one dimension is usually tantamount to effectiveness in the other. But groups can be effective only to the extent that they perform tasks that are appropriate to a group. In this way, they take advantage of the uniquely social elements of group decision making.

An analysis of the communicative process reveals both structural (space-oriented) and functional (time-oriented) elements. Chapter 3 (Group Communication—Structural Elements) and Chapter 4 (Group Communication—Functional Elements) discuss these characteristics of the communicative process as they are specifically adapted to the group setting. The structural elements of group communication (for example, feedback responses, networks, gatekeeping, breakdowns, and barriers) are the most commonly known, but the functional elements may be more significant to understanding the process of group decision making. Chapter 4 illustrates how the communicative process can be viewed from a pragmatic perspective. These functional elements (for example, feedback sequences, analysis and punctuation of interaction sequences, and the content-relationship dimensions) are vital to our understanding of group decision making.

Chapter 5, The Process of Group Decision Making, traces various approaches and models which have been used to understand group task performance. This discussion emphasizes a four-phase spiral model of decision emergence, a process defined in terms of punctuated interaction sequences. This descriptive model indicates not so much that groups *make* decisions as that decisions *emerge* from the ongoing group interaction.

Developing standards for members' behavior unifies the participating persons within a functioning social system. Chapter 6 emphasizes the two most common group standards—roles and norms—and discusses them in terms of communicative behaviors. In the same sense that decisions "emerge" from group interaction, so too do group norms and each member's role.

Chapter 7, Leadership and Status, focuses on the most common of all group roles—that of leader. The discussion utilizes the functions perspective of leadership, a perspective that is consistent with the view of communication and group process. Furthermore, the process of leader emergence is described as a counterpart of decision emergence, discussed in Chapter 5. In fact, this description suggests that as group members succeed in arriving at consensus on group decisions, they develop a status hierarchy and leadership at the same time and as a part of the same process.

Chapter 8, Social Conflict and Deviance, adopts a functional approach in explaining group phenomena typically regarded as socially disruptive and therefore to be avoided or resolved. The process view of group decision making employed throughout this book suggests that conflict and deviance are really quite typical components of the group process. Therefore, they should be expected and even considered to be "normal" aspects of the entire group process. This chapter emphasizes *managing* (rather than resolving) conflict and deviance in order to take advantage of their positive functions and to avoid excessive fear of them as inherently destructive to the group process.

Chapter 9, Improving Effectiveness of Communication and the Group Process, provides general guidelines to group members. These guidelines must be quite general because of the inherent impossibility of providing the "ten easy steps" to effective group decision making. Then, too, viewing communication and group as a process emphasizes the importance of timing. Actions that would be very effective at one point in the group decision-making process would probably be quite disruptive at another point. Within these limitations, however, exist a few principles of effectiveness that stem directly from an understanding of the nature of the process.

The three appendixes provide additional information that allows the reader a deeper understanding of the process of group decision making. Appendix 1, Anatomy of a Decision, illustrates the "flavor" of group interaction during the four phases of decision emergence described in Chapter 5. This appendix includes samples from the interaction of a real decision-making group and illustrates the interaction sequences typical of each phase of group decision making. These interaction sequences provide a verbal picture of what group decision making actually looks like.

Appendix 2, Analysis of Small Group Interaction, introduces techniques for observing group interaction. Any student of group decision making should have some "feel" for observing and analyzing the interaction of group members in the process of actual group decision making. This appendix is not intended to make anyone an expert observer, but the reader who uses it can gain the sensation of observing and analyzing real-life group decision making in action.

Definitions of important concepts and terms are included at various points in the book as they are introduced, but they are rarely set off typographically so as to be handily memorized. *Defining* a concept is easy. *Understanding* it is more difficult but infinitely more valuable. But if anyone is compelled by some inexplicable urge to memorize definitions, Appendix 3, A Reader's Guide to Jargon, provides thumbnail definitions for most of the specialized terms used throughout the book.

You may decide, during your classroom study of group decision making, to omit some chapters and emphasize some chapters more than others. Or you may rearrange the chapters to fit your specific purposes. No book is sacred in the sense that no changes in its content or organization should be made in adapting to specific classroom purposes. Indeed, I expect to rearrange some chapters and to include supplemental information not contained in any chapter when I teach group decision making. All chapters of this textbook emphasize an understanding of how a group is structured, how it functions, and how it evolves through the process of human communication.

Understanding is the key to effective participation in group decision making. Central to that understanding and to effective participation is human communication in the group. One must always keep in mind that, however members of a small group may differ from one another as human beings with a unique combination of personality and abilities, they all have one thing in common: they are communicating individuals. But no one can really *teach* effective communication and group process; it can only be *learned*. I hope the truth of that seemingly paradoxical statement will become apparent during your reading of *Small Group Decision Making: Communication and the Group Process.*

# The Group Process

Robert Stroud, better known as the "birdman of Alcatraz," was truly an amazing person. Without previous background or professional training in ornithology, he became an expert on birds and bird diseases while a prisoner in solitary confinement. For most of us the most astonishing part of Stroud's story is not his self-developed expertise in ornithology but the fact that he could endure so many years of solitude. We cannot even imagine the interminable tedium of loneliness—no one to talk with day after day, no one to laugh with or argue with or just sit in silence with year after year. Most of us would probably prefer death to an indefinite sentence of absolutely solitary confinement.

One of the techniques associated with brainwashing involves social isolation. The prisoner is separated from all other prisoners and cut off from all communication with family, friends, or even the author of a book. It is not surprising that the prisoner often develops an interpersonal bond akin to friendship with the jailer. Satisfying the compelling need for companionship is preferable to insanity. The feeling of being absolutely and totally alone is simply intolerable for a normal human being.

The human is indeed a social animal. Few of us could exist as a social hermit, and we generally consider those few hermits who do exist to be crazy. This is not to say, however, that humans crave to live in huge metropolitan communities, although a glance at any of our overcrowded and smog-ridden megalopolises would seem to indicate that many do. But a person can feel just as alone in a large city as in solitary confinement. Humans have developed a need for intimate social relationships. In other words, we have developed a need to belong—typically to a small group.

The small group is the oldest and most common of all social organizations. Nations and entire civilizations have come and gone, but the small group has continued throughout all recorded history. We belong to family groups of close friends, groups of associates at work, recreational groups, ad infinitum. While our membership in some small groups may involve only interpersonal friendship and serves no purpose other than the gratification of social needs, our membership in many small groups serves a much broader purpose. Work groups in an office or a factory exist in order to perform some task within the larger social organization. Political action groups attempt to work collectively toward the solution of social problems.

Groups generally exist to accomplish some purpose. Their members perform some task which requires cooperative effort for the group to be productive. The goal of the group is, to some extent, the goal of each individual member. Without such task groups, the larger society would shrivel and die. After all, what is a society other than the sum of coordinated and interconnected small groups existing within it? Thus, groups not only have purposes, but they carry out purposes and even shape the purposes of the larger society of which they are a part.

We are concerned with small groups that exist for a definite purpose. For the moment, let us not quibble about how small a small group must be. Certainly the group must be small enough so that every member is able to know and communicate with every other member. We are also concerned with communication. A group, however large or small, cannot and does not exist without communication among its members. Communication and only communication binds individual human beings together into group membership. Communication and only communication allows group members to fulfill the group purposes.

Communication, for our purposes, inherently includes speech or oral communication. Of course, people communicate nonverbally as well, through gestures, movement, and space. But speech is the basic mode of communication in every small group. Furthermore, for our purposes, the communicating members of a small group are in a face-to-face situation. While it is theoretically possible for a group to exist by communicating only through letters or telephone, the face-to-face situation is far more typical in this society.

But our primary concern involves a more specific purpose—the purpose of making decisions. While many aspects of a small group are common to numerous types of groups with a greater variety of purposes, group decision making not only is more common but also allows for greater sophistication in developing the group process. We shall, of course, be interested in other group purposes from time to time as they contribute to our understanding of group decision making, but the emphasis of the book remains on decision making.

"Group" and "process" are two words common to nearly everyone's daily vocabulary. We use these words flippantly as though we understood them thoroughly. And, for the most part, this understanding is sufficient for everyday conversation. But writers of textbooks use these words and others as though they and their readers understood the words in the same way. I want to take no chances in this textbook.

This chapter is devoted to providing a working definition of "group process." Essential to this definition is an understanding of each of the two words individually. To provide these working definitions requires a certain amount of courageous self-assurance. Although the words are common, definitions for them abound. The reader will discover in this chapter (and in others to follow) that the viewpoint expressed in this book is in substantial agreement with some other authors and in substantial disagreement with perhaps even more.

## "PROCESS" DEFINED

A single sentence is not sufficient for an adequate definition of "process." As with most terms, process cannot be *defined* nearly so easily as it can be *understood.* A dictionary provides several elements of "process" that offer a starting point for such an understanding. According to any good dictionary, four elements are inherent in a process—*action* or acts, a continuous *change in time,* advancement or *progress* over time, and a *goal* or result. Thus, process clearly implies a time dimension as well as a space dimension in which action occurs in a continuously changing progression toward some goal.

David Berlo (1960, p. 24), discussing the process of communication, offers an excellent and often quoted definition of process:

> If we accept the concept of process, we view events and relationships as dynamic, on-going, ever-changing, continuous. When we label something as a process, we also mean that it does not have *a* beginning, *an* end, a fixed sequence of events. It is not static, at rest. It is moving. The ingredients within a process interact; each affects all of the others.

Berlo's definition is richer than the dictionary's and emphasizes the time dimension as a fluid, ever-changing evolution of ingredients. Because it is so deeply imbedded in the time dimension, any beginning or end of a process is an arbitrary point in time since the "something" is different from one instant to the next. Berlo also provides a clue to why the process is continually changing: interaction among the ingredients. Each ingredient affects and is affected by every other ingredient. The ingredients, then, are interdependent; that is, any change in one of the ingredients affects all the other ingredients.

Clearly implied in the nature of process is a marriage of the space and time dimensions—structure and action. For example, "wooden table" is a statement about the *structure* of various pieces of wood. But the *process* of "wooden table" requires an explanation of how wood was sawed from a felled tree (an arbitrary starting point in time), the sequence of steps involved in cutting and assembling those pieces of wood, applying the finish, etc., until the finished table appears (an arbitrary stopping point in time). Thus, process involves not only structure but also how and why structural changes come about during the passage of time.

## "GROUP" DEFINED

### A Smorgasbord of Definitions

Marvin E. Shaw (1976, pp. 6–12), in his integration of the research knowledge of small group phenomena, summarizes the various approaches to defining "group." Most of the definitions cited by him indicate that members of a group *share* something in common. And it is that common something which defines the existence of a group. One definition considers a group to be any collection of individuals with shared perceptions. That is, a group is composed of individuals who perceive the existence of a group and their membership in it.

Perhaps more familiar is the definition which stipulates the sharing of a common motivation or goal. Thus, workers unite to form a labor union since they have a common need to satisfy—for example, higher wages and better working conditions. The collective strength of the union, then, possesses the common purpose of securing those goals.

Still another definition based on commonality specifies the sharing of a common fate. That is, a basketball team or a debate team wins or loses as a group and not as individuals. The outcome affects all members of the group as a whole and not each member individually.

Other definitions imply that commonality is insufficient for an adequate understanding of "group." This class of definitions looks to the structure of the group—the relationships and ties among group members which bond them together into a group. Such an organizational definition perceives the social organization as the "glue" of group structure. Thus, roles, norms, values, status hierarchies, power relations, etc., are laws which govern the behavior of group members and tie them to the group. The presence of these ties defines the nature of the group.

A final category of definitions perceives the central element of a group to be interaction among its members so that the members are interdependent among themselves. It is this type of definition that Shaw (1976, p. 11) finds most acceptable—" . . . a group is defined as two or more persons who are interacting with one another in such a manner that each person influences and is influenced by each other person." (Although not everyone agrees, this book uses "interaction" and "communication" interchangeably. The two terms are considered to be synonymous.) The notion of mutually reciprocal influence among members embodies the concept of interdependence among members of a group. Although for the purpose of this book Shaw's definition is incomplete, it forms the basis for our definition of "group."

### The Principle of "Groupness"

Common sense should tell us that not every collection of individuals who talk with one another and who even exert minimal influence on one another is a "group" in the strictest sense of the term. Consider several individuals who congregate in an elevator or at a bus stop. They may carry on a conversation, but they do not constitute a real group.

Arguing whether a particular collection of persons makes up a group is about as worthwhile as arguing about the number of angels who can dance on the head of a pin. But identifying those characteristics which differentiate a group from a collection of individuals does provide insight into a more complete understanding of the nature of a group. John K. Brilhart (1978, pp. 20–21), for example, specifies five characteristics of a group:

**1**  A number of people sufficiently small for each to be aware of and have some reaction to each other . . . .
**2**  A mutually interdependent purpose in which the success of each is contingent upon the success of the others in achieving this goal.
**3**  Each person has a sense of belonging or membership, identifying himself with the other members of the group.
**4**  Oral interaction (not all of the interaction will be oral, but a significant characteristic of a discussion group is reciprocal influence exercised by talking).
**5**  Behavior based on norms and procedures accepted by all members.

You will note that Brilhart employs the smorgasbord of definitions within his five characteristics—common perceptions (1 and 3), common fate and common goal (2), interdependence and interaction (4), and organizational structure (5). Brilhart adds to the interaction characteristic the stipulation that a significant proportion of communication will be through speech, thereby virtually requiring that the group be in face-to-face confrontation. He also places a general limitation on size, which is assumed within the framework of a *small* group.

But Brilhart is more concerned with illustrating the principle of groupness, which he considers a property that groups possess and collections of individuals do not. According to Brilhart (1978, p. 21):

> "Groupness" emerges from the relationships among the people involved, just as "cubeness" emerges from the image of a set of planes, intersects and angles in specific relationships to each other. One can draw a cube with twelve lines (try it), but only if they are assembled in a definite way. Any other arrangement of the lines gives something other than a cube. Likewise, one can have a collection or set of people without having a group . . . .

Brilhart emphasizes that a group exists as something apart from the persons who constitute the membership. Just as the twelve lines form "cubeness" when placed in the proper relationships to one another, groupness forms from the relationships among the members. As the individual lines lose their individual identity when "cubeness" is perceived, so do members lose their identity as individuals when groupness is perceived. Shaw (1976, p. 14) appears to be making a similar observation when he states, ". . . a group is real to the extent that it is perceived as an entity."

For several scores of years a controversy existed among sociologists regarding the existence of a "group mind." In oversimplified terms, a group was thought to have a "mind" of its own—a way of thinking and a pattern of emotions quite separate from those of the individual members. The "group mind" idea was rejected several decades ago on the basis that the group could not be substantially different from the individuals who made up its membership. A group simply cannot have a mental life external to the mental lives of its members. In analogical terms, a finished product is limited by the raw materials of its composition. Without sulfur, oxygen, and hydrogen, for instance, sulfuric acid cannot exist.

Although a "group mind" is not implied, a group does possess an identity of its own apart from the identities of its individual members. In fact, individual members often take on the identity of the groups to which they belong as part of their identity as individuals. For example, John Doe is identified as a Democrat, a student, a communication major, a suburbanite, a Kiwanian—all groups with corresponding identities and with alleged characteristics of their own. We shall return to this point later, when we discuss the law of partial inclusion.

## The Group as a System of Behaviors

The identity of a group apart from the identities of its individual members—groupness—has been established. A more common method of expressing this same principle is literally a cliché—that is, a group is "more than the sum of its parts." This principle of nonsummativity assumes that individual components constitute a single entity and, further, is characteristic of a "system."

An entire body of theoretical knowledge, commonly known as "general system theory," may be beneficial to furthering our understanding of the group process. A "system" may be defined simply as an entity which behaves as an entity because of the interdependence of its component parts. A group system, then, is a group which behaves collectively as a group because of the interdependence of its members. Every system possesses three elements which describe its existence—structure, function, and evolution.

The *structure* of a system may be regarded as the physical arrangement of components in space at any given point in time.

The *function* of a system may be defined as the relationships among components in time. The function of a system provides order and regulation of the system. The complex of structure and function combined is necessary to describe the process of a system's operation. The function of a system is the day-to-day operation of the system. Our society provides laws which allow the system to function in a desired (that is, normal) manner. As structure refers to relationships among a system's components in space, function refers to the relationships among those components in time.

The *evolution* of a system embodies the history of the system—its progressive and possibly regressive changes through time. Every system needs a history—time to develop into an orderly structured and functioning system. The behavior of the system contains that history. Open systems, of which a group is one, possess the capacity of self-determination. Hence, the system itself may artificially accelerate the process of systemic development.

The principles of "groupness" and "process" are consistent with the evolution of a system. It takes time for a collection of individuals to form groupness. And the process of forming a group from a collection of individuals is embodied in the evolution of the group system. Those evolutionary changes as the group changes its character are also included in the evolution of the system.

If the point is not yet clear after the discussion of the many definitions of a group, I shall be explicit now. None of the definitions of a group is false or incorrect. That is, each definition is true and correct. As Shaw (1976, p. 6) says, "It is evident that different authors are simply looking at different aspects of the same phenomenon." It is a fact that the observation of reality must always proceed from the perspective of the observer. And perception is always fragmentary. Remember the story about the blind men who encountered their first elephant. The point is that none of the blind men was incorrect. Each perceived the same phenomenon from a different perspective and generalized about the whole phenomenon on the basis of his perceived information.

The truth is that reality is quite elusive. It is not so much *discovered* as it is *constructed* and manipulated. When considering human behavior from a process perspective, we confound even further the problems involved in constructing reality. Berlo (1960, p. 25) explains:

> The basis for the concept of process is the belief that the structure of physical reality cannot be *discovered* by man; it must be *created* by man. In "constructing" reality, the theorist chooses to organize his perceptions in one way or another. He may choose to say that we can call certain things "elements" or "ingredients." In doing this, he realizes that he has not discovered anything, he has created a set of tools which may or may not be useful in analyzing or describing the world. . . . The dynamic of process has limitations; nevertheless, there is more than one dynamic that can be developed for nearly any combination of events.

In "constructing" a definition of the "reality" of a group, each author attempts to organize perceptions by emphasizing those elements that he or she considers most significant. By creating a "set of tools," the author has used only one "dynamic" for describing a group and has based the definition of "group" on that perspective.

The perspective of this book is communication. It should not be puzzling, then, that our definition of a "group" will utilize that perspective. The common method of defining a group has viewed individual human beings as the components of the group system. The definition which follows does not deny that human beings constitute the group, but the individual person is not the primary unit of analysis. Rather, what the individual does—how he or she behaves—constitutes the set of tools used to describe, analyze, and define the group.

If components of a system are interdependent, they influence and are influenced by one another. Unless we consider some form of supernatural power, the only means by which one person can influence another is by behaviors—that is, the communicative exchanges among people provide the sole method by which influence or effects can be achieved. Our emphasis, then, is on what group members do and less on what they think and feel. Thus, the components of our group system are the communicative behaviors produced by individual members.

Karl Weick (1969, p. 46), in discussing "collective structure," stresses the point that as people organize into a group system, they organize their behaviors:

> . . . the elements potentially available for a collective structure consist of the behaviors that can be produced by *A* and the behaviors that can be produced by *B*. . . . The collective structure can involve only those behaviors that *A* and *B* are capable of producing. A collective structure exists when behaviors of two or more persons become interstructured and repetitive. The unit of analysis now becomes the interact or double interact and *not* the act. To identify instances of collective structure, we look for instances in which, with regularity, *A* emits an act which is followed predictably by an act from *B*, and *B*'s act then determines *A*'s subsequent act.

A collection of individuals, then, develops into a group as each member interlocks his or her behaviors with those of the other members. Consider an analogy of a basketball team. All the previous definitions of "group" are applicable to the team. But for our purposes, the team possesses "groupness" to the extent that the behaviors of the players are interdependent, interstructured, and predictable. Sportscasters are fond of saying that a team has played together so long that the players "know each other's moves." To rephrase this cliché, players can, on the basis of their own acts, predict what other players will do next and what they themselves will do subsequently. A "fast break" or "out-of-bounds play" is based on structuring the players' behaviors interdependently so that the result of the cluster of interdependent behaviors is a player "free" to take a shot. On the other hand, some basketball teams are characterized by "free-lancing," which may be another way of saying that the players' behaviors are not interdependent but are based on each player's behaving as an individual. Hence, a free-lance team is more a collection of individuals than a group.

Weick expresses more concern, however, with the "interact" or "double interact" and less with the single act. In fact, interacts and double interacts are simply groupings of acts. An interact is composed of two contiguous acts, while a double interact is a combination of three contiguous acts. A emits an act (a single act), which is followed by an act from B (an interact), which is followed by a third act from A (a double interact). If the emphasis is on interdependent acts, the more important unit of analysis is the interact or double interact. In this way, acts are seen within the context of preceding and succeeding acts. The structure of the group, then, is defined by those sequences of acts which recur so often that one can predict what kinds of acts tend to follow or precede other kinds of acts. Because interdependence of individuals is achieved by mutual influence through communication, the organizing element of the group system is communication. And communication and communicative exchanges—acts, interacts, and double interacts—are the ingredients for analyzing the system—not the individual members.

Viewing a group as a system of behaviors may be disconcerting to some. A system of behaviors is not tangible. You can't touch or hold a behavior. It doesn't exist in space. Hence, a group seems somewhat mystical as a result. In a way, this is very true. Groups are less tangible than we often believe. But communicative behaviors can be observed— unlike such internal phenomena as interpersonal liking, beliefs, and feelings. And communicative behaviors are apparently the only method by which interdependence or mutual influence can be achieved or observed.

As the discussion of communication in Chapter 4 will illustrate, the processes of communication and of group merge into virtually a single process. In this sense, the subtitle of this book, *Communication and the Group Process,* refers not to two different elements but to a single process. The process of communication is virtually indistinguishable from the process of group. The element that unifies the communicative process and the group process is, theoretically, the broad framework of general system theory—a popular theoretical view within the study of groups and social organizations.

Therefore, a group will be defined as a collection of individuals whose communicative behaviors—specifically, acts, interacts, and double interacts—become interstructured and repetitive in the form of predict- able patterns. To the extent that the communicative behaviors of group members are interstructured, the attributes used to characterize a group may be assumed to exist.

### The Leaderless Group Discussion (LGD)

For the purpose of understanding fully the "natural" process of a group, this book will consider the leaderless group discussion (LGD) as the prototype of a group. Contrary to the implication of its name, the LGD is not a group of talkative people who do not have a leader. The characteris- tic that distinguishes an LGD from other groups is the group's capacity for self-determination. That is, an LGD is affected or influenced by a minimum of authority or forces which are external to the group. For example, a committee formed within a larger organization is subject to the demands and pressures of the larger organization. The organization imposes on the committee certain assigned duties, deadlines for task completion, etc., and the activities of the committee are restricted by the need to meet the needs and goals of the organization. The LGD, to the contrary, has a broader capacity to decide for itself its own goals, its own norms, its own roles, and its own status hierarchy. Rather than having its leadership assigned by some external authority, the LGD determines its own leader. Hence, "leaderless group discussion" implies not the absence of leadership altogether but the absence of externally assigned leadership.

A second characteristic of an LGD concerns the external pressure on all status levels. I shall assume the membership of the LGD to be peers at the time the group is formed. A large organization endows its members with status and structures those status levels into a hierarchy. A corporation, for example, has directors, managers, assistant managers, supervisors, and assembly-line workers. A committee formed within this corporation would reflect the status hierarchy of the larger corporation. Consider the military—perhaps the most status-conscious of all human organizations. Members of the military visibly display their status on their sleeves or shoulders. Understandably, a group composed of military personnel would be highly susceptible to the status demands of the larger organization. But to avoid the external pressures of a larger organization's status hierarchy, the LGD is generally thought to consist of members with the same initial status.

For our purposes, we shall also consider an LGD to be a "zero-history" group. That is, our LGD is observed from its first formation—the point of zero history. It has already been established that the process of developing groupness takes time. So that the complete process of group formation can be observed, observation of the group must begin at the point of its inception as a collection of individuals. The zero-history group, then, embodies the total history of the group.

To the extent that external forces impinge upon the self-determination of the group members, the "natural" group process is incomplete. This is not to say that a group which is subject to external pressures is not natural. Indeed, most groups in the real world are probably not "pure" LGDs. But an LGD embodies the entire group process—the development of its entire group culture. Our purpose is to look at the entire group process. The LGD allows us to do that. A non-LGD reflects something less than the whole process with a portion of the group process predetermined by external authorities. Thus, the LGD reflects the group process in its "pure" or "natural" state.

Realistically, of course, no group is either totally free from external authority or totally controlled by external forces. In fact, forming a true LGD in a classroom is practically impossible. Every classroom group is subject to external restrictions—the presence of the instructor, the "captivity" of the classroom, the status distinctions from the student culture, the environmental pressure of classroom assignments and the end of the quarter or semester, or the due date for a group project. Even if the instructor does not assign a specific task but allows the classroom group to select its own, the group is "forced" to choose its own task rather than voluntarily forming around a common need "felt" by the group members. But even though a classroom group is not truly an LGD, external restrictions are or can be quite minimal. Although the LGD is defined in its "pure" form, realistically we expect that the LGD in real life is to some extent "impure."

One might ask at this point why we are employing the LGD as the model for a group when it is so "unrealistic." Such a reaction, however, misses the point. Every group is, to some extent, an LGD. In other words, being an LGD (that is, having the capacity to regulate itself, free from the constraints of an external authority) is not a characteristic which a group possesses or lacks. It is a continuum—a characteristic which every group possesses to some degree. In a "pure" LGD, the capacity for self-regulation is highly prominent. The members are keenly aware of their own self-regulatory powers. In groups which are not LGDs to any significant extent (that is, groups whose regulation by external authority structures is strong, such as groups within a larger organization and families), *some* self-regulating capacity is still present. On the other hand, members of such groups are less keenly aware of their power to govern themselves. Their "informal" structure may not be recognized or approved by the external authority, but it is often much more powerful than the official or "formal" structures of authority.

Later chapters will briefly discuss specific types of "real-world" groups which are not LGDs to the same extent as the "pure" form that might exist in the classroom. But the self-regulating capacity of all groups is still present in these "realistic" groups when the group is viewed as a process. Often the group process is delayed, and occasionally it is thwarted, by overly powerful external authorities. However, with some exceptions (for example, the military, prisons, and some bureaucracies), the decision-making group is an LGD to a considerable extent and is thus capable of a good deal of self-regulation. To the degree that external authorities usurp the group's capacity, the entire group process is not allowed to develop.

Therefore, to utilize the LGD in its fullest possible sense is to provide a benchmark against which other groups can be compared. At that point, it becomes possible to evaluate whether any group (depending on the nature of the task and whether the group can function effectively to perform that task) should have more or less self-regulating capacity.

### The Size of the "Small" Group

Our definition of "group" as a process and as a system of behaviors does not include the characteristic of size which seems to be implied by the word "small." You will recall, however, that Brilhart's (1978) five characteristics of "groupness" include the characteristic that the group be small enough so that each member knows, and is able to react to, every other member. Beyond this very general limitation, however, the criterion of size is rather trivial in defining group as process.

Sociologists have long defined various levels of human society— individual, dyad, group, organization, society (or culture). Communication specialists have also found these distinctions popular in separating the field of communication into various sociological settings—that is, intrapersonal communication, interpersonal communication, group communication, organizational communication, and mass communication. Within the study of communication, at least, these distinctions are decreasing in importance, so that the process of communication is typically viewed as the same, regardless of the sociological setting in which it occurs. Under any circumstances, the distinction between one sociological level and another, on the basis of size alone, is virtually impossible to determine. For our purposes, at least, I intend to draw no distinction between what is typically called "interpersonal" communication and group communication. The process of communication in both settings is the same.

Given the nature of group as process, then, I cannot provide any upper limits of size. That is, I will not provide any size limitation at which a group, after having increased to that size, becomes an organization. I shall adhere to Brilhart's very general characteristic that a group is sufficiently small for each member to be able to know and react to every other member. At the lower limit of the size criterion, however, I will stipulate that a group includes at least three people.

Although a dyad (that is, two persons) is similar in many respects to a group, it is a much simpler—that is, a less complex—social system. The difference created by adding even one person to a dyad (thus involving three members instead of two) provides a much more complex social system. Even a three-person group embodies many characteristics not present in a dyad. For example, in a dyad only one channel exists to "connect" the communicators. In other words, a dyad cannot have a communication network in the sense that some channels are used more often than others. A network in a dyad is impossible. In a three-person group, however, three channels are possible (A-B, A-C, and B-C). Thus, a network involving channel selectivity is possible.

It is also impossible for a deviant to exist in a dyad. Any norm that exists between two persons must have the recognition and consent of both members, otherwise, it ceases to exist as a norm. On the other hand, a norm in a three-member group may result from the imposition of the norm by a majority or coalition of two members on the third member.

Mortensen (1972, pp. 267–268) also indicates several characteristics of dyadic interaction that are quite different from interaction in a group. For one thing, he says that the dyad is "a highly unstable, tension-producing form of interchange. It is unstable because everything depends on the continuous reactions of only one person—either A or B." In other words, either member of a dyad can stop all the interaction by simply withdrawing. In a three-member group, however, interaction does not cease because of the whims or the actions of only a single person. That is, no one person has the power to destroy or disrupt completely the entire social system.

Mortensen goes on to indicate that dyads are also vulnerable to a highly complementary interactive relationship. That is, the dyad tends typically to gravitate, for example, toward a dominant-submissive relationship between the two participants. A dyad in the form of an interview exemplifies such a relationship. One of the members is quite active, and the other member is quite passive. In other words, one person asks the questions, and the other person answers the questions. But, because the dyad is so vulnerable to the activities of either person, the passive member also has ultimate veto power over the relationship. The passive member can, at any time, void the relationship by refusing to respond. As a result, the dyad is much more unstable than a group of three or more members.

Mortensen summarizes the distinctions between dyadic and group interaction. He suggests that, particularly in a task-oriented situation, a dyad exhibits more tension and is more unstable than a three-member group. Furthermore, the proportion of verbal activity and the nature of the verbal activity are quite different from the interaction that occurs when three or more members are present.

Perhaps the most significant difference between the dyad and the group is the feeling of identification with the larger system—a feeling that is seldom present in a dyad. One member of a classroom group verbalized this feeling of interdependence most vividly in responding to the group's interaction during a specific group meeting. She described her personal reactions in her diary: "A group project, such as this, creates a great amount of tension in those involved, because how you do certain things may be quite different from someone else. And yet, you're dependent on each other for the overall success or failure. And you feel a responsibility for success of the others as well as yourself."

This feeling of mutual interdependence, the feeling of interpersonal responsibility for the success and failure of other members as well as for yourself, is highly similar to Brilhart's second characteristic of "groupness." He specifies that groupness implies a mutually interdependent purpose so that individual success is contingent upon the success (or failure) of the entire group. The responsibility for success is, furthermore, a two-way responsibility. Members of a group tend to feel responsible for the success of the entire group as well as to develop even greater resentment toward any other group members who do not share their portion of the responsibility.

In a group, then, individual members tend to be highly aware of their responsibility, whether it stems from social pressure or the fulfillment of a personal need. Nevertheless, that feeling of interdependence in a group is much stronger and more vital than it is in a dyad. In the two-member social system, any responsibility is toward only one other person and not toward an entity apart from the individual members—that is, the group.

Our definition of "group" is now rather complete—three or more individuals whose communicative behaviors become interstructured and repetitive in the form of predictable patterns. I hasten to reiterate that, although the group process includes a minimum of three people, the process of communication in a group is not unlike the process of communication in a dyad. In fact, what is true of a dyad is undoubtedly true of a group. The reverse, however, is not so evident. Many characteristics of a group are not present in a dyad. Nevertheless, discussions of the social and task dimensions of a group (in Chapter 2) will also reflect what is known about dyadic interaction. I shall continue to assume that what is true of dyadic interaction is also true of group interaction.

## THE INDIVIDUAL AND THE GROUP

Each human being is, to some extent, unique. Every man and woman possesses a self that is uniquely his or hers. Some people may believe that engaging in group decision making will have little impact on one's self or self-concept; therefore, the group is little more than a reflection of the summed self-concepts of those persons who make up the group membership. On the other hand, another school of thought might conclude that the individual self-concept is forced to conform to the overwhelming power of the group itself. Therefore, the self-concept becomes subjected to the social pressures of conformity and is influenced *by* the group process rather than influencing it.

In actuality, it is more probable that both these explained relationships between self-concept and group are fundamentally inaccurate. For one thing, each explanation assumes a linear relationship between group and individual—either that the group influences the individual or that the individual influences the group. In all likelihood, any influence which exists in the group process is not totally linear or "one-way." The self-concept of each individual member and the group process as a whole undoubtedly develop simultaneously, each influencing the other and being influenced by the other. Certainly, individual members will affect the performance of any group. Moreover, the nature of the group will affect the self-concepts of any and all members within it. But rather than providing a simple choice between which influence is stronger (the group or the individual selves), the relationship between the two is more accurately understood as a *mutual* development. The selves of the individual members nurture and grow with the group just as the entire group process nurtures and grows with each individual self.

## Social Comparison

Leon Festinger (1950, 1954), a social psychologist, believes that every human being possesses a need to evaluate self. That is, each person's self-concept embodies within it some quest or desire for evaluation. For example, a person with a certain opinion is generally dissatisfied unless or until that opinion can be judged to be correct. A person feels he or she has certain abilities and needs to know how good those abilities are. Often the need to evaluate one's own self-perceived abilities and qualities leads to comparing those abilities and qualities with those of other people. Simple nonsocial and objective means for comparison are often unavailable or do not exist at all. Festinger therefore developed his theory of "social comparison."

Festinger suggests that people are most likely to compare themselves with other people who are quite similar and with whom they are in close interpersonal contact. It would be foolish, for example, for junior high school students to compare their intellectual achievements with those of college graduates. The comparison with another person would most likely involve another junior high school student, probably a friend or classmate. In other words, the evaluation of the self will be more accurate when the differences between oneself and others are relatively small.

In the case of extreme dissimilarity between the persons being compared, Festinger suggests that the man or woman engaging in social comparison can still cope merely by avoiding situations that are very dissimilar. In other words, social comparison also includes the notion of selectivity. That is, a person chooses to engage in social comparison with similar persons and tends to avoid comparison with those who are extremely dissimilar.

This selective phenomenon of social comparison thus leads to the formation of groups which are quite homogeneous—that is, whose members have similar opinions, abilities, and qualities. In this way, liberals tend to associate with other liberals and, consequently, compare their own liberal qualities with those of their fellow members. Conservatives associate and compare themselves with other conservatives and succeed in maintaining their own conservatism.

Festinger's theory of social comparison, then, may explain why and how self-concepts remain relatively stable over long periods despite the vast amounts of social interaction. Those interactions involve comparisons with people who have similar selves so that the person's self-concept is maintained and even reinforced through social comparison.

Of course, any change in a person's "life space" (for example, a move to a new town, a transfer to a new job, a change in schools) will bring that person into contact with a different—and unfamiliar—social situation. The new situation will thus lead to new social comparison processes because of the reduced capacity to exercise choice or selectivity in objects for social comparison.

The point is this: When social comparison processes are functioning and a person is attempting to evaluate his or her own abilities, opinions, and qualities, the self-concept remains quite stable and unchanging, owing to the selection of appropriate objects (persons) and social situations used for comparison. These persons and situations are considered to be "appropriate" to the extent that they are quite similar to one's present self-concept. Nevertheless, changes in social situations, perhaps due to normal life changes during the process of living in our mobile society, often bring the person into contact with new social situations and, thus, with other persons to be used as objects for social comparison. In that case, the self-concepts change, sometimes quite drastically.

## Self-Disclosure

Each person possesses many different "selves" rather than a single, uncomplicated self-concept. One differentiation among these selves is that between "public self" and "private self." That is, each person possesses a self that is visible to, and known by, friends and acquaintances. At the same time, parts of the self remain private in the sense that they are qualities of which others have little or no knowledge. Of course, the closer a friendship, and thus, the greater the communication between two persons, the greater the proportion of each individual self that will be public to the other.

A person who is providing information to someone else about the private self may be said to be engaging in "self-disclosure" or "self-disclosing communication." It is important to note, however, that self-disclosures do not necessarily include anything and everything that one may relate to another about oneself. Self-disclosing communication is said to occur when the information about self that is given to another person includes some information that the other would not know or be able to discover through other means. In Culbert's terms, "Self disclosure refers to an individual's explicitly communicating to one or more persons information that he believes these others would be unlikely to acquire unless he himself discloses it" (1967, p. 2).

One significant characteristic of self-disclosure is the phenomenon of reciprocity. That is, as one person makes self-disclosures to another, the other typically responds with self-disclosures. In fact, in reviewing research on self-disclosure, Pearce and Sharp (1973, p. 418) call reciprocity the "best documented characteristic of self-disclosing communication." In other words, as *A* self-discloses to *B, B* tends to self-disclose to *A*. This reciprocating self-disclosing communication, then, results in something of a snowball effect. As communication contains a certain amount of self-disclosure, more self-disclosure will be contained in further communication in ever-increasing amounts. Thus, if B reciprocates A's self-disclosure with further self-disclosing communication of his or her own, A will typically reciprocate and engage in even more self-disclosing communication, thereby influencing B to engage in additional self-disclosure, and so on.

Consider a hypothetical example of unreciprocated self-disclosure. You tell an acquaintance something about yourself which you consider quite private. Your acquaintance appears to be interested in this information but doesn't give you any intimate information in return. You are unlikely to continue exposing your private self to the other person unless you get something in return. This communicative procedure is analogous to an economic transaction in which you have invested something of yourself but feel that the other person has invested nothing. Self-disclosure, then, is similar to a financial transaction in which information about the self is the commodity being transacted.

Although self-disclosing communication tends to escalate over time—that is, to increase steadily during the formation of a social relationship—there is reason to believe that this escalation does not continue indefinitely. That is, self-disclosure early in a social relationship is rather slight but soon increases as a result of reciprocated self-disclosing messages of the participants, up to a point at which self-disclosure, in terms of both amount and reciprocity, decreases. Therefore, a mature social relationship between two close friends or husband and wife, for example, contains less self-disclosure than during an earlier time when their relationship was still being developed. This decrease in self-disclosing communication appears to be intuitively sensible. After so much self-disclosure during the development of a close relationship, each person's private self contains less information of which the other person is unaware. That information has, during past self-disclosure, become part of the public self. Consequently, there is less information about each person's self to be disclosed to the other. Furthermore, there is little necessity for self-disclosing communication in the sense that the closeness or the intimacy of the relationship already contains within it large investments or commitments by the participants. Having made those commitments, each person needs progressively less self-disclosure in order to maintain the relationship.

A further characteristic of self-disclosing communication is appropriateness. A self-disclosure may be appropriate or inappropriate in *timing:* that is, *when* the act of self-disclosure takes place. Indeed, the timing of certain communicative behaviors is a highly important factor in communication and the group process and will be discussed again and again throughout this book. There may also be appropriateness or inappropriateness of *content.* Before discussing appropriateness of self-disclosing communication, it is necessary to note differences in content between various kinds of self-disclosure. One self-disclosing comment is not necessarily the same as another self-disclosing comment. For example, certain topics are much more easily disclosed than are others. If I inform you that I once taught in South Dakota high schools, I am engaging in self-disclosure. That is information about myself which you would probably not know (or care about, for that matter) unless I told you. This topic is "safe" and is quite appropriate as self-disclosing communication to an early acquaintance. On the other hand, some topics (such as my sex life or love life) would be highly inappropriate. Furthermore, within any given topic area, the "depth" of self-disclosure can vary considerably. That is, I could make self-disclosures about my sex life or love life in a very intimate or a nonintimate manner. A simple statement, "I dated my wife for three years before we were married," is a self-disclosure about my love life; but it is not a very intimate statement. (I am not willing to provide an example of a statement with high intimacy on this particular topic.) Altman and Taylor (1973) list thirteen topics or subjects which differ (for most people) in the level of intimacy. These topics include religion; marriage and children; dating, sex, and love; parental family; physical condition and appearance; money and property; politics; emotions; interests and hobbies; interpersonal relationships; personal attitudes and values; school and work; and demographical or biographical characteristics. Keep in mind, also, that specific self-disclosing communication within any of those thirteen topics ranges from a very intimate statement to a not-so-intimate remark.

It is now possible to discuss the appropriateness of self-disclosing communication itself. We often tend to believe, quite erroneously, that self-disclosure or "openness" of communication with others leads to a close interpersonal relationship and generally more effective communication. Although self-disclosure is quite common and typical of (perhaps even essential to) friendship and close interpersonal relationships, the timing of self-disclosing communication is nonetheless highly significant. Horenstein and Gilbert (1976) conducted some research which discovered, for example, that when strangers engage in communication for the first time, self-disclosure leads to a dislike of the self-disclosing person and a desire to avoid further interaction with that person. While more intimate self-disclosures would probably lead to greater anxiety and increased discomfort in that person, the researchers suggest that any self-disclosure between strangers (that is, first acquaintances) tends to make the other person feel uncomfortable, experience anxiety, and therefore avoid further interaction. This reaction may be similar to embarrassment and a feeling that "I don't know you that well."

Those who suggest that direct and open and self-disclosing communication is essential to healthy relationships and one's own well-being must remember that the openness of communication—particularly of self-disclosure—is effective only when it is appropriate to the situation. And of particular significance to appropriateness is the timing of self-disclosure—that is, when self-disclosure occurs. Too much self-disclosure too early in a relationship will probably lead to dislike and thus to the early disintegration of the relationship.

Altman and Taylor (1973) also assert that reciprocity of self-disclosure is more important in forming interpersonal relationships than the actual amount of self-disclosure. That is, the interpersonal relationship is never "one-way." It is the result of each communicator's investment in the relationship, so that one person's self-disclosing communication leads to self-disclosure by the other person and back again. Thus, when someone tells you something about himself or herself, this disclosure is your cue to reciprocate, to engage in your own self-disclosure, if you want the relationship to continue to grow.

Reciprocity is also important in terms of level of intimacy. If a self-disclosure is very intimate and the response to it is not nearly so intimate, the person who made the initial self-disclosure will feel that it has not been reciprocated. The converse is also true: if one person discloses information which is relatively "safe" (that is, not very intimate), and the response is on a much higher level of intimacy, the person responding runs the risk of the "too much too soon" problem discussed earlier. In other words, an appropriate response to a self-disclosing comment is not simply another self-disclosure, but self-disclosure at a similar level of intimacy or a similar depth of response.

The phenomenon of self-disclosure as a part of human communication is a highly popular topic among communication scholars. It bridges the gap between the self and the group by providing one significant interpersonal aspect of the individual self. Central to the notion of self-disclosure is the realization that, as noted earlier, each person has a part of self which is public as well as another part which is private. The person, then, is able to choose whether to reveal a part of that private self to the other person. Furthermore, the person possesses the capacity to choose how much of the private self will be revealed to the other person. In making the revelation, the person is investing or committing a part of self to the relationship. And that investment is likely to result in further investment, further commitment. Moreover, the relationship comes to take on significance to the act of human communication. The relationship thus becomes greater than the self of each individual communicator. This phenomenon of the social relationship embodied in every act of human communication is implicit in the characteristic of "groupness."

### Interpersonal Trust

According to Gulley and Leathers (1977, p. 213), "Interpersonal trust is that relationship that exists when the interactants base their behavior on the expectation and prediction that each will act in mutually beneficial ways as they strive to achieve objectives that involve some degree of risk." Interpersonal trust is a characteristic of every successful decision-making group. Without trust among members, groups are destined to substandard performance.

Keep in mind that trust characterizes the *relationship* rather than an *attitude* held by any of the persons. Trust is not "one-way" but involves all members in the situation engaging in the same relationship called "trust." If A trusts B but B does not trust A, then trust cannot be said to characterize the relationship. Rather, it would refer to a person's attitude.

Developing interpersonal trust is, like a group, a process. It takes time. In order for each person to develop some expectations of the other person and to be able to predict that person's behavior, trust must include some past history of interaction among the members of the relationship. A trusting relationship cannot develop overnight. It is not an immediate occurrence, but, rather, it emerges from the relationship after it has endured for some time.

Furthermore, the mutuality of interpersonal trust involves the achievement of goals and objectives. No one engages in a trusting relationship with another for purposes of self-satisfaction or self-aggrandizement. Rather, interpersonal trust involves objectives that are shared by, or common to, all participants in the situation. Typically, such a goal is one that either cannot be accomplished or can be accomplished only with utmost difficulty by one person functioning alone. A team or group is, then, essential to accomplishing the goal.

Pearce (1974) suggests a further characteristic of interpersonal trust that will become even more important when the social and task dimensions of the group process are discussed in Chapter 2. According to Pearce (p. 242), ". . . even if the trusted person is well-intentioned and knowledgeable . . . , he must be perceived as capable of performing the appropriate behavior to be trusted." If you go swimming on the "buddy system" with a fellow swimmer, the expectation is that you will help if your buddy gets into trouble and that your buddy will save you if you get into danger in the water. Nevertheless, if either of you is a poor swimmer, interpersonal trust cannot exist to a significant degree. Despite your respective good intentions and helpful attitudes, the capability of performing the necessary lifesaving behaviors essential to the trusting situation of the buddy system may be highly questionable. Consequently, the expectations and predictions of the other person's behaviors must include some expectation and predictability of that person's capability of performing the trusting behavior appropriate to that situation. All the good intentions in the world are not likely to increase your trust in your swimming buddy unless you also believe in his or her capability to save you should the need arise.

Interpersonal trust, then, is inevitably a characteristic of the entire social situation. It involves not just the attitudes of one or more individuals but, also, mutually other-directed definitions of the relationship. And those definitions are reciprocated by all participants in the situation. Furthermore, the situation must involve some history of past interaction, the development of a set of expectations and predictions of one another's behaviors. Of course, this predictability of one another's actions is based on what occurred during the past interaction. The situation of interpersonal trust also allows for the possibility of alternative options as responses to each person's invitations to engage in trust.

In this respect, as Pearce (1974) points out, to talk about interpersonal trust with any understanding is to consider the interdependence involved in the situation, the attitudes and expectations of all participants, and the mutuality and reciprocity of those attitudes and expectations, as well as behaviors and reciprocated behaviors during human communication.

### Risk

Scholars who write about self-disclosing communication often discuss the "bus-rider phenomenon": the tendency of human beings to reveal more of their selves to strangers whom they never expect to engage in further interaction (such as a fellow bus-rider) than to an acquaintance whom they do expect to see again. The bus-rider phenomenon emphasizes the fact that interaction with strangers whom one will probably not meet again involves very little risk to the person. There is simply no commitment to the relationship or to developing the relationship. Therefore, anything you say in the relationship will not come back later to haunt you. Consequently, such communication involves little commitment to any social relationship and, hence, is of little importance to the social self.

The concept of commitment will arise again in future chapters dealing more specifically with communication and the group process. Fundamental to any commitment, to any development of a group, is the element of risk that is present in the situation. Commitment to any group, to any loyalty, to any person, inherently and inevitably involves the risk of being wrong, of appearing foolish in the presence of others. It is easy to do things when you are alone which would be extraordinarily difficult or embarrassing if done when you are with others. Engaging in group decision making requires the ability to risk, and if necessary to endure, frustration, disappointment, and ridicule or shame. Without that commitment by all or nearly all members of a decision-making group, little will be accomplished; and decisions, if made, will be of predictably poor quality.

We are all probably familiar with the saying "It is better to keep your mouth shut and be thought a fool than to open it and remove all doubt." That cliché contains the questionable advice to avoid risk, to avoid commitment, to be safe when interacting with others. Such advice not only reveals a naive view of social interaction but—more important—is incredibly bad counsel for prospective members of decision-making groups. Nevertheless, many people implicitly adhere to this axiom in social relationships and avoid the risk inherent in committing themselves to a group or a social environment.

When we engage in social risk, we are essentially gambling on a successful outcome. When one "hides" self and avoids risk, one is refusing to gamble. But if committing oneself to a social situation risks the possibility of failure, avoiding that commitment positively assures the lack of success. Social commitment and risk-taking also allow for the possibility of success and increased self-esteem as well as, for example, successful decision making in a group. Avoiding commitment and refusing to gamble assures failure. There is no possibility of success for either the self or the group process.

The element of risk cannot be overemphasized in the group process. Anyone who engages in communication with another person, if that communication is to be effective and meaningful, must inevitably assume some risk of self. Communicators, to be right, must risk being wrong. Of course, everyone who takes a risk must be aware that the consequences may be negative. But avoiding negative consequences will accomplish little. Moreover, achieving positive results more than compensates for any earlier feelings of risk. I am reminded of the biblical parable concerning the servant who buried the talents he was given. He thus avoided losing his money, but he did not profit either. Stated another way, to avoid any situation that includes an element of risk is ultimately to lose.

Engaging in risk, increasing vulnerability to fellow members of a group, is prerequisite to an effective group process. To avoid risk, for whatever reason and with whatever strategy one wishes to employ, is to deny the group its ability to function with maximum effectiveness. Furthermore, it is to deny your own self the opportunity to grow and to develop your own abilities and qualities. It may well be a form of social paranoia, although probably not in any psychopathological sense that would require therapy. Rather, such paranoia is a common neurosis that discourages the development of the human potential and fosters ineffective communication and inadequate group functioning.

## SUMMARY

Understanding the nature of group process requires an understanding of the nature of "group" and "process." Process involves the dynamic relationships of events in an ongoing, continuous sequence of time. Each ingredient of the process affects, and is affected by, every other ingredient as changes in the process evolve through time. Although many perspectives have been used to define "group," this book utilizes the perspective of interdependence and interaction. A collection of individuals develops "groupness" over time so that the identity of a group exists apart from the separate identities of its individual members.

A group is conceived to be a system characterized by its structure (the pattern of relationships among components at any given point in time), its function (the regulatory, recurring day-to-day relationships among components through time), and its evolution (the continuous changes of structure and function over a long period). Rather than perceiving individual persons as the components of the group system, this book considers communicative behaviors as the units for defining, observing, and analyzing the group system. Thus, a group is a collection of individual persons whose communicative behaviors—specifically acts, interacts, and double interacts—become interstructured and repetitive in the form of predictable patterns. The prototype group that embodies all the elements of group process and is minimally inhibited by external or environmental constraints is the leaderless group discussion (LGD).

Individual persons join groups as a result of social-comparison processes. Successful group decision making is thus a direct result of each person's integration into group membership. Central to this integrative process are the mutual and reciprocal functionings of self-disclosure, interpersonal trust, and risk.

Chapter 2

# Dimensions of
# the Group Process

Our society has long tended to draw rather clear distinctions between allegedly opposing phenomena. For example, we classify a person as a liberal or a conservative, a Democrat or a Republican, a blue-collar worker or a white-collar worker. It is no wonder, then, that we differentiate between two dimensions of group decision making—task and social. Because people are involved in a group, the social dimension is evident. And because the group is expected to come to agreement on a decision, the task dimension is also important.

It is unfortunate but true that the task and social dimensions of group decision making are often viewed in conflict with each other. This view seems to reflect the hackneyed conflict between reason and faith, science and the humanities, classicism and romanticism, logic and emotions. There have been numerous attempts to provide detailed plans and instructions for making a group decision which avoids social or emotional influence. The assumption underlying these proposals is apparently that a decision is better when based on an impersonal and critical evaluation of the facts. We are cautioned against emotional reactions in the apparent belief that such reactions lower the quality of the group decision.

The purpose of this chapter is to provide an insight into the task and social dimensions of group process. Consistent with the perspective of interdependence involved in group process, these two dimensions will be viewed as inseparable. This chapter attempts to illustrate how the social dimension affects group decision making and, consequently, how group decision-making tasks are, or should be, fundamentally different from decision-making tasks performed by individuals.

## INTERDEPENDENCE OF SOCIAL AND TASK DIMENSIONS

Both task and social dimensions are inherent in the process of group decision making. No decision-making group exists without both dimensions. It is vitally important to understand each of them in order to understand effective group decision making and to participate effectively in a decision-making group. "Task dimension" refers to the relationship between group members and the work they are to perform—the job they have to do and how they go about doing it. "Social dimension" refers to the relationships of group members with one another—how they feel toward one another and about their membership in the group.

For some reason the task and social areas of the group process have typically been viewed separately. Tuckman (1965), for example, indicates that two problems continuously confront a group during its period of development—group structure (social) and task activity. Thus, group members deal with each type of problem separately throughout their existence as a group. According to Tuckman, certain comments aid in developing the group structure, and other comments are directed toward accomplishing the group's task. Robert F. Bales's (1950) system of classifying behaviors or acts of group members—"interaction process analysis" (IPA)—specifically labels every comment as oriented toward either the social area or the task area. Such a total separation is probably unwise. Common sense should tell us that a comment such as "Aw, you don't know what you're talking about!" implies not only an outright rejection of a contributed idea (a task comment) but an impact as well on the social relationship of at least two members. Bales's (1970, pp. 471–491) revision of his IPA categories of acts seems to reveal second thoughts about drawing such a clear distinction between social and task comments.

This viewpoint agrees with the position of Kelley and Thibaut (1954, p. 736), who feel that the task and social dimensions of group process are highly interdependent—in fact "virtually indistinguishable" from each

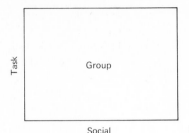

Figure 2-1   "Dimensions" of the group process.

other. That is, one may separate the two from a theoretical perspective, but the interaction between the two makes them virtually inseparable in practice. Cattell (1955) and Bales (1953), on other occasions, have also emphasized the interdependence of the two dimensions.

There is a reason for using the term "dimension" to refer to the task and social areas of group process. Figure 2-1 illustrates the two-dimensional existence of a plane geometrical figure. A rectangle exists in two dimensions—height and width. Height cannot be separated from width without destroying the rectangle itself. Although the height or width may be observed and measured separately, the two dimensions are inseparable within the definition of the rectangle. The same inherent and inseparable relationship is true of the task and social dimensions of a group process. Without either dimension, the group process does not exist.

Several people have attempted to separate the task from the social dimension in order to observe more closely the behavior or acts of group members related to the task dimensions. Scheidel and Crowell (1964) attempted to observe those acts specifically related to the development of ideas. Fisher (1970a) sought to isolate those acts directly related to the making of group decisions. In terms of an actual separation of the task from the social dimension, both attempts were probably abortive. It would probably be more accurate to say that Scheidel and Crowell and Fisher viewed a single interdependent group process from the perspective of the task dimension. In other words, group members make a decision and develop ideas at the same time and in the same manner that they develop a group structure and get along together.

### Productivity and Cohesiveness

You can probably remember being a member of a group which you thoroughly enjoyed. There was an esprit de corps among the members, a spirit of camaraderie, a feeling of close personal ties. You undoubtedly felt the group was worthwhile and rewarding to you, and you felt a sense of loyalty to the group—a personal commitment. In a group such as this, members are proud to be members. Occasionally such groups evolve from classroom groups. The following comments for example, are selected from the final entries in diaries kept by members of a group formed within a class studying group communication. Their feelings were unanimous:

> "I feel a close bond with the other members of our group and would like to continue working with each one."
> "I am very grateful for this group experience and feel a very close bond of friendship and understanding with each member."
> "What I really want to emphasize is the way that we learned to function as free-thinking people unacquainted, really, with the others (at the beginning of the term) and evolve into an extremely cohesive group."
> "I developed a great amount of respect for and a relationship of oneness or unity with each member individually and the group as a whole."
> "It may sound a little corny, but I feel [list of the other members' names] are good friends and, when this class is over, I will feel, if nothing else, that I have made some friends for life."

On the other side of the coin, you have perhaps been involved with groups which were less than appealing. There may have been bickering among some members, but probably you were more bored than hurt by the group experience. Rather than feeling a sense of commitment or pride in the group, you probably searched for excuses to avoid group meetings. If you had any choice in the matter, you probably dropped out of the group. Otherwise, you endured it only as long as you had to. One comment from a final diary of another classroom group illustrates this type of group: "One thing that really affected the development and behavior of our group was not being able to get together for a meeting. It seemed that the five of us could never find one time that was good for everyone. But as they say, you can always find time for the things that are important."

The two types of groups just described illustrate a difference in "cohesiveness"—the ability of group members to get along, the feeling of loyalty, pride, and commitment of members toward the group. It would not be inaccurate to say that cohesiveness is, more than anything else, the degree of liking that members have for one another. To the extent that members like one another, they are committed to the group and feel loyal and proud of their membership status. Cohesiveness may also be viewed as the output of a group's social dimension. That is, cohesiveness is not a process so much as a state of being. As groupness emerges from group interaction, the group may be characterized at some level of cohesiveness. Such a characteristic describes the outcome of the process in the group's social dimension.

In a similar fashion, the output from a group's task dimension may be described as "productivity." To the extent that a group accomplishes its task, it is productive. Like cohesiveness, the amount of productivity is not always easily determined. Of course, the productivity of a group on a manufacturing assembly line may be measured by counting the number of products its members complete in a given time period. Or the productivity of a basketball team may be determined by the number of games it wins. But what of a decision-making group? The number of decisions is seldom a good indication of productivity. A jury, for example, may have only one decision to make—the guilt or innocence of the defendant. As in most decisions, quality rather than quantity is the best determinant of a decision-making group's productivity. And the quality of decisions is exceedingly difficult to measure.

Despite the difficulties of observing and measuring productivity and cohesiveness, they serve as useful concepts to describe the general success of a group along its task and social dimensions. Caution must be exercised, however, in utilizing these descriptive terms. Cohesiveness and productivity are not qualities that a group does or does not possess. Each is a characteristic which describes to some degree the success of the group process in every group.

In every group, both cohesiveness and productivity exist in some amount. That is, a group's productivity or cohesiveness should each be visualized as some point along a continuum. For example, in terms of cohesiveness a group may be low, moderately low, moderately high, high, and so forth. Another analogy may illustrate this point. Height is a characteristic of every person. We measure height conveniently in feet and inches, and everyone has height to some degree. We may describe someone as tall or short, but we would never say that a person has no height. In the same way, we may describe a group as "low" with respect to cohesiveness or productivity, but it is foolish to say that the group is "not productive" or "not cohesive." Even though we commonly use such expressions to characterize a group, we must keep in mind that we actually mean that the group is rated at the lower end of the continuum of either productivity or cohesiveness.

Since the interdependence of the task and social dimensions has been established, it seems reasonable that the outputs of these dimensions— cohesiveness and productivity—should also have an interdependent relationship. Although we can visualize a group whose members hate one another but are able to be quite productive, this type of group is unusually rare. Common sense would dictate a direct relationship between productivity and cohesiveness—that is, the more cohesive a group is, the more productive it is likely to be. And this dictum is true—up to a point. As a group raises its level of cohesiveness, the more likely it is to raise its level of productivity. Conversely, the more productive the group, the greater the likelihood that it will be more cohesive. However, the relationship

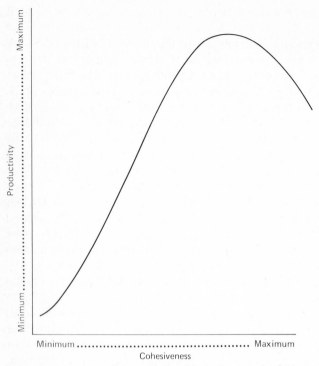

**Figure 2-2** The curvilinear relationship between cohesiveness and productivity.

breaks down toward the upper end of the two continuums. Figure 2-2 illustrates this curvilinear relationship between cohesiveness and productivity. According to this diagram, extremely cohesive groups are more likely to have moderate to low productivity. Although the productivity of highly cohesive groups probably doesn't sink to the level of groups that are extremely low in cohesiveness, such groups are not nearly as likely to be as productive as groups with moderately high cohesiveness.

Several explanations account for this phenomenon. First, the group may have been together so long that its original purpose—its task—has suffered simply because the members enjoy one another's company too much. Many local community service organizations find that over the years the primary purpose of their organization has changed from assisting their community to having a good time. The greater proportion of their activity, then, is socializing rather than working on community service. I am familiar with one group whose purpose, at the time the group was formed, was to raise money for an annual charity drive. As far as I know, that group still raises money annually; but the group continues to meet regularly during the year to play cards, eat dinner, and generally entertain itself. The greater proportion of its effort is social enjoyment, not raising funds.

Another explanation is advanced by Clovis R. Shepherd (1964, pp. 94–95). He indicates that a group which is highly cohesive but has low productivity has a great deal of "reserve productivity." That is, the group is capable of much more productivity but simply does not expend the effort to be productive. Hence, its productivity lies dormant or in reserve. The classic example is the extremely bright student who does just enough work to earn a passing grade but doesn't earn an A. Teachers, parents, and friends would say that this student isn't working to capacity. Another example is the athletic coach of a losing team who bemoans the fact that the players are capable of winning every game but just aren't playing to the level of their abilities. In either case, the assumption is that the group or the person is capable of superior productivity but actually achieves only average or below-average productivity—hence the term "reserve productivity." If actual productivity and reserve productivity were added together, the total would be a superior level of productivity.

Whatever the explanation for the curvilinear relationship between cohesiveness and productivity, the point to remember is that the outputs of the two dimensions of group process affect each other reciprocally. For example, an increase in productivity tends to increase the cohesiveness of a group. Recall the Green Bay Packers football team coached by the late Vince Lombardi. The coach and the team possessed all the characteristics that would normally lead to low cohesiveness. The coach was aloof from his players—highly dictatorial and a "slave-driver." The players were forced to perform behaviors they would normally find abhorrent. They were subject to stringent training rules more appropriate for Little League juveniles than mature adults. They endured torturous practices above and beyond the normal practice routines. But they won games. They ruled the National Football League during the decade of the 1960s and became famous for their "Packer pride." Apparently the team was a tightly knit, highly cohesive group. We can only wonder how cohesive it would have been had it been a losing football team.

Conversely, an increase in cohesiveness generally precipitates a corresponding increase in productivity. The classic example of this phenomenon is commonly known as the "Hawthorne effect." Deriving its name from a series of investigations performed in the Hawthorne plant of the Western Electric Company, the Hawthorne effect generally refers to the increase in productivity that results from an environmental change in the social dimension. Organizational managers may single out a work group within the organization and give that group special attention or special favors, such as enlisting its aid in a research situation. That group is likely to increase its productivity as a result. Athletic coaches talk about getting their players "psyched up" for the big game with a great deal of group activity, shaking hands, yelling together, and so forth. They believe their teams play better in the proper socioemotional atmosphere. Examples, based however vaguely on the Hawthorne effect, are familiar to all of us. The background music in an office is intended to make the social environment more pleasant so that the office workers are more productive. I have an uneasy feeling that when we are customers in a store with soothing background music piped in, we are expected to purchase more products in the pleasant environment of that store.

Occasionally, however, the increase in productivity precipitated by an increase in cohesiveness may be more a rationalization by the group members to account for their otherwise low level of productivity. That is, the group members probably realize that their group has accomplished little in its task dimension, and so they rationalize that the group actually accomplished more than it did. One method of rationalization is to change the nature of the task. Members of a classroom group often feel that their decision-making task was not very worthwhile, anyway, and so they arbitrarily change their perceptions of what the task really was. The following excerpt from a classroom group's final self-analysis illustrates this rationalization:

> Because our information would not be used for anything of real importance, we felt we were wasting our time to meet. . . . The only real purpose in our group was to get in the assignments. . . . As it turned out, our group was more a social group than anything else. We never really got into any real conflicts. But we felt some very important things came out of the experience of being in a group. We learned better how a group functions and why. . . . All the different topics that we had discussed in class about what happens in a group became clearer to us as we related to each other about what had happened in our group. This gave all of us a better understanding of group methods.

In reality, little groupness ever emerged for these group members. They experienced a spurt of social success toward the end of the term and began the process of rationalizing their previously low productivity. Although they did perceive the "real task" of the classroom group, these members were probably attempting to impress the instructor rather than actually describing their group's level of productivity. It is, unfortunately, probably true that comments like these are more typical of the classroom group than the comments of the extremely cohesive group cited earlier.

### Groupthink

Irving Janis (1972), a social psychologist, has discussed the phenomenon of "groupthink," which provides further evidence for the strong interdependence between the social and task dimensions of the group process. Groupthink occurs only in highly cohesive groups. Although it is related to the association of cohesiveness and productivity, it is relevant less to the *amount* of task effort (that is, productivity) than to the quality of the group's task performance.

Janis suggests that highly cohesive groups may be victims of groupthink. The independent judgments of individual members are affected by the group's level of cohesiveness. Members seek the group's judgments in the belief that the judgments on which group members concur are inevitably superior to judgments made by any one member. In this way, members employ group thought as the basis or standard for determining their own individual thinking. Members thus suspend their own critical thinking in favor of the thinking which stems from concurrence.

Groupthink is not merely conformity of members to group pressures. Rather, it is characterized by defective or ineffective judgments that are precipitated by the tendency of members to seek concurrence with other members at all costs. Conformity generally implies that deviant members are pressured by other group members to conform to their judgments, but groupthink provides more of a "prior constraint" on individual thinking. Group members are not so much deviants as they are willing pawns of the group. They suspend their own beliefs in favor of group beliefs. They probably feel implicitly that their group is invulnerable to bad decisions. One of the characteristics of groupthink is strong in-group loyalty and a belief that persons outside their own group are less capable and less aware of important information.

Also, unlike pressures for conformity, the phenomenon of groupthink instills in members an illusion of unanimity. Members are unanimous in their judgments, have always been unanimous, and will probably always be unanimous. The group is so cohesive that members have little doubt, if any, about their own commitment to the group decisions. Any doubts they might have had are quickly and thoroughly rationalized or otherwise dispelled by the members themselves, so that the illusion of unanimity quickly becomes a reality.

Groupthink typically implies ineffective or poor decision making. The ineffectiveness of the decision-making process results from the members' suspension of their critical faculties en route to consensus. A period of interaction involving conflict over ideas and critical idea testing is normal and typical of the group process. Groupthink thus short-circuits the natural group process and is likely to result in decisions of poor quality. Of course, groupthink is possible only in groups that have achieved an extremely high level of cohesiveness.

Typically, members of such groups are not aware of groupthink. On the other hand, some highly perceptive members may have the feeling that something is wrong. One person in a classroom group suffering from groupthink clearly perceived that something was wrong. She wrote in her diary after one group meeting, "Everyone in the group gets along almost *too* well. Ideas that come about, therefore, are shallow and unclear. Members of my group are afraid to challenge or question ideas."

As the following chapters will emphasize, one characteristic of the group process, which endows the group with its capacity to make high-quality decisions, is conflict—specifically, conflict over ideas, the substance of the group's task efforts. Groupthink is a phenomenon which inhibits conflict and thus results in defective and low-quality decisions which achieve consensus.

## THE SOCIAL DIMENSION

Our society has long recognized the worth and dignity of the individual. The individual's right to life, liberty, and the pursuit of happiness is inviolate. Advertisements sell products by appealing to the wish to "get away from the crowd" and assert individuality. Laws protect each person's rights to privacy, to earn a living, to gain an education—in short, the right to be an individual. But we also recognize that the human being is a social being. Although a few people choose to be hermits, most human animals seek the company of other humans and apparently need membership in a variety of social systems.

To understand a group is to understand the relationship of the individual and the group. Moreover, to understand this relationship is to understand the individual. This section deals with the reciprocal relationship between the individual and the group. Specifically, the development of the miniculture, which constitutes a group, entails the development of a climate that socializes the uniqueness of the individual into the social system of the group. The term "socioemotional climate" refers to this merger of individual and social system.

### Perspectives on the Socioemotional Climate

The most common perspective used to discuss the socioemotional climate of a group is cohesiveness. But cohesiveness is a very general and abstract concept which is virtually synonymous with socioemotional climate. Understanding how cohesiveness develops is indeed equivalent to understanding the development of a group's socioemotional climate.

**Interpersonal Attraction**   One common approach to discussing cohesiveness is to discuss how and why people are attracted to one another, that is, how and why people like one another. The assumption is that people who like each other develop a cohesive group. So a cohesive group is cohesive because members develop interpersonal liking.

Numerous factors have been associated with interpersonal attraction. One rather consistent factor is similarity, particularly similarity of attitudes. Typically people with similar attitudes toward objects tend to congregate and reinforce one another's attitudes. ("Birds of a feather flock together.") Such reinforcement is evidently a pleasing experience, so that people with similar attitudes tend to like one another.

Theodore M. Newcomb's (1953) "AtoBreX" system provides one explanation of this phenomenon. Figure 2-3 shows the minimal AtoBreX system in which A and B are persons with positive or negative attractions toward each other and with positive or negative attitudes toward some object X. If A and B have similar attitudes (either both positive or both negative) toward object X, Newcomb postulates, they will experience a "strain toward symmetry," so that their attractions toward each other will be positive. A symmetrical AtoBreX relationship involves positive attractions between A and B along with similar (both positive or both negative) attitudes toward X. Newcomb's approach also emphasizes the importance and even the necessity of communication in order for A and B to inform and to influence each other about their attitudes.

A second factor associated with interpersonal attraction is frequency of interaction. As people communicate with one another more often, they increase their mutual attraction. There is little way of knowing, however, whether greater frequency of interaction is a cause of interpersonal attraction or its effect. That is, are people attracted to each other because they communicate more frequently? Or do they communicate more frequently because they like each other? One certainly tends to communicate most often with friends and is more apt to be friends with those with

**Figure 2-3** The coorientation model. *(From Theodore M. Newcomb, "An Approach to the Study of Communicative Acts,"* Psychological Review, **60:***393-404, 1953. Copyright 1953 by the American Psychological Association, and reproduced by permission.)*

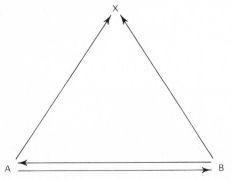

whom one communicates most often. At the very least, we can say that interpersonal liking cannot be achieved without some interaction. And, in addition, we probably decrease the frequency of our interaction with people we don't particularly like.

A third factor associated with interpersonal attraction is the perception of reciprocated attraction. Interpersonal liking is a two-way street. We tend to be attracted to people who we can see are attracted to us. (This phenomenon of reciprocal attraction is consistent with the norm of reciprocity to be discussed in Chapter 6.) Perception of the other person's attitudes and feelings is certainly important to interpersonal attraction. And our perceptions can be based only on what we see and hear the other person do or say. In other words, communication provides the data—the raw materials—on which we build our perceptions of others.

One additional variable often associated with interpersonal attraction is also directly linked to communication—self-disclosure. Self-disclosure may be defined generally as statements made to another about one's self—what one thinks, feels, believes, wants, needs. Erving Goffman (1959, 1963, 1967) discusses the presentation of one's self to another as a normal phenomenon of human interaction. Although he does not explicitly discuss self-disclosure, he assumes that presenting or disclosing one's self to another is an inevitable and unavoidable experience. A person who communicates with someone else is engaged in an act of self-disclosure to another. Goffman assumes further that the self may be "presented." That is, communicators attempt to manipulate the perceptions or impressions of others by presenting data through communicative behavior that is designed to present them as they want to be perceived.

Brenda Robinson Hancock (1972), in a pilot research project, has discovered some important implications concerning self-disclosure by communicative behavior. Hancock's results indicate that although groups of friends and groups of acquaintances tend to discuss many of the same topics, friends tend to discuss intimate topics for longer periods and use much more intimate language. That is, friends tend to engage in more self-disclosing communicative behavior than acquaintances do.

Whether self-disclosure, like frequency of interaction, is a cause or an effect of interpersonal attraction is quite unclear. But self-disclosure through communication must be regarded as one of the factors linked to interpersonal attraction.

**Member Satisfaction**     Cohesiveness may also be viewed as the extent to which members enjoy, or are satisfied with, their group experiences. Rather than viewing an individual's relationship with another individual, this perspective on cohesiveness attempts to view one element of an individual member's perception of the group as a whole. Although the term "satisfaction" may imply that group membership satisfies some "need" of an individual, it is used here in a much broader sense to refer to morale, loyalty, or any way in which individual members are pleased with their group membership.

Heslin and Dunphy (1964) summarized 450 studies linked to satisfaction and discovered three variables which explain most instances of members' satisfaction with their groups. Heslin and Dunphy labeled these three factors "dimensions of member satisfaction." They include "status consensus," "perception of progress toward group goals," and "perceived freedom to participate." Status consensus implies the degree of agreement among members on the identity of the leader or other high-status members. If all members rank the same individual or individuals high, then status consensus is said to be high.

Significantly, the actual progress toward group goals and actual participation are not clearly associated with member satisfaction. Group members can manipulate their perceptions of group productivity. Thus, it is the perception of progress, rather than actual progress, that is important to satisfaction.

Common sense should tell us that not all members in a group participate equally. Furthermore, members probably should not do so. Some members have more ability than others and should be greater participators than those of lesser ability. Nor do all members have an equal need to participate. Some people are more extroverted than others. What is important, however, is not equal participation but the perceived freedom to participate. If members feel that they have an equal opportunity to participate, whether they choose to do so or not, they are satisfied with the group. Clearly, group members do not all participate equally. It should be equally apparent that perceived freedom to participate and not equal participation should be the goal of a group whose members are happy with their group experience.

**Group Identification**   Another perspective from which to view individuals and their relationship with the group is the extent to which they identify themselves with that group. Many scholars discuss group identification as the member's internalization of group goals—the extent to which the group goals become the goals of the individual members. Group identification here implies a broader meaning. To the extent that each group member feels a part of the group or recognizes membership in the group, group identification may be said to exist.

There are some observable manifestations of a growing group identification even in the classroom group. Student members will change their classroom seating patterns and begin to sit beside or near their fellow group members. The member will begin to refer to the group in the first person as "my" group or "our" group. When members keep diaries of their reactions after each group meeting, the diaries themselves reflect a developing group identification. A diary in the early stages of the group meetings will include a reference to another member in the third person, for example, "I am having trouble with one of the people in this group. He seems to criticize everything I say." Later, that same member will use first names exclusively in referring to fellow group members—"Steve is still the critic of our group. But I am beginning to realize that he just wants us to think about what we are saying."

Occasionally group members have difficulty establishing group identification, so an impetus is needed to stir their feelings of unity. An example from one such group indicates a possible impetus for increasing group identification. One group member, frustrated by the obvious apathy of his fellow group members, sought help from his instructor. This group, as might be expected, was not very productive and had received a rather low evaluation on a preliminary group project. The members were naturally disappointed over their low grade. The instructor and the student arranged a conference at which time the entire group complained, as a group, to the instructor about the low grade. During the conference the instructor remained firm and proceeded to justify the low mark, often using rather shaky grounds for his justification. The conference proved to be successful in that the group developed much closer ties of group identification. They became united against a common "enemy"—the instructor. At the end of the term, when they were informed of the contrived incident, the group members had almost forgotten it. Group identification, in this instance, was spurred by conflict with some external foe. But, more important, the feelings of increased group solidarity were maintained in the absence of the foe.

### Social Tension

The feeling of tension is familiar to all of us. A person who feels tense is nervous and irritable. Television commercials have endowed tension with a certain fame, along with its accompanying headache. But tension does indeed have its physiological signs—contracted muscles, the familiar sweaty palms, the averted eye gaze. This is the tension experienced by an individual person. Social tension is not unlike the tension experienced by an individual. Persons in a group suffering from extreme social tension may exhibit many of the signs of individual tension. Extreme social tension is characterized by an electric atmosphere. The very air seems charged. The individual members are uncomfortable. All in all, extreme social tension is not a pleasant experience.

**Primary and Secondary Tension**   Bormann (1975) distinguishes between two types of social tension—primary and secondary. The difference is one of kind rather than degree. During the initial period of a group's formation, primary tension is inevitable and to be expected as a normal occurrence. One might compare primary social tension to stage fright. Social inhibitions create a lack of assurance on how to behave. Comments are quietly spoken and very tentative. Long pauses occur between comments. Members rarely interrupt one another; and if two members should speak at once, profuse apologies reveal the extent of primary tension present.

Overall, group interaction during periods of primary tension is of very low intensity. Members are overly polite to one another and overtly strive to avoid anything which might involve social repercussions. But a group needs time and activity to "break the ice." After all, a social system does not yet exist, and members do not know what to expect or what is expected of them. Primary tension is normally overcome without great difficulty as interaction is allowed to continue, although it may recur briefly at the beginning of each group meeting—particularly if a relatively long period of time elapses between meetings. Generally, once the ice is broken, a group need worry no more about social problems stemming from primary tension. Typically, such tension is not a serious problem in a group's socioemotional climate.

Secondary tension is potentially much more serious. Unlike primary tension, it is not always predictable or easily overcome merely through the passage of time. The hallmark of secondary tension is typically an abrupt departure from group routine. Sometimes a sharp increase in tension begins with an outburst from one of the members. There may be a heated exchange between two or more members. A flurry of verbal activity will be followed by an unbearably long pause. During the heated exchange members may attempt to shout over one another's comments for extended periods. Usually two or three members will do most of the talking while other members remain rigidly silent, staring at the floor. Extreme secondary tension is definitely an unpleasant sensation and, if uncontrolled, threatens the social health of the group.

The causes of secondary tension are many and varied. Overt interpersonal conflict, occasionally even a personality conflict, may precipitate severe secondary tension. Environmental pressures, such as a shortage of time to accomplish the task, will cause it to rise sharply. Quite often, a feeling of frustration among the members foments tension. Such frustration may stem from an acknowledged lack of success in task accomplishment or the feeling that the group performance was far short of expectations. A nonconforming member might cause frustration—particularly one who is habitually tardy or absent from group meetings or who consistently fails to fulfill promises made to the group. Whatever the cause, extreme secondary tension, once experienced, must be brought under control if the group is to survive.

**Managing Social Tension**    Up to this point we have discussed tension as harmful and destructive to a group's socioemotional climate. Certainly excessive tension is harmful to the group, but some tension is both normal and essential. In fact, some tension is always present in a functioning group. Tension implies activity. An actor, for instance, is not relaxed when performing but, rather, is tense, concentrating on the performance. The successful athletic team is "up for the game." After a group overcomes the natural social inertia in the early stages of group development, the members experience tension. They are alert, on their toes—tense. The functioning group is not at rest but active and hence is experiencing some degree of tension.

In point of fact, it is tension that holds the group together. While excessive tension may act as a centrifugal force which threatens to tear the group apart, controlled tension functions as a centripetal force which holds the group together. Place the opposite poles of two magnets together and they will be drawn toward each other. I am sure you have seen the simple experiment of placing a sheet of paper on the magnets and sprinkling iron filings on the paper in order to see the activity of the lines of attraction bonding the two magnets together. Although the magnets seem at rest, they are in fact exerting force which holds them together. Another demonstration of the bonding characteristic of tension is to bend your elbows and place your palms together in front of you. Push your palms together, exerting as much pressure as you can. You may notice your hands quivering, but they are essentially still, held together through the tension of pressure. In a similar manner, tension holds the members of a group together and allows them to function effectively as a social system. Members interact, and interaction inherently implies some level of tension.

The problem of social tension, then, is not that it exists, but that it may exceed an optimal level. Every group has a "tolerance threshold" of social tension above which it cannot function effectively. If the tension level is below that threshold, the group is able to function well. But when the tension level rises above the group's tolerance threshold, it becomes the overpowering priority in the group's socioemotional climate. The group must reduce that tension level before it can do anything else.

Of course, the tolerance threshold varies from group to group. Some groups can tolerate a rather high level of tension. That is, some groups are able to function effectively although a rather high level of tension is present. Another group whose tolerance threshold is lower will find that level of tension intolerable. Just as some individuals can endure more pain than others, some groups can endure more tension that others. The problem for the group, then, is to develop successful mechanisms for reducing tension when it rises above the tolerance threshold.

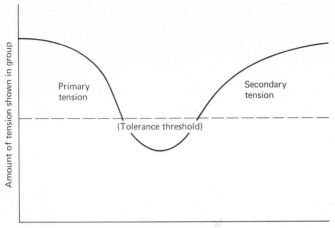

**Figure 2-4**   Tension curve of a hypothetical group: uncontrolled secondary tension. *(Figures 2-4 through 2-7 adapted from Ernest G. Bormann,* Discussion and Group Methods: Theory and Practice, *Harper and Row, New York, 1969, fig. 11, "Secondary Tension Curve," p. 172.)*

Figures 2-4 through 2-7 illustrate graphically the rise and fall of a group's tension level. Of course, tension cannot be measured very accurately, and so these graphs serve only illustrative purposes. The group illustrated in Figure 2-4 overcame the initial primary tension but was unable to control secondary tension. Thus, the secondary tension level remained above the tolerance threshold, and the group was unable to function effectively throughout. For the members of this group, the socioemotional climate was extremely unpleasant. No group can withstand indefinitely the pressures of secondary tension above the tolerance threshold. One can predict that the life expectancy of this group is quite short. The members will probably disband their group rather than suffer this social agony much longer.

Figure 2-5 illustrates an unusual type of group but one that occasionally occurs. Members of this group were never able to overcome their initial primary tension. Obviously there was very little groupness. They remained a collection of individuals. Members did not identify with the group; they exhibited extraordinary apathy, and had virtually no commitment to either the group or the task at hand. One is reminded of the community meeting called to protest apathy, but no one showed up at the meeting. This group—or, more accurately, collection of individuals—will not exist long either. If the members do continue to meet (in the event that they are a "captive" aggregation compelled to meet), they will accomplish little.

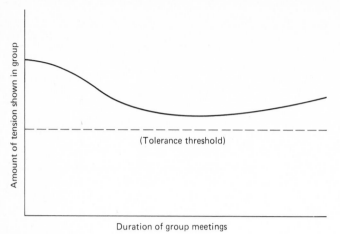

**Figure 2-5**  Tension curve of a hypothetical group: uncontrolled primary tension. *(From Bormann, 1969.)*

Such groups are quite atypical. Communication among even "captive" individuals generally produces some degree of interdependence among members. But one classroom group did correspond to this graph quite closely. In approximately 20 hours of meetings, all of which were recorded on audiotape, their interaction patterns in their first hour of meeting time resembled closely the interaction of nearly every other hour of meeting time. They continued to speak with extremely low intensity and never interrupted one another. Pauses between comments were long and painful, some 30 seconds or more in duration. Needless to say, this group also showed little outward sign of group identification, nor was it very productive.

At first glance, the group illustrated in Figure 2-6 seems ideal. The members overcome primary tension and never suffer from secondary tension above their tolerance threshold. They seem to be a happy, healthy group of contented people. And that may be true. More likely, however, members of this group either are bored stiff or are suffering from an abnormal fear of social tension. It is simply not healthy, perhaps not normal, for group members never to experience secondary tension above their tolerance threshold. One explanation for never doing so would assume that they just don't care enough to get excited about anything. As a result, members do what they are told but have little commitment to the group's activities. Another plausible explanation would assume the members to be hypochondriacs about social tension. They fear tension so much that they conscientiously avoid any stimulus which would raise the tension level above the tolerance threshold. Hence, members retreat or

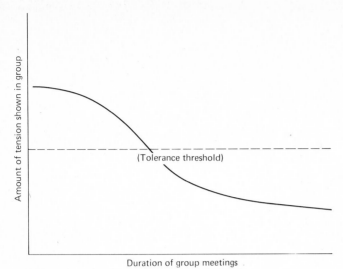

**Figure 2-6**  Tension curve of a hypothetical group: absence of secondary tension. *(From Bormann, 1969.)*

take flight from any potential source for a social problem. Rather than solving their social problems, they ignore them and hope they will go away.

Of course a "perfect" social system exemplified by Figure 2-6 might exist. The members might be entirely compatible, so that social tension just never rises. Or their tolerance threshold may be so high that the tension level never exceeds it. Nevertheless, the group develops no history in its behavior pattern as a system that would indicate its success in alleviating social problems when they arise. If their environment were a Garden of Eden, perhaps problems would never appear. I can only wonder, though, what would happen to such a group if and when the going gets rough. Without successful past behavior, its ability to cope with excessive social tension remains highly questionable.

The group illustrated in Figure 2-7 is most likely to enjoy the ideal socioemotional climate. This group has frequent moments of secondary tension above its tolerance threshold, and it consistently dispels the excess of tension. This group successfully manages its social tension and obviously has no fear of secondary tension. Its past behavior is a series of instances of successful management of tension. The members have obviously developed mechanisms for successfully coping with secondary tension and have incorporated them into their system's function patterns. The social fabric of this group is strengthened with each success in

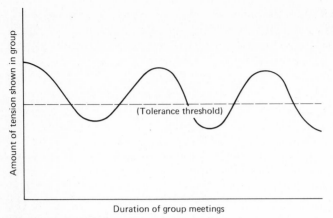

**Figure 2-7** Tension curve of a hypothetical group: frequent periods of secondary tension. *(From Bormann, 1969.)*

managing social tension. The socioemotional climate is vibrantly healthy, and the members undoubtedly find the group exciting and stimulating.

Lest the point is not yet clear, I must emphasize that the *amount* of social tension above or below the tolerance threshold is relatively insignificant. What does matter is the ability of the group to manage its tension level successfully. Thus, the group in Figure 2-7 is characterized by the *frequency*, and not by the amount, of excessive social tension it experiences. Each period of tension above the tolerance threshold is quite brief. Members do not suffer extended periods of excessive tension but invoke tried-and-true mechanism-functions for reducing the tension when they need to. Unlike the group illustrated in Figure 2-6, this group has the devices at its disposal—that is, within the system's function patterns—to cope with actual and potential problems of social tension.

It should be apparent at this point what a healthy socioemotional group climate looks and sounds like—at least as far as managing tension is concerned. A healthy group is apt to be noisy. Its members are uninhibited and probably not governed by norms of politeness. There are frequent disagreements, arguments, and constant interruptions which reflect the members' eagerness and commitment to their group—high group identification. Members who are not major contributors to the group's verbal interaction are actively a part of the group. They are alert and nonverbally appear interested in the comments of others.

The mechanisms developed by successful groups for reducing excessive tension are also many and varied. Moreover, what works in one group may be totally unsuccessful in others. Often one or two persons assume the role of tension-relievers, and the group looks to them for help when the time arises. Sometimes a tension-reliever is a jokester—a person who is carefree, is happy-go-lucky, and makes people laugh. But laughter is not always a clear sign of tension release; it may even signify excessive tension. When members laugh at comments that are really not funny, they are probably exhibiting, rather than releasing, tension. Quick, abrupt, high-pitched laughter is generally a sign of tension rather than tension release. One group successfully relieved primary tension through a member who constantly told jokes, often at her own expense. But when secondary tension arose, her self-deprecating jokes were totally unsuccessful. In fact, the other members resented her carefree attitude and finally demanded that she take a more serious attitude toward their task. Thus, the behavior that dispelled primary tension was unsuccessful in coping with secondary tension, even in the same group.

Another tension-relieving role may be a mediator between two conflicting members. When secondary tension erupts from such an interpersonal conflict, the conciliator who is respected by both the conflicting members is a tension-reliever. Sometimes excessive tension is reduced by finding a scapegoat as a mediating agency. When tension arises from frustration over environmental or task pressures, that frustration must be vented at someone or something. In a classroom group, the instructor serves as a convenient scapegoat. In a business organization, the "boss" becomes the outside "enemy." The successful scapegoat is generally outside the immediate group membership. Most important to the group, though, is not *how* it manages tension but *whether* it does.

The key to successful tension management is distressingly and deceptively simple. *The successful group confronts social problems head on.* More problems are created by avoiding or ignoring potential problems than by facing them squarely. Such overt action is rarely easy, however, and generally requires old-fashioned guts! But the social benefits are worth the momentary and perfectly normal reluctance. One member's diary, written immediately after a particularly productive group meeting, emphasizes the wisdom of confrontation:

> But almost everyone got the hippie-stereotype impression of me. It goes to show, first impressions are really terrible, because everyone is so different from what I thought. I told them all exactly what I thought of them and they told me. I thought this would be a total disaster, and everyone would end up hating each other. But it brought us very close together, I think. This meeting is a great accomplishment for our group. Now I think we can start moving.

Whatever the social problem, the importance of confronting it head on cannot be overestimated. Occasionally the group is in for a painful period of agonizing tension during this confrontation. But in the long run the group not only survives but becomes stronger. One classroom group provides a fantastic example of extreme measures used to confront a social problem centered in a single person. This example also demonstrates equally fantastic results which accrued in the group's socioemotional climate. This five-member group was composed of four women and one man. For a variety of reasons the man was considered a male chauvinist by the women members, a thorn in their side. They deeply resented what they considered to be his domineering behavior, although they had not directly verbalized their resentment. At one climactic meeting they finally decided to let him know—clearly and forcefully. The following excerpts from the male member's paper analyzing his group most clearly illustrate what happened during the confrontation and its aftermath:

> Then there was the meeting when one of the members hit me with the comment, "Go to hell, you egotistical creep!" It was then that I began to realize the value of this class and how our group reacted. There was, of course, a great deal of tension that day. I was very nervous and uncomfortable. . . . In being blasted I, more than anyone else, I think, felt what a brutal force and what brutal pressure can fall on someone in the social dimension of a group when people begin to attack you.
>       . . . It was exciting to have each member of the group become confident enough to bare his or her soul to the rest of the group.

A comment from another member of the group corroborates the positive effects of this extreme confrontation:

> My first reaction to Marilyn's "Tom, go to hell" was that it was uncalled for. I thought that that type or degree of honesty was not needed. However, it was exactly what was needed because it opened the door to real communication. We all became very sober and honest with each other. . . . By the end of the meeting my mind was so elated that I felt completely free of anxiety or pressure, and I felt very much at peace with myself and with the world.

Granted, not every confrontation will have such immediate and such positive effects. Nor will every confrontation be centered on a single member or even on a person at all. But avoiding potential social problems will have even fewer immediate effects and many less positive ones. Social problems do not go away if they are not solved. They simply remain and fester. It takes guts to confront social problems as squarely as this last group did. It is exceedingly difficult to cast off natural inhibitions so quickly and so completely. But, of course, most confrontations would not be nearly so extreme or painful either. The important point, again, is not the extreme measure used by the group to confront its problem but the fact that it did overtly and conscientiously decide to confront the problem.

But what of compromise as a solution? Surely problems are not always win-or-lose propositions. A group should be able to effect some sort of "golden mean." The spirit of compromise is healthy. No one should belittle the wisdom of the spirit of compromise. Nor should one assume that compromise is the cure for all social problems. Often compromise is a tactic used by a group to avoid facing its problems. The following excerpt from a classroom group's final self-analysis reflects this point:

> It was surprising that our first task was completed because we had competition within the group that became disruptive. In order to achieve the task we had to compromise and stop competing. . . . However, compromise never was the ultimate solution, as we were to learn. Our group suffered from tension because we did compromise. The only thing our first compromise did was to produce a paper but leave the members with a sub-conscious feeling of "something is wrong." We concluded that compromise is an easy way of dismissing tensions that could go beyond the threshold—an escape from facing the ultimate questions that have to be answered for group survival.

In this group, compromise was a substitute for the solution of social problems. The members compromised as the easy way out. Rather than facing up to their problems, they escaped from them through compromise. We must conclude, then, that compromise is a useful mechanism for tension management. But compromise should come *after* the group confronts its social problems and should not be used as a substitute for facing up to its problems.

In summary, there is one vitally important point to remember. The successful and socially healthy group is not characterized by an absence of social tension but, rather, by successful management of social tension. No group should expect, or even hope for, an absence of problems caused by social tension. Instead, a group should expect social problems to occur, should confront those problems, and should develop mechanisms for their control. This means that the members must learn to overcome their personal inhibitions, be honest, and require or demand the same behavior from other members. Such "good advice" is, of course, deceptively simple. It is more easily said than followed. But a successful group requires not only time for development but also the overt effort of its members to make it a success. One student group encapsulated this good advice in a pithy slogan that may be worth repeating: "The group that fights together stays together." A later version of this slogan may be even better: "The group that fights, unites."

## THE TASK DIMENSION: DEFINITION

The nature of the task dimension of the group process has long been a topic of considerable concern among scholars of small group phenomena. In many respects, the task of groups in the "real world" (that is, outside the classroom) is generally imposed on the group by some external authority—that is, some authority outside the group. For example, the legal system assigns its decision-making task to a jury after a courtroom trial. A group in a business organization which must decide, for example, how to market a specific product is assigned that task by some organizational superior for the purpose of furthering the goals of the larger organization.

Occasionally, however, individuals form into a group for the purpose of performing some task that can be accomplished more productively with group effort. For example, political action groups are often formed by persons who wish to respond as a group to some perceived problem, such as improving environmental quality, lobbying for specific legislation, or electing a candidate to political office.

Roby and Lanzetta (1958) have discussed how certain types of tasks will place different "critical demands" on group members in terms of specifying what behaviors or procedures they need to perform in order to accomplish those tasks adequately. Other scholars have attempted to specify those "critical demands" by listing the various types of tasks actually performed by groups. Hackman (1968), for example, has identified three types—production tasks, discussion tasks, and problem-solving tasks. A production task calls for the presentation of ideas concerning some stimulus, such as "Write a critical analysis of *Othello*." A problem-solving task requires the group members to specify an action to be taken regarding some pressing need—for example, "What should be done to resolve the problem of insufficient parking on campus?" Hackman's discussion task, the most general of his three types, deals with an evaluation of issues that typically have no right or wrong answer. For example, "Is the American economy truly free enterprise?"

The task dimension of the group process central to our interests involves the more comprehensive task of decision making. In virtually any group's decision-making effort, all three of Hackman's tasks (production, discussion, and problem solving) will be involved. Although later discussions in Chapter 5 will indicate some minimal differences between problem solving and decision making, the task efforts of decision-making groups resist any clearly specifiable restrictions as to the nature of the group task.

Much more significant, however, is the tendency to view any task as one which can or even should be performed by a group. I shall take the position that in order to maximize the quality of task performance, certain tasks should be performed by groups, and other tasks would be best performed by expert individuals. My distinction, then, is based less on what types of tasks are given to groups and more on the particular type of task most appropriate to the group process.

## THE TASK DIMENSION:
## INDIVIDUAL VERSUS GROUP DECISION MAKING

Surely the process of making decisions in a group differs from that of one person working alone. This statement should not be too startling. After all, a group is different from a single individual. For one thing, there are more people in a group. This bit of wisdom contains several important implications. A group possesses a greater variety of resources. There are more minds to contribute to the decision-making effort, more sources of information. Unlike the lone individual, a group is able to divide labor among its members so that, for example, members can work on their own specialties.

On the other hand, a group possesses potential problems not inherent in individual decision making. The problem of achieving consensus is present in a group. The many examples of hung juries are ample evidence of the existence of this problem. And, with the addition of more people, there is greater opportunity for conflict. At the same time, there are many more sources to generate new ideas. Also, there are more viewpoints from which to evaluate critically those ideas. In other words, a critical exchange of ideas is much more easily accomplished by a group.

### The Risky Shift

Among the differences discovered when individual and group decision making have been compared is the phenomenon commonly known as the "risky shift." Simply stated, the risky shift refers to the fact that groups tend to gamble more than their individual members do if each were making the decision alone. That is, a group tends to select an alternative that has a bigger payoff but a lower probability of attainment. If groups and their individual members were to place bets on a horse race, for example, the risky shift would predict that the group decision would be more likely to place the bet on the 100-to-1 shot than would any of the decisions made by the members deciding alone. Although there are exceptions to this rule (as there are to almost every rule), the proof is quite conclusive that a given person is more likely to make a decision involving greater risk when in a group than when making a decision alone. Thus, group interaction apparently stimulates individual members to take greater risks and to be less conservative than they would as individuals.

Much time and effort have been expended in order to explain the risky shift. Shaw (1976, pp. 70–77) documents the major results of those efforts. Although it is not my purpose to provide a detailed account of the various explanations, I shall summarize them briefly and critically. One explanation asserts that risk taking is a personality trait of individuals. Thus, groups composed of high risk takers will tend to make riskier decisions. This explanation may be true, but the findings indicate that generally *all* groups make riskier decisions than their members do individually.

A second explanation stipulates that risk taking is a value shared by members of a certain culture. This may also be true—particularly if the culture is composed of mountain climbers. But this explanation does not account for the fact that groups generally tend to make decisions even riskier than those of individual members of the same culture.

Another hypothesis explains that the group's risky shift can be attributed to the influence of a risk-taking leader. Such an explanation is simple to understand and too easy to believe. But not only does some research indicate that this explanation is probably not true; the nature of group leadership, to be described in Chapter 7, casts serious doubt on the credibility of this hypothesis.

A final explanation, and one which probably has the greatest evidence to support its acceptance, attributes greater risk taking in a group to a diffusion among group members of the responsibility for the group decision. Such an explanation corroborates the conventional wisdom gained from the experience of viewing a lynch mob in a western. Each of the good citizens of the frontier town wouldn't think of lynching the man in the jail. But in the anonymity of the mob and the overwhelming feeling of group support, "mob fever" results. Examples of "mob fever" and "leaping on the bandwagon" should readily come to mind with a minimum of thought.

The fact is fairly well established that groups do make riskier decisions than individuals. We should probably accept that fact and expect a group decision to involve greater risk. But *why* groups make riskier decisions may be a moot question. It is certainly less important than determining *how* groups make riskier decisions, that is, discovering what *behaviors* in the group lead to greater risk taking and how these behaviors are interlocked with one another in a pattern of interaction unique to group decision making. Unfortunately, knowledge of these phenomena is not totally available to us at the present time. One plausible explanation of the risky shift based on interaction patterns may be that the communicative patterns of social conflict alleviate the fears and initial conservatism of individual members. Those conflict patterns will be discussed in Chapter 8.

**Efficiency and Speed**

Few people have accused a group of being efficient. Referring a proposal to a committee in order to kill it is a well-known parliamentary tactic. Simple arithmetic should illustrate that, in terms of hours expended, groups are destined to be less efficient than individuals. Assume that one person can perform a task in 1 hour. A three-person group would be required to perform that task in 20 minutes in order to equal the 1 hour expended by the individual. If the task is decision making, a group would probably spend more than 1 hour—hence, an excess of 3 "one-person" hours.

Compared with individuals, groups are abominably slow. You will recall that it takes time for "groupness" to evolve. The group must establish a history before it can function effectively as a decision-making system. For a group member, patience is an important virtue. Inevitably, group members become highly frustrated, particularly in the early stages of group development, over the group's apparent lack of progress. Members are anxious to "get the show on the road," to quit wasting so much time and attend to the task at hand. Although these feelings of frustration and discouragement are typical, they should not be considered serious. Progress is not very visible in the early stages of group development, but the seemingly rapid progress later is a direct and cumulative result of the activities which have come before. (Chapter 5 discusses the process of group development during decision making.)

David Berg (1967) provides one possible explanation for the apparent inefficiency and slowness of group decision making. In his analysis of the duration of themes discussed during group interaction, he discovered that a group's effective attention span is quite small. In fact, the average length of time a group discusses a single theme is only *58 seconds.* In other words, groups tend to jump from topic to topic very quickly without dwelling on any one topic for very long. As described in Chapter 5, groups tend to make decisions in spurts of activity, whereas an individual may be more capable of lengthy periods of sustained effort.

At this point one may be tempted to ask, "If groups are so slow and inefficient as a decision-making system, why bother with them at all? Let individuals make all the decisions." If efficiency and speed were the sole criteria by which decision making is judged, no one should bother with groups. But the *quality* of the decision is infinitely more important than the time expended to make it.

Although it is difficult and often impossible to measure the quality of decisions accurately, there is a deep-seated feeling that in many cases groups will make better decisions than individuals. Our jury system, for example, is based on this premise—that a group of peers is more likely to arrive at a better or more accurate verdict than a single individual, even a judge. The principle of a democracy also operates on this assumption. If it didn't, we would disband the Congress and the Supreme Court and make the President a dictator.

Common sense tells us, then, that in some cases a group, even an occasional group of nonexperts, will make higher-quality decisions than a single individual—even an expert individual—will. It is this feeling, perhaps, that sustains our interest in group decision making. But it is more than a mere feeling. There is incontrovertible evidence that some situations virtually demand decisions made by groups and not by individuals. Our next problem is to identify those situations.

### The Group Task

For years small-group researchers compared individual decision making with group decision making, attempting to determine whether, in fact, two heads are better than one. After numerous studies and conflicting results, researchers revised their perspective. As Collins and Guetzkow (1964, p. 57) point out, "It seems more profitable to ask, 'On what kinds of tasks and in what environments will the group perform better than its individual members working separately?'" It seems reasonable that the impact of the social dimension of a group (for example, more information resources, capacity to divide labor, social conflict, critical analysis, demands of consensus) would give the group a distinct advantage for some decision-making tasks.

James H. Davis (1969, p. 33) distinguishes some characteristics of the group task which are different from those of a task for individuals.

> Some tasks could reasonably be presented either to individuals or to a group. A word puzzle, for example, presents a challenge to an individual person as well as to a set of persons who cooperate in its solution. This type of task is defined in terms of individuals but the definition remains applicable to groups as well. On the other hand, a number of tasks are impossible, or undefined, for individual persons apart from a group. For example, the major chore facing a group may be reaching agreement on some political issue. An individual subject may have no doubts as to his own position, but be distressed to find others in disagreement. The resolution of this disagreement in order to achieve consensus may represent a formidable task for the group, but there is no counterpart to this task for the isolated individual.

It is clear that some tasks, such as an algebra problem or a crossword puzzle, may be performed by either an individual or a group. But the social dimension of the group process could add nothing to the solution of such a problem. Nevertheless, as Davis points out, some tasks require the critical exchange of conflicting viewpoints, such as a political issue. In this task a group has a distinctly superior advantage.

Zaleznik and Moment (1964, p. 143) provide further direction in our search for the group-decision situation. They point out that a group functions under a condition of "psychological interdependence" so that the productivity of the group is more than the sum of the outputs of the individual members. If a group were to perform a task that could be just as easily performed by an individual, the output would be merely the total of the outputs from all the individual members. If one of the members were absent one day and the other members continued working at their same rate, the productivity of the "group" would decrease. In other words, the activity of any of the members would have no influence on the group activity. There would be no interdependence among members. The authors go on to say:

> The output of the problem-solving group is of an entirely different nature. The contributions of the individual members do not accumulate by simple addition to determine the group's output. The output is *more than* the aggregate of individual contributions, or in some instances less. *Such a group deals with the kind of problem that actually requires group activity for its resolution* [emphasis added].

The principle of nonsummativity (that is, that the whole is greater than the sum of its parts) which Zaleznik and Moment call "psychological interdependence" is described by Collins and Guetzkow (1964, p. 58) as the "assembly effect." According to Collins and Guetzkow:

> *An assembly effect occurs when the group is able to achieve collectively something which could not have been achieved by any member working alone or by a combination of individual efforts.* The assembly effect bonus is productivity which exceeds the potential of the most capable member and also exceeds the sum of the efforts of the group members working separately.

The importance of the principle of nonsummativity cannot be over-estimated. If a group performs a task which an individual could just as easily perform, the group cannot surpass the efforts produced by its most competent individual member. But if group activity is *required* to make the decision, the group can easily exceed its most competent member. The most capable individual in the group is still incapable of producing the critical exchange of ideas developed by the demands on the group to achieve consensus.

We should now be able to define the type of decision situation that is unique to the group process. For our final assistance we turn to Norman R. F. Maier's (1963) distinction between the type of decision that requires high-quality technical expertise and the type of decision that requires acceptance and commitment from the group. To illustrate this distinction: The solution of a sophisticated mathematics equation requires a person who has considerable expertise in mathematics. You or I would be at a loss to solve the problem, since we simply do not possess that extent of mathematical expertise. For such an individual task there exists only one "correct" answer or one "best" answer. On the other hand, if our problem involves deciding who should be the next President of the United States, we are dealing with a totally different kind of problem. Experts in political science or economics have no greater voice in this decision than you and I. Their votes count the same as ours. For such a problem no single "correct" or "best" answer exists (although each of us is probably convinced that one person would be a better President than any other).

The solution to the group task, moreover, has no external means by which the correctness of the decision can be validated—unlike the mathematics problem, which is wholly determined by the technical laws of mathematics. The sole criterion for validating the group decision is group acceptance or group commitment to the decision once it is made. Thus, the only criterion for validating the decision is whether it achieves consensus. Of course, the passage of time would allow a better judging of the quality of the decision. But remember that the decision situation changes from one point in time to another. What was a "good" decision during the campaign might prove to be less "good" after the elected candidate has been in office for a few years. Because decision situations change, incumbents are sometimes defeated in bids for reelection.

Of course, it is not always easy to distinguish among group decision situations and individual decision situations. For example, a person suffering from a heart ailment would be well advised to follow the diagnosis of the most expert heart specialist. This decision situation obviously requires high-quality technical expertise. But if several equally qualified heart experts disagree on the diagnosis, should the patient determine which physician is the most expert or ask the specialists to come to some form of group consensus? Such questions are rather academic. But they do illustrate that the distinction between an individual and a group task is not always black and white.

An important point to remember is that neither groups nor individuals are superior as a decision-making system. One person with expert qualifications should be expected to outperform a group on an individual task, and a group should be expected to outperform a single person on a group task. If the task requires high-quality technical expertise, the available individual who is most expert in that technical specialty should perform that task. If the task requires group commitment or validation by consensus, a group should be expected to perform that task. And unlike individual tasks, group tasks do not have a single "correct" or "best" answer that can be verified by some source external to the group. Many problems arise when groups are asked to perform a task which can just as easily be performed by an individual. Few will deny that there are too many "committees" in the world. But when the situation warrants it, a committee decision is essential if the decision is to be of highest quality.

## SUMMARY

The group process embodies two dimensions—the task dimension and the social dimension. Despite numerous attempts to separate them and a pervasive tendency to consider them in conflict with each other, the task and social dimensions of a group process are inseparable and interdependent. Although they may be separated theoretically, the task and social dimensions exert mutual and reciprocal influences on each other so that they are virtually inseparable in practice.

Productivity and cohesiveness may be considered the outputs of the task dimension and social dimension respectively. A curvilinear relationship exists between task and productivity so that as the cohesiveness of a group increases, its productivity also increases to a point of diminishing returns. As a group approaches extremely high cohesiveness, it tends to decrease in productivity. Thus, the group with the highest productivity is generally a group with only moderately high cohesiveness. Consistent with the interdependence of the task and social dimensions, productivity and cohesiveness are also interdependent, each exerting influence simultaneously upon the other.

One result attributable to the interdependence of a group's task and social dimensions is the phenomenon of "groupthink." Groupthink occurs in highly cohesive groups and results in lowered quality of the group's task performance. Members of such a group tend to suspend their individual critical thinking in favor of judgments on which other members appear to concur. Groupthink results in an illusion of unanimity and in less effective decision making.

There are several ways to view the socioemotional climate of a group. All deal in some way with a perception of the cohesiveness of a group. The most common method is to view the extent to which group members like one another. A second perspective involves the degree to which members are satisfied with their group experience. Similar to member satisfaction is group identification—the extent to which members are committed to their membership and exhibit loyalty to the social system.

The socioemotional climate of a group is, to a great extent, dependent upon the social tension experienced by the group. Social tension is of two types—primary and secondary. Primary tension refers to the normal period of tension in early stages of group development caused by the absence of a social structure and the normal inhibitions of members new to a developing social system. Secondary tension occurs during group interaction as disruptive periods in group routines of activity. Of the two types of tension, only secondary tension is generally a problem to a group's effective functioning.

Although some degree of social tension is inevitable and, in fact, vital to a successful group, tension may rise above a group's tolerance threshold and keep the group from functioning efficiently. A socially healthy group experiences frequent periods of social tension above its tolerance threshold and develops mechanisms for reducing tension to a tolerable level. Although devices used to reduce excessive tension vary widely and include anything that works, all devices seem to possess one attribute in common. Each device involves a direct confrontation of the social problem, facing it squarely without attempting to avoid or ignoring it.

A vast quantity of investigations have compared individual decision making with group decision making. Although the group process embodies two dimensions (task and social), the individual process has only the task dimension. The two-dimensional nature of groups results in several points of comparison with individuals. Groups tend to make riskier decisions than do their individual members making decisions alone. And, compared with individuals, groups are inefficient and slow. But for many situations group decisions are virtually necessary because of the superior quality of the decisions.

There are some tasks that can just as easily be performed by individuals or by groups. For those tasks group activity adds nothing to the efforts of the most capable member. These tasks are those whose accomplishment requires high-quality technical expertise and for which there is one "correct" or "best" answer validated by the subject matter of the technical specialty.

Other tasks, however, require group acceptance or group commitment for successful performance. For such tasks no single answer may be externally validated as "best." The sole means of validating this type of decision is whether it achieves consensus. These situations relate to the type of task which may be uniquely labeled the "group task." A group decision, because of the "assembly effect," will undoubtedly be superior to the decision made by even the most competent group member working as an individual.

# Chapter 3

# Group Communication —Structural Elements

Chapter 1 discussed the nature of process, a merger of structure and action. As you will recall, "structure" and "action" refer to the space and time dimensions of communication. Undoubtedly, communication is a process which contains both structural and actional (that is, functional) characteristics. It is quite impossible to discuss comprehensively the process of group communication without including both attributes.

This chapter focuses on those structural elements significant specifically to communication in a group setting. I do not intend to imply that the functional aspects are to be ignored in our view of group communication, but merely to deemphasize them here in order to focus on a group's communicative structures. In fact, most of the discussions in later chapters will place greater emphasis on the functional elements. Chapter 4 will, in turn, focus on the functions of group communication and concomitantly downplay the structural dimension. A comprehensive understanding of group communication obviously requires knowledge of both structural and functional elements, covered in both this chapter and the following one.

## FEEDBACK RESPONSES

Most of you, in your conventional wisdom, will interpret the concept of feedback as a response or reaction to a previously transmitted message. Indeed, we typically consider feedback in this way. You send a message to another person. That message travels along a channel to the other person who, in turn, receives it and responds to it. That is, the receiver reacts. The receiver "feeds back" information to you, which you then interpret as feedback because you interpret it as a reaction or response to your previously transmitted message. And the cycle continues indefinitely, or at least as long as you continue to interact with the other person.

We tend, also typically, to think of feedback responses as very significant during a communicative event. More realistically, however, we should consider feedback as inevitable. Regardless of which perspective is used to understand the nature of communication, in the same sense that one cannot *not* communicate (a fact that will be discussed in Chapter 4), one cannot avoid making a feedback response. For example, if you are waiting in line at a supermarket checkout counter, you are often surrounded by strangers. Nevertheless, you and all the other shoppers are involved in a common situation—waiting in line.

Assume that a stranger in front of you turns to you and remarks, "They sure are slow at this time of day, aren't they?" Your response to that statement is inevitably a feedback response. You have numerous responses available to you, such as the following: (1) You could agree and respond by saying, "They sure are." (2) You could disagree, offering a statement such as "Oh, I don't know. The line seems to be moving rather quickly, even though they are quite busy." (3) You could be noncommittal or perhaps even change the subject—"I hate standing in line" or "I'm in a hurry" or "That other checkout counter seems to be moving faster." (4) You could ignore the original statement by turning or looking away from your new acquaintance. Whatever you choose to do in responding to the stranger's initial statement, you are engaged in providing a feedback response. Even your attempt to ignore the other person and not engage in communication is a feedback response.

The fact is that you are involved in that communicative event, that common situation, whether you want to be involved or not. Even response 4 (ignoring the other person) is a feedback response. You have, in essence, "said" to the stranger, "I am not interested in continuing this communication. I don't wish to speak with you." Your behavior, both verbal and nonverbal, is a feedback response that conveys information to the other person about yourself, about that other person, and about your relationship to each other. Even your attempt to ignore the other person leads to some interpretation. The stranger may consider you something of a snob, an unfriendly person. The relationship is not likely to be interpreted as a desirable one or to be continued. Furthermore, the other person's self-concept may be damaged to some small extent. He or she may wonder whether body odor or bad breath has stimulated your antisocial reaction.

Since a feedback response is absolutely inevitable within a communicative event, the common notion of "one-way" or "two-way" communication would appear to be of limited usefulness or importance—at least when one is talking about communication in a face-to-face setting. Once two or more people are involved in a common social situation, even strangers who are standing in line together at a supermarket checkout counter, any behavior performed by any of these strangers is potentially communicative. Furthermore, any behavior performed by a receiver after a source's message is naturally interpreted as a feedback response. How, then, can one-way communication occur in a face-to-face communication setting? The answer is that it cannot. For purposes of communication and the group process, there is no such thing as one-way communication. All communication is inevitably and inherently two-way. All behavior following another person's behavior is inevitably and inherently a feedback response. Thus, feedback responses are constantly occurring throughout the interaction among group members.

One's self-concept, or one's beliefs and attitudes about self, also develop through communicating with others. Every person is constantly receiving new information, which then serves to validate or invalidate one's own beliefs and self-concepts. Every feedback response provides some information to the source about his or her self-concept. Such responses provide information about how others view us.

I do not mean to imply that every statement or feedback response that is received always contains specific information about self. Rather, information that is conveyed to the source must be interpreted. If you disagreed with the person in the checkout line at the supermarket, that may have had an effect on the person's self-concept. For example, that person may have had a friendly, outgoing self-image and taken pride in having the ability to relate to other people very well. Your disagreement (or, even worse, your failure to answer) may have damaged this self-concept or cast it into doubt.

One of the problems in interpreting feedback responses is to determine how honest or authentic those feedback responses are. How sincere is the person who is providing the feedback response? Is the other person merely trying to "make us feel good" while actually masking or hiding true feelings? Some people may believe that all feedback responses should always be honest, genuine, and reflect "true" feelings, if the communication is to be effective. If we reflect upon such a belief for a moment, however, we will probably not accept it as a universal principle.

In a situation in which a genuine feedback response might be harmful to another person, we often provide a response that is less than authentic—in reality, a lie. Often those dishonest feedback responses occur because we do not wish to hurt anyone's feelings unnecessarily. In other words, we often interpret our friendly relationship with the other person to be more important than the honesty of our feedback responses.

I can recall attending a play directed by a friend of mine. I thought the production of that play was horrendous. The actors were awful; the stage movement was equally awful; the pace was agonizingly slow. In short, I thought my friend had failed miserably in his direction. Nevertheless, when I talked with him after the production, I told him what a fine play it was and how much I enjoyed seeing the production of well-written drama. If I had provided a truly honest feedback response to his "How did you like the performance?" his feelings might have been hurt. More important for me, he might have wondered about the future of what was then a friendly relationship. My dishonest response may have been a compliment, not so much to his directorial abilities as to his status as a friend. I valued our relationship more than I valued the principle of honest and authentic feedback responses.

The stronger the relationship, the more valuable the feedback responses. The closer the ties of interpersonal liking (cohesiveness) among members of a group, the more honest and authentic will be these responses. Typically, feedback responses among close friends will include more negative evaluations than will the responses among acquaintances, although many positive responses will also occur during the interaction among friends. One might summarize this discussion by suggesting that the most effective feedback responses occur in groups or social relationships which are strong and in which the interactants like one another. On the other hand, honest and authentic feedback responses do not necessarily cause or lead to interpersonal liking. Rather, because persons like each other, they are more likely to be more authentic. That is, interpersonal liking allows for the probability of more authentic and genuinely honest feedback responses.

Nearly everyone is familiar with the process of response reinforcement in the familiar sense of psychological "conditioning." We are all aware of Pavlov's classical experiments in which the dogs were conditioned to salivate at the ringing of a bell, even without the presence of food. In a very simple sense, all of us are "conditioned" throughout our lives in the sense that we have been trained to perform behaviors that are appropriate to our culture. We have been taught to say "Please" and "Thank you," to eat with a fork, etc. This acculturation into our society in which we learn manners or appropriate behavior is, in a way, a certain kind of conditioning. After all, we were rewarded when we remembered the appropriate action and punished when we failed to behave in the socially approved manner.

Conditioning, however, is not the major thrust of this discussion. Rather, we are more concerned with feedback responses. But feedback responses may reinforce the behaviors which precede them. That is, our reactions or responses may or may not be favorable to the preceding comment. We may nod, smile, say "Uh-huh," "I agree," or "Yes," or express approval in some other way. On the other hand, our feedback response may be negative and may express disapproval. We may shake our heads, scowl, or say "No," "I disagree," and so forth. When we express disapproval through our feedback responses, those responses tend to inhibit or extinguish that behavior. In this way, we have negatively reinforced the other person's behavior. When our feedback responses express approval, they tend to enhance or encourage continuation of that behavior—positive reinforcement. Therefore, a feedback response may serve as a positive or a negative reinforcement of the preceding behavior.

Many people fear the potential effects of such reinforcement patterns when the power to condition members of a society is in the hands of an unscrupulous leader or tyrant. We fear being manipulated or controlled or even "brainwashed" by a government, an advertising agency, or a group leader. We are all too aware of the fictional accounts of some futuristic society of conformists who are conditioned to accept the will of some "big brother." Books and movies such as *1984, Logan's Run, Brave New World,* and *Soylent Green* depict the future in depressing and apocalyptic terms. We worry about being "conditioned" by violence on television, by manipulative advertising that will control our buying and even our voting habits. In short, our society suffers from a rather irrational fear of the alleged power of psychological conditioning.

Of course, the human being is not a machine and is not so easily manipulated or so easily conditioned as the writers of fiction would have us believe. Basically, the human being is highly obstinate. The human is able to decide what messages to receive, what messages to believe or disbelieve, what messages to remember, what portions of messages to be received or remembered, distorted or revised. In short, the control over the message (and over feedback responses, too) lies in the hands of the receiver. In fact, some scholarly research (McDavid and Sistrunk, 1957; Nokes, 1961) has discovered that feedback responses which seemed obviously positive in their reinforcement (and were intended as such) were interpreted by some receivers as being negative. Furthermore, some receivers interpreted negative feedback reinforcement as being rather positive. We should not underestimate the awesome power of each human being as a processor of information.

Discussion of group processes in Chapter 6 will emphasize the tremendous "power" which the social unit of the group has over the members individually. At the same time, however, the discussions of group process will illustrate the capacity of the individual members to shape the formation and the functioning of the group. Feedback responses (as positive or negative reinforcement) certainly do affect our behavior. And through feedback responses, we also affect other people's behavior. At the same time, however, we must keep in mind that feedback responses (as attempts to influence) can, and often are, successfully resisted by receivers of those responses.

The psychological function of feedback responses or communicative reactions as reinforcement emphasizes feedback as a means to control human behavior. The discussion of feedback in Chapter 4 as a more functional (rather than purely structural) aspect of communication will also emphasize feedback as a means of "control," although in a much different sense. In both cases, however, we need to keep in mind that feedback as reinforcement is only an *attempt* to control and cannot be an omnipotent influence on defenseless and unsuspecting human beings.

## CHARACTERISTICS OF MESSAGES

Mechanistically speaking, when people communicate, they exchange messages with one another. I encode a message and direct it to you. You decode that message, provide some understanding or interpretation of it, and then encode a message in response. In this way, communication occurs as messages flow back and forth between source-receivers, members of the group. The message in this mechanistic framework of communication is a structural phenomenon. That is, the message is conceptualized as some *thing* that is transmitted across space on a channel and received at another point in space. This mechanistic framework emphasizes the structural elements of communication in which message and channel are indeed the central elements.

From such a mechanistic view of communication, it seems reasonable to think of effective or "good" communication as the exchange of "good" messages. When I tell a new acquaintance that I am a faculty member in a university department of communication, that person often responds with a statement such as, "I had better watch what I say." Conventional wisdom dictates that the messages we transmit and receive have certain characteristics which render them desirable, effective, or "good." A structural approach to group communication might, therefore, include those attributes or characteristics or qualities which a "good" message comprises.

Harnack, Fest, and Jones (1977, pp. 94–96) offer a list of eight "characteristics of desirable contributions" in group discussions and entreat students of group communication to use it as a checklist for improving their contributions to the group interaction. Those eight characteristics are relevance, relatedness, good timing, sufficient length, clarity, informativeness, openness to evaluation, and provocativeness.

You will probably note that not all these characteristics refer to structural elements of messages themselves. For example, "openness to evaluation" is more an attitude of the source than something contained in a message. Then, too, a message is "provocative" only to the extent that the receiver interprets the message as a stimulus to further discussion. If the later discussions continue the train of thought contained in the "provocative" message, one could assume that that message may have provoked it. It is difficult, however, to determine structurally if any message is "provocative" at the time it is first uttered. Of course, the message has "relevance" only if it can be compared with the earlier messages during the group discussion and seen to be on the same topic.

The most important one of these eight characteristics may be "good timing." As later discussions in ensuing chapters on the group process consistently illustrate, what is said, how it is said, and even who says it may not be nearly so significant to the group process and to effective decision making as *when* it is said. Therefore, it is difficult to determine whether any single message, in isolation, is structurally desirable or undesirable in terms of its characteristics alone. When the message is placed within its context of the ongoing group interaction, it can be assessed as to its appropriateness or inappropriateness, relevance or irrelevance, relatedness or unrelatedness, good timing or bad timing.

Gulley and Leathers (1977, p. 31) also discuss the "codability" of messages during group communication. The codability of messages is very similar to the characteristic of "clarity" advocated in the list of desirable contributions noted above. The important point of the message is how easily it can be interpreted by the receiver. On the other hand, it is difficult to think of the meaning of a message being contained *in* the message. Rather, we typically tend to think of the meaning of messages as being within people—a property of the process of interpretation. We have even coined clichés which illustrate that meaning is located within the person and not in the message—"Meaning is perception" and "Words don't mean; people do." Phrased another way, the meaning of the message is *assigned* by the human interpreter and does not exist in the coded message itself. Nevertheless, a message may be encoded in such a manner as to increase the likelihood that it will be interpreted quickly, easily, and in a manner similar to the meaning intended by the source.

Gulley and Leathers suggest that messages during group communication are often highly ambiguous or unclear or, in their words, that they possess "low codability." Moreover, they suggest that the members of groups frequently appear to be very tolerant of these ambiguous messages and do not often seek clarification of them. Naturally, ambiguous messages have communicative advantages as well as obvious disadvantages. In terms of the disadvantages, an ambiguous message may drastically affect the efficiency of group conversation in the sense that members may argue at length before discovering that they are in agreement all along but are unaware of that fact because they are using messages of low clarity or low codability. The same can be true of a group in apparent agreement on an ambiguous issue, although there may be much disagreement that remains unexposed because of a lack of sufficient clarity.

On the other hand, ambiguous messages often occur early in a group's interaction history and are used by the group members as a means of coping with the group's decision-making task—that is, with the problem to be solved. As discussion in Chapter 5 concerning the decision-making process will illustrate, highly ambiguous messages (that is, messages whose codability or clarity is low) are neither "good" nor "bad" in and of themselves. There are times when such messages are quite typical of, and beneficial to, the making of decisions by a group. At other times during the group process, however, they may be quite inappropriate and detrimental to the group's decision-making efforts.

Under any circumstances, it is difficult to make once-and-for-all statements concerning what specific characteristics should be reflected in messages exchanged during the entire process of group decision making. Generally speaking, in terms of the eight characteristics listed earlier, I might suggest that messages exchanged by members of decision-making groups should probably be informative, sufficiently long (actually, quite brief, as in normal conversations), and relevant to the task and to prior interaction. I shall not, however, advance any hard-and-fast rules concerning the characteristics that *all* messages should contain throughout the group's interaction. Subsequent discussion of group decision making in Chapter 5 should render abundantly clear the overriding significance of the timing of messages (when they occur) rather than the characteristics they may contain.

## NETWORKS

The most common structural approach to communication is the pattern of channel linkages among individual members of a group. Such patterns consider a group in terms of which members transmit and receive messages to and from one another. Network patterns generally disregard the specific content of the messages, how they are transmitted or received, and the sequence of the message transmissions. Patterns of channel linkages are commonly known as communication "networks."

In many groups the communication network exists before the formation of the group. Generally some outside authority establishes the network to be used by the newly formulated group. Groups within large organizations, for example, employ legitimate and formal networks established by legitimate authorities within that organization. Although informal networks may arise during the process of interaction among organizational members, the organization recognizes the formal network as the optimum one for that group's task performances. One often refers to communicating through the formal legitimate network of communication within an organization as "going through channels"—that is, utilizing those channel linkages formally recognized as the primary communication network of the organization. Going through channels, however, does not always include face-to-face confrontations with every communicating member of the formal network.

The LGD (leaderless group discussion) contains no formally established network indicating which members can or cannot communicate with one another. Nevertheless, as the process of group interaction continues, members use some linkages very frequently and others quite sparingly. Thus, a network emerges during group interaction and reflects the developing social structure of that group. Figure 3-1 illustrates four common networks that may structure five-member groups. The all-channel network is really not a network at all. Since a network emerges during group interaction, the all-channel network implying relatively equal usage of every possible interpersonal channel linkage is the status of the communicative structure before a network has clearly emerged from the interaction.

Distinguishing among networks typically involves using the concepts "centrality" and "distance." The communicative distance from one member's position in the network to another member's position is the sum of the communicative links required for a message to be sent and received along the shortest possible route. In a five-member group the maximum distance is four, as illustrated by the distance between A and E in the chain network. The minimum distance, of course, is one—for example, the distance between A and E in the circle network.

The relative centrality of any member's position is the sum of distances between that position and all other positions in the network. The most central position in any network is the position with the lowest number representing relative centrality. For example, C's position in the wheel network needs only four communicative links to be able to communicate with every member in the group, while each of the other

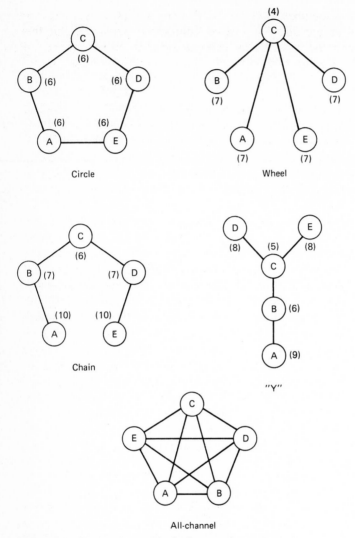

**Figure 3-1**  Common networks in five-member groups.

positions requires seven links to accomplish the same purpose. Therefore, C is the most central position in the wheel network. Figure 3-1 includes the relative centrality figure for each position in each of the four networks.

Many studies comparing communication networks have revealed numerous differences among various networks using a variety of points of comparison. For example, in terms of speed and efficiency, centralized networks, such as the wheel and the chain, are superior to decentralized networks, such as the circle (the least centralized network). But this discovery is tempered by a further comparison in terms of accuracy of problem solving. For solving simple problems, centralized networks are much more accurate, but decentralized networks are more accurate for solving complex problems.

Regarding the morale of group members, the members of decentralized networks experience greater satisfaction with their group experiences than do members of groups employing a centralized network. In short, centralized networks are considered superior in accomplishing tasks, at least simple ones, although decentralized networks foster more cohesive groups and appear to have an advantage in performing more complex tasks.

Results from past comparisons of communication networks, however, may not be particularly significant to LGD decision making. In the first place, nearly all such comparisons have been performed in research laboratories under rigidly controlled conditions. The laboratory context itself is no reason to dismiss comparison results as insignificant. But one of the typical laboratory controls has unfortunately been the severe restriction of time allowed for group interaction. A few studies which allowed more time for group interaction, such as that performed by Cohen, Bennis, and Wolkon (1961), revealed that the differences among groups using different network patterns diminished significantly over time. (Network research has also typically restricted other aspects of communication, such as sending only written messages without face-to-face confrontation. But the restriction of time may be a more significant restriction of the group process.)

A group needs time to develop any satisfactory organization. As soon as the group members accustom themselves to the network they are using, the particular pattern or network they employ should be of little consequence. The success of centralized networks in the task dimension of the group process should increase the cohesiveness of group members over time. Time is absolutely essential for the natural interdependence of the two dimensions of group process to assert itself. And, too, the social success of decentralized networks should also allow members to strive harder in the task dimension and thereby increase their speed and efficiency of task performance. Whatever the reason, the differences among networks as to speed, efficiency, accuracy, organizational stability, and group morale appear to diminish to the point of insignificance over time.

The importance of time has been emphasized earlier but is still worthy of mention. When a group does not have sufficient time to establish its social organization, the members begin to compensate. Under severe time restrictions, they compensate by short-circuiting the group process. One shortcut method used by groups in the absence of a clear social organization is to substitute the simple majority vote for the process of validating decisions by consensus (Hall and Watson, 1970). Group members functioning under severe time pressure simply don't have sufficient time to proceed through all the steps of decision modification in order to achieve consensus on their decisions. Therefore, they resort to shortcuts to decision making, such as majority votes. The inevitable result, of course, is false or superficial consensus. Members allegedly perform their tasks and make their decisions, but they do not commit themselves to carrying them out. Decisions may be "made," but they have not achieved consensus.

The purely structural view of communication networks does contribute to the understanding of group process in some respects. Centrality is a concept which has been consistently related to leadership and status. The most central position in an emergent network is most apt to be the position occupied by the emergent leader. The various levels of centrality generally reflect the status levels of the group's hierarchy.

Figure 3-1 illustrates two status levels (levels of centrality) in the wheel network. The relative centrality of C is four, and the relative centrality of all other positions is seven. Three status levels are reflected in the chain network. C is the apparent leader with a relative centrality of six, B and D are the second status level with relative centralities of seven, and A and E are the third status level with centrality figures of ten. The Y network illustrates four status levels, a rather uncommon status hierarchy to emerge in a five-member group. Only the circle network has a single status level and illustrates another extremely improbable network to emerge in a decision-making group.

The network that finally emerges from extensive group interaction is not the only network employed by the group during the process of decision making. A group may employ one network at one stage of the process and shift to a different network later on as the group enters a new phase of the process. In this respect, centrality does not necessarily reflect leadership or even high status during the intermediate stages of the group process.

The verbally active "problem member," for example, may at some point during interaction be the recipient of influence from every other member verbally attempting to modify the problem behavior. During this period of group interaction, the network would probably reflect the deviate in position C in the wheel network—a highly central position. This network, reflecting a problem member in a central position, is undoubtedly temporary. A problem member or extreme deviate who does not modify his or her behavior will be ignored by the others and excluded from their interactions. Such action virtually expels the extreme deviate from the network and from effective group membership. Centrality, then, is often linked to leadership and status in the network that finally emerges from group interaction. But network centrality during intermediate stages in the process of group decision making may also indicate an extreme deviate under group pressure to conform.

Another stage of network development involves the coalitions or subgroups formed during various phases in the group decision-making process. The network used at that time generally reflects the existence of coalitions. To illustrate, the Y network might reflect the presence of two coalitions, one composed of three members (C, D, and E) and the other composed of two members (A and B). We might hypothesize further that the three-two coalitions have formed around two leader contenders. The two most central positions, B and C, would then reflect the two contenders representing each of the two coalitions.

Discussing network structures of group communication would not be complete without mentioning the limited number of networks included in the discussion above. Obviously there are more possible network combinations than the four (omitting the all-channel network) shown in Figure 3-1. But other combinations are simply variations of these basic models. For example, the wheel and chain networks can be combined by adding to the wheel network two additional channel linkages between A and B and between D and E. The same network can be formed from the chain network by adding channel links between A and C and between A and E. This wheel-chain network is then a network variation formed by combining channel linkages included in two of the basic network models.

Further variations should be obvious. The important point is that emergent network structures can be observed in a small group and that these structures provide insight into various aspects of the group process of decision making.

A final point to remember concerning network structures involves the nature of a process. Interaction patterns change through time as the group moves from one phase to another in the decisional process. Network structures also change. Structural change should reflect processual changes so that the developing network structure can be viewed as an emergent process changing over time and culminating in the final emergent network characterizing the group's status hierarchy. Thus, action (time) attributes are added to the otherwise purely structural (space) attributes of the network.

The discoveries based upon comparing the different purely structural attributes of the various networks can probably be dismissed as rather trivial and irrelevant to developing a richer understanding of the process of group decision making.

## CHANNEL CAPACITY

A field of study known as "information theory" also approaches communication from a structural perspective. While highly specialized and restrictive as a comprehensive view of human communication, information theory has provided some fresh insights into the process of human communication. One of those insights is "channel capacity" and, simply speaking, refers to the maximum number of information items a human can effectively handle.

According to one authority on information theory, George A. Miller (1956), the number of information items that an individual can identify and deal with effectively is incredibly small. Miller indicates the maximum limit (or channel capacity) is probably seven, plus or minus two. While information theorists vary slightly in their estimates of channel capacity, from fewer than seven to more, all agree that our capacity to process information is limited and generally very small.

Information theory has also discovered that the human being can increase channel capacity significantly by combining items of information into larger classes of items. That is, you can combine several items of information into a larger class of items and identify that class as a single unit. For example, rather than process items, "747," "Chevrolet," "Pontiac," "DC9," "Ford," you can combine the five individual items into two representative classes—"automobiles" and "airplanes." Thus, you increase your channel capacity by treating groups of items as individual items.

In the jargon of information theory, a single item of information is known as a "bit." A class of information items formed by combining several "bits" has been labeled a "chunk." The point is that humans can learn with experience to increase their individual channel capacity by reclassifying and grouping unitary items of information.

If one individual can increase channel capacity with experience, it seems logical that a group of individuals should be able to increase its channel capacity, also. Lanzetta and Roby (1957) discovered the existence of that very phenomenon. Over a period of time a group learns to increase the amount of information it can effectively handle. Apparently during the process of group interaction, members develop the ability to process an ever-larger number of information items. According to the precepts of information theory, the group members effectively increase their channel capacity through a normal process of grouping and classifying different information items into "chunks," thereby remaining within their channel capacity but effectively handling a greater quantity of information "bits."

The group process of decision modification illustrates an apparent increase in channel capacity integral to the group process. Group members introduce numerous decision proposals, many of which are continually reintroduced for further discussion. Rather than modifying those proposals directly and increasing geometrically the number of information items that group members would have to identify, the members reformulate old proposals when they are reintroduced. If group members modified each proposal through direct amendment, they would be required to deal with each original proposal and each amendment separately. A reformulated proposal, however, is a single item that replaces the former proposal and does not increase the number of information items to be discussed. Moreover, a reformulated proposal may combine several earlier proposals into a single proposal that reduces the number of information items discussed by group members. The group process of decision modification, then, allows the group members to increase the amount of information they can effectively identify and discuss during group interaction. (Chapter 5 includes a more complete discussion of the group process of decision modification.)

Some evidence has indicated that the quality of group decisions increases in proportion to the number of ideas members generate during group interaction. This may be true, but there is certainly a point of diminishing returns as the number of contributed ideas approaches the limits of the group's channel capacity. The group's limitations on the amount of information it can identify may explain why some research studies indicate no significant increase in the quality of final group decisions when members did generate more ideas. The structural attribute of channel capacity is, like network structures, also related to the process (both structure and action) of group decision making.

## GATEKEEPING

Viewing communication structurally (as the transmission and reception of messages on a channel) reveals a further structural characteristic of communication. The networks illustrated in Figure 3-1 provide a graphic depiction of the concept of "gatekeeping." You will note, for example, that some group members in each of those networks (except for the all-channel network) do not communicate directly with every other member of the group. In the wheel network the person occupying position B does not communicate directly with the member occupying position D. Rather, B exchanges messages with the member in position C, who, in turn, exchanges messages with D. Member C, in all networks except the all-channel network, is the intermediary or link in a chain of communication channels between members B and D. That is, B communicates with D only through C's intermediation in the circle, the wheel, the chain, and the Y networks.

The member who occupies that middle link in the network is in a position of greater (i.e., lower) relative centrality. In the Y and chain networks, for example, member B is the gatekeeper between A and C. In the chain network, member D is a gatekeeper between C and E. In the wheel network, member C is a gatekeeper between every possible pair of members—A and B, A and D, A and E, B and D, B and E, and D and E. In other words, all messages sent and received in the wheel network are transmitted either to or by the group member who occupies position C. For this reason, the wheel network is the most centralized network of all.

It seems reasonable, then, that a gatekeeper is a person who occupies a position of considerable potential influence. This member receives more messages from more different sources than members who are in less central positions in the network. Given this informational advantage over other group members, a gatekeeper (in the sense of a centralized position in a small group network) often becomes a group leader or, at least, a member with above-average influence. The concept of leadership will be discussed in more detail in Chapter 7.

When persons sit around a table in a face-to-face situation—for example, a group in a classroom setting—the notion of networks seems somewhat artificial. After all, there appears to be nothing that would prohibit any group member from exchanging messages with every other member in the group. Thus, the all-channel network should be the network used by virtually every "real" group. Nevertheless, networks typically emerge in face-to-face groups after a period of time. They are characterized by a predominant usage or neglect of certain channels. That is, some members tend to communicate more with some members and less with others.

The gatekeeping role in classroom groups may also be a factor in activities that occur outside the face-to-face situation. Therefore, gate-keeping is not readily apparent in the actual group meetings during the performance of its decision-making task. One classroom group, in particular, contained one member—Marilyn—who performed an important gatekeeping role, but that role was apparent only in situations outside the face-to-face meetings of the group. Marilyn was neither a leader nor a particularly high contributor during the group's discussions at its meetings. Nevertheless, she, probably more than any other single member, was responsible for the group's successful decision-making performance.

Marilyn's group had a problem. That problem was Carol. Carol proved to be quite irresponsible in her interactions in that group. She was often absent from the meetings, usually with a legitimate excuse (employment and other classroom pressures). But reasons for absences from group meetings are of little concern to a functioning group. Quite reasonably, the other group members resented Carol's absences because she was not doing her part to help the group do its work—a task that placed it under considerable time pressure. Regardless of the legitimacy of Carol's absences, the other group members found themselves having to assume a heavier burden in the group's task efforts. Carol just didn't accept her share of the group's responsibility. Moreover, she also had what appeared to be a personality conflict with a few of the group members, a conflict which probably stemmed from a radical disagreement over religious beliefs.

During the meetings that Carol did attend, her contributions were not frequent and were not directed to any one member of the group more than others. When she was unable to attend the meetings, she consistently contacted Marilyn outside class meetings, often giving her material to bring to the meetings. Soon Marilyn was the person who spoke for Carol during group meetings and who explained Carol's absences or reported on her progress. In other words, Marilyn became the gatekeeper between Carol and the other group members. While the others resented Carol's lack of commitment to the group, they considered Marilyn to be a valuable member. Through Marilyn, they came to accept Carol as a member of what developed into a rather cohesive group.

The gatekeeping role does not necessarily imply influence in a group, although it often does. Nevertheless, this role serves a valuable structural position in the processing and dissemination of information among all members of the group. Moreover, the position carries with it enormous responsibilities for the exercise of judgment of what information should be relayed from one person to another, what information should not be retransmitted, and what information should be augmented or emphasized.

When gatekeeping occurs in the exchange of messages in a group, communication is mediated in the sense that communication between a source and a receiver "goes through" a mediator. On the level of an entire society, we often refer to this phenomenon of mediated communication when thinking of the mass media—radio, television, newspapers. Our mass media serve as the go-between for informational sources and the larger society—us, the consumers of information. Mediated communication is, thus, rather efficient in terms of mass information processing. Too many data are available in our informational environment for us to process or consume them all—that is, to interpret all the data as meaningful information. The gatekeeper plays a structural role that reduces considerably the quantity of data available. By relaying information to the receiver, the gatekeeper converts much data into a manageable amount of information and typically conveys this information in a more understandable form.

Gatekeepers possess an awesome responsibility. They must make many crucial decisions before relaying or retransmitting the messages. For example, should information be transmitted in the same manner and the same form in which it is received? Often, relaying identical information is quite impossible. There is simply too much of it to be relayed. The gatekeeper must then reclassify the information into larger "chunks." At this point, the selectivity of the gatekeeper becomes highly significant. Mass media, and particularly newspaper and television news reporters, have often been accused of allowing their biases to dictate what information they select and retransmit to the public.

Gatekeepers have no choice but to exercise their selective processes. They must recognize, interpret, and then retransmit information. The gatekeeper who uses the selective processes adequately is called "objective"—as in the "objective news reporter." More often, however, the objectivity of a news reporter is determined by the extent to which the information received is consistent with the biases of the reporter in the gatekeeping position. But before we hasten to condemn, keep in mind that this use of the selectivity processes in information processing is quite normal.

A gatekeeper not only retransmits information but also withholds information, thereby not allowing it to pass through to the next receiver in the chain. In the same sense that a dam holds back some amount of water in a reservoir and allows only a portion of the water over the spillway, a gatekeeper also holds back some information from the receiver and allows only certain other information to "spill over." Withholding certain information and retransmitting certain other information must also be a part of the gatekeeper's process of selectivity. Although information may not necessarily be distorted, the omission of some information may lead to a different interpretation of the information that *is* received. In this sense, a gatekeeper who does not perform the role adequately may be guilty of both an error of commission (distorting information in the retransmitting) and an error of omission (withholding pertinent information).

The gatekeeping role in a small group has another aspect which has not yet been discussed. Benne and Sheats (1948) include in their list of "group-building and maintenance roles" the role of gatekeeper. They also equate that role with the role of "expediter." According to them, then, the gatekeeper's role is "to keep communication channels open by encouraging or facilitating the participation of others," as well as by regulating the flow of communication.

Bonnie Johnson (1977, p. 234) refers to the facilitating nature of gatekeeping in terms of an "attitude" that members of a group should possess. This attitude leads members to attempt actively to encourage and solicit the participation of other group members. I have just noted the tremendous responsibility of gatekeepers because of their possession of informational influence. Johnson, as well as Benne and Sheats, emphasizes the gatekeeper's acceptance of that responsibility by advocating the adoption of an attitude which facilitates the information-processing capabilities of the entire group. This attitude would also deemphasize the possible misuse of the natural informational advantage by an unscrupulous gatekeeper.

Relating gatekeeping to the earlier discussion of channel capacity, we should be aware that persons in gatekeeping positions (such as, for example, member C in a wheel network) must also cope with an enormous amount of information. Member C receives all the messages from all other group members and must process every message exchanged during group interaction. This gatekeeper may be inundated with far too much information to process. After all, any human being has only a limited capacity to process information. That capacity can easily be exceeded during normal exchanges of information in a wheel network.

When the member in a gatekeeping position must deal with information that exceeds his or her capacity to store and retrieve information, the result is called information "overload." Information overload is more of a problem in a large-scale organization (which would involve many more people and much more information in various forms—for example, written memoranda, oral conversations, formal letters, market reports, sales reports) than it is in a small group. The face-to-face interaction of a decision-making group would normally use information in the same limited forms—verbal and nonverbal speech.

Furthermore, as discussions in Chapter 5 concerning the process of decision modification will illustrate, groups soon develop methods of coping with too much information. They handle many different pieces of information for very brief periods of time rather than simultaneously discussing those same items over a long period. Information overload, then, rarely is a problem during small group decision making, although it may be much more significant within a large organization. Most important, overload occurs, not throughout the entire group or organization, but at a specific point or position in the network. And that position must be relatively central—that is, a gatekeeping position.

## SOCIAL STRUCTURE

The social structure of roles and status levels in a group also affects the communication among the group members. The members communicate with one another in different patterns and networks, dependent to some extent on the status levels (such as leader and followers) in their group's social structure.

Collins and Guetzkow (1964, pp. 170–177) have adequately documented the finding that the social structure in a group does affect the structural aspects of its communication. Leaders and other high-status persons, for example, are major participators during group interaction, both as initiators and respondents of messages. Low-status members communicate for a disproportionately large amount of their time with high-status members, thus affirming that network centrality is linked with leadership and status. The typical explanation for this structural phenomenon in the group's use of networks involves the individual member's desire to aspire to higher status. An individual who finds it impossible to rise to high status through his or her own achievements will substitute for actual status a vicarious membership in a higher status by communicating upward in the status hierarchy.

During the process of leader and status emergence, however, the structural patterns of communication change over time. During early stages of the emergent process, contenders appear to communicate most often with their lieutenants and not with one another. Such a communicative structure is consistent with the assumption that coalitions form around leader contenders. The communication network also reflects those coalitions. After a group completes its process of leader emergence, however, the leader tends to initiate and receive messages to and from all group members and assume a central position in the network.

Certainly the status of the group member affects the messages he or she initiates and receives. *Who* says it is as important to perceiving the relative importance of the message as *what* is said. Status endows a message with value. In the study of persuasion and attitude change, the "ethos" or credibility of the communicator appears to be a significant factor in how people attend and react to persuasive messages. Thus, the communicative structure in a small group affects, and is affected by, the social structure of the group members. Communication structure and social structure exert a mutual and reciprocal influence on each other and may therefore be considered interdependent.

## BARRIERS AND BREAKDOWNS—A FALLACY

Too often, instances of ineffective communication are dismissed as the result of communication barriers or breakdowns. This mechanistic rationalization of communicative failures has enjoyed widespread popularity in everyday usage and even in group communication research (Black, 1955). It is not necessary to dwell on this common misconception of the communicative process. Dennis Smith (1970), among others, has already illustrated the fallacy in the reasoning allegedly justifying the existence of barriers and breakdowns in communication.

Briefly, a communication barrier or breakdown is a purely structural attribute of communication, on the assumption that messages travel through space from one person (a source) to another person (a receiver). Thus, communication is not so much a process as a linear flow of messages across space. A "barrier" is a "dam" which blocks the flow of messages so that the receiver cannot receive an initiated message. A "breakdown" assumes that the connecting link between communicating individuals ceases to exist—in the same sense as a broken telephone line. In any case, the concept of barriers and breakdowns depends on the idea that a linear flow of messages across space is the central feature of communication.

The basic analogy of communication barriers and breakdowns is the machine in which a barrier (for example, a clogged fuel line) or a breakdown (say, a broken fuel line) could certainly be said to exist. If human communication were so mechanistic, it would certainly be much less complex than it is. Fortunately, human beings and their social systems do not correspond accurately to the mechanistic analogy.

The assumption of linearity is contrary to the principle of interdependence. Communicators don't send and receive isolated messages; they engage in a process—the development and maintenance of an interpersonal relationship. And that relationship is defined by the recurrent, sequential patterns of messages in the context of the entire interaction. Communication as an interaction process denies the possibility of its being partially blocked or breaking down. Can an interpersonal relationship be blocked or break down? In group communication that interpersonal relationship is groupness, inextricably interdependent with the process of group communication. As long as any vestige of groupness exists, communication continues to exist. A barrier or breakdown assumes an absence of communication, but it ignores the more important problem of ineffective communication.

Furthermore, later discussions in Chapter 8 will demonstrate the normality of social conflict and deviance. If the linear flow of messages is central to group communication, social conflict and deviance must by definition be inherently disruptive. That is, conflict will lead to closed channels and communication barriers or breakdowns. That social conflict disrupts the free flow of messages is blatantly false for much, if not most, social conflict and deviance.

Occasionally, members of an unsuccessful group believe that social conflict is harmful and disruptive. Because of their belief, the members overtly avoid conflict until their tension level and suppressed hostility become so extreme that communication barriers and breakdowns do seem to exist. Such a group illustrates a classic example of the self-fulfilling prophecy in action. If group members believe that conflict is disruptive and harmful, they tend to behave as if it were and eventually succeed in disrupting effective group communication and harming the group process.

To take seriously the notion of communication barriers and breakdowns is to regard communication mechanistically, to be sure. More important, however, too much emphasis on barriers and breakdowns subverts even a mechanistic conception of human communication—at least when it occurs in a face-to-face situation, such as in group decision making. Thinking of effective and ineffective communication is much more valuable and beneficial than believing in the myth of noncommunication.

Subsequent discussions in this volume will ignore the possibility of barriers and breakdowns in human communication. The book will emphasize, instead, the improvement of communicative effectiveness and the effectiveness of the group process. What you might have otherwise considered to be a communication breakdown, at least in terms of the conventional wisdom you continue to possess, will be treated as communication, but ineffective communication. Try to reconceptualize barriers and breakdowns and interpret them in the sense of a communication process that is not operating adequately or effectively but is working nonetheless.

Too many common misconceptions about communication and the group process prevail in our society. One step in improving the effectiveness of communication is for all members to discard their misconceptions about groups and about communication. Truly, understanding communication and the group process includes not *mis*understanding it.

## SUMMARY

Communication, viewed as a process, contains both structural and functional dimensions. Structural elements are consistent with a view of communication as transmitting and receiving messages on channels. Feedback responses, one structural element of communication, are unavoidable and occur continuously during the give and take of group interaction. Effective feedback responses during group interaction depend upon the cohesiveness of the group members and the interpretations of those feedback responses by the persons who receive them.

Certain characteristics of the messages that constitute the group interaction are important to decision making. However, the timing of the messages may be more significant to effective group decision making than the content of the messages.

Viewed structurally, group communication has been perceived as a network—the pattern of channels that link members of the group. Networks are distinguished from one another by relative centrality and distance among network positions. The most central position in a network has been linked with leaders and with deviants who are under extreme social pressures to conform. During the process of group decision making, several networks generally emerge from the group's interactive patterns and reflect coalition formation and leadership at various stages in the group process.

Channel capacity—the structural restraints limiting the amount of information that can be processed effectively—illustrates a potential reason underlying the group process of decision modification. Furthermore, the person who occupies the gatekeeping position in the network is responsible for receiving, transforming, and retransmitting information to other members of the group. The gatekeeper is often subjected to information overload, that is, to receiving more information than is humanly possible to process and relay to others. On the other hand, barriers and breakdowns of communication are considered as untenable concepts which are inconsistent with viewing communication as a process.

# Chapter 4

# Group Communication —Functional Elements

You have undoubtedly been trained in various aspects of communication throughout your experience in elementary and secondary schools and in college. You have probably mastered, to some extent, the syntactic dimension of communication, its grammar. For example, you know about placement of nouns and verbs, agreement between subject and predicate, etc. The semantic dimension is also emphasized in our schools, generally in the sense of finding a referent for a word in order to decipher its meaning. That is, a word stands for something. Early in your educational career, you learned to use the dictionary and provide definitions for words—semantics. The dimension of communication that rarely appears in our schools' curricula, however, is the pragmatic dimension.

The pragmatic aspect of communication deals with the relationship of the symbols (the words, for example) to the user (the person, the communicator). Another way of understanding the pragmatic dimension of communication is to think of the functions performed by a message or a unit of communication. That is, what does the action *do* in the communicative process? Beyond the grammar of the sentences and the meanings of the words is the pragmatic notion of how the action functions in the communicative situation as, for example, a bluff, a threat, a plea, or an expression of intimacy.

The major emphasis of this chapter is on the pragmatic functioning of human communication. To discuss communication in terms of what it does rather than what it looks like is to emphasize the functions of communication. Moreover, it will soon become apparent that the same comment (even using the same words, said in the same manner) may perform different functions, depending upon when it occurs in the sequence of interaction. In other words, the function of any particular communicative act is often determined by the acts that precede or follow it during the normal process of ongoing human communication.

The ideas contained in this chapter are not particularly complex. However, they may appear to be more difficult than they are, probably because understanding the functional elements of communication requires revising the way we normally think of communication. In the pages to follow, for example, the concept of messages and their transmission and receipt on a channel is of little relevance. The emphasis is now on the entire group or social system, taken as a whole—a single whole, composed of all the members of the group. The focus is on the group as a system—a single information-processing entity of which each individual person is a part. In other words, the whole (the group) is different from the sum of its parts (the individual members). Rather than focus on the individual human being (for example, on self-concept, attitudes, values, beliefs), we will concern ourselves with the social relationship, the organization of individuals into a single unit called a "group."

## PRAGMATIC CHARACTERISTICS OF COMMUNICATION

Some people distinguish between "communication" and "interaction." Erving Goffman (1969, p. ix), a sociologist, defines communication as a term which "obviously and centrally applies" to "socially organized channels for transceiving information." To Goffman, communication can be viewed only as transmitting and receiving messages on channels. He reserves the term "interaction" to designate the conduct or behavior of human beings in relationship to one another in face-to-face settings. For fully understanding communication and the group process, however, such an artificial distinction is self-defeating. For our purposes, and consistent with the opinions of most communication scholars, I shall use the terms "communication" and "interaction" interchangeably. They refer to the same process and are considered to be synonyms.

### Communication Defined

You will recall that the definition of "group" in Chapter 1 emphasized the group as a system of behaviors composed of identifiable patterns of interactions. The definition of communication is consistent with that earlier definition of "group" to the extent that the process of "group" and the process of communication are considered to be precisely the same process. In this respect, the subtitle of this book, *Communication and the Group Process,* implies a single perspective of small group decision making. I have emphasized the group as the focus of attention, and I view the communicative process from that focus—the group as a holistic system.

When the focus of communication shifts from the individual human being to the social system (the group), the most significant elements of communication become the *relationships* among group members rather than the internalized feelings, attitudes, emotions, or beliefs of individual members. The only way in which two persons can establish a relationship with one another is to act toward one another, to engage in communicative actions. How A "feels" about B cannot affect their social relationship unless and until that feeling becomes observable to B and to other group members—that is, until that feeling is expressed in the form of action, a communicative behavior. Although that internalized feeling may be highly important to A, it is significant to B and to other group members only to the extent that they are able to become aware of it. In other words, private elements of a person's self can be important to the group system (and to group decision making) only if they become public and knowable or if they affect behaviors that are then public and observable. In either case, the focus is on the communicative actions, the behaviors.

Peter McHugh (1968, p. 132) emphasizes this fundamental aspect of the group communicative process. He states flatly, "Nothing of interest to us is private and hence unobservable." He goes on to state (p. 134), "Definitions are not owned, . . . hidden away in the recesses of mind and self. They are *performances,* applied and validated, and thus public and observable. . . . "

Any behavior that a person can perform is based on a choice from among alternative behaviors available to each communicator. Every person is capable of performing any of a vast array of possible actions. The action that is performed at any given instant is inevitably a product of some choice process, a process of choosing to perform one or more behaviors from among the enormous repertoire of available behaviors. In this sense, everyone possesses a repertoire of behaviors capable of being performed at any given time. The performance of a behavior is thus a result of each person's choice.

Why do we choose to perform some behaviors and not others in any given situation? Although we are capable of free choice and free will, this fact does not imply that our choice is random, that we choose to behave in a purely happenstance or capricious manner. Rather, we choose to behave on the basis of what we consider to be appropriate to a given situation. Stated another way, our repertoire of choices is *constrained* in the sense that many alternatives are eliminated and are thus not available to be chosen in any given situation. As paradoxical as it may seem, we have the capacity of choice among behaviors at the same time that our behavioral choices are subject to numerous constraints that limit the range of alternatives available to us. In many instances, we are only vaguely aware, or even unaware, of any of these constraints, but we submit to them nevertheless. For example, we wear clothing in public rather than appear nude. We speak in a language that contains specific rules of syntax and semantics and conform to those rules (although often rather loosely), even though we may not be aware of the rules that operate to constrain our choices.

Often constraints occur as a result of a particular social situation in which we find ourselves. For example, in your family group the constraints that fellow family members place on your behaviors are quite different from the constraints present when you are in a group of close personal friends. Furthermore, either of those situations will place constraints on your actions that will be different from those constraints evident in a group of strangers or new acquaintances. We will communicate in one way with a boss or an employer and in a different way with a close friend or fellow family member. The social environment places many constraints on our behavioral repertoire and significantly influences the communicative process.

The principal origin of the constraints on our behaviors is the previous interaction itself. That is, constraints result from our past behavioral choices during interaction as well as the past behaviors of others. When communicating with someone, you *must choose* to perform some behavior. That is, you have no alternative but to choose and thereby perform some behavior. Regardless of what your initial behavioral choice is, your subsequent behavior in the situation is thus constrained as a result of what you and the other communicators have elected to perform in past communicative behavior. Watzlawick, Beavin, and Jackson (1967, pp. 131–134) refer to this phenomenon as the "limiting effect of communication" and describe it as follows: "In a communicational sequence, every exchange of messages narrows down the number of possible next moves" (emphasis deleted).

An example may illustrate this limitation principle of communication more clearly. Several months ago, I was riding to campus on a city transit bus when an elderly gentleman boarded the bus and sat beside me. After a few minutes, he remarked that it was shameful that the city had cut down so many of the big trees along the street on which we were riding. Without really thinking, I responded, "Yes, it sure is." That single exchange of messages functioned to place both of us in a communicative situation that limited my subsequent behavioral choices. At the very least, I experienced some degree of involvement in this casual relationship. That involvement, virtually involuntary on my part, proceeded directly from my agreeable response to his initial attempt to make conversation. He went on to ask me whether I lived in that neighborhood. I replied that I lived farther south in another suburban area. My involvement became deeper, and the conversation became less one-sided. Our conversation continued until the bus arrived at the university campus and I was able to excuse myself.

That particular conversation was a casual one. I have not seen that person since our brief encounter. During that time, however, we engaged in a relationship in which we influenced each other and were influenced by our communicational choices. Some relationship is present, inherently and inevitably, in every communicative event. Every exchange of messages constrains our further interaction behavior. In the few moments on the bus, my first comment seemed rather innocuous at the time but proceeded to commit me to that conversation. I did not really want to engage in conversation, but I did not wish to appear rude, either. Consequently, I responded to the man's first comment and then felt trapped. Moreover, this involvement and entrapment in subsequent interaction occur every time we communicate. Had I chosen to ignore the man's first comment, disagree with it, or redefine it, the ensuing interaction would have been quite different because it would have placed different constraints on the later sequences of messages. Nevertheless, subsequent interaction is always constrained by previous acts.

Each time a person enters into a communicative situation, he or she brings to that situation some preliminary definition of the relationship and of the situation. The exchange of messages (i.e., the interaction behavior) that occurs during the communicative event defines the communicative situation more clearly until a single definition of the situation exists. The definition is characterized by a particular variety of message exchanges. In other words, our definitions of the situation that we bring to the relationship are redefined in conjunction with those of the other communicator.

A communicative relationship thus evolves during the process of interacting with others. Each communicator soon learns which behaviors are appropriate to that situation and which behaviors are inappropriate. The interaction soon stabilizes, if the communication continues for a sufficient time. Stated another way, each person in every communicative situation learns how "to play the game," what the rules are that govern the communication. As a result, the individual communicators constrain their behavioral choices until an identifiable pattern of message exchanges evolves to characterize or define that relationship.

Communication is thus a series of actions. That is, communication becomes a sequence of events which occur in time. An action is not a "thing." It has no material existence; it is not extended; it does not take up any space. A behavior is fleeting. It exists only in time and is thus related to other behaviors or other events in time. Communication, viewed in this manner becomes somehow less "real" than the structural elements of communication discussed in Chapter 3. We can easily visualize, in a physical sense, messages being transported on a channel from one place in space to another place in space, from source to receiver on a channel-path. These elements are all conceptually "thinglike" in the sense of a material existence of the elements of communication. However, communication as a sequence of behavioral events reflects no comparable physical quality.

Despite the absence of physical communicative elements, a pragmatic perspective of communication is understandable as certain sequences of acts become familiar. That is, certain acts tend to follow other acts so frequently and are repeated so often that we come to expect the next act in the sequence even before it occurs. The interaction becomes familiar because it has been repeated so often in the past. In this way, past interaction sequences constrain future interaction even though the communicators themselves may be unaware that their actions are being constrained. Communicative relationships are thus characterized by what sorts of actions are performed by communicators who are familiar with the appropriate sequence.

I have certain friends with whom I engage in mutually insulting behaviors. Either one of us will insult the other. That insult is a clear sign that the next act in the sequence will be another insult in response. Some of my other interpersonal relationships are characterized by argumentative interaction. That is, virtually anything either of us can say will be followed by the other's disagreement. For me, these sequences of interaction with these particular people are symptoms of very close interpersonal friendships. I would never have dreamed of insulting or disagreeing with my companion on the bus, however. That sequence was characteristic of a casual first acquaintance. Insults and disagreement would have been quite inappropriate in such an early stage of interaction. The close relationships characterized by mutual insults and argument have developed over a long period and are based upon frequent exchanges of similar behaviors in the past. Those past sequences are now familiar to us and constrain our present interaction. If we were to be polite and agreeable with each other at the present time, we would find the interaction unfamiliar and feel that something was going wrong with our relationship.

Each person's behavior, then, is a reflection of the relationship with other people. Since one's relationship with others changes, often drastically, from one social situation to another, one's "style" of communicative behavior is also subject to different constraints because of the different social relationships. A different combination of communicators (a different group) would prompt a different set of communicative behaviors.

This view of communicative functions does not ignore a person's self. Rather, such a perspective considers the behaviors performed by a person (particularly those behaviors performed in sequence with the behaviors of other persons) as a very adequate representation of the self. In other words, every person's self grows, develops, and possesses an identity in relationship with other people. It does not exist in isolation. Furthermore, relationships with other people are defined and characterized as sequences (interacts and double interacts) of communicative behaviors or actions. As behavioral sequences (determined by past interactions) become familiar to the communicators, the social relationship becomes identifiable and "comfortable" to the communicators.

Communication, then, is a series of events, each one following the other in a stream of ongoing actions or behaviors. These actions performed by the communicators are "connected" with one another within this ongoing stream. Therefore, we think of the "connectedness" among the various actions rather than each individual action in isolation. We talk about *inter*action or communication to signify the entire conversation, the entire process of communication.

The process of communication, then, involves considering the entire conversation or discussion of the communicators (for our purposes, members of a decision-making group) as a single process. It is in this sense of a single "system" of communication that Birdwhistell (1959, p. 104) characterizes communication as an entire process or system in which an individual participates. An individual "does not originate communication" but rather "engages in or becomes part of communication." Viewed pragmatically, the communication process emphasizes the interconnections between the actions performed by the individual communicators. Together with their connections, all the actions by the individual communicators form the entire system or process of communication. For our purposes, the communicative system is the group and the group process.

Group communication, then, involves a sequence of the actions that are contributed by individual members. As a sequence, each action follows after, or precedes, another action. The person, when engaging in, or becoming part of, communication, contributes actions or behaviors to the overall process of communication. In a sense, each person takes turns in contributing actions, particularly in the form of verbal utterances in a face-to-face conversation or discussion. For some period of time, any individual group member gets the floor and later relinquishes his or her turn to another member who then has the floor for some additional period of time.

Communication or interaction is the sequence of the actions contributed by the communicators in the sense that they take turns in contributing to the sequence. Each person's action is connected in some manner to the action that precedes it and the action that follows it. An example of such connectedness occurs when we say that a comment following a question may be regarded as an answer. Rather than think of each individual action separately, we think of the *connections* between actions and thus view the communicative process as a *system* of communication rather than as actions and reactions by individual persons.

### One Cannot *Not* Communicate

When communication is viewed as a sequence of behaviors, one factor becomes immediately apparent—one cannot *not* communicate. It is literally impossible not to behave. For example, try this exercise: For the next 10 seconds, *do not behave.* Your first reaction should be the realization that such an instruction just doesn't make any sense. The idea of *not* behaving is nonsensical. Even silence or remaining motionless is behavior. Sleeping is behavior. Breathing is behavior. Lying or standing still is behavior. Thus, if behavior has no opposite, and if communication is defined as behavior, then communication also has no opposite. Hence, one cannot *not* communicate.

Watzlawick, Beavin, and Jackson (1967, pp. 48–51) were probably the first to coin the now familiar phrase, "One cannot not communicate." This catch phrase has often been the object of considerable misinterpretation. For example, is all communication to be considered behavior? The answer to this question is affirmative. (No problem so far.) On the other hand, is all behavior communication? The answer here is less clear.

Certainly not all behavior can be communication. On the other hand, any behavior performed during communication potentially has some message value. That is, any behavior is potentially communicative in the sense that it can affect subsequent interaction. But any behavior that is not public or observed (such as random foot-tapping or fidgeting under a table, out of view) is not a significant part of the communicative situation. Moreover, such behavior *cannot* be significant precisely because it is not public or capable of being observed.

Any behavior, though potentially communicative, may eventually prove to be insignificant. To understand communication, then, is to discover those parts of the interaction, the particular kinds of actions, that are the most significant elements of the interaction. Other behaviors would be considered rather unimportant, but not necessarily noncommunicative. Is all behavior communication? Not necessarily. But any behavior that is public and thus observable within the ongoing interaction is potentially communicative.

The impossiblity of not communicating also suggests that communication need not be intentional or successful to be definable as communication. We sometimes believe that communication takes place only when it is effective—that is, when source and receiver have interpreted the message similarly or are "on the same wave length." But in the event that interpretations are not similar, we tend to believe that communication has not even occurred. For example, we often say, "We talked to each other, but we did not communicate." Such an observation apparently suggests that communication has not been totally successful or has not fully resolved disagreements. Obviously, such a communicative situation may not be particularly effective or successful. But to suggest that no communication has taken place is absurd.

When people are talking (that is, behaving verbally and nonverbally) with one another, they have no choice but to become involved in a series of behavioral exchanges. These interactions are, by definition, communication. It is not, however, necessarily effective communication. Indeed, misunderstanding may characterize many communicative situations. But its presence does not mean that no communication has taken place, although it may imply that the communication was not particularly effective in establishing a mutually satisfactory relationship.

### Content and Relationship Dimensions

To this point, our discussion has focused on behaviors and actions performed by individual communicators. I have said little or nothing concerning the interpretation of those actions or what those actions might contain. Assume that any action or behavior performed by any person during a communicative event can be called a "message." As such, it contains information. Pragmatically, that information involves two dimensions—a content dimension and a relationship dimension. As dimensions, content and relationship aspects of communication are inseparable and are always present in every communicative behavior.

Gregory Bateson (1935), a social anthropologist, first discussed the concept of two aspects of language which he termed the "report" and "command" characteristics. His original analysis of language has since been extended to communication, generally, as content and relationship dimensions. The content dimension of communication refers to the aspect of behavior that deals with specific data. The content is the topic of conversation, the subject matter. The relationship dimension refers to that property of communicative behavior that provides direction as to how the message's content is to be interpreted. It enables the members of the communicative situation to develop some definition of their social relationship.

The content and relationship dimensions of communication may be compared, respectively, with the "information" contained in a message and the "style" in which the information is expressed. To express a message that contains some information is to express that message *in some way*. Stylizing a message is absolutely unavoidable. In other words, a message will contain some content, and it will also be "stylized." We teach children early in their formative years to stylize messages in order to develop satisfactory relationships. We call such training in stylizing messages "being polite" or "having good manners." The child soon learns not to say, "Gimme the potatoes." Instead, we teach children to ask, "Please pass the potatoes," along with other stylizations including "Thank you," "You're welcome," and "Excuse me." The *content* of the two messages requesting potatoes is precisely the same, but the relationship dimension within the two messages differs significantly.

In every exchange of messages in a sequence of interaction, the content and relationship dimensions of communication are present. Within group decision making the two dimensions are even more apparent and probably more meaningful than in normal everyday conversation. I hasten to add that these dimensions are no more important in group decision making than in other communicative situations; but because of the task and social nature of decision-making groups, those dimensions seem more obvious and are directly involved in the effective functioning of the group process. Ultimately, these dimensions are related to effective decision making. Members of decision-making groups are, therefore, more likely to be aware of the content and relationship dimensions of communication than are communicators in other situations.

It is important to remember that whenever communication occurs, the communicators are dealing with information at the same time that they are developing a social relationship. That relationship dimension of the communication may develop into one of friendship, enmity, cooperation, equality, superior-subordinate, or any of many possible social relations. Moreover, these relationships develop during the sequence of interactive behaviors and may or may not be consistent with expectations arising from the situation. I am sure that you have had communicative relationships, for example, with some "bosses" who interacted with you as though they were indeed superior to you. Another boss, however, may have been more of a colleague or an equal in your interactions. Many husband-wife pairs interact in the form of a superior-subordinate relationship, while others have developed a more equal relationship. Inevitably, the relationship (together with the content) is an inherent part of, and is reflected in, the communicative behaviors exchanged by the participants during group communication.

Group decision making is clearly a social enterprise. While members are communicating with one another, they are simultaneously attempting to achieve consensus on decisions and establishing a social relationship that unites individuals into a functioning group. Thus, group members perform their decision-making task at the same time that they are developing their group relationship. Every act of communication performs a content (informational) function as well as a relational function.

Consider the following excerpt abridged from the interaction of a classroom decision-making group. The students were discussing the pros and cons of establishing a coal-burning plant to generate electricity in southwestern Utah.

*Tim:* Well, the environmental groups are certainly opposed to a power plant so close to the national park.

*Jack:* Frankly, I think that the environmentalists are all a bunch of nuts.

*Mike:* I don't think I understand. What do you mean?

*Jack:* They just don't seem to care about the people who live in that area. The residents want the plant.

*Mike:* Don't care? You've got to be kidding. They care more about the future of those people than lining the pockets of a few utility companies.

*Jack:* But look at all the jobs that will be created.

*Mike:* And look at all the pollution that will float into the park.

*Jack:* What *are* you? Some kind of Sierra Club freak?

*Mike:* What are *you?* A Bircher?

*Tim:* Does anybody know what time it is?

This brief excerpt illustrates the interplay of content and relationship functions within the interaction. Jack and Mike are engaged in an argument over specific information related to the topic at hand. Apparently their argument includes relational overtones, as well. Their conflict over the content issues leads to a rather competitive relational conflict. Their final comments are as much a personal attack on the relationship level as they are inquiries into the ideational basis for each other's opinion.

Tim's last comment illustrates clearly that the content and the relationship dimensions are simultaneously functioning during the interaction. In terms of the content of that final statement, Tim is asking a question that seeks information concerning the time of day. The question changes the subject matter of the discussion on the content level. In fact, one of the other group members responds and tells him the time according to her watch. More important to the relationship dimension of the interaction, however, Tim's request breaks the tension which has been developing in the group as a result of the informational and interpersonal conflict between Jack and Mike. Tim's abrupt change of topic leads to the release of relational tension created by Jack and Mike's interpersonal rivalry.

Similar to the social and task dimensions of group process, in every act the content and the relationship functions of communication always operate simultaneously during the process. Every act of communication contains information in the content dimension as well as some additional indicators as to how that information should be interpreted (that is, the relationship dimension). Sometimes the relational dimension is reflected in the manner in which the words are said (in the inflection, vocal emphasis, etc.) or, perhaps, in the choice of words used to express the information or even in the movements, gestures, or facial expressions during the utterance of the words. Under all circumstances, then, the content and relationship functions of communication occur simultaneously in every act.

These two dimensions of communication should not be construed as a difference between kinds of acts or types of behaviors. In other words, one act of communication is no more content-oriented or relationship-oriented than another. The content and relationship functions of communication are inseparable and inherent within each and every act of human communication.

### Analysis of Interaction

One method that attempts to understand the ongoing stream of interaction during group decision making involves classifying or categorizing each participant's contribution to the communicative process. In this way, any action contributed by an individual member is perceived to be of a certain type. Chapter 5 includes this method of understanding group communication in order to facilitate a fuller understanding of how group members make decisions (task dimension) and relate to one another (social dimension). The practice of interaction analysis, in which categories or classes of actions are used to analyze the ongoing process of group communication, is also the subject of a more detailed discussion in Appendix 2.

Of course, any action performed by an individual group member fulfills different functions. For example, the conversation excerpted from the decision-making group's discussion of the power plant near a national park (page 102) provides several examples of multifunctional comments.

Tim's final remark, for instance, serves several functions. He is not only requesting information, but he is also releasing the social tension that has developed because of the increasingly personalized conflict between Jack and Mike. Also, Tim's comment serves to change the topic of conversation.

The point of understanding group communication, then, is not to identify which function is the most important one served by any given action. We should recognize that each individual action performs several functions in the communicative and group process. The categories used to analyze interaction focus on specific classes of functions in order to let us understand the interaction from a restricted viewpoint. Another list of categories, however, may focus on other functions and lead to an understanding of the interaction from the perspective of a different set of functions. Therefore, one can regard the interaction of the same decision-making group from the viewpoints of several different category systems. Combining the results from such analyses will provide a more complete description, explanation, and understanding of the process of group decision making.

Using different category systems to understand the ongoing interaction appears to be quite sensible. We wouldn't think of looking at a painting in only one way in order to understand it completely. A study of the colors and the artist's combinations of them in the painting would provide only one way of understanding the work of art. Concentrating on the composition of figures and objects in the frame would be another way of looking at the painting. We might also consider such factors as the mood or impression created in the painting, the artist's purpose and style, the school of art which the painting represents, the reactions of critics and the public, and so forth. Communication is understandably a complex phenomenon. It is multifaceted and involves many different functions. Thus, different classes or categories of human actions are necessary in order to achieve the fullest possible understanding of communication and the group process.

Later in this chapter I shall discuss specific lists of categories or functions of communication that have been used to analyze ongoing interaction in group decision making. Keep in mind that any list of categories of interaction must inevitably reflect some way of understanding that which is considered most important in the communicative process. If we look for certain functions in group communication, we will find those functions. But in doing so, we must also ignore other functions. In a sense, the categories that are used to analyze interaction are spectacles or eyeglasses through which we look in order to view the communicative process. Using a different set of categories to analyze interaction, then, is similar to looking at communication through a different set of spectacles and thus seeing something different.

## Punctuation of Interaction

I suggested earlier that the functional view of communication seems less "real" or less "actual" than a view of communication as messages traveling along a channel. The ongoing sequences of communication, because they are events, are certainly less real in the sense that they are not tangible. They are not objects but occurrences, events in time. Moreover, as a series of events, interaction continues indefinitely in an ongoing stream of continuous occurrences. After all, time doesn't stand still; it moves forward in only one direction—toward the future. Some events may be of longer duration than others, but duration does not necessarily make an event more or less important. Furthermore, how does one interpret an event, a behavior, or a message within an ongoing stream or sequence of communication? Recall that, as a process, a stream of communicational behaviors has no beginning and no end other than one that is arbitrarily selected.

An analogy may best illustrate how one can organize, and thus derive meaning from, a sequence of communicative acts. Consider a stream of letters of the English alphabet strung together, unorganized and ongoing, such as the following: *aneatdeskisasignofasickmind.* These letters are contained in a sign which, quite appropriately, hangs over my desk in my home office. The sign, however, does present those letters in organized groups of words. That is, the letters are punctuated (organized) into words by placing spaces between the letters. The groups of letters are more understandable, more meaningful, than the letters by themselves. Properly punctuated, the sign reads, "A neat desk is a sign of a sick mind." Punctuation thus involves grouping or organizing an otherwise incomprehensible series of letters into understandable letter-groups called words, and the words into phrases, sentences, paragraphs, and so forth.

Punctuating is nothing more than organizing or grouping elements in order to enable one to interpret their meaning more easily and more meaningfully. The letters themselves have no intrinsic meaning or significance. But the words (punctuated groups of letters) do endow the elements, in combination with other elements, with an interpretable meaning and, hence, significance. Furthermore, if you change the punctuation rules, you tend to change the possible interpretations of the sequence of elements. Several years ago, after discussing punctuation of interaction sequences, a student attended the next class meeting with a hand-lettered sign on his shirt. The sign consisted of the "words," *toti emul esto.* He asked us to interpret the phrase. Not one of us was sure, but we all felt that the phrase was vaguely Latin. Since none of us knew Latin, we were unable to decipher the three words. His response was to punctuate the apparently Latin phrase into four English words. He did not change the sequence of the letters. He merely revised the punctuation rules of the sequence. Hence, the phrase was transformed into nonsensical English—"to tie mules to." I have often wondered whatever became of that student. If that one incident was characteristic of his potential as a scholar of communication, he is presently either a tremendous success or a dismal failure. I suspect the latter.

Clearly, then, no specific behavior, action, or message has any definite meaning by itself. Rather, the meaning of communication, both content and relationship dimensions, is understandable only within a sequence that has been punctuated or organized into groups of messages or actions. The punctuation, then, allows for a meaningful interpretation of the meaning or significance of communication. We are all familiar with the famous experiments of Pavlov, who conditioned dogs to salivate at the ringing of a bell even without the presence of food. On the other hand, *that* punctuation of the sequence of events was the scientist's interpretation. If one of Pavlov's dogs had been able to speak, it might have said, "See how I have this dumb human trained! Every time I feel hungry, I just salivate. Then he rings the bell and gives me food." Pavlov himself, the dumb human, punctuated the sequence of events quite differently. He thought Fido was the one who was conditioned.

If a single behavior of an individual group member is an act, then groupings of acts result from punctuating the interaction sequence. At this point, it is necessary to introduce two terms that are admittedly jargon, but that are convenient labels I shall use to denote specific groups of acts. We already have terms to designate the grouping of letters of the alphabet in the written mode of communication. We call those groupings "words." Groupings of words are called "sentences," and groupings of sentences are called "paragraphs." Our present purpose requires similar terms to designate groupings of actions or behaviors within an ongoing sequence of interaction during group decision making.

The "act," then, is the contribution to the discussion of a single individual. One act following another act (that is, a pair of acts) is called an "interact." Thus, an interact is composed of two contiguous acts. A "double interact" is a combination of three contiguous acts in the interaction sequence. Member A emits an act (a single act), which is followed by an act from member B (thus, forming an interact), which is followed by a third act from member A (a double interact). Because our emphasis is on communication or *inter*action, the more important unit of analysis is the interact or the double interact—that is, the connectedness of acts to form interaction. In this way, the individual acts are always within the context of the communicative process—the preceding and succeeding acts.

The earlier excerpt of interaction from the group composed of Tim, Jack, and Mike comprises a total of ten acts. Those ten acts also contain nine interacts or possible combinations of two contiguous acts. Tim's first remark followed by Jack's comment is one interact; Jack's comment followed by Mike's subsequent comment forms another interact; and so on. If one numbers those ten acts from 1 through 10, then the nine interacts are composed of 1-2, 2-3, 3-4, 4-5, 5-6, 6-7, 7-8, 8-9, 9-10. Each individual act, then, is the second act of one interact (in combination with the preceding comment) and the first act of another interact (in combination with the following comment). The same is true in forming eight double interacts from the same list of ten acts. The eight double interacts are 1-2-3, 2-3-4, 3-4-5, 4-5-6, 5-6-7, 6-7-8, 7-8-9, 8-9-10.

The question remains as to which groupings of acts (interacts and double interacts) are to be regarded as the appropriate ones. The rules for punctuating acts within the interaction sequences are less explicit and less readily identifiable than the punctuation rules for grouping letters into words, phrases, and sentences. The punctuation of the sequence of letters, discussed earlier, into *toti emul esto* does not conform to those familiar punctuation rules. The alternative punctuation (*to tie mules to*), however, does conform to those rules. The latter punctuation reveals four recognizable English words. The former punctuation produces no recognizable English words among the three. And why are the words recognizable? One reason is that they are familiar in common usage. That is, we have used these words so often in the past that they become recognizable when we use them again.

Although the rules are not quite so specific in punctuating acts into interacts and double interacts, some sequences of interaction are recognizable as sequences. Consider the following list of three acts which are scrambled (that is, out of sequence), in terms of a recognizable double-interact pattern:

"Fine."

"Fine, thank you. How are you?"

"Hi. How are you?"

Clearly this double interact is in reverse order. The sequence is recognizable as the "greeting ritual of our American culture." The sequence is so familiar, so patterned, and has appeared so often in the past (and is, thus, familiar) that we respond to the question as a ritualistic greeting and not a realistic inquiry into the state of our health.

Some time ago, members of my family visited some friends of ours. Their preschool son had just returned from the emergency room of a hospital where he had received treatment for a perforated eardrum and an ear infection. He was clearly a sick boy and could do little more than lie on the couch. But even even at his young age, he had already mastered the ritualized greeting of our society. When asked the question. "How are you?" he immediately responded, "Fine." The response as a report of his obvious state of health was ludicrously inappropriate. But as a response to the ritualized greeting, he responded typically and normally. He recognized the punctuation rule and participated in the interaction sequence appropriate to that rule.

How, then, are interaction sequences punctuated into interacts and double interacts? One common method of punctuating is to organize sequences into interacts and double interacts which are familiar. And interacts and double interacts become familiar to the extent that they have been repeated often in the past. The more frequently that certain acts follow or precede other acts, the more familiar those interacts become. The more familiar they are, the more they are recognizably punctuated. Punctuation of interaction sequences, then, is typically a matter of sheer redundancy. The more often they have occurred in sequence in the past, the more we are able to expect them to occur again in the future, and the more we will tend to punctuate them as recognizable sequences in the present.

The later discussions of the decision-making process and the development of social relationships are based upon the punctuation of interaction sequences in terms of their past frequency of occurrence—that is, their repetitiveness or redundancy and thus their recognizability as sequences of interacts and double interacts.

Generally speaking, members of a successful decision-making group will agree (although not necessarily at a high level of awareness) on how their interaction is punctuated. Typically, the punctuation or organization of acts within a meaningful pattern is a matter of familiarity—that is, how often those particular sequences have occurred in the past.

Occasionally, breaking the familiar sequence and substituting a novel or unexpected action has greater impact than would normally be expected. Its information value is enhanced precisely because it is out of the ordinary, unexpected, and novel. These are characteristics of human communication that will become increasingly important as we delve more deeply into the analysis of communication and the group process.

## The Theoretical Perspective

I shall continue to emphasize throughout this volume the fact that our understanding of communication and the group process (and anything else, for that matter) depends upon the perspective with which we choose to view it. In this sense, the perspective precedes a definition. Given a certain way of looking at communication and the group process, a definition will follow and will reflect that specific viewpoint. Therefore, to understand how the perspective is used to view communication and the group process is to be able to provide a definition. But to formulate a definition prematurely (that is, before understanding the viewpoint used) is to short-circuit the process of understanding. I continue to emphasize understanding rather than solely definitions or solely knowledge. To understand is to know not only *what* you know, but also *how* you know and *why* you know. Without understanding, knowledge includes only *what* you know.

By now, it is obvious that we could have employed many perspectives to view small group decision making. Not all perspectives lead to the same conclusions, and no single perspective has achieved anything approaching universal popularity. Stated in other terms, there is presently no unified theory of small groups, nor is there any unified theory of communication. Anyone who purports to describe and analyze small group communication must necessarily select that perspective which seems most useful and advantageous.

Selecting a single unifying theoretical perspective of small group communication necessitates omitting the others. And a great many partial theories and models and descriptions of small groups and communication have been necessarily ignored in previous chapters. For example, the theoretical perspective selected has virtually disregarded Kurt Lewin's (1951) field theory of small groups, Robert F. Bales's (1953) equilibrium model, George C. Homans's (1950 and 1961) external and internal "systems," Peter M. Blau's (1960) social integration model, and Thibaut and Kelley's (1959) social exchange model. While later chapters will allude to certain aspects of some of these perspectives, they will essentially ignore the basic precepts of those perspectives and consistently emphasize another perspective of the process of group decision making.

The theoretical perspective employed throughout this book is taken from general systems theory, more specifically, modern systems theory. While many fields of endeavor, ranging from biology to computer science, have employed versions of systems theory, the particular systems approach used has been specifically adapted to communication and group decision making. More specific discussions of the theoretical underpinnings of systems theory applied to group communication appear elsewhere (Fisher, 1971 and 1975; Fisher and Hawes, 1971), but a few basic principles of this theoretical perspective should explain in part the basis for my present discussion of the group decision-making process.

Perhaps the most basic of all systemic principles is that of "wholeness"—that every component of the system affects, and is affected by every other component and that a change in one component necessarily effects changes in all other components. Every system, including a small group, possesses some degree of wholeness. Analyzing each component part of the system individually destroys the essence of the system. For instance, analyzing the personality traits of each group member is inconsistent with the principle of wholeness, which would neglect a comprehensive analysis of individual members in favor of a comprehensive analysis of the group as a single entity.

The principle of nonsummativity—"the whole is different from the sum of its parts"—is integral to the principle of wholeness. To analyze components individually denies the interdependence of those components. A particular act or message by itself is virtually meaningless. No act or message possesses any intrinsic meaning in isolation. It takes on meaning and significance only in the pattern of acts and interacts in the social system. If it rains today, there is no particular meaning or significance in that event. But if we have planned a picnic in the city park, the rain takes on meaning in that system's context. If the farmer's crops have been suffering from a drought, the rain possesses a different significance and meaning in that system's context. The isolated behavior of the individual member is quite unimportant by itself. It is the pattern of behaviors which constitute the system and provide its identity as a systemic whole.

## FEEDBACK SEQUENCES

Structurally, feedback was defined in Chapter 3 as a response or reaction to a previous action. In a functional, pragmatic view of communication, feedback is not merely a response but an entire sequence of actions in the form of a double interact. This conceptualization of feedback stems directly from the field of cybernetics, which has been credited with coining the term "feedback." Cybernetics involves the study of control—how machines (and humans) develop normal functioning by controlling any deviations or departures from what is considered "normal."

An analogy may explain this notion of cybernetic control and the way in which feedback functions to maintain the steady or normal operation of the system. Figure 4-1 depicts a feedback sequence that is often used to illustrate the notion of cybernetic feedback. You will note that feedback, as a sequence, involves a cycle of events, each one of which affects the next event in the sequence. In this way, any change in any one event will precipitate a change in every succeeding event, including itself.

For example, assume that the thermostat of Figure 4-1 is preset at 68°F. Beginning at any arbitrary point on the cycle, we should be able to visualize a change or deviation in the normal operation of the thermostatic mechanism. Perhaps the termperature of air in the room falls to 65°F.

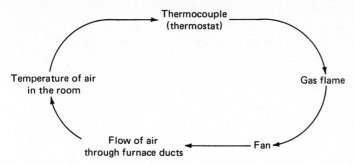

**Figure 4-1**  The feedback cycle of a thermostat.

This change is a deviation from the "normal" functioning of the system, with the "normal" temperature defined by the preset temperature of 68°F. That deviation from the preset temperature causes the thermocouple to close, thus completing the electrical circuit and opening the gas jets in the forced-air furnace. The pilot light ignites the gas flame, thereby super-heating the air in the furnace chamber, which in turn causes the fan to turn on, which in turn increases the flow of air through the furnace ducts to the room, which in turn raises the air temperature in the room. The feedback cycle is then complete.

Note that the "cause" of the rise in room temperature is the original decrease in room temperature. In other words, feedback as a cycle is self-reflexive. The effect of feedback is to reflect back on itself by setting in motion a sequence of events. Each of these events affects the next event in the sequence until the cycle is completed by returning to the original event. At this point, the feedback cycle begins again in a never-ending cyclical pattern of self-reflexive regulation of the temperature in the room.

Because feedback is a cycle, any deviation in any one event sets off a chain reaction that reflects back on that original deviation. Thus, the dropping of the room temperature caused the thermocouple to close which caused the gas to ignite, which caused the fan to turn on, which caused the air to flow through the ducts, which caused the room temperature to rise. Feedback is inherently a self-reflexive (reflecting back on itself) cycle of actions or events.

Feedback as a sequence is not simply a knee-jerk reflex to some antecedent stimulus. In fact, feedback is not a single action at all. Rather, feedback is a self-reflexive process initiated by some deviant action. The deviant action (that is, some change in a preset "normal" standard of actions) sets in motion a sequence of actions, each of which stimulates the next action in the sequence until the sequence closes the cycle by exerting influence on the original source of the deviation. Feedback is a self-

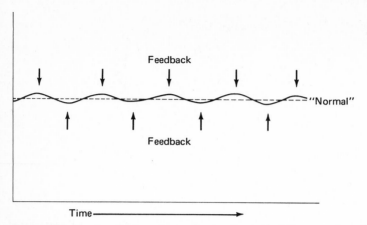

**Figure 4-2**   The functioning of negative feedback (deviation-counteracting).

reflexive cycle or loop—self-reflexive because the deviant action exerts influence on itself through direct influence on each link in the chain of events contained in the cycle.

Feedback loops are of two varieties—positive and negative. Negative feedback is a self-reflexive process which counteracts the deviant actions. Figure 4-2 illustrates how negative feedback functions to counteract any deviation from the standard or "normal" functioning of the system. The thermostat is an example of negative feedback—a deviation-counteracting cycle. If the dotted line in Figure 4-2 indicating normal operation of the system can be assumed to be 68°F and the solid line is the real room temperature over a period of time, the figure illustrates that negative feedback counteracts any deviation from 68°F. The feedback cycle functions to lower the temperature if it goes above the standard and to raise the temperature if it falls below the standard. Thus the temperature in the room remains relatively constant. It is 68°F, plus or minus some allowable amplitude. Deviation in either direction from the standard is counteracted so that the actual range of temperature is very small—say, from 65°F to 71°F or 68°±3°F. In summary, negative feedback counteracts deviant behavior in a system and functions to keep the system operating within a rather narrow range of "normal" behaviors.

Positive feedback is, of course, the opposite of negative feedback. The positive feedback loop initiated by deviant actions sets in motion a cycle that reflects back on the deviant action by amplifying the deviation and thus causing even greater deviation. Figure 4-3 illustrates how positive feedback functions to increase or amplify deviation in the same direction (away from the "normal" standard). In the positive feedback shown in Figure 4-3, the original deviation escalates above the normal

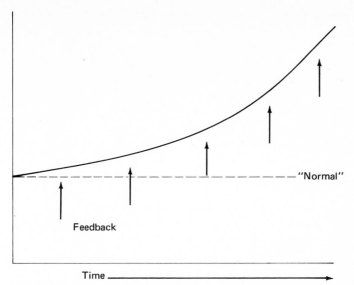

**Figure 4-3**   The functioning of positive feedback (deviation-amplifying).

standard governing the system. Positive feedback thus serves not to counteract but to amplify and encourage additional deviation in that same direction. While Figure 4-2 showed feedback forces operating in both directions to counteract deviation so that actions returned to normal, positive feedback forces in Figure 4-3 function to increase deviation in only a single direction—away from the "normal" standard. Any deviation sets in motion a positive feedback loop that causes even greater deviation.

The urbanization process illustrates graphically the amplification of deviation through positive feedback. In brief, farmers occupy a rural area and create a demand for services such as machinery repair, sale of agricultural products, groceries, a post office, medical care, and so forth. Soon a small village blooms in the middle of the rural area. Soon a company builds a small factory near the town because of the available supply of labor. More people move to the town in order to secure jobs at the factory. With more people available for work, the market for more services is larger, so more stores selling consumer goods are necessary. Shopping centers and more factories are built as more people move to the city. The small town booms to form a megalopolis. Each deviation from the originally rural area stimulates more and more deviation in a classic illustration of positive feedback.

The international arms race is another classic example of positive feedback loops. The spiraling arms race has brought an extraordinary amplification of innovations in weapons development leading from the invention of gunpowder to dynamite, to the atomic bomb, the hydrogen bomb, the cobalt bomb, to the ICBM and MIRV, ad infinitum.

Progress, growth, and change in a social system can occur only through amplifying deviant behavior by means of positive feedback cycles. Naturally the social system must devise methods to manage positive feedback, along with progress, growth, and change, or the deviation gets out of hand. Urbanization may symbolize much progress in our nation, but unmanaged urbanization has created the serious problems we have only recently faced. The severity of these problems, such as air and water pollution, urban decay and blight, urban crime, inadequate civic services, and overpopulation, has prompted the observation that a megalopolis, such as New York City, may be totally ungovernable. Nations, too, have recently attempted to set limits on the current arms race through treaties and multilateral agreements. And arms limitation talks among the powerful nations of the world will probably continue for some time.

Progress and change in a social system are both desirable and essential for the survival of that system. But the system must learn to manage them so that the benefits from progress can be realized. Management of social change leads to the development of new negative feedback cycles and the strengthening of old negative feedback cycles, allowing progress to occur gradually in manageable proportions and at a manageable speed. That our society has not successfully managed progress in recent years is ingeniously portrayed by Alvin Toffler in his book *Future Shock,* in which he illustrates how we are physically living in the present while intellectually remaining in the past. Changes have been too frequent and too fast for us.

The normal process of managing conflict and deviance in a small group through positive and negative feedback loops is a focus of Chapter 8. For the moment, it is sufficient to postulate that innovation, progress, and change in a social system require the existence of social conflict and deviant behavior. Moreover, the successful social system develops both appropriate positive and appropriate negative feedback mechanisms in order to manage social progress for the benefit of all members of the system.

As later discussions will illustrate, group decision making (in both task and social dimensions) involves feedback sequences of both types— positive and negative. Both are necessary in order for the group to complete its task and achieve group solidarity, as well as to control deviation of members from consensus on the decision and the level of group cohesiveness. When progress and change are occurring in the group, positive feedback cycles are functioning more strongly than negative feedback cycles.

It should also be apparent that progress and change, if they remain uncontrolled, are ultimately harmful to the group. Negative feedback cycles must reassert themselves in order to control the final decision and group solidarity. But if these negative feedback cycles are stronger than the positive feedback cycles at all times, little progress or change will occur in the group. Consequently, the group will tend to stagnate. It will not be innovative or creative. It is eminently sensible, then, that both positive and negative feedback cycles should characterize the ongoing process of group decision making. Nevertheless, either variety of feedback cycle may be stronger than the other at a given point during the process of group decision making.

The functional view of feedback (that is, feedback cycles or sequences) is probably more valuable as a means of understanding feedback in communication and the group process. The notion of feedback as response is not so much unimportant as it is only a partial view of feedback in the context of group decision making. Feedback as simply response seems more important to the individual member and less significant to the group as an entire social system. Because this book stresses group decision making (specifically, communication and the group process), the greatest emphasis in Chapter 5 will be on the positive and negative feedback cycles during the process of group interaction during the making of decisions. Chapter 5 will therefore illustrate more specifically those feedback cycles that function during group interaction as groups go about their task of making decisions.

## DIMENSIONS OF COMMUNICATIVE BEHAVIOR

Earlier in this chapter, the two dimensions of communication—content and relationship—were discussed. As you will recall, content refers to the specific subject matter or information of communication, and the relationship dimension indicates how the information is to be interpreted. That is, every communication serves to establish some identifiable social relationship among the communicators regardless of the content or the subject matter of the communication. From the previous discussion of interaction analysis in this chapter, you will remember that any category system used to analyze communication focuses on specific functions performed by communicative actions. Thus, it is possible to focus on the content or the relationship aspect of communication with a given category system while still recognizing the fact that both content and relationship dimensions are present in each communicative act. The following paragraphs will attempt to illustrate how we can view the ongoing interaction of decision-making groups in terms of either the content dimension, the relationship dimension, or both. Such analyses, of course, involve using different category systems to analyze communicative behavior.

The most common category system used to classify interaction behavior is probably that of Robert F. Bales (1950). His system of twelve categories is known as "interaction process analysis" (IPA). Figure 5-1 includes the categories of the IPA, along with the various classes of categories. Bales's IPA classifies acts into two broad categories—the task area and the socioemotional area. This separation corresponds closely with the content and the relationship dimensions of communication. In essence, Bales's perspective of the interaction process suggests that the content and the relationship dimensions (that is, the task and the socioemotional areas) can be separated in the interaction so that a particular act is assumed to be oriented exclusively to the task or to the socioemotional area. One can infer from Bales's category system that a given act may be classified as either a content act or a relationship act, but not both.

Although Bales's IPA system will be discussed in more detail in Chapter 5, it is important to note here that the perspective Bales employs to view decision making differs significantly from the viewpoint or perspective used in this volume. In referring to content and relationship as "dimensions" of communication, I have adopted the view that *every* act contains both a content aspect and a relationship aspect, although I may focus on only one of the dimensions in a given category system to analyze interaction. Therefore, any attempt to separate acts into those that are primarily oriented to either content or relationship is quite impossible.

Earlier discussion has also indicated that this viewpoint is in substantial agreement with those of some scholars and in substantial disagreement with those of some others (Bales, for example). This observation is still another way of saying that one's understanding of communication and the group process depends upon the viewpoint or the perspective used to understand it. One can safely assume, then, that the perspective adopted in this book is quite different from that of Bales.

Viewing the content and relationship dimensions of communication pragmatically, we are able to examine different lists of interaction categories that emphasize one or the other dimension. Some of these lists of categories will be discussed in this chapter, with the purpose of providing an explanation of those specific category systems—specific lists of functions performed by communication during the process of group decision making. The results obtained from actually observing the interaction of decision-making groups will be discussed in Chapter 5.

### The Content Dimension

One way to view the interaction of decision-making groups is to consider each act in terms of how it functions to influence the opinions of other group members toward a specific issue being discussed. Central to such a category system is the concept of "decision proposal." Each issue or topic of discussion during group decision making is potentially a decision that the group can make. In other words, each topic of conversation is a proposed decision that may be incorporated in the final consensus or that must be resolved as a preliminary step to achieving consensus on a final decision.

For example, a jury whose decision-making task is to determine the guilt or innocence of a defendant undoubtedly discusses many issues preliminary to that final verdict. That is, the jury members may need to determine whether a specific eyewitness is credible, whether the prosecution proved beyond a reasonable doubt the existence of motive, whether extenuating circumstances were sufficient to excuse the defendant from a crime, and so forth. In this way, each individual act during the jury's deliberations functions on a given proposal in such a way that it attempts to influence the perceptions of other members toward that proposal.

Once a decision proposal is identified, the categories of interaction provide a list of functions performed on that potential decision. This analytical system, based on decision proposals, includes the following categories:

1. Interpretation
   f. Favorable toward the decision proposal
   u. Unfavorable toward the decision proposal
   ab. Ambiguous toward the decision proposal, containing a bivalued (both favorable and unfavorable) evaluation
   an. Ambiguous toward the decision proposal, containing a neutral evaluation
2. Substantiation
   f. Favorable toward the decision proposal
   u. Unfavorable toward the decision proposal
   ab. Ambiguous toward the decision proposal, containing a bivalued (both favorable and unfavorable) evaluation
   an. Ambiguous toward the decision proposal, containing a neutral evaluation
3. Clarification
4. Modification
5. Agreement
6. Disagreement

Even the act that initiates the decision or introduces a topic for discussion functions on the proposal in some way. It may *interpret,* favorably, unfavorably, or ambiguously, with or without substantiation. But, under any circumstances, every act functions on a decision proposal in terms of how that idea should be viewed by the group members. This category system, based on the concept of decision proposals and used to observe the interaction of actual decision-making groups in real life, provides the categories for the model of decision emergence that will be discussed extensively in Chapter 5.

Significant to this category system are the favorable, unfavorable, and ambiguous categories of interpretation and substantiation. A comment that is classified as favorable is a comment that functions on the decision proposal by expressing a favorable attitude toward it and, thus, implicitly attempting to influence the perceptions or opinions of other members toward a favorable position regarding the proposal. Similarly, a comment that is unfavorable toward the proposal attempts to influence other members to reject the proposed idea.

It is possible, however, to interpret or substantiate (that is, to interpret with evidence) a decision proposal ambiguously. An ambiguous comment is one in which the speaker's attitude or opinion is not explicit in the act itself, either because it is neutral (for example, "That's interesting") or because it contains both a favorable and an unfavorable evaluation (for example, "That's a good idea, but it needs a lot of work before it is acceptable").

Using this category system to observe the earlier excerpt showing the interaction of Tim, Jack, and Mike provides some indication of what that interaction is like. Even without being thoroughly familiar with these interaction categories, one can clearly see that the interaction between Jack and Mike reflects a sequence of favorable and unfavorable interpretations or substantiations of the decision proposal regarding the establishment of the power-generating plant so near a national park. Their resulting interaction is a sequence of favorable-unfavorable-favorable (*f-u-f*) interaction—a clear indication of conflict over ideas or over the subject matter of the discussion. This conflict arises over a decision proposal—a conflict in the content dimension of communication. Whereas Tim's comments may reflect a neutral or ambiguous attitude toward the proposal, the comments of Jack and Mike are definitely not ambiguous.

Mike's first comment, in which he asks for clarification of Jack's preceding act, is the only act of either member that reflects neither a favorable nor an unfavorable interpretation or substantiation of the decision proposal. Mike is merely asking for more information in order to determine "where Jack is coming from." When Mike finds out from Jack's subsequent comment, he solidifies his position and takes a clear ideational stance on the decision proposal.

This category system for analyzing interaction is specifically related to the content dimension of decision-making tasks. It is probably an analytical system that is less relevant or less appropriate to interaction of other types of groups. But because our emphasis and our interest here are on group decision making, this system for analyzing interaction based on decision proposals is altogether appropriate and directly within the focus of our interest. In specifically exploring the process of group decision making in Chapter 5, the discussion will refer explicitly to these categories of decision-making interaction. You may wish to refer back to these categories when you read the discussion of the model of decision emergence in that chapter.

## The Relationship Dimension

There are certainly many ways to view the possible relationships that can unite the individual members within a group. Such relationships may be defined in terms of one or more previously discussed interpersonal factors. For example, we can define a relationship in terms of its level of intimacy, how much interpersonal trust is present, or how much self-disclosure occurs and is reciprocated among members. The category system of social relationship to be discussed in this section, however, defines the relationship in yet another manner.

We must recognize that the nature of a relationship is also definable within a variety of different perspectives and, hence, different systems of interaction categories. The present category system has been used more extensively than any other to show the nature of social relationships in groups. It is presented here, not necessarily because it is the best way to view a social relationship, but because it has been used most often. Therefore, our knowledge of social relationships is greatest within this perspective.

Gregory Bateson, a social anthropologist, is an important scholar in the content and relationship dimensions of communication. He has defined "relationship" (1972) in terms of what he calls "control modes" of communicative actions. We often use this same concept of control-mode relationships in everyday conversation when we describe the game of "one-upsmanship." We often characterize a conversation, for example, by suggesting that someone is trying to "one-up" the other. "One-upsmanship" means an attempt by one person to control the other, to achieve a higher social status than the other, and in some respects to be "dominant" over the other.

Viewing communication in terms of control modes involves three basic categories:

↑ One-up: Attempt to restrict the behavioral options of the other person
→ One-across: Attempt at mutual identification
↓ One-down: Attempt to relinquish one's own behavioral options to the other person

At the risk of oversimplifying these categories, we can look at certain examples of how an individual may contribute a one-up, a one-down, or a one-across act. Actually, however, the only way to define a comment as either one-up, one-down, or one-across is to consider that comment in relation to the interaction sequence, particularly the comment preceding it. For example, returning to the Tim-Jack-Mike interaction, Mike's comment "You've got to be kidding!" is probably a one-up act. Mike is relationally saying to Jack, "I am not going to allow you any behavioral options other than the one of agreeing with me." His statement is highly imperative; it is didactic. Mike commands Jack to change his mind and conform to Mike's own opinion.

Jack might have responded by saying to Mike, "Yes, I guess you're right. You've convinced me." If he had done so, he would have clearly relinquished his behavioral options to Mike in making this one-down comment. In reality, however, Jack responded by arguing with Mike. That is, he refused to relinquish his behavioral options to Mike and responded with another one-up comment.

Another example of a one-down comment is the question or inquiry asked out of ignorance and relinquishing the control of the interaction to the person with the knowledge. Such an inquiry is not a request for clarification, such as Mike's initial query. The one-down inquiry is a request for information because the person who is asking doesn't know information.

A one-across comment does not attempt to control the other person. Nor does such a comment acquiesce to the other person's control. Such an act serves to define the relationship as one of equal status. An example of such a one-across act may function to restate, repeat, or clarify the previous act. Some group interactions, particularly encounter or training groups, encourage one-across actions. Often such a comment is preceded by the ritualistic and explicit declaration that the comment is restating for the sake of clarification: "What I hear you saying is . . ."

Obviously a single utterance by one person cannot hope to establish a social relationship. The relationship is definable only by a sequence of individual acts. A one-up comment does not establish a social relationship, but in the context of other acts (that is, interacts and double interacts), it can be part of a relationship. In this sense of a social relationship, it becomes apparent that a person "engages in" or "becomes part of" communication (that is, the relationship). No one individual can unilaterally define a communicative relationship. Rather, it is defined by individual actions in concert with the actions of other persons.

Bateson (1935) discusses two identifiable social relationships under the general headings of "symmetry" and "complementarity." The minimal instance of one of these relationships is, of course, an interact. A symmetrical relationship, therefore, is an interact in which the antecedent and subsequent (first and second) acts in the sequence are the same function—either $\uparrow\uparrow$, $\downarrow\downarrow$, or $\rightarrow\rightarrow$.

A complementary relationship is an interact in which the antecedent and subsequent acts "fit together" to form a complete relationship. In the same sense that two angles that together form a right angle (90°) are called complementary angles in geometry, two acts that "fit together" to form a complete social relationship are called a "complementary social relationship." Thus, a complementary relationship involves one person's attempt to assert control over the other and the other person's acceptance of that control—↑↓ and ↓↑. A complementary relationship may take the form of any of the following common social relationships: dominant-submissive, question-answer, buying-selling, giving-receiving, employee-employer, parent-son or parent-daughter, superior-subordinate, husband-wife, teacher-learner, source-receiver, etc. I do not mean to imply, however, that these social relationships are "complementary" in their use of control modes; rather, they are complementary in the sense that they "fit together."

The two forms of complementary relationships (↑↓ and ↓↑) are essentially the same. One is a mirror image of the other—that is, the reverse of the other. Member A is dominant and member B is submissive, or member A is submissive and member B is dominant. The three forms of symmetry (↑↑, ↓↓, and →→), however, are quite different from one another. The ↑↑ symmetrical relationship is one of competition—competitive symmetry. Each person is trying to "one-up" the other. They are competing with each other, as shown in Mike's and Jack's interaction.

Submissive symmetry (↓↓) is not so overtly competitive, but it may reflect an underlying competition, nevertheless, in the sense that each person is attempting to force the other person to take the initiative. If you have ever played chess, you will know that it is sometimes to your advantage to force your opponent to attack or to make the initiating moves. A boxer who is a strong counterpuncher may want the opponent to lead with the punches. Submissive symmetry is also apparent in an interaction which I am sure is familiar to each of us. It is the conversation that occurs in situations, for example, which involve decisions such as how to spend the evening. The conversation may go something like this:

"What do you want to do tonight?"
"I don't know. What do *you* want to do?"
"I don't care. It's up to you."
"No. Really, you decide."
"But I really don't care."
"Neither do I."

Relationships characterized by submissive symmetry are often the most difficult and frustrating relationships of all.

Equivalent symmetry (→→) is characterized by the establishment of a peer relationship—equal partners. Equivalent symmetry, according to a commonsense interpretation, would probably characterize a democratic relationship, for example, a decision-making group composed of equals and led by a democratic leader. We must be careful, however, to avoid thinking of any relationship, including equivalent symmetry, as the most desirable type of social relationship. In certain contexts, one kind may be more valuable than another. I doubt, for example, that a relationship of equivalent symmetry would be highly desirable in a group of soldiers in combat or in an orchestra or a flight crew. Such situations probably call for a highly symmetrical relationship between officer and enlisted men, between conductor and players, and between captain and crew.

It should be obvious that not all these relationships can be sustained for an indefinite period. For example, competitive symmetry ($\uparrow\uparrow$) must be resolved in some manner, or the relationship will be highly uncomfortable. Mike's and Jack's competition was apparently so unpleasant that Tim found it necessary to relieve the social tension with his innocuous comment asking for the time. Submissive symmetry ($\downarrow\downarrow$) is also not likely to be sustained for any long period. The participants simply won't get anywhere. No progress will be made. It is a relationship that is temporary at best.

The complementary relationships ($\uparrow\downarrow$ and $\downarrow\uparrow$) and equivalent symmetry ($\rightarrow\rightarrow$) are, on the surface at least, relatively stable. They appear to be those that can characterize a relationship over a longer period of time. Although such a conclusion seems consistent with common sense, it is probably not the case, however.

Bateson (1972, p. 70) states that a healthy social relationship is neither "purely symmetrical or purely complementary but that every such relationship contains elements of the other type." He suggests that a purely symmetrical or purely complementary relationship is prone to a phenomenon which he calls by the tongue-twisting word "schismogenesis." This phenomenon is simply the escalation of either a symmetrical or a complementary relationship to the extent that the relationship dissolves because of mutual hostility engendered by "too much" symmetry or "too much" complementarity.

A "healthy" relationship, then, probably contains some symptoms of several kinds of relationship—competitive symmetry, submissive symmetry, complementarity, etc.—at various times during the course of the interaction. As we shall see later, the healthy and most cohesive social relationship is often characterized by periods of conflict. A decision-making group without conflict is undoubtedly quite boring and incapable of sustaining itself. Equivalent symmetry is by no means the most desirable social relationship in every circumstance if "most desirable" implies the exclusion of other kinds of symmetry or complementarity.

## A Note on Terminology

One of the problems in the attempt to explain relatively new and complex material in a textbook is the required use of many new terms. You have undoubtedly been aware of the use of unfamiliar jargon in the preceding paragraphs. I do not apologize for it. Jargon is necessary and eminently worthwhile; and learning the jargon of a discipline is essential for students new to that discipline—it is probably tantamount to learning a foreign language.

I am digressing here in order to show you that I am aware of having used jargon. Further, I am aware that you may be experiencing difficulty in learning this new vocabulary, and even of the possibility that you may resent it. I can assure you that I am not coining new words for the purpose of making simple material more difficult. Rather, the discussion includes concepts that cannot be expressed, or can be expressed only with difficulty and with undue ambiguity, in everyday or familiar terms. Jargon (such as "symmetry," "complementarity," and "schismogenesis") will occur again in later chapters without the explanations that have been presented in the preceding pages. I have included Appendix 3 as a reference to jargon; it gives explicit definitions of terms as they are used in this volume. Develop the habit of referring to Appendix 3 ("A Reader's Guide to Jargon") as you continue to use this textbook.

## GROUP INFORMATION PROCESSING

We probably know a great deal already about how persons process information individually. That is, we know that each person selects and interprets information from among the vast quantity of data available in the environment. Chapter 5 will discuss more specifically how members of a group deal with information, particularly information that is associated with making group decisions. At this point, however, it is important to know that some attributes of information processing are unique to the group, that is, to the *social* process or the *social* system of group decision making.

In the first place, according to Grunig (1969), members of decision-making groups tend to seek new and additional information in order to assist their efforts in performing decision-making tasks. That members seek information, however, does not imply that they utilize that information in the most rational and efficient manner. In fact, Pruitt (1961) and Lucas and Jaffee (1969) found that decision-making groups often, perhaps typically, do not use new information very rationally.

One might realistically assume that not all items of information available to the group are consistent with each other. Accepting one item of information necessarily involves rejecting other items that disagree. Nearly every jury must decide which witness to believe when the plaintiff's and defendant's witnesses contradict one another's testimony. For example, one defense psychiatrist might testify that the defendant did not realize the difference between right and wrong and was legally insane. A psychiatrist called by the plaintiff might testify that the defendant was legally sane. The jury must then exercise its judgment as to which item of information—that is, which witness's testimony—is most acceptable or credible.

The process of group interaction during group decision making includes many such judgments. Often group members make those judgments on nonrational bases. A common basis for judgment compares the new information with the previously established position of the group. If the item of information conflicts with the group's already-established position, the members tend to reject the new information out of hand. At such times the members consider the information irrelevant or of inferior quality, whether it is or not. Thus, group members sometimes treat information nonrationally. Occasionally they will be irrational and reject obviously relevant information on the ground that it is irrelevant. In either case, members reject the information first. They then search for a basis for rejecting it, after the fact, to rationalize the judgment they have already made.

The nonrational approach to information processing in group decision making emphasizes the importance of timing. The point at which an information item is introduced is sometimes more important than the quality of the information itself. If the information is introduced after the group has already established an ideational position, the quality of that information will certainly have little impact on the process of group decision making.

It is vitally important that members submit information important to a comprehensive discussion of the decision proposals relatively early in the group interaction. Information takes on its greatest significance during the period in which members are "testing" ideas and are engaged in conflict over them. During that period, members cannot so easily dismiss information on nonrational bases. During this idea-testing period (which will be discussed in Chapter 5 as the conflict phase), members utilize information to support their own positions or to review critically the positions of other members that are opposed to their own. In this conflict phase, the critical testing of new ideas is at a maximal level and demands a generous amount of information. But after this period of conflict and idea testing, new information tends to lose its impact (Holder and Ehling, 1967).

## SUMMARY

Communication, in terms of pragmatic functioning, is viewed as a pattern of behaviors in which the acts of each communicator constrain, and are constrained by, the pattern created by his or her own and others' behaviors. All people who engage in communication develop to some degree an interdependent relationship with one another, a relationship that embodies both structural and actional (functional) attributes of a process. This interdependent relationship is the process of communication.

Viewed as sequences of actions, communication is unavoidable in the same sense that one cannot *not* behave. In this way, all communication is behavior, and the understanding of communication focuses on the social system—the connectedness of actions performed by individual group members in an ongoing, turn-taking sequence. Furthermore, every communicative action contains both a content dimension (information) and a relationship dimension (how the information is to be interpreted), analogous to the interdependence of the task and social dimensions of a group process. Thus, communication and the group process are defined similarly and may be said to constitute a single process.

The ongoing stream of communicative behaviors can be understood by analyzing each action as being of a certain type of function performed. Every communicative act can then be analyzed within a category of communicative functions. All the categories for analysis thus constitute a list of functions that can be performed by communication. To understand the ongoing process of communication, one must focus on the connectedness of those categorized actions. Acts are thus punctuated (organized or grouped) into recognizable sequences of interacts or double interacts on the basis of their familiarity or recognizability. And certain sequences become recognizable as interacts or double interacts on the basis of their frequency of occurrence during the history of past interaction.

As recognizable sequences, communicative feedback may be understood (within the perspective of systems theory) as positive or negative functions. A negative feedback sequence functions to control any deviation within the group system, and positive feedback sequences function to amplify deviation. In this way, negative feedback controls the operation of the system and keeps it functioning normally; positive feedback leads to progress and change. Feedback sequences are recognizable in both the content and relationship dimensions and are definable as punctuated, frequently recurring double interacts composed of the categories of interaction analysis. Finally, members of a social system process information in ways that are different from those used in information processing performed by a single, isolated person.

# The Process of
# Group Decision Making

The past several decades have witnessed a growing concern over the allegedly clandestine nature of some decision-making groups in our society. The specter of a decision-making group in the proverbial smoke-filled back room is familiar to all of us. More often, the group making vital decisions is quite visible, but entrance into the group is highly restricted. Thus, concern has been concentrated on gaining a voice in the group decisions. For example, the "student power" movement of the 1960s resulted in student representation on most university committees, faculty senates, and even boards of regents. Now that a voice in the decision-making process has been, or is being, secured by previously powerless minorities, the problem might appear to be solved. Unfortunately, nothing could be further from reality.

The sentiment of one newly named student member of a university's governing board aptly described the persistent problem. He stated that he had worked long and hard for student representation on that board, but now that the students' voice could be heard he didn't know what to do about it. The fact is that membership in the decision-making group is necessary but not sufficient for effective decision making. A knowledge and an understanding of the process of group decision making are absolutely essential for effective membership. Hundreds of business organizations seek assistance from professional consultants so that their management personnel can function effectively in decision-making groups. Being a member of a group is simply not enough. An understanding of how groups actually make decisions—the process of group decision making—is necessary for effective participation in group decision making.

The purpose of this chapter is to describe the process that characterizes group decision making. So that the reader doesn't expect more than is offered in this chapter, an unfortunate but true state of affairs must be emphasized. There is no formula which a group can learn and employ to ensure "good" decisions. Nor is there a convenient list of do's and don'ts that group members can memorize to improve their participation in group decision-making situations. All such lists (and there have been many) are universally unacceptable and doomed to failure when applied universally to all decision-making groups.

It is hoped that by understanding what knowledge of the group process is available, the group member will be more sensitive to, and aware of, what is occurring during group interaction. Such understanding and perceptiveness allow the group member to function at maximum effectiveness in a group situation. Awareness of the process without the use of "cure-all" principles of behavior, then, should be the goal of a prospective group member. But even awareness of the group process is no guarantee of group success, although the chances for such success are much greater. Such a view may be overly pessimistic, but it is probably realistic.

## AN OVERVIEW OF KEY TERMS

Preliminary to reading the ensuing discussion of the group decision-making process, one should have a full understanding of several key terms that will be used extensively in this chapter. All these terms are familiar and prompt immediate definitions. But, in a sense, these terms are jargon. That is, each of them specifies a rather precise meaning, probably narrower than the meaning used in everyday conversation. It is for the sake of precision, then, that the following definitions are included.

The relationship between *decision making* and *problem solving* is not a source of universal agreement. Some view the two terms as virtually synonymous; others draw rather clear distinctions between them. Our concern is with all decision making, which, for our purposes, includes some types of problem solving while excluding others. Recall the earlier distinction between tasks more appropriately performed by individuals and those uniquely adapted to the group process. The basis for that distinction also differentiates between two types of problem solving. One kind of problem possesses a "best" or "correct" solution, which is determined by external and objective means. Such problems may be typified by a mathematical problem for which only one solution is acceptable, a logic puzzle governed by the invariable rules of induction and deduction, or a crossword puzzle. Certainly these problem-solving tasks are not within the province of group decision making.

On the other hand, some problems have no solution that is subject to external validation. The solutions to these problems can be discovered only through group acceptance—the willingness of the members to commit themselves to implementing the solution. Thus, the only possible check of the validity of the solution is whether it achieves group consensus. Such problems would include determining how to combat pollution or crime most effectively, questions of penal reform, the rising costs from inflation, and so forth. The value of such solutions may ultimately be determined by how well they work after they have been put into practice. But at the time of their achieving consensus in the group, only validation through group consensus determines their worth.

Some decision-making tasks, of course, are not strictly within the scope of problems to be solved. Juries make decisions on questions of value and unverifiable facts. Voters make decisions on candidates for political office. These decisional situations do not stem directly from problems that require solving and include even such prosaic decisions as what clothing to wear tomorrow, what the theme for homecoming should be, what color to paint the house, and what brand of toothpaste to buy. Certainly decision making includes some types of problem solving and much more.

A *decision,* ultimately the outcome of group interaction, is inevitably a choice made by group members from among alternative proposals available to them. Rarely, if ever, does a group make a single decision in isolation. Although only one decision is sometimes apparent, such as a jury's decision of guilty or not guilty, many preliminary decisions are essential to that final decision and are made by the group on its way to achieving consensus on the final decision. The jury, for example, must decide which witness to believe, which piece of evidence is stronger, whether there is a reasonable doubt, and so forth. Group members, then, focus their attention on various proposals during their interaction and choose, from among those alternative proposals, which ones they will accept or reject. The sum of the accepted proposals constitutes the productivity of the group.

Although quantity of proposals initiated during group interaction is not a reliable measure of productivity, the fact remains that only those proposals that are initiated during interaction are available for final decision making. It is not yet clear whether more decision proposals yield higher-quality decisions. Results of research efforts aimed at answering this question, particularly those efforts studying brainstorming techniques, are varied and conflicting. Common sense indicates that quantity of ideas proposed and quality of decisions achieving consensus are somehow related, but one must not neglect the factors of social conflict and intermember influence during interaction. As members discuss alternative proposals, they attempt to influence one another, directly and indirectly, to accept or reject a given proposal. The process of reciprocal influence during group interaction is one focus of this chapter.

A group reaches a decision as members achieve consensus on a proposal. The term *consensus* implies a variety of differing meanings. Some think of consensus as the will of the majority which results from democratic voting procedures. Some believe unanimous agreement is necessary for consensus. Often consensus implies the absence of a formal vote but implicit agreement not necessarily verbalized by the group members. Obviously, a consensus decision is one on which members typically agree, but agreement is often a necessary, but not a sufficient, condition for consensus. That is, members may agree with a decision, even unanimously, but may not achieve consensus.

For our purposes, consensus implies not just agreement but commitment to the decision reached. In fact, members may be committed to a decision to the extent that they work to put it into effect without ever fully agreeing with it. Zaleznik and Moment (1964, p. 142) clarify the nature of consensus as commitment:

> Our meaning of consensus lies in the degree of personal commitment the members feel toward the group decision after it is reached. This means, for example, that even though some members might disagree with the decision on principle, they will accept it and personally carry out their part. Their emotional commitment to the group is measured by willingness to put the plan decided on into effect, in their own personal behavior.

Simple agreement on a decision proposal, then, does not necessarily guarantee that the decision has achieved group consensus. In fact, group members who submit to pressures or external authority might express agreement without really accepting the proposal itself. In such instances the decision achieves false or superficial consensus, that is, agreement masquerading as consensus. The phenomenon of consensus without real agreement is not extraordinarily rare. For example, unsuccessful candidates for their party's nomination for political office often campaign strongly for the winning candidate. People may disagree on a new law or new tax passed by their elected representatives, but they generally obey those laws and pay those taxes.

The prime requisite for consensus, then, is not agreement with the decision, although agreement is highly common and even typical. The essential ingredient of consensus is the extent of group loyalty shared by members. To the extent that the members are cohesive or have developed groupness, the decisions reached by that group are most likely to achieve consensus as well as agreement. Thus, the rather cohesive group is more likely to be effective as a decision-making body.

The interdependence of the task and socioemotional dimensions of a group is again evident. As Zaleznik and Moment (1964, p. 155) point out, "Although this [consensus] may seem to be a purely task requisite, it is clearly a connecting link between task and social-emotional problems."

Consistent with the emphasis on communication and group process, the concern of this chapter is the *process* of group decision making. That is, this chapter is most concerned with questions of *how*—how groups achieve consensus on decisions over time; how members try to exert influence on one another during various periods of group interaction; how members' communicative behaviors occur in interstructured patterns during interaction. In short, the process perspective will emphasize how members interact during discussion of decision proposals and how certain proposals achieve consensus during group interaction.

## PRESCRIPTIVE AND DESCRIPTIVE APPROACHES

Using an agenda as a step-by-step outline to guide the group's decision-making efforts provides a prescriptive approach to group decision making. That is, the agenda illustrates how groups *should* make decisions. A prescriptive agenda provides guidelines, a road map, to assist the group in achieving consensus. In one way, such a prescriptive approach is based on an assumed "ideal" process. It implies that there exists a "right" or at least a "best" way to make decisions. The agenda then leads the group members to conform to that best or ideal process. Whether such an ideal process of group decision making exists is clearly a matter of conjecture. Certainly no evidence exists that would support any conclusion regarding an ideal process, one way or the other.

Prescriptive approaches to group decision making rest on several inherent assumptions. First, prescriptive methods typically assume all members to be consistently rational. These methods generally outline an agenda which lists the various steps a group goes through in making decisions. The various types of evidence are detailed along with methods of evaluating each type of evidence. The prescriptive method warns against emotional appeals or other nonrational aspects of group interaction, assuming that such techniques disrupt efficient group decision making. In other words, prescriptive methods often distinguish clearly between the task and socioemotional dimensions of the group process and assume the latter to be disruptive. Not only does this assumption deny the interdependence of the two group dimensions, but it delimits the primary advantage of group decision making over individual decision making—the socioemotional dimension.

A second assumption underlying prescriptive methods of group decision making is an attempt to improve the quality of the group's decision-making outcomes. Similar to a physician's prescription of medicine for an ill patient, prescriptive group methods assume that using the method will lead to a happy, healthy, and productive group. Although research efforts to discover the truth of this assumption are not in unanimous agreement, their results tend to cast doubt on its validity. Many researchers, including Bayless (1967) and Pyke and Neely (1970), have discovered little significant difference in group productivity between groups using different methods of decision making. Assisting groups to achieve higher-quality decisions is definitely a worthy goal. Apparently, however, present prescriptive methods have failed to achieve that goal.

Undoubtedly the most common prescriptive method used in group decision making is the "reflective thinking" model suggested by John Dewey (1910) some seven decades ago. Although Dewey intended his model of reflective thinking to apply only to an individual's mental processes, his model has been widely employed as a guide to group decision making as well. Briefly, Dewey's model includes the following six steps:

*Step 1:* A difficulty is felt or expressed.
*Step 2:* The nature of the problem is defined.
*Step 3:* The nature of the problem is analyzed.
*Step 4:* Possible solutions are suggested to solve the problem.
*Step 5:* The solutions are compared by testing each against selected criteria, and the best solution is selected.
*Step 6:* The best solution is implemented, that is, put into effect.

Dewey's model serves as a universal agenda to guide a group toward consensus in an orderly, step-by-step progression. The group is expected to discuss and complete each step before moving on to the next step in the sequence. Steps are intended to be followed in sequence without omitting any or reversing their order. Dewey's model also clearly applies to problem solving, assuming that decision making and problem solving are not significantly different. It is equally clear that Dewey's model assumes the superiority of rationality and omits consideration of a group's socioemotional dimension. But of course Dewey intended "reflective thinking" for individuals. When used to guide group decision making, the model does not allow for the socioemotional dimension.

One of the factors that led to developing the model of decision emergence (to be discussed later in this chapter) was my somewhat accidental observation that classroom groups, trained in the use of a specific decision-making agenda (modeled after Dewey's reflective think- ing), did not seem consistently to adhere to the step-by-step guidelines of the agenda. As an instructor in a group decision-making class in which I taught the use of the agenda, I soon found that members of the groups seemed to be making decisions *despite,* rather than *because of,* their step-by-step outline-agendas. I even attempted an experiment in one class in which I assigned the same task to different groups and asked one set of groups to use an agenda based on Dewey's reflective-thinking pattern. I gave no such instructions to the other groups but left them on their own. All the groups arrived at consensus on similar decisions. More important, each group appeared to reach those consensus decisions in a similar manner, with or without the assistance of an agenda. At that time, I came to believe that a natural process is present in all or nearly all successful decision-making groups, whether they use an agenda or not.

The approach to the group process of decision making, to be discussed later in this chapter, is a descriptive approach. Such an approach attempts to document not how groups *should* make decisions, but how they *do* make decisions. As its name implies, a descriptive approach involves observing actual groups interacting for the purpose of social decision making. The descriptive method seeks to describe the interactive process that is common to those groups. Whereas a prescrip- tive approach is based on an "ideal" process, the crux of the descriptive approach is the "reality" of observation.

Several assumptions underlie a descriptive approach to group deci- sion making also. Probably most basic is the assumption that a "natural" process of group decision making does indeed exist. That is, groups develop their own interdependent task and socioemotional dimensions in a normal and fairly consistent interactive pattern that leads to validation of decisions by consensus. The process is assumed to be "natural" (that is, normal) because it occurs in all, or nearly all, effective or successful decision-making groups.

The natural process of decision making is, of course, present to some extent in all groups engaged in performing decision-making tasks. On the other hand, that process is also inhibited to the extent that the group is subject to some undue influence imposed on the members by some source or authority external to the group itself. That is, the natural process is overtly present to the extent that a group is an LGD (a leaderless group discussion). To the extent that an external authority inhibits the group's freedom (for example, to choose its own leader, to establish its own norms, or to develop its own network of roles), the group deviates somewhat from this natural process.

The presence of an external authority, however, does not preclude an LGD. Rather, it serves only to inhibit the full functioning of the LGD process and to "drive it underground" so that it is less visible. When the natural process functions "underground," the group is subject to a system of leadership, roles, norms, etc., that is "formal" (consistent with the external influence) and "informal" (consistent with the natural group process).

The perspective of communication and the group process is probably best served by emphasizing the descriptive approach to group decision making. This approach will also focus on observing the interaction patterns of group members—their interlocked communicative behaviors—as they occur and change over time. I shall attempt to trace these patterns and changes in patterns of interaction as the group members proceed from the initiation of their task performance to their achievement of consensus.

I also recognize the fact that many people may feel more comfortable when using some step-by-step guidelines in the form of some agenda-outline, typically a reflective-thinking model. I do not discourage the use of an agenda. Indeed, it is often quite beneficial in assisting a group's decision-making efforts. Nevertheless, using an agenda in no way implies that a natural process of group decision making will not be present in the group's interaction patterns. Consequently, I shall take the position that the group members themselves should decide whether an agenda is used.

## EARLY MODELS OF GROUP DEVELOPMENT

Although formal instruction in group decision making is probably a twentieth-century phenomenon, the historical roots of group communication probably date back to the classical age of Greece and the philosophical origins of dialectic. The ancient Greek philosophers viewed the practice of dialectic as the search for truth through the exchange of opinions or arguments in free discussion. While the classical philosophers regarded dialectic as a branch of philosophy (specifically, logic), the contemporary view of group decision making is more closely aligned with the social sciences.

Sociologists, psychologists, and psychotherapists, as well as communication scholars, have long been concerned with studying how groups develop over time from a mere aggregate or collection of individuals into full-fledged groups. A few of those early models of group development are described in the following paragraphs in order to provide some background and perspective for the "spiral model" and the model of "decision emergence" which constitute the major thrust of this chapter. The discussion of other models of group development includes only a few of the more commonly known ones. For a more comprehensive discussion of group development, see Hare (1976, pp. 88–112).

## Equilibrium Models

One conceptual approach to the study of groups is to explain the group process in terms of a balance or an equilibrium between two opposing forces. Such a balance model or equilibrium model is popular in many social-psychological explanations in the sense of an "approach-avoidance" conflict (opposing forces favoring and disfavoring some course of action), cognitive dissonance (simultaneous knowledge of positive and negative information concerning a course of action), along with numerous other explanatory models.

Such equilibrium models are popular, perhaps because they are easily conceptualized and easily adapted to structural elements of social behavior. They are conceptually consistent with physical phenomena. That is, the equilibrium principle is evident in the axiom that actions have equal and opposite reactions, in the balance scale, in positive and negative forces of magnetic energy, etc. Furthermore, such models of group decision making implicitly assume the rationality of human beings, an assumption that has been discussed earlier in this chapter as difficult to sustain in explanations of human behavior.

Although Robert F. Bales is best known for his development of the categories for "interaction process analysis" or IPA (Bales, 1950), he also developed an equilibrium model to explain group behavior. His IPA categories were probably developed as a way of observing actual interactive behavior in terms of an equilibrium between task and social forces. Bales (1953) hypothesized that every group has a problem of adapting to its environment. During this adaptation, it develops social mechanisms that serve to differentiate members from one another—for example, differences of roles, differences of status, and the development of a leadership structure. As a result of this emphasis on differences among group members, the social dimension of the group (in terms of its cohesiveness and interpersonal solidarity) suffers.

According to Bales's equilibrium hypothesis, then, work that the group performs in accomplishing its task leads to a deterioration of the group's social structure. Conversely, as the group attempts to increase the interpersonal ties among its members and to perform work in the social dimension (that is, to raise the level of cohesiveness), its work on the task suffers. Groups tend to fluctuate back and forth between task and socioemotional activity, that is, between attempting to solve their task problems and maintaining group solidarity.

Bales's IPA categories (see Figure 5-1, page 137) are consistent with the equilibrium hypothesis. You will note that the twelve categories are divided equally between the task dimension and the socioemotional dimension—six categories each. Note further that the twelve categories are also divided equally between polarized or mutually opposed categories oriented to specific problems in either the task or the social dimension. Bales thus conceptualizes each and every act as directed toward solving some task or social problem confronting the group. Furthermore, every action that a member contributes to the group discussion is oriented to either a task problem or a social problem, but not both.

According to Bales's equilibrium hypothesis and his IPA categories, then, group members may engage in interaction toward performing their task. But when they do, they are ignoring the socioemotional problems of the group. Furthermore, when group members are working on socioemotional problems, they are neglecting task performance. Thus, according to Bales, every group is caught between the opposing forces of task activity and socioemotional activity. To engage in interaction in one area is to ignore the other area. The result is the equilibrium problem. Groups must then learn to solve this problem by including within their deliberations an appropriate balance of both task interaction and socioemotional interaction. Moreover, this interaction swings back and forth between periods of task interaction and periods of socioemotional interaction, rather than the interaction pattern's reflecting a homogeneous mixture of task and social acts.

One of the problems associated with using equilibrium models in order to understand the group process is the difficulty in separating clearly those forces that allegedly oppose each other. Bales, for example, views task activity and socioemotional activity as separable in the interaction itself. That is, he believes that any given action performed by one of the members can be considered *either* a task-oriented act *or* a socioemotional act. The discussions of group interaction throughout this book, however, consistently illustrate how the task and socioemotional dimensions of communication and the group process are interdependent. One affects the other so significantly that any attempt to understand the group process from only the task or the social dimension is tantamount to observing the entire interdependent process through one set of spectacles. But in no event can one sustain the assumption that task activity and socioemotional activity are independent of each other.

A second problem arises in attempting to discover what specifically constitutes equilibrium or the point of balance between the two opposing forces. Clearly, equilibrium does not mean, for example, an equal amount of task actions and socioemotional actions. Using the categories of the IPA, Bales and Strodtbeck (1951) discovered that group interaction achieves an apparent equilibrium between task activity and socioemotional activity by exhibiting a 2 to 1 ratio in the interaction. That is, the interactive behaviors of the group members contain about twice as many task comments as socioemotional comments. The problem of determining when equilibrium is achieved in the interaction is thus extremely difficult.

The best way to use the equilibrium models is probably to understand the group process in terms of the continuing presence of its two dimensions—task and social. While progress is being made in the socioemotional area of group activity, it is also being made in the task area of the group process. We can focus our attention on one of the dimensions in order to understand it more specifically, but we should keep in mind that our view is restricted to the spectacles we are using to understand the group—the single dimension of the group process. Furthermore, to understand the group solely in terms of either the task or the socioemotional dimension is a matter of which spectacles we use to view the group process. But the group process is functioning continuously in both dimensions, even though we may not be seeing both of them functioning at the same time. The dimensions remain interdependent and inseparable. Only our understanding or viewpoint of the group process is restricted.

## Phase Models

The most popular approach to understanding the developmental process of groups over time is to describe group activity moving through a sequence of different kinds of interaction. This sequence develops into stages or phases of group interaction from the beginning of a group's activity as an "aggregate" to its eventual maturation as a group and the establishment of full-fledged groupness. From a task-oriented perspective, the phases of group development chronicle the group's interaction from the beginning of a group's task performance to the achievement of consensus on decisions. Although numerous models of group development have appeared throughout the past several decades and reflect differences in their authors' interests, the following brief survey of some of these models should also reveal remarkable similarities in their description of the phases of group development.

The most familiar of all descriptive models of the group process is the three-phase model advanced by Bales (1950) and Bales and Strodtbeck (1951). These authors discovered that decision-making groups, most of which were problem-solving groups, tend to discuss different kinds of task-related problems at different periods of time in their group interaction. Their three phases may be briefly described as follows:

*Stage 1:* Emphasis on problems of *orientation* (deciding what the situation is like)

*Stage 2:* Emphasis on problems of *evaluation* (deciding what attitudes should be taken toward the situation

*Stage 3:* Emphasis on problems of *control* (deciding what to do about it)

Bales and Strodtbeck base their three phases of the group decision-making process on data compiled from using Bales's (1950) system of interaction process analysis. Figure 5-1 illustrates this system (see also Appendix 2). The IPA classifies each communicative behavior performed by members during group interaction. The classes of behavior include

**Figure 5-1**   Bales's categories for "interaction process analysis."

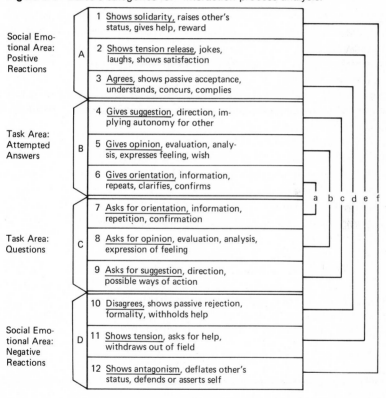

Key:

a Problems of orientation      d Problems of decision
b Problems of evaluation       e Problems of tension-management
c Problems of control          f Problems of integration

twelve categories—in reality, six bipolar pairs of categories. Each category in the pair is the antithesis of the other, for example, "agrees—disagrees," "shows solidarity—shows antagonism." The IPA also separates the group's task and socioemotional dimensions by labeling three pairs of categories in each area. And each bipolar pair of categories is assumed to deal with a particular kind of problem confronting the group. Each of the first three types of problems—orientation, evaluation, and control—is emphasized in order by each decision-making group in three successive phases during group interaction.

Bales and Strodtbeck's analysis of the group decision-making process indicates that members predominantly give and ask for orientation in the first phase, give and ask for opinions in the second phase, and give and ask for suggestions in the third phase. The authors also discovered that both positive and negative reactions also tend to increase progressively from one phase to the next. However, the third phase, "control," appears unique among the three in this respect. Although increasing amounts of negative reactions are characteristic of the first part of the final phase, the latter stages of the control phase include predominantly positive reactions.

Bales and Strodtbeck also emphasize the cyclical nature of the three phases of group decision making. As a group completes one decision-making task by progressing through the phases of orientation, evaluation, and control, it tends to recycle back to the initial orientation phase as it performs each subsequent task. Thus, according to Bales and Strodtbeck, the three phases characterize each performance of a single group decision-making task.

Dunphy (1964) also depicted a sequential analysis of group development. He advanced a four-phase model of group development in terms of emotionality cultures:

*Stage 1:* Dependency (group members look to the leader for direction of their activity)
*Stage 2:* Fight-flight (group members resist the leader's directions and develop their ability to work independently of a leader's guidance)
*Stage 3:* Pairing (group members demonstrate a marked increase in group cohesiveness)
*Stage 4:* Work (little emotionality of any type appears during the final stage of group activity)

You will note that Dunphy's developmental model is highly similar to Bennis and Shepard's (1956 and 1961) model of levels of work, which will be discussed in the following paragraphs. Dunphy also emphasizes the socioemotional dimension of the group process. This emphasis clearly reflects his interest in training groups rather than in groups specifically oriented to decision-making tasks.

Bennis and Shepard developed a four-phase model to describe group development. Their observations were much more subjective and interpretive than the direct observational method of interaction analysis. They derived their description from the reactions of nonparticipant observers. Their findings, according to the authors, also reflect their interpretations over a five-year period of teaching classes in group dynamics. The following four phases of group development are labeled according to the level of work the group is able to accomplish:

> *Phase 1:* One-level work. Personally need-oriented—not group-oriented (Dependence and Authority Relations).
>
> *Phase 2:* Two-level work. Maintaining the group task. Group-oriented and necessary—but routine (Resolution-Catharsis and beginnings of feeling of interdependence).
>
> *Phase 3:* Three-level work. Group-focused work with new methods of attack, goal establishment, idea-testing (Interdependence with group focus and sense of direction).
>
> *Phase 4:* Four-level work. Creative and integrative interpretation with immediate relevance to present problems of group task (Consensual Validation and maximum Productivity). (1956, pp. 753–755)

Several interesting observations emerge from Bennis and Shepard's model. For example, it illustrates a group's progressive ability to do more sophisticated work. This ability is apparently gained in successively progressive stages as the group develops interdependence among its members. As the group begins its process of development, it is dependent upon some external authority responsible for the group task. In a T-group, that authority is the trainer; in an organization, it is the boss; in a classroom, it is the instructor. The group can do two-level work only as the members begin to reject the external source of authority. By the time the members are able to do three-level work, they have completely rejected their dependence on the external authority.

Bennis and Shepard's model also maintains a clear separation between work and emotionality—the task and socioemotional dimensions. Although recognizing their close relationship, the authors emphasize the importance of achieving social interdependence as a prerequisite to task accomplishment. They feel that a group accomplishes the major part of its task during the period of four-level work.

Bennis and Shepard also discuss the phenomenon of flight behavior—the group's tendency to escape from its task, often as a result of social conflict among members or with the external authority. Generally the group begins settling these conflicts during the resolution-catharsis period of two-level work and has them well in hand during the social interdependence of three-level work. Bennis and Shepard observe that running away from the task is an attempt by the group to avoid some unpleasant stimulus, such as social conflict. The phenomenon of flight behavior will be discussed in more detail in Chapter 8.

Tuckman (1965) employed still another method for observing groups as he devised his four-phase model for group decision making. In fact, he himself did not observe any groups but synthesized the results of other published observations. He notes that groups simultaneously confront two kinds of problems in each phase of decision making. He labels these two problem types: *(a)* group structure (how to get along) and *(b)* task activity (how to proceed). Essentially, these two types of problems are "social problems" and "task problems," thereby denying the inseparable interdependence of the two dimensions of group process. Tuckman characterizes his four phases and their corresponding social and task problems with a catchy rhythm of four rhyming words:

*Phase 1:* "Forming." (a) Testing and independence; (b) attempting to identify the task.
*Phase 2:* "Storming." (a) Development of intragroup conflicts; (b) emotional response to task demands.
*Phase 3:* "Norming." (a) Development of group cohesion; (b) expression of opinions.
*Phase 4:* "Performing." (a) Functional role-relatedness; (b) emergence of solutions.

Tuckman's point of departure, like Bales and Strodtbeck's, is the type of problem under discussion at various stages in group interaction. He also clearly separates the members' communicative behavior into task and socioemotional areas. And, like Bennis and Shepard, Tuckman assumes that the group accomplishes most of its productive output in the latter stages of the decision-making process.

Despite the different methods used to observe group behavior, these three descriptive models possess characteristics in common. Although the perspective of each observer is quite different, they agree on many elements of the decision-making small group. Quite naturally, all three descriptions reflect a greater emphasis on the socioemotional dimension than on the task dimension. But this emphasis should be expected, since all the authors are psychologists or social psychologists whose primary interest is personality and social structure—not communication.

Consistent with the emphasis on the socioemotional dimension, all three models perceive a stable social structure as prerequisite to task productivity. Of course, this observation is possible only when one considers the two dimensions to be separate and even antagonistic to each other. Then, too, this observation denies the mutual influence of these dimensions. The result of this separation is an emphasis on explaining *why* groups are capable of making decisions rather than *how* groups actually do achieve consensual validation of decisions. The admitted emphasis of this book is on the "how" rather than the "why."

Although the three descriptive models do not completely agree on the nature of each phase, there seem to be four discernible phases of group decision making. Bales and Strodtbeck delineate only three phases, but they describe the control phase as including successive emphases on negative reactions and positive reactions in the early and latter portions of that final phase. Thus, four distinguishable phases seem to characterize group decision making.

Although the three descriptive models do not reflect identical characteristics of each phase, several phases include characteristics common to all three models. That is, the first stage of group decision making in all three models is a period of orientation—a period in which members adjust their individualities to group membership and accustom themselves to the task at hand. This orienting period generally involves a search process in which members search for ways to view their task with no particular focus or established opinion toward the task.

One of the middle phases in each of the models includes a period of social conflict among members, differences of opinion on task ideas and social norms. This similarity seems to confirm that social conflict and deviance are indeed a normal part of the group process. Moreover, social conflict and deviance are normal during only one period of group interaction. And that period of normal conflict is near the middle of the process and not near the beginning or the end of group task performance. Thus, the norm of social conflict and deviance characterizes a specific intermediate phase in the process of group interaction that ultimately leads to validation of decisions through consensus.

A final stage of interaction in which members apparently accomplish most of their work on their task is common to all three models, although the exact nature of that stage is not abundantly clear. Bales and Strodtbeck indicate the final stage is characterized by a maximum number of positive reactions. The other two models indicate that the group becomes capable of creative and effective task performance. But all three models agree that the group members achieve consensus and thereby validate their decisions during this last phase.

One final observation is appropriate concerning the descriptive approach to group decision making. Although two people may observe the same phenomenon and agree on many points of comparison, they may also disagree fundamentally on what they have observed. The perspective of the observer significantly influences what is observed and what conclusions are drawn from the observations. I can recall my initial adolescent attempt to dive from the high board at my local swimming pool. When I looked up at the board from the water below, it didn't seem high. But when I first looked down from the vantage point of standing on the board itself, it seemed astronomically high. One must remember that observation of reality is not reality. Observation is subject to the perspective of the observer and the tools used to observe.

The descriptive model discussed in the remainder of this chapter agrees with some elements contained in the previous models and disagrees with some others. Discrepancies among observers should not be of significant concern when one understands the differences among observational perspectives. The process of communication is the perspective employed in the following model.

## THE SPIRAL MODEL

Although the prescriptive and descriptive models described earlier are different in many significant respects, they are all "linear" models. Each model is based on a step-by-step progression toward the completion of task objectives. The steps in the linear model assume a given order. A group completes discussion of one set of problems before moving to the next. Each model assumes that solving one set of problems is prerequisite to solving the next set of problems. That is, the group is incapable of solving the second set of problems until it solves the first, and so on. Groups cannot or should not deal with problems out of sequence. Any step out of sequence would be considered a lack of group progress and an error of that group. The linear model outlines progress toward task accomplishment as a methodical progression along a straight line.

Thomas M. Scheidel and Laura Crowell (1964) discovered that group interaction aimed at developing ideas does not correspond to a linear model. Using a system of interaction analysis (see Appendix 2) as their observational scheme (Crowell and Scheidel, 1961), these authors describe the group process of idea development as a "spiral" model. (See Figure 5-2.) One member introduces an idea, and other members respond with agreement or disagreement, extension or revision. The idea is the object of discussion, and it develops over time to reflect the group's viewpoint. When an idea is developed to the point that it is an object of agreement by all group members, the group anchors its position on that idea and introduces new preliminary ideas progressing from that anchor point of agreement. The spiral process, then, involves "reach-testing" forward from an anchored position of agreement. If the reach-tested idea

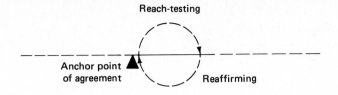

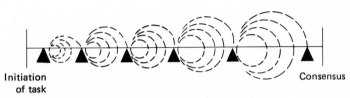

**Figure 5-2**   The spiral model of decision making.

is affirmed by the group, a new anchored position is established, and reach-testing proceeds from there. If the new idea is rejected, the group returns to its anchored position and reach-tests another new idea from that same anchor point.

The spiral process of anchoring and reach-testing is not linear in that the group constantly retraces its path of idea development. Groups develop new ideas not in linear sequence but cumulatively. One idea leads to another. One idea is progressively modified and remodified during the course of group interaction until the group achieves validation of its final decisions by consensus. The spiral process is cumulative and progressive, reflecting continuous modification of ideas and backtracking to agreed-upon ideas as members reconfirm positions.

As noted earlier, several descriptive models indicate that the bulk of the group's task activity occurs in the final stages of interaction. The spiral model denies that allegation but explains the appearance that groups accomplish more work during the final stages. The spiral process is cumulative, and all ideas developed in the latter stages of interaction are the direct result of earlier agreements and anchored positions. But in the final stages, the group has acquired a vast background of many agreed-upon positions. Reach-testing in the final phase therefore proceeds from a broader base of agreement with increasingly diminishing need to back-track to earlier anchor positions.

A children's springlike toy known as a "Slinky" illustrates this point. As you stretch the Slinky, you will notice that the spirals can be compressed at one end with relatively wide spaces between spirals at the other end and in the middle. But the spirals are all interconnected in a single continuous band of spring steel. In this way, the spirals of reach-tested ideas are compressed during the final period as consensus decisions become increasingly obvious to the group members. But those decisions are possible only because of the previously anchored positions of agreement developed in earlier phases. The process is cumulative rather than linear.

The spiral model also accounts for the apparent inefficiency of group decision making regarding the use of time. Every beginning geometry student knows that the shortest distance between two points on the same plane is a straight line. But group decision making apparently does not conform to a straight line of a linear model. Rather, the group process is more like a spiral of anchoring and reach-testing. But the spiral process is certainly not a disadvantage of group decision making. Anchoring and reach-testing ideas illustrate the group's superiority when performing decision-making tasks requiring high acceptance.

Other descriptive models depict the group decision-making process globally in terms of task and socioemotional dimensions. But the spiral model describes the group process in terms of the interaction patterns among members. The following model assumes the existence of the spiral process.

## THE PROCESS OF DECISION EMERGENCE

Chapter 7 will discuss the phenomenon of leader emergence—the fact that groups do not "select" leaders so much as the leader and other roles "emerge" during group interaction. If the task and socioemotional dimensions of group process are truly interdependent, it seems logical that the decision-making process should be similar to the leadership process. Moreover, group decision making, like leadership, possesses no single "best" or correct answer to be discovered in a "Eureka!" or "Aha!" manner. It is reasonable to conclude that groups do not *make* decisions. Decisions *emerge* from group interaction.

If you were to observe a decision-making group as a participant or as a nonparticipant attempting to determine the point at which the group makes its decision, you would find such a task extraordinarily difficult if not impossible. During some period of the group's interaction, the decision is probably apparent to you even though the group members continue their discussion.

The process of emergence is gradual and cumulative. A specific point in time at which decisions are made is not apt to be found. In fact, the emergence process presupposes that groups achieve consensus on their decisions *after* those decisions appear to have been made. The very final stage of interaction, then, fulfills the purpose of procuring members' public commitment, the essence of consensus, to decisions already reached.

### Phases of Decision Emergence

Using interaction analysis (see Appendix 2) as the method for observing group decision making, Fisher (1970a) discovered four phases in the process of group decision making. Unlike other observational schema, Fisher's method identified each alternative decision proposal suggested during group interaction and attempted to observe the process whereby preliminary ideas are transformed into consensus decisions. Thus, each member's communicative act functions on the decision proposal under discussion by expressing some opinion (favorable, unfavorable, or ambiguous) toward that proposal, providing evidence to support that opinion, modifying the proposal, clarifying it, and agreeing or disagreeing with another member's opinion. The group interaction is thus anchored to the subject matter of the group interaction—the decision proposals—and to members' attempts to influence the perceptions of other members toward those proposals.

The observed pattern of communicative behaviors—acts and interacts—indicates four rather distinct phases of group decision making, each characterized by a different pattern of interaction. Those phases are orientation, conflict, emergence, and reinforcement.

**Orientation Phase**   A group's early problems of socializing and excessive primary tension affect the interaction patterns in this early phase. Members clarify and agree most often in this phase. As members are unaware of their social position initially and not sure of how to handle the task, they do not quickly or strongly assert themselves or their opinions. Consequently they make assertions tentatively in order to test the group and they agree with virtually everything. For example, a member states an ambiguous opinion toward the decision proposal, a second member agrees with that ambiguous opinion, which is followed in turn by another ambiguous opinion. Since members agree even with comments serving only to clarify points of information, agreeing with another member's comment seems to function in the orientation phase not so much to reinforce other members' beliefs and opinions as to avoid disrupting the developing social climate.

Group members in the orientation phase search tentatively for ideas and directions to aid their decision-making efforts. They are unaware of the direction the group will eventually take, so they don't commit themselves, favorably or unfavorably, to the newly introduced decision proposals. Rather, they express attitudes that are ambiguous toward proposals—attitudes that don't really take a stand one way or the other.

Many of the ambiguous opinions expressed in the first phase probably reflect favorable attitudes in the making. That is, since members assert opinions and arguments favoring the proposals with increasing intensity as the discussion progresses, those opinions must be in the preliminary stages of formation during this orientation phase. As the issues become clarified and as the social climate becomes more conducive to the honest statement of one's true position, many members apparently change their ambiguous opinions to opinions favoring the decision proposals.

Characteristic of the orientation phase, then, is getting acquainted, clarifying, and tentatively expressing attitudes. This stage is a period of forming opinions, not rocking the boat, and getting rid of social inhibitions—in short, the orientation phase.

**Conflict Phase** The second phase of group decision making is characterized by dispute—ideational conflict over decision proposals. In the orientation phase, members only tentatively express their opinions, typically ambiguous. In the conflict phase they appear to have made up their minds. Members are now aware of the direction the group is taking toward the decision-making task and of the relevant decision proposals emerging from the group deliberations. Thus, members typically express either a favorable or an unfavorable attitude toward those proposals. Gone is the tentativeness of ambiguity. Gone, too, is tentativeness due to social inhibitions.

Polarization of attitudes means disagreement and conflict. In the conflict phase, expressing a favorable attitude is generally followed by another member's expressing an unfavorable attitude (and vice versa). Members have different opinions and express them in argument with one another. Not only do members express less ambiguous attitudes, but they also express them more tenaciously. They now provide data and evidence to substantiate their beliefs and engage in full-fledged debate with other members.

The interaction patterns of the conflict phase reflect the formation of two coalitions resulting from polarization of beliefs. That is, two coalitions are present in this phase—one favoring and one opposing those decision proposals that ultimately achieve group consensus. To illustrate, members A and B favor the proposals and reinforce each other's favorable opinions; C and D oppose the proposals and reinforce each other's unfavorable opinions. Expression of ambiguous attitudes or the presence of a "mugwump" member is not normal in the conflict phase.

The norm is dissent, controversy, social conflict, and innovative deviance. In fact, mugwumps are deviates in the conflict phase in that they do not participate in the debate over ideas and opinions.

It is quite probable that the coalitions centered around leader contenders are the same coalitions formed by polarization of ideas during the conflict phase. The interdependence of the task and socioemotional dimensions seem to confirm that explanation.

**Emergence Phase**   Social conflict and dissent dissipate during the third phase. Members express fewer unfavorable opinions toward decision proposals. The coalition of individuals who have opposed those proposals which eventually achieve consensus also weakens in this phase. The interaction patterns in the emergence phase reflect significantly less positive reinforcement of one another's unfavorable attitudes. A few residues of overt social conflict remain, but they are not significant. Comments expressing unfavorable attitudes are not only not reinforced by subsequent agreement or more unfavorable attitudes from other members in the coalition; they are not expressed so tenaciously either. That is, opposing members typically assert unfavorable opinions without including supporting evidence or reason to substantiate them.

The hallmark of the emergence phase is the recurrence of ambiguity. As in the orientation phase, some members express opinions ambiguous toward the decision proposals and tend to reinforce them by responding with further expressions of attitudes ambiguous toward the proposals. Thus, ambiguity toward decision proposals is prominent in the orientation phase, declines significantly in the conflict phase, and rises again during the emergence phase.

But although the proportionate number of comments expressing ambiguous opinions and interacts reflecting reinforcement of ambiguous comments does not differ substantially from the orientation phase, the function performed by ambiguity in the interact patterns of the emergence phase is significantly different. During orientation, members express opinions tentatively in the form of ambiguous attitudes toward the decision proposals. Some of these ambiguous comments are undoubtedly the initial expression of favorable or unfavorable opinions in rudimentary form of development. But group members have no reason to be tentative in the emergence phase. They are certainly no longer searching for attitude direction. They have plotted that direction in the orientation phase and debated it during the conflict phase. In the emergence phase, task direction is obviously no longer at issue. It is quite unreasonable to conclude that expressing an ambiguous opinion at this late point in the discussion reflects a tentative expression of a developing opinion.

The key to the function of ambiguity in the patterns of group interaction lies in associating the emergence phase with the conflict phase. Ambiguous communicative behavior functions in the third phase as a form of modified dissent. In the conflict phase, members either favor or disfavor the decision proposals. In the emergence phase, the bimodal distribution has shifted to favorable or ambiguous attitudes toward these same proposals. That is, the group member who expresses opposition to decision proposals in the conflict phase is in the process of changing from disfavor to favor through the mediating step of expressing ambiguous opinions.

Members expressing ambiguous opinions in the emergence phase have already committed themselves to a stand of opposition in the conflict phase and cannot be expected to change their opinions so abruptly. Thus, their dissent changes to assent by way of ambiguity. A dissenting member in the conflict phase responds to another member's comment favoring a proposal with an opinion disfavoring it. In the emergence phase, in the same situation the response will be an opinion ambiguous toward the proposal. Opposition to the proposal is still being expressed, but opposition is dissipating as attitudes are modified.

The two coalitions present in the conflict phase also dissipate during the emergence phase. The coalition of dissenting members opposing the decision proposals does not immediately disintegrate but turns to ambiguous comments as a final form of dissent. Just as the exact point in time at which a leader or a decision emerges cannot be pinpointed, neither can one determine the exact moment of the death of the dissenting coalition. The dissipation of dissent and the dissipation of the coalition are gradual and mediated by ambiguity. In the absence of outright social conflict, decisions may appear to have been reached. But the expression of ambiguous opinions, while not totally unfavorable, is not yet favorable. As disfavor dissipates to ambiguity, however, favorable opinions toward the decision proposals increase concomitantly.

The third phase is probably the crucial stage in the group process of decision making. During this third phase the eventual outcome of group interaction becomes increasingly more apparent. Therefore this third phase is called the "emergence" phase.

**Reinforcement Phase**   While group members tend to reach decisions during the emergence phase, they achieve consensus on those decisions during the reinforcement phase. Substantiating one's opinion toward the decision proposal is no longer necessary. After all, the ideas were thoroughly tested during the conflict phase, but members continue to provide evidence and reasons to support their opinions favoring the decision proposals, thus adding additional fuel to the fire of emerging consensus. Members constantly and consistently express opinions favorable to the proposals and positively reinforce one another's favorable opinions with expressions of agreement and additional social support. This overwhelming preponderance of interaction patterns that favor the decision proposals and positively reinforce those favorable opinions clearly identifies the final phase of group deliberations.

Dissent has all but vanished in the reinforcement phase. This phase includes the lowest number of comments opposed to the decision proposals and virtually no interacts of social conflict—that is, a favorable comment followed or preceded by an unfavorable comment. Of course the orientation phase contains few interacts of social conflict, too. But whereas the low level of conflict during orientation reflects the members' conscious avoidance of conflict due to social inhibitions, the reinforcement phase reflects unity of opinion among group members. The dissipation of dissent, both direct (unfavorable opinions) and modified (ambiguous opinions), is virtually complete in this phase of group interaction.

Pervading this final phase in group decision making is a spirit of unity. All members seem to agree and strive to show that agreement through positively reinforcing one another. Their interaction patterns reflect virtually no tension as members are jovial, loud, boisterous, laughing, and verbally backslap each other. This is the phase of developing members' commitment to those decisions that were the object of conflict in the second phase and that emerged during the third phase. This is the reinforcement phase.

Orientation, conflict, emergence, and reinforcement, then, are the four phases of decision emergence. They have been described here in terms of characteristic patterns of interaction. Where possible, they have been associated with elements of the socioemotional dimension. The original purpose of the investigation that revealed these four phases was to observe verbal task behavior free from the confounding variables of the socioemotional dimension. That purpose, of course, was doomed to failure. The two dimensions are interdependent. Attempting to view only one dimension can only provide a perspective from which to recognize the interdependence of both.

The descriptions of the four phases are admittedly rather general and provide no examples of group interaction. In order to illustrate the phases more clearly and reveal the "flavor" of group decision making from the viewpoint of members' communicative behaviors, Appendix 1, Anatomy of a Decision, provides detailed examples of interaction patterns from an actual decision-making group. Appendix 1 should clarify most questions raised in the preceding general description.

### The Group Process of Modifying Decisions

The spiral model of idea development, described by Scheidel and Crowell (1964) and affirmed in the phases of decision emergence, reveals that group decision making is a process of cumulative development of consensus decisions. Groups achieve consensus on decisions through interaction patterns which modify, reject, accept, or combine previously introduced decision proposals. However, the specific nature of the interaction patterns that cumulatively modify decision proposals until they appear in consensus form is not evident in the discussion of either the spiral model or the phases of decision emergence.

Studying the interaction patterns of decision-making groups, Fisher (1970b) discerned a pattern of cumulative, step-by-step modification of decision proposals. That is, groups do not typically modify preliminary decision proposals by clear and direct amendments but in sudden jumps to different formulations of the same root proposal. Consistent with Berg's (1967) discovery of a group's rather brief attention span, Fisher found that groups apparently do not discuss each proposal for an extended period. Rather, a group member introduces a specific decision proposal, members discuss it for some length of time, drop it in favor of discussing another decision proposal, and reintroduce the first proposal later during the group deliberations.

Often groups reconsider the proposal in the same form. But on those not infrequent occasions when the initial formulation of a proposal is not precisely the one that eventually achieves consensus, members reintroduce the proposal in modified form. Sometimes a proposal is reintroduced several times, each with further modification. Thus, groups achieve consensus on decision proposals not in a consistent evolutionary pattern but, rather, in spurts of energy.

Following this pattern of decision modification, a member introduces a decision proposal which the members discuss briefly and then drop from consideration. Later, a member reintroduces this same proposal in substitute form, and the group proceeds toward consensus in a cumulative and cyclical manner.

An example may illustrate this pattern of modification more clearly. A corporate management training group (four men, here called A, B, C, and D) was engaged in making decisions regarding the management of a hypothetical corporation. One of their consensus decisions was to concentrate their sales and advertising campaigns for their mythical business in two market areas—one urban and one rural. Member B initially introduced this decision proposal in its rudimentary form—to withhold all attempts to sell their products until after the results of a market analysis had become available. The following excerpt is from the group's interaction at that point:

*B:* This is going to be our plan initially, to get this market analysis. I feel we should consider holding our market in inventory and not sell the first quarter until you find out where the market is.

*A:* What would you do with the sales representatives, then? Just let them sit around?

*B:* Pay their salary—$8,000.

*A:* But you're not getting any return on your money.

*D:* You've got to put them out in the field.

*C:* Put them out. It wouldn't cost us anything.

*A:* All right. What should we do about advertising?

The group members did not respond favorably to B's proposal, and they quickly moved to another, as yet unrelated, proposal concerning advertising. Later, C reintroduced a substitute decision proposal regarding how to allocate the company's sales representatives:

*C:* As a matter of fact, if we were to take one area and blanket it with our sales reps and take another area for our market analysis, we might be able to calculate a second area based on the results of our sales.

*A:* We might be able to. At least it's a better possibility than. . . .

*D:* It's an indicator.

*C:* An indicator. You've got more information.

*B:* We need to get a job description of the chairperson.

The group members responded favorably to the substitute proposal. Yet they dropped the second proposal, too, before coming to a final decision and before exhausting their discussion of it.

The decision proposal to concentrate their sales representatives in two market areas came closest to the form of a direct amendment to the decision proposal while it was being discussed:

*C:* Our first shot at sales is really to obtain a market coverage.

*B:* What do you mean by "market coverage"?

*C:* I'm sorry. A market forecast.

*B:* That's what we were saying. Get a forecast on each region and try to cover sales in each.

*C:* But I don't think we can do that. I think we can blanket only one area.

*B:* If you put two sales reps in each area, you use six sales reps. But I don't think you want to do that.

*D:* No. We can't reallocate. If we put two in each one of those areas and reallocate one of them to the other area, then we cover it.

*B:* You're covered if the first guy gets a sale.

*A:* You've got to gamble a little bit, but I don't think you want to throw your whole sales staff into one area. I think we ought to distribute three and three. [By allocating the six sales representatives "three and three," A proposes to distribute them equally in two market areas. He appears to amend the earlier proposal to concentrate them in a single area.]

*C:* Three and three?

*A:* Three and three. And then see what the results of our market analysis are. On the basis of this knowledge, we can better reallocate.

*D:* Where are we going to do our market analysis anyway?

Member A initiated a new decision proposal largely by amending the proposal under discussion—to concentrate all six sales representatives in one area—and introducing it in amended form—to distribute them equally in two areas. But, without exhaustively deliberating this proposal, the members quickly shifted to another decision proposal regarding the area of market analysis.

Earlier the group had discussed the decision proposal of whether the company should advertise:

*B:* How much for advertising?

*C:* Mr. Marketing, would you recommend two pages of advertising for each of the areas we are going to cover?

*D:* Yes. I think that's the least we can do. If we are going to put sales reps in an area, we ought to support them.

*B:* Remember, we haven't got much cost there.

*C:* You can't make money unless you spend it.

*B:* No. But we are just finding out where the market is right now. Why spend it for advertising?

*C:* But what if the other people spend? We'll find out, of course, if we lose a sale to the competitors.

*B:* Let's not advertise.

*C:* We ought to advertise something.

*D:* I think we should have one page.

*C:* One page, at least.

*B:* But we don't have the money.

*A:* How are we doing in formulating our long-range objectives?

Unlike the previous examples of decision proposals dropped after initiation and brief discussion, members responded to this proposal with a direct conflict of opinions. But without resolving the conflict, the group again shifted to a totally different proposal—formulating the company's long-range objectives. The two decision proposals to concentrate their sales force in two areas and advertise in both areas were combined later in a further reformulation of the decision proposals:

*A:* With the marketing advantage you have getting this information, you'd better spend as much as you can on advertising and sales in that place and ignore the rest.

   *B:* I don't know if we want to go into two areas or not. We aren't going to have enough to cover.

   *C:* I would suggest that we take a shot at two areas. If we hit area 4, which is urban, and pick area 2 right above it, which is. . . .

   *A:* Strictly rural.

   *C:* If we hit area 4 and area 2, we can draw conclusions and see if there really is a difference between the urban and rural markets.

Member C's addition of "urban" and "rural" to differentiate the two market areas is not so much a modification of the proposal as it is an observation on the advantage of concentrating advertising and sales representatives in two areas. This point seemed to win over the obviously reluctant member B. And this configuration was the decision proposal that eventually achieved group consensus.

   Each of the reformulations of the initial decision proposal is introduced, discussed, and dropped several times. The excerpts included above illustrate only those moments in the group's interaction in which members initiated the proposal in a modified form and does not include other reintroductions of the same proposal. Thus, members modify decision proposals by leaps or jumps rather than continuously by direct amendment and prolonged discussion.

   In short, reformulations or modifications of the initial decision proposal do not typically emerge from direct criticisms of the proposal while it is being discussed. Rather, group members appear to wrestle with the proposal, sometimes with conflict and sometimes without, and then put it aside temporarily until one of the members experiences an insight and suggests a reformulation that seems closer to what the group really wants.

   It seems clear that the process of decision modification reveals an interaction norm of a start-and-stop deliberation of decision proposals. Group members normally cease deliberations regarding a specific decision proposal and abruptly switch to another proposal. This norm is often frustrating to inexperienced group members. One classroom group's self-analysis reveals just such frustration:

> We would be talking about one subject and then all of a sudden in midstream change and start talking about something else. Our group has the trait of going around in circles.

This perceptive comment reflects the concern of a group member who considered this "going around in circles" as indicating some failure in group interaction. Unfortunately, the members of this group never realized during their interaction that they were behaving quite normally. Only their frustration was disruptive.

The tendency of a group to cease deliberations abruptly and switch to another topic is similar to the phenomenon of "flight behavior" discussed earlier in this chapter. The term "flight" usually implies an attempt to avoid some unpleasant stimulus such as interpersonal conflict or extreme social tension. Yet groups exhibit interaction patterns characteristic of flight behavior whether there is dissenting social conflict or not. Each of the 163 decision proposals observed (Fisher, 1970b) was introduced, discussed, dropped, reintroduced, discussed, dropped again, and so forth, in essentially the same pattern. Rather than indicating that the group is "fleeing" from some unpleasant social problem, the spasmodic progression toward consensus seems to be an inherent and quite normal characteristic of interaction patterns during the process of group decision making.

The group norm of "flight" during decision making probably serves the purpose of managing tension as well as progressively modifying decision proposals. Because a group normally does not consider any decision proposal for an extended period of time, social tension does not easily or quickly rise to intolerable levels. Certainly participating in group interaction, continuously susceptible to social pressure, is by its very nature a highly intense experience. The pressures on each person, due simply to group membership, cannot be sustained indefinitely.

Some level of secondary tension is normal throughout group interaction. The spurts of task activity probably indicate the natural tendency of a group to manage its social tension by frequently conserving energy through abrupt transitions to different decision proposals. Thus, the spiral model of the group decision-making process, though generally intended to describe the process of task performance, is closely interrelated with the group's social dimension as well.

**Social Conflict and Decision Modification**    Although the evidence is not conclusive, there is a justifiable basis for believing that the patterns of decision modification do reflect the influence of social conflict over decision proposals. That is, when members consistently respond to initiated proposals with a conflict of opinions, the successive reintroduction of those decision proposals follows a distinctive pattern. And when members experience little conflict of opinions toward initiated proposals, the successive reintroduction of those proposals corresponds to a different pattern.

The pattern of decision modification characterized by little social conflict is generally a process of lowering the level of abstraction of the language phrasing the decision proposal. That is, each successive reintroduction of a substitute proposal is slightly more concrete than the previous one. The example of the corporate management training group corresponds to this essential pattern. Another example of this pattern of lowered abstraction appears in the interaction of a group of nursing experts planning a workshop-conference for educators in public health nursing.

Early in the nursing group's weeklong deliberations, the members discussed the present status of public health nurses and observed that public health nurses felt they were downgraded by the rest of the nursing profession. The group then felt that the public health nurses attending the conference would be defensive and would resist new proposals. Later, a member initiated a substitute proposal to begin the conference with "a nonthreatening something." After being discussed and dropped, the substitute proposal was reintroduced, proposing to "get the conference feeling good and then change them." A later substitute proposal suggested that they begin the conference "on common ground." Eventually the proposal was reintroduced in the form that achieved consensus—"Begin the conference with a history of the contributions which public health has made to the field of nursing."

Each reformulated decision proposal follows from the previous one, and none elicited much dissent from the members. Furthermore, each succeeding decision proposal was more concrete or specific than the previous one. Thus, without social conflict, group members modify decision proposals in an evolutionary and methodical process of lowering the level of abstraction of each successive proposal. This pattern might be illustrated in the following methodical sequence:

*Statement of the problem*—"Public health nurses feel their lack of status and will therefore be defensive and resistant to change."
*Criteria for the solution*—"Begin the conference with a nonthreatening something." "Get the conference feeling good and then change them."
*Abstract statement of solution*—"Start the conference on common ground."
*Concrete statement of solution*—"Begin the conference with a history of the contributions which public health has made to the field of nursing."

In the absence of social conflict or significant dissent, the lowering-of-abstraction pattern of decision modification seems to be painless, systematic, and eminently reasonable. But not all emergent decisions follow such a methodical route to consensus.

The presence of social conflict and dissent stimulates a different pattern of decision modification in which members introduce successive decision proposals at essentially the same level of abstraction. The same nursing group proceeded through the following reformulations of another initial proposal. The final reformulation achieved group consensus and was prerequisite to several other decisions to include specific programs in the conference:

1  "The public health nurse is engaged in treatment of pathology."
2  "Public health nurses should have more clinical work with patients."
3  "Public health nurses do perform tasks that require clinical nursing skills."
4  "Clinical skills are required for working with patients in the home as well as in the hospital."
5  "Public health nursing is a clinical nursing specialty."

This second pattern also reflects the characteristic start-and-stop cumulative development of a consensus decision. But unlike the lowering-of-abstraction pattern associated with minimal conflict and dissent, this pattern reflects substitute decision proposals which are virtually restatements of each other. Each proposal is essentially the equivalent level of abstraction of every other.

The lowering-of-abstraction pattern is methodical in that members express little disagreement on the credibility of each decision proposal. In the absence of social conflict, group members apparently perceive their task as one of seeking or "discovery"—in this case, discovering what to include in the conference that would solve their problem and meet their established criteria.

The second pattern including social conflict seems to reflect a different task for the members. To some members of the nursing group, public health nursing is a form of community social work or civil service in a government-sponsored clinic. To others, public health nursing is a clinical nursing specialty equivalent to, for example, psychiatric nursing. The issue produced disagreement and significant social tension among group members. Rather than being perceived as a task of discovery, the task in the presence of significant social conflict was perceived to be "persuasion" or attitude change in order to secure intragroup agreement. Whereas creativity is required to perform a task of discovery, persuasion is required to secure agreement.

Social conflict, then, does not affect the basic start-and-stop process of decision modification but apparently does result in a distinctive pattern of that decision modification. With little substantive conflict, members methodically reintroduce substitute proposals in a pattern which consistently lowers the level of abstraction of that proposal. With little interpersonal conflict, members see their task as one of search or discovery. When a decision proposal precipitates social conflict among members, that proposal is typically reintroduced at essentially the same level of abstraction in successive equivalent restatements of the root proposal. In the presence of dissent, the group members perceive their task to be one of persuasion in order to secure agreement among all group members.

Jumping from proposal to proposal with little or no transition and without exhausting the discussion of a given decision proposal is characteristic of the process of group decision making. And the level of interpersonal conflict, along with the members' perception of the nature of their group task, influences the extent to which the process of decision modification is systematic in lowering the level of abstraction of the language in which the proposals are phrased.

## FACTORS OF GROUP MEMBERSHIP

Groups are composed of human beings, and human beings can be characterized in a multitude of ways. Specific groups, then, may be composed of literally thousands of different combinations of persons. Any attempt to discuss comprehensively all those possible combinations would be a gargantuan undertaking. Frankly, I do not wish to take on such an awesome responsibility. Group members can be differentiated according to age, sex, physical characteristics, intelligence, abilities, aptitudes, and a host of different personalities. Two decades ago, Mann (1959) indicated that there were over 500 different measures of personality alone. Certainly, over the past 20 years, even that figure has increased enormously.

The following paragraphs concerning the influence of factors of group composition on the task dimension are not intended to be either comprehensive or even representative of all compositional factors. Rather, the discussion will include only two factors of group composition. These factors are important and increasingly popular among scholars of group communication. To the reader who wishes to know more about the impact of compositional factors on the group process, I recommend the discussion by Marvin E. Shaw (1976, pp. 163–192).

### Abilities of Members

It would be foolish to say that abilities of members have no impact on group decision making. Certainly, groups composed of intelligent members will make more intelligent decisions than groups of less intelligent persons. Similarly, groups of more capable or more expert members will make more capable or more expert decisions than will less qualified groups. It would also be foolish to attempt to discuss in any definitive sense the possible combinations of different abilities among members of decision-making groups. Shaw's discussion is the place to look for a more comprehensive discussion. My present purpose includes discussing only a very few abilities that members may possess and that are relatively important to the process of group decision making. These abilities are not necessarily more important than others, but they seem intriguing in terms of their potential impact on the outcome of group decision making.

Earlier discussions have illustrated Dewey's (1910) model of reflective thinking as it is typically used—as an agenda to guide group deliberations. Indeed, this is the typical and traditional use of reflective thinking in group decision making. Nearly forty years ago, however, Alma Johnson (1943) talked about reflective thinking as an ability possessed by human beings. She devised a test designed to measure a person's reflective-thinking ability. Later researchers applied her reflective-thinking test to measure the abilities of specific group members performing decision-making tasks.

Such research (for example, Pyron and Sharp, 1963; Pyron, 1964; Sharp and Milliken, 1964) revealed that members ranking high in reflective-thinking ability were perceived by their fellow members as more capable and as contributing more to the group's decisions than members who ranked low on this ability. Moreover, the researchers indicated that groups composed of members with high reflective-thinking ability tended to make higher-quality decisions.

We can surmise, from this knowledge that comes from scholarly research, that reflective thinking may indeed be an ability that is possessed by humans, just as critical thinking, analogical thinking, or intelligence is an ability. And there are tests available to measure each one of these abilities. We can also conclude with assurance that groups composed of members with greater ability will be able to make better decisions. "Consequently," according to Goldberg and Larson (1975, p. 28), "it is tempting to assume that if a group collectively follows a reflective thinking pattern [as an agenda] the quality of its problem-solving deliberations may improve. This is not necessarily the case." It is probably better to think of reflective thinking as an ability that some people possess to a greater degree than others, much as we think that some people are more intelligent than others. But reflective thinking as a prescriptive approach to improve the quality of group decision making has not been as well documented.

Edward DeBono (1968) has discussed another personal ability that may be directly related to improving the quality of group decisions. DeBono illustrates two different types of thinking, which he calls "vertical thinking" and "lateral thinking." He describes vertical thinking as "the only respectable type of thinking in our society." It is consistent with logic, rationality, and reason. Mr. Spock of "Star Trek" is probably the fictional archetype of the ideal vertical thinker.

Lateral thinking, on the other hand, is less rational and logical. It deals with new and quite arbitrary ways of looking at problems. Lateral thinking is highly creative in the sense that it explores new and unorthodox views of familiar situations. It is less rational in the sense that vertical thinking deals with a step-by-step approach to problem solving with emphasis on the greatest probability of success. Lateral thinking involves leaps of the imagination and lack of concern with probabilities for success.

To illustrate the difference between vertical and lateral thinking, an example may be in order. You may be familiar with the puzzle concerning the cannibals and the missionaries crossing the river in a single boat. It goes something like this: Three missionaries and three cannibals must cross a river. They have but one boat, which will carry only two people. Since the river is filled with crocodiles and piranhas, no one can swim the river. The problem, however, concerns the cannibals' latent tendency to eat people. The missionaries are safe as long as their number is equal to or greater than the cannibals. But if the cannibals outnumber the missionaries on either side of the river, it's good-bye missionaries. How can all six people safely cross the river in the single two-person boat?

The exclusively vertical thinker may find this puzzle somewhat difficult to solve without numerous trials. The more lateral thinker, however, experiences little difficulty and typically uncovers the solution immediately. In case you have not discovered the answer, the step-by-step solution follows:

1   One cannibal and one missionary cross the river. The missionary returns with the boat.
2   Two cannibals cross the river. One of them returns with the boat.
3   Two missionaries cross the river. *Both a missionary and a cannibal return with the boat.*
4   Both remaining missionaries cross the river. One of the cannibals returns with the boat.
5   Two cannibals cross the river. One of them returns for the remaining cannibal.

The key to solving this little problem lies in step 3. The vertical thinker, concerned with efficiency and achieving the goal in the most direct manner, is apt to overlook the possibility of having *two* people return with the boat. But such a step is necessary if you are to keep the cannibals from outnumbering the missionaries on one or the other side of the river. The lateral thinker, on the other hand, is not blinded by the constraints of efficiency and "rationality at all costs." Such a thinker quickly sees the key to the solution and solves the puzzle with little difficulty.

You may be tempted to believe that lateral thinking is superior to vertical thinking or vice versa. Such a conclusion, however, would be quite mistaken. DeBono is emphatic in asserting that vertical and lateral thinking are complementary modes of thought. In some situations vertical thinking will be superior, but at other times lateral thinking will prove to be more useful in solving problems. It would be wise, then, for everyone to develop abilities of both vertical and lateral thinking. Unfortunately, while vertical thinking can be, and is, learned and taught in contemporary classrooms, lateral thinking can be learned only through experience and revelation. It defies any formalized description or instruction and can be acquired only through experiences with the novel, the creative, and the unexpected.

## Sex Differences

The psychological and behavioral differences between men and women have long been a popular subject of social researchers. Even though the results from such research have been rather ambivalent and inconsistent, it has long been commonly believed that men are better problem solvers and women are more concerned with the social relationships and are more easily persuaded. Explanations of such alleged differences have consistently attributed them to the sex-role stereotypes of men and women in our culture. Women are considered to be "feminine," and men are supposed to be "masculine." Therefore, men and women are socialized and trained at an early age to display these role characteristics. Girls receive dolls as Christmas and birthday presents, and little boys receive trucks and G.I. Joe paraphernalia. Girls take home economics classes, and boys take shop classes. Boys become athletes, girls become cheerleaders.

The renewed interest, precipitated by the women's movement, in sex-role stereotyping has led to numerous changes in our cultural views of men and women. Socialization processes in our society are becoming less oriented toward sex roles. It is not uncommon in recent years for boys to enroll in cooking and sewing classes and for girls to enroll in woodshop classes. Women's athletic teams, once a rarity in American high schools, are now very common. The apparent psychological and behavioral differences between men and women are becoming less distinct as well.

More important, those differences are probably less associated with the physiological distinctions between males and females and more attributable to the self-concepts of masculinity and femininity of either men or women. That is, a woman may have a masculine or feminine self-concept in terms of psychological orientation. In a similar manner, men may be more masculine or feminine in their self- concepts. Such a notion of masculinity and femininity as a self- concept should appear quite acceptable. It makes little sense that merely because someone possesses a womb, she is less capable of solving complex problems. And why should men be any less socially aware and sensitive to other persons?

Milton (1957) found consistent support for associating a difference in problem solving with self-concepts of masculinity and femininity, regardless of whether the problem solvers were males or females. That is, men who considered themselves masculine were better problem solvers, and women whose self-conceptions were "unfeminine" were also better problem solvers. When masculinity and femininity are conceptualized as elements of a self-concept, rather than a physiological difference, any conclusion which suggests that men differ (psychologically or behaviorally) from women becomes highly suspect. In fact, traits of masculinity and femininity are now associated with certain roles in our society rather than with the maleness or femaleness of the persons who occupy those roles. Stereotyping a person on the basis of that person's sex is rapidly becoming outdated.

To illustrate our society's tendency to stereotype sex roles, numerous feminist puzzles have become popular in recent years. One such puzzle, which is probably quite familiar to you, involves the story of the teenage boy who was involved in a serious automobile accident. His father was driving the car and was killed instantly. The boy was rushed to the hospital in critical condition. The doctor in the emergency room took one look at the boy and screamed, "My God! It's my son!" The puzzle, then, concerns how the critically injured boy could be the doctor's son when his father had been killed in the same accident. Of course, the answer is that the doctor was the boy's mother.

Sandra Bem (1974) has developed a psychological test that attempts to discover whether a person's self-concept is masculine or feminine. She discovered, from administering this test to numerous persons, that many people are androgynous. That is, many people possess a self-concept that includes characteristics which our society has judged to be masculine (for example, ambition, assertiveness) as well as allegedly feminine characteristics (for example, affectionate nature, understanding).

Recent research into sex differences in communication has employed the self-concept of androgyny with some rather explanatory results. These results suggest strongly that sex differences in communication are related more to self-concepts than to physiological differences of gender.

(See, for example, Montgomery and Burgoon, 1977; and the entire 1977 convention program of the Speech Communication Association which includes papers by Watson; Patton, et al.; Greenblatt, et al.; Montgomery and Burgoon; Eman; and Morse.)

Some communicative differences between males and females should be noted. These differences may or may not be related to self-concepts. Specifically, males and females differ regarding their amounts of self-disclosing communication. For example, women disclose more on the basis of liking the other person, and men disclose more on the basis of interpersonal trust. (For a more comprehensive discussion of sex differences in self-disclosure, see Gilbert, 1976a and b.)

Aries (1976) discovered that the interaction patterns of males and females differ when they communicate with their same sex and when they interact in groups of both sexes. She also provides an important implication in interpreting any sex differences among males and females in interaction patterns, stating that these differences "reflect the sex-role demands of conventional society." She goes on to say, "Despite the new ideology developing about sex roles, it was not yet incorporated into the patterns of social interaction. If the movements from liberation from sex roles are successful, we should find in time more variation in interpersonal styles in both one-sex and mixed groups."

In Chapter 7 and elsewhere, the subject of sex differences affecting communication and the group process will be discussed. It is difficult to draw any definitive conclusions concerning any interactive differences between males and females in the group process. We can, however, come to some tentative conclusions: (1) Any behavioral differences between males and females is probably associated with the sex-role stereotypes that are dominant in our American society. (2) Apparent sex-role differences probably stem from each person's self-concept—either masculine, feminine, or androgynous. (3) The increased awareness of sex-role stereotypes engendered by the women's movement will probably lead to social changes and eventually to minimal, if any, noticeable behavioral or psychological differences between males and females. Indeed, the research that has discovered such differences between males and females is probably outdated and obsolete even by the time it is published.

Partially as a result of my own feminist tendencies (even though I am male) and unsystematic observation of classroom groups during years of teaching group decision making, I strongly believe that any differences between male and female interaction are perceived to be greater than they really are. In other words, I hold a rather firm belief with almost no empirical support. And that belief is that we tend to *perceive* that men and women communicate differently. But the actual differences in the communicative behaviors of men and women are probably quite minimal, if they exist at all.

## SUMMARY

Decision making includes problem solving, which requires a high acceptance of the solution. Decision making also includes other types of decision making that are not clearly classified as problem solving. A decision is a choice among alternative proposals, the sum of which constitutes all or part of the group's task performance. Consensus signifies the commitment of members and their willingness to implement decisions reached by the group.

Prescriptive views of the group decision-making process attempt to illustrate how groups should make decisions. They assume rationality on the part of the group members, an ideal process of decision making, and improved quality of group decisions. Doubt is cast on the credibility of those assumptions. The most commonly used prescriptive method of group decision making is John Dewey's "reflective thinking" model.

Descriptive models of the group decision-making process attempt to illustrate how groups *do* solve problems and assume the presence of a natural or normal development of consensus decisions. Such models differ on the basis of the perspective of the observer and the tools used to observe the group process. The most commonly used descriptive model is the three-phase model from Bales's IPA. Other descriptive models using different observational techniques reveal significant similarities with the three-phase model, but few models employ the perspective of group interaction patterns.

Unlike linear models of group decision making, a spiral process assumes a pattern of anchored group positions of agreement and reach-testing forward to develop new ideas. In this way group members refine, accept, reject, modify, and combine ideas progressively and cumulatively until the idea reflects the group consensus. The spiral process, normal to the group process, accounts for the apparent inefficiency of group decision making as well as the influence of the social dimension in achieving higher-quality decisions.

Decisions are not so much *made* by a group as they *emerge* from group interaction. This emergence of decisions is illustrated in the four-phase model of orientation, conflict, emergence, and reinforcement, each phase characterized by a distinctively different interaction pattern.

Group decisions achieve consensus in a spasmodic and cumulative modification of decision proposals in which proposals are introduced, discussed, dropped, and reintroduced in slightly modified versions until the proposal appears in a form that achieves group consensus. Although this start-and-stop process of decision modification is typical of all introduced decision proposals, the presence of social conflict affects the pattern of reintroduced decision proposals and the members' perception of their group task. In every case, the spasmodic process of decision modification reflects the normal interaction patterns of group members and influences both the task and socioemotional dimensions of the group.

The individual characteristics of the members of the decision-making group may also affect the group's task performance. For example, a higher ability level (particularly of reflective and lateral thinking) of the group members will probably lead to a higher-quality group decision. However, the differences in contributions made by males and females may be less significant than conventional wisdom would assume.

# Chapter 6

# Behavioral Standards
# —Roles and Norms

Developing the socioemotional climate of the group is essentially a process of acculturation. Typically, the process of acculturation implies a new member's joining an already established culture, in the sense of a Vietnamese immigrant's coming to the United States to live, a Midwesterner's moving to New York, or a Southerner's relocating in the North. Certain modes of behavior are acceptable within a given culture, and others are unacceptable. Previous members of a culture have established certain expected patterns of doing and thinking. These patterns must be learned by the newcomer.

One familiar example of the impact of cultural differences on behavioral expectations is that of the North American in a Latin American country who arrives at 2:30 for a 2:30 appointment. The North American, considering the arrival to be "on time," is unable to comprehend why the Latin American should consider it rude to arrive so "early." Each culture develops its own rules for guiding behavior, and these rules may be quite different from those in another culture. The alien newcomer, then, must adapt to the new behavioral patterns or face the consequences of "culture shock."

Every group develops its own standards to guide the behavior of its members. Even those groups that have formal requirements to direct members' behavior also develop informal rules during the process of group interaction. Every group thus establishes its own rules for guiding the behavioral patterns of its members. Of course, the development of those standards is typically cumulative and implicit, but it is nonetheless evident.

Members of every group soon realize that their membership in that group constrains, to some extent, their freedom to choose their own behaviors. That is, each member possesses a range of behavioral choices that are available to him or her. But the process of group development narrows this range of acceptable behaviors so that some behaviors are appropriate and others are inappropriate within the group context. Each member soon learns what is expected of him or her and what is expected of others. In regard to the informal rules, at least, every member has had a voice in formulating those expectations.

You will recall that the discussion of groupness in Chapter 1 states that one of the characteristics of groupness is the development of behavioral standards. That is, one of the characteristics of groupness is "behavior based on norms and procedures accepted by all group members" (Brilhart, 1978, pp. 20–21). Although the rules that guide the behaviors of group members are seldom formalized in the sense of a written code, the members of groups soon develop expectations of how each member is to behave during group interaction. The normal process of group development leads to these expectations and the developing groupness.

This chapter will discuss the two most common standards for group members' behavior—roles and norms. Some roles and norms may be beyond the control of the group members themselves. That is, external standards may, in some respects, be stronger than the group's ability to devise informal norms and roles. Remember that every group is an LGD (a leaderless group discussion) to some degree. Nevertheless, the development of informal roles and norms creates an extremely potent force which guides group interaction. The primary emphasis of this chapter, then, is on the development of those informal roles and norms.

## ROLES

Comparing the concept of a social role to the dramatic role portrayed by an actor on stage is all too familiar. Even Shakespeare believed that all the world is a stage and life is just acting out one part after another. But we must not conform too closely to this analogy if we are to capture the richer meaning of the social role. The stage actor does create a role but is limited by the playwright's lines and the foreknowledge of the play's conclusion. The actor must also divorce the self, to a large extent, from the character portrayed. One's social role, on the other hand, is a direct reflection of one's self, and the specific behaviors that constitute the social role are much more spontaneous. And, of course, one cannot rehearse most of these behaviors beforehand.

## Roles Defined

The sociologist Erving Goffman (1961, p. 87) refers to role as "the basic unit of socialization." As each individual member of any social system (a group, a culture, a society, etc.) identifies with and becomes identified with that system, the member assumes a role in that system. Goffman suggests, "It is through roles that tasks in society are allocated and arrangements made to enforce their performance." Role, for our purposes, may be defined as a position in an interlocking network of roles which make up the group. But to define role solely in terms of "position," relative to the "positions" of other members of a group, is to fail to comprehend fully how members function in their performance of roles and, ultimately, how the group functions as a decision-making system.

Hare (1976, p. 131) defines role as the "set of expectations which group members share concerning the behavior of a person who occupies a given position in the group." According to Hare, then, the role involves the behaviors performed by one member in light of the expectations which other members hold toward those behaviors. Hare's definition also includes, to some extent, the tendencies to behave which emanate from the person's own personality, but which may or may not be expressed in actual role behaviors.

Considering role in terms of the expectations of other members, we can understand that the behavior of each individual member can be either consistent with the member's role or inconsistent with it. In other words, if the behavior of the member is similar to what other members expect, that behavior can be considered to be role behavior. Surely you know certain persons who create within you certain expectations that they will behave in a specific way. But if one of those persons were to do something which you didn't expect, you would probably describe such behavior as being "out of character." In other words, the behavior was not consistent with your expectations of that person's role.

To think of role solely in terms of "position" in a group network of roles is to provide only a partial picture of a group's social structure. Often a group which is subject to external pressures (e.g., a group within a larger organization) is also subject to a network of roles (within the larger organization) which is imposed on the group. A leader may be designated because of the status, seniority, or position which that member holds within the larger organization (for example, the company president and a group of advisors, or a supervisor and a group of subordinate workers). In this formal structure, each role position exists somewhat independently from the person who occupies that role. That is, when the person leaves the group, the position (or role) remains unfilled.

Furthermore, the person's behavior in such a formal role may not be consistent with the other member's expectations of the behaviors that *should* be performed by a person occupying such a role. Then, we say that the person occupying the position is not fulfilling the role obligations. For example, the leader is not doing the leading. Defined in terms of behaviors *and* position, role becomes inherently behavioral. Furthermore, a behavioral role exists only when a person is performing behaviors within a role. And those behaviors, in combination with the expectations of other group members, constitute our working definition of the role in a decision-making group.

Each role must be defined, to some extent, in terms of the behaviors performed by the member occupying that role. The definition of role solely as some preordained position which exists apart from the identity of the person occupying the position is incomplete. If we were to view role in its broader sense, we might consider "president" of a government or a large organization to be a role. This type of role, defined solely as a position with attendant duties and privileges, exists independently of the person who actually serves as the president. Such a role definition governs many of the behavioral choices of the person filling that position. In addition, the position exists within the organization's structure despite the identity of the person who occupies it and continues to exist whether or not any person occupies it.

The role of "father" in a family group is also determined by factors other than behavior. The role of father is determined biologically (or legally, in the case of adoption) rather than simply by the actual behaviors performed. On the other hand, we also refer to the behavioral functions of the role of "parent," regardless of who performs them. Therefore, an older child, for example, may perform "parenting" functions (that is, behaviors identifiable with the parent's role) even though that child does not occupy the formal position of parent, determined legally or biologically. The role, determined by behavior, is the informal role of parent.

To the extent that each group is capable of developing its own roles, norms, and social system, the members develop a system of informal roles. Such a system is created in addition to any preestablished network of roles which is "passed out" to the members by some external authority. Thus, each member (together with the other group members) works out his or her role through performing communicative behaviors. Each member's role, along with that role's relationships with the roles of other members, must be defined principally in terms of the behaviors performed by that member in combination with fellow group members.

Later in this chapter I shall discuss specific types of roles which exist in many different groups. However, it is quite impossible to formulate a complete list of the roles which are performed in nearly every group. One member may perform several different roles, and several members may perform the same role. But informal roles are quite idiosyncratic to a particular group. One five-member group may have a network of roles totally unlike the role network of another five-member group performing the same task. No role appears to be universally present in all (or even most) groups, with the probable exception of the role of leader. But because the leadership role is unique and so significant to the group process, Chapter 7 is devoted entirely to it.

Bormann (1975, pp. 292–308) provides one possible explanation for the idiosyncracy of informal roles in decision-making groups. His stimulus-response model of role emergence suggests that roles develop over time, owing to a pattern of response reinforcement during group interaction. As a member performs a given behavior, other members either encourage or discourage its continued performance through their reactions. If the other members encourage this role function (that is, positively reinforce the behavior), Bormann's model postulates that the member will be likely to repeat that behavior until it becomes a full-fledged role function. If the other members discourage the behavior, however, the person will probably cease performing such a behavior during subsequent interaction. Thus, each individual member develops a role by consistently performing those behaviors which receive positive reinforcement from other group members. Furthermore, the other group members develop a set of expectations concerning a given member's role behavior on the basis of that person's repeated performance of similar behaviors.

Whether the reason for the idiosyncratic nature of roles has to do with response reinforcement or some other factor seems a trivial issue. Bormann's model of role emergence provides one plausible explanation of how roles develop during the process of group interaction. Clearly, however, we know that roles are generally idiosyncratic to a specific group. The reinforcement of spontaneous behaviors provides one explanation for such variation of role networks among different groups.

Typically, group members acknowledge the roles of individual members and develop a set of expectations about each member's role retrospectively. That is, *after* the behaviors have been performed and the expectations have been developed, the role of each member becomes more easily identified. The identity of each member's role becomes more apparent to the group, and each member is increasingly seen as different from the other group members. Often the group's expectations and the role networks develop without the individual members' being aware of the role each is performing in the group. Nor are they necessarily aware of the expectations which other members have of them while the process of role emergence is taking place.

One member of a classroom decision-making group was informed by her fellow group members that they believed her role to be that of "blocker." She responded in her report of the group meeting, "I was considered a blocker. I can't figure out why." Her role behaviors during past group meetings, even though she was apparently unaware of them, were consistently critical of the group's directions and its potential decisions. She consistently characterized the progress made during previous meetings as "Not much." Hence, the role consists not only of the behaviors performed by each individual, but of those behaviors in conjunction with other group members' behaviors and expectations. After the fact, then, the members are able to discern the behaviors that are "typical" (that is, consistent with the role) and come to expect them.

Each member's role "belongs" less to the individual member than to the group as a whole. Each person's role is a product of the entire group interaction—the combination of the behaviors performed by the individual member and the behaviors performed by other members. The result of such group interaction is that the group as a whole works out the role, both in terms of behaviors and expectations, of each individual member. A specific person's unique personality may affect his or her behavioral contributions to the group interaction. But this effect is limited.

One member of a classroom group, in her diary of group meetings, wrote the following about her own role: "It is really nice to know that I have a role now, so that I can play it. Everyone says that I am a supporter and harmonizer. . . . I really enjoy my group, and this has really helped me to understand people in groups. Before, I have been so scared of interacting. This class [group] has helped me come out of my shell more than usual." While a person's private tendencies will affect behavior to some extent, every person's behavior in a group is more the product of the group interaction, taken as a whole, than it is a product of the person's own tendency to behave in a certain way.

Each individual member develops that pattern of behaviors which constitutes his or her role in conjunction with fellow group members. Thus, the role—the behavior pattern—that a person develops in one group may be quite different from that same person's role in another group. A role, then, is not wholly determined by someone's innate personality traits. The human being does not carry a role from one group to another. A role is more like a suit of clothes which is put on or taken off to suit the occasion. The group's demands on the individual member's behaviors change because the group itself changes.

### Role Performance

Goffman (1961, p. 85) discusses role performance in terms of "the actual conduct of a particular individual while on duty in his position." If we think of role as a formal position in a network, the performance of that role by the person who occupies it is determined largely by the informal development of role behaviors in conjunction with the other members of the social system. Moreover, each person possesses an implicit notion of being "on duty" when performing that role. When on duty, the person is likely to perform role behaviors. But when a person is "off duty," his or her behaviors are less likely to conform to the expectations of other members of the social system.

I recall one classroom group in which the members recognized one of their group as their leader. At the same time, they resented somewhat his overbearing and arrogant approach to performing that leadership role. He talked constantly and tended to override any objections by other members to his directions. That same person rarely spoke during the meetings of the entire class. He never volunteered a contribution to classroom discussions. When called upon, he was very soft-spoken and acquiescent. Apparently he considered himself to be "on duty" as a "leader" only in his smaller group. In the larger classroom, he was "off duty" and felt no need to conform to the group's expectations of what a leader should do.

Goffman (1959, pp. 106–140) distinguishes role performance in terms of "regions" of behavior. In other words, a person performs a role when he or she is before the audience appropriate to that role (the "front region"). On the other hand, when the person is "backstage" (in the "back region"), there is apparently no perceived need to perform the role. Consequently, role performance is quite inconsistent with other people's expectations when the performer is in the back region; it is consistent with the expectations of others only when the performer is in the front region.

I once read a magazine reporter's impressions of a beauty pageant. The reporter seemed amazed that the reigning Miss Something-or-Other, while waiting backstage for her cue to go on, stood with no smile on her face and was observed to be actually picking her nose. I too was amazed that this beautiful young woman could engage in a behavior so inconsistent with her performance in her role. After all, Miss America simply does not pick her nose. Also, Burt Reynolds, discussing his macho image and his advancing age, is reported to have said that he was getting tired of constantly having to hold in his stomach.

It is important to remember that every person in every group performs some role. That is, every member occupies a position in a network of roles that is consistent with the set of expectations which other members have in regard to that person's behaviors. Furthermore, the person who is occupying that position actually communicates with other group members and performs that role in the process of engaging in the group interaction. But the role performance of a person in that particular group and that person's own personality or position in another group are not necessarily the same.

The member who is confronted with the expectations of other group members and is "on stage" in the performance of that role can be expected to engage in behaviors (that is, to communicate) in a manner consistent with that role. But that member, when backstage (that is, not subject to the expectations of other group members), may contribute communicative behaviors that are quite different from the expected role performance. The actual role performances by individual group members are truly products of the group and the group interaction. Role performance should not be confused with behaviors or personality characteristics that are identified solely with an individual group member and with no one else.

### Role Conflict

Occasionally role strain or role conflict occurs in a group in which a member finds that the demands of the group on her or his behavior are more than can be performed (role strain) or that the role behavior in that group is contradictory to her or his role performances in other groups (role conflict). Typically, the informal role structure is virtually free from patterns of role strain, since every member works out a certain role performance in combination with other group members. Rarely does a person become committed to an emerging pattern of role behaviors which that person is unable to perform adequately.

Not typically but occasionally, an individual member will perceive a conflict between role performance in the group and role performance consistent with the member's own personality or self-concept. One such member expressed just such a conflict in her reactions to a classroom group meeting. She wrote, "I started out with the feeling that I was going to remain passive and not contribute to the group—just to see if anyone would try to get things going. I was tired of trying to spark everyone and get them moving. I couldn't do it. I guess my personality is not suited for that role." Another individual expressed a similar role conflict when she confided, "I became very embarrassed when the group described my role (as they saw it) in the group. . . . I guess I'm not too 'hep' on confrontations as well as tension. I can't confront others unless it's positively."

These students, although not typical of most group members, discovered that the group's expectations of their role performances were not consistent with their own perceived capabilities and self-concepts. Therefore, they experienced some role conflict between their own self-perceptions and their group's expectations of their role performance.

One student in a classroom group apparently experienced a similar feeling. She was the member delegated by her group to confront another frequently absent member with the group's ultimatum: "Put up or shut up." She wrote in her diary of her reaction to the group's decision to appoint her as the confronter. She considered herself a friendly and amiable person—one who was unable to perform such an aggressive task. Nevertheless, she did just that during the next group meeting. Her diary, written at the conclusion of that meeting, included the following comment: "I felt that my role [as confronter] in the group meeting had a stifling effect on me, but I felt that we accomplished a lot." Her successful performance, then, evidently compensated for her internal struggle with the role.

A more likely and perhaps more typical strategy of a person who is placed in an incongruent role is to modify perceptions of that role. Such a strategy may result in perceiving the role as something it is not or in perceiving the self in a different role. Another classroom group may provide a classic example of role-self perceptions that were quite unrealistic and quite inaccurate in terms of the individual member's perception of his role in the group. Bob, as I shall call him, perceived himself as a natural leader and certainly the leader of his classroom group. After one meeting he wrote his personal reactions to that meeting in his diary (a class requirement): "I sort of felt insecure in my role as leader. I let John take it mostly, and he finally came to terms with the task and analyzed it well. However, everyone was unanimous in their support of me, so I guess they feel good about me as leader."

John's reactions to that same meeting appeared in his diary: "I do not object to Bob's trying to control every meeting. But if he slips or does something I do not agree with, I jump in and take control." Another member, after that same group meeting, wrote, "Bob tried to dictate to us again today, but I thought John handled him very well, under the circumstances." A meeting two weeks later brought the following comments from two other group members. One member wrote, "The meeting was short, but we accomplished everything we needed. I guess I'm feeling a little less annoyed with Bob." The other member wrote, "I was especially pleased with this meeting because Bob and I did not conflict as we did in the past. Perhaps this is due to two factors. First, he realized my right to have an opinion and respected my opinions more. Second, though, I might have been too tired to assert myself." Bob's reaction to that same meeting reflected quite a different perception of the situation: "My position as leader was more firmly established." Incidentally, at the end of the class when the group members voted on who they thought had led the group, John received every vote—except one (probably Bob's).

A more typical variety of role conflict is the inconsistency between a person's behaviors in the role of group member and a role in another group. One member of a classroom group, an older woman who described herself as "old enough to be the mother of any of my fellow members," found herself in role conflict in her group. The particular role conflict she perceived might have been something of a "generation gap." During one meeting especially, she found this role conflict to be virtually unbearable and described her reactions in her diary: "Because of the subject of the discussion [premarital sex], I am still reacting as a parent rather than a 'free-thinking' individual. I shall try to 'cure' this habit. Carefully taught and long-ingrained standards make it hard to compromise. They never change completely."

This particular member was quite committed to both groups (her family and her classroom decision-making group) and the ideals of the two groups. She earnestly wanted to engage in appropriate role performances in both groups but found the carryover from one to be in conflict with the other. Consequently, she wanted to believe in opposite sides of the same issue. She never did completely resolve this role conflict.

One reason for the different roles developed by the same person in different groups is the interdependence of the social dimensions. The nature of the task stimulates certain expectations or requirements so that the network of roles is affected along with all elements of the social dimension. An example from a classroom group may illustrate this phenomenon. One woman, whom I shall identify as Margie, felt her contribution to a group was limited to follower and information giver. Although bright, Margie was extremely shy and found it difficult to assert herself in any social setting. In a classroom group discussing problems of educationally disadvantaged children in urban ghettos, she found her behavior pattern quite different from what her personality traits might have predicted. Her fellow members discovered she had had summer experience in social work and consistently turned to her for critical advice. They recognized her expertise based on personal experiences. Margie became a critic-evaluator and by far the most frequent contributor to her group. Rather than being a follower, Margie found herself in a role of dominance because of the nature of the task and her relationship with it. Of course, her personality was unchanged. She remained shy and nonassertive. But in the role network of this particular group working on this particular task, Margie's behavior pattern was assertive and her role was quite dominant.

In contrast to Margie, Steve was a BMOC ("big man on campus")—a starting member of the football team, an officer in his fraternity, handsome, and loaded with personal charm. It was impossible to dislike Steve. Everyone liked him from the first meeting, including his fellow classroom-group members. Steve was used to being a leader and seemed to have the knack of exerting the forcefulness of his personality on whomever he came in contact with. But as the pressure of time to complete their task impinged upon the group members, they became increasingly disenchanted with Steve's role behaviors. He discovered that his personality and charm were insufficient to meet the demands of task accomplishment. Bewildered by the social ostracism from his fellow group members and frustrated because his contributions were consistently rejected or ignored, he uncharacteristically remained silent and became a habitual absentee. For Steve, the experience of being in that group was obviously socially painful.

Role conflict can certainly occur, as it apparently did in Steve's case. Generally, however, a person is able to keep the role in one group quite distinct from that in another group. At a commonsense level, your behavior at home with your family group is different from your behavior with a group of your close friends. And both behavior patterns are different from your behavior in a classroom. You behave differently at a football game and a fancy restaurant. If role strain or role conflict does occur, the LGD (leaderless group discussion) irons out the problems with a minimum of difficulty. Implicitly, and often without consciously doing so, we make changes in our role patterns and performances as we move from group to group. And we do so as easily as we change shirts. This is the nature of social roles.

Baird and Weinberg (1977, pp. 164–168) summarize three different types of role conflict: "intrarole conflict, where someone experiences conflict while playing a single role; interrole conflict, where one person is simultaneously required to play two different roles; and interpersonal role conflict, where two or more individuals compete for the same role." The problems of role conflict, particularly those of intrarole and interrole conflict, are most pronounced in the network of formal role positions imposed by external sources on a group. The informal network of roles, developed by a group in its capacity as an LGD, typically avoids the intense role conflicts. The individual person and the group are able to devise their own role network and expectations in a form that is comfortable for most group members. In other words, role conflict is rarely a problem, except in the structure of formal roles. Any problems of role conflict that are evident in the formal structure are often ameliorated in the informal role structure worked out by the group members during the process of group development.

The problem of interpersonal role conflict, in which two or more persons attempt to perform the same role, is more evident in the leadership role. The problems associated with developing the leadership network of a group will be the subject for discussion in Chapter 7. Interpersonal role conflicts regarding nonleadership roles are extremely rare in either the formal or the informal role networks.

The problems of intrarole and interrole conflicts are usually worked out by each individual member. The resolution of such conflicts often involves determining appropriate regions of role performances. That is everyone must, to some extent, perform different roles that conflict with one another or roles that are in conflict with one's self-concept. The resolution of such a conflict is typically the delineation of boundaries or regions for performing each role. In this way, the individual separates his or her self from role performances and remains consistent with the expectations of differing social systems. The specific demands of a given role at a given time and in a given social system are separated from the demands on role performance in another social system or at another time. Thus, each person determines the limits for each role performance and delineates clearly which role is more salient or more significant at a given time.

In this way, you communicate or behave in your family as a son or daughter, a parent, or a spouse in a role performance which is different from (and even inconsistent with) your role performance in a group of close friends. Each person works out the multitude of roles he or she performs in different groups by determining the regions of each role performance. Every person knows when to be "on stage" or "on duty" in the performance of each role. In this respect, every human being is to some extent a social chameleon, responding to the expectations of individual people in social systems. Maintaining a clear separation of those social systems and the respective roles within them is a typical method of coping with potential role conflicts.

### Role Differences

As individual group members work out their own roles in cooperation with other group members, each member takes on a role which differentiates him or her from the other group members. That is, even though each member's role behaviors depend on the behaviors of other members, the resulting pattern of interactive behaviors distinguishes each member's role from those of other members. The group is thus composed of a network of roles, but each group member individually possesses an identity that distinguishes that member from other members. Group members, therefore, come to expect an identifiable set of certain behaviors from one person and a different set of behaviors from another person. In this way, each member maintains an identity as an individual, and the network composed of all individual identities becomes identifiable as the group.

Although it is impossible to formulate a complete list of all possible roles in a group, Benne and Sheats (1958) have classified some roles commonly observed in training groups. Their classification scheme includes three types: group task roles, group building and maintenance roles, and individual roles. Although we will find it difficult to sustain such a clear distinction between roles that serve only task functions and those serving a purely social function, these three role types indicate that some roles are not oriented toward group goals but apparently fulfill some purely individual needs. While the following list of roles cannot be considered comprehensive it may clarify some typical examples of roles that often develop during the process of group interaction:

*Group task roles*

Initiator-contributor
Information seeker
Opinion seeker
Information giver
Elaborator
Coordinator
Orienter
Evaluator-critic
Energizer
Procedural technician
Recorder

*Group building and maintenance roles*

Encourager
Harmonizer
Compromiser
Gatekeeper and expediter
Group observer and commentator
Follower

*Individual roles*

Aggressor
Blocker
Recognition seeker
Self-confessor
Playboy
Dominator
Help seeker
Special interest pleader

This list of roles, formulated by Benne and Sheats, certainly does not exhaust the list of all possible roles that can occur in groups performing decision-making tasks. An additional role, common to many groups, is that of "joker." Depending on the specific interaction, a joker may be a harmonizer, a follower, a tension reliever, a playboy, or even an information giver (although the joker's information is typically phrased in a humorous way). In cloaking information in humor, the joker may allow the group to accept information which would otherwise be unacceptable.

The joker may play a role which benefits the group process by relieving tension. Because of the humorous style of the role, the joker may succeed in being an excellent critic-evaluator of others' ideas. Such criticism would be disguised by humor and may be more likely to gain a hearing in the group without arousing defensiveness.

We may tend to think of the role of joker as being associated primarily with the socioemotional dimension and less relevant to the task. That association may possibly be valid. When the joker's role as the group clown arouses a set of expectations that the joker is not serious about the task or is disinterested in helping the group achieve consensus, however, the role is probably more disruptive than beneficial to the group process. Every role is inevitably relevant to both the task and socioemotional dimensions of the group process. In a decision-making group, any role performance (such as that of the joker) that leads group members to believe that the member is not serious about completing the task is likely to be detrimental to the most efficient functioning of the group process.

The "silent member," or low participator, is another role that may have important functions in the group process. As Chapter 7 will illustrate, a member who participates little in the early portion of the group interaction may, later in the discussion, serve to identify the leader of the group. If a member is characterized by other group members as a silent member, they often come to believe that the silent one is not fully committed to the group or the group task. On the other hand, a silent member may develop into an important contributor to the group process if the group members do not perceive low participation as a symptom of low commitment.

One classroom group contained a silent member who later played an important role in that group's development, even though the total amount of talk he generated remained well below the average of all group members. His later contributions, though infrequent, consisted of volunteering to do the group's outside activities, to research materials, and generally to perform the less desirable legwork of the group. Not only did the other group members come to view his role as quite valuable; the member himself became much more satisfied with the group and his membership in it. One of his reactions to a group meeting late in the class expressed his increased satisfaction: "I felt I made some very important, objective contributions . . . I have moved from being a low participator to an important, candid one. Meetings are more fun now."

Some groups tend to assign roles to certain group members. These assignments are, of course, in addition to the roles normally emerging from continued group interaction. Certain assigned roles are often beneficial to the group's progress, as long as the group does not attempt to assign the entire network and thus substitute some "formalized" role network in the belief that the assigned roles will replace the informal roles.

Jenkins (1948) believes that one assigned role may well enhance the progress of a group that is sincerely and seriously interested in self-improvement. He suggests that groups appoint one of their members to be a "group productivity observer." This member then takes on the responsibility, in addition to the informal role developed through normal group interaction, to report at the end of each meeting on the progress the group appears to have made during that meeting.

To benefit from the possibility that a group productivity observer may be beneficial to the group process, the other group members must be open to the criticisms and observations of the observer. Moreover, they must have faith in the objectivity of the member they choose to be the observer and must be willing to trust that member. Of course, the person who is assigned the role of group productivity observer must be frank, candid, and honest in observing the group interaction and must give the group an accurate assessment of its productivity. If your group wishes to assign this role to one of your group members, you may find such a role performance quite helpful. But the group productivity observer is beneficial only to the extent that you are all willing to accept the member's observations and strive actively for self-analysis. On the other hand, if your group appears to be functioning quite normally and acceptably, you will find little reason for assigning such a role to anyone.

Probably because of the influence of the women's movement, a great deal of recent interest has emphasized the roles played by males and females in the group process. Much of this interest has been directed at the influence of sex-role stereotypes on group functions, but some investigations have attempted to discover potential role differences between males and females in terms of their role performance and their influence on the overall group process. One such study (Williams, Gray, and Broembsen, 1976) observed differences between all-female groups and all-male groups as to their role differentiation and stability of role networks. The findings suggest that all-female groups exhibit less differentiation among the members' roles than do all-male groups, at least in the way that each group reacted to the laboratory situation.

The research findings suggest further that role differentiation does not necessarily lead to greater productivity. That is, the female groups tended to outperform the male groups in performing their assigned tasks. Williams, Gray, and Broembsen suspect that these differences may be due to the past experiences and socialization patterns rather than to the biological differences between males and females. For whatever reason, however, females may find it less imperative to make clear distinctions among the roles performed by group members, while males tend to expect greater differences among role performances.

Under any circumstances, one should expect that nearly every group will develop a network of roles which also differentiate members from one another. Such an observation should not appear too controversial. After all, individual human beings are typically quite different from one another. We typically tend to distinguish one person from another and say that each possesses a unique personality and is an individual in his or her own right. At the risk of appearing undemocratic, we might even affirm the truism that all people are not created equal. Although all people may have equality of rights and privileges, some persons are more capable than others and have different kinds of capabilities. As a result, the roles that individuals perform during group interaction will probably lead to observed and expected differences among group members. Such role differentiation should not be considered "good" or "evil" but quite normal in human interaction.

## NORMS

Conformity by members to certain behavioral conventions, specified or unspecified, is a normal and consistent phenomenon of every social system. The punishment for nonconformity is often not clear, but the pressure to conform is strong nonetheless. We consistently follow the changing fashions of dress and music, for example. What was conformist yesterday may be nonconformist today, but we continue to heed the changing social whims in an overt drive to avoid being abnormal.

The human animal apparently possesses a strong desire to follow the herd. At one time or another, you have probably proved this point with some variation of the "emperor's new clothes" prank. I can recall several instances when, as a teenager, I went downtown with a group of friends on a Saturday night. We would stop at a busy corner and stare upward at a purely arbitrary point in the sky. We would engage in totally meaningless but animated conversation about this imaginary phenomenon we were allegedly observing. We would point to it, "oohing" and "aahing" over the magnificence of the sight. Within minutes a crowd of people would have gathered, all of them staring and pointing to the sky. When we felt the crowd was sufficiently large, we would quietly slip away and congratulate ourselves on our remarkable ability to manipulate human behavior.

As standards for behavior, norms vary considerably in the extent to which they are known. Some norms, such as laws or bylaws of a formal organization, are very explicit. The members of that particular social system are well aware of what the laws of that system are and what the punishments are for violating the laws. Laws are easily recognized and understood. Other norms, however, are less explicit. Members of the system may not realize they exist until they are violated. I recently overheard two students in the hall of a classroom building. One student was condemning her friend for wearing clothes that were out of fashion. The unfortunate student who was violating this unwritten norm of fashion was clearly unaware that she was "behind the times." I feel quite sure that the ridicule which she suffered was likely to result in her contributing some perfectly good clothes to the Salvation Army thrift store.

It is also true that certain behaviors are normal (that is, consistent with the social norms) to certain roles, while people in other roles abide by different norms. Norms are simply not applicable equally to all members of the social system. Some people in certain roles are not allowed to do things that are quite normal for people in other roles. For example, a child is not allowed to watch television as much as older children in the family system do consistently. I can recall that my own norm as a youngster was to go to bed before 10 P.M. My older brother was allowed to stay up long past that hour. I apparently accepted that norm with the full realization that, as soon as I assumed the role of "adult," I would be subject to a different bedtime norm.

On a larger sociological scale, roles are also governed by different norms. A business executive who may be engaging in "normal" behavior when playing golf and joining the "right" country club would be behaving abnormally when drinking beer with the "hardhats" in a saloon after work. Certain norms may apply to all members of a group, but other norms may apply only to certain members because of the roles they occupy.

### Norms Defined

The most obvious definition of a norm includes some characteristic of necessity or obligation—"oughtness." According to Homans (1961, p. 46), norms describe how "members ought to behave in a certain way in certain circumstances." The degree of oughtness may vary from situation to situation and from role to role, and it may also determine the extent of the punishment to be meted out for deviating from the norms. That is, when one belches at a party, one is behaving contrary to some norm. But the punishment for this deviation is not likely to be as severe as the punishment for violating some codified norm, such as robbing a bank. Under any circumstances, however, to behave contrary to a norm is to do something which the system decrees one ought not to do.

Davis (1969, p. 82) distinguishes between formal norms and informal norms, a differentiation that is particularly relevant to our study of group decision making. Formal norms include those which are explicit and are intentionally adopted by the group—for example, the procedures the group adopts or the rules it abides by in its meetings. Robert's *Rules of Order,* for example, would constitute a set of formal norms. Informal norms, on the other hand, emerge during the interaction of the group members and become "knowable" as the interaction continues. Group members may be aware of both formal and informal norms, but the informal norms are more changeable as the members continue to interact with one another.

Some norms, which may be either formal or informal, also originate from the values of members. Davis refers to a value as "a basic belief or assumption about what is good, right, or proper." Such values probably originate in a larger culture or society to which the specific group members belong. The values of a business organization, for example, would be imposed on the members of subgroups within that organization. After all, the group members are also members of the larger organization. Members may also possess values which they bring to the group from the larger society to which they all belong—the university community, a church, a national culture, etc.

Norms may thus originate in a larger society, in the group's interaction, or in the procedural rules officially adopted by the group. In this way, they may be imposed on the group as well as created or formulated during the process of group interaction. Like other behavioral standards (such as roles), norms may be formal or informal. In summary, norms may be imposed on the group from an external authority or may be developed by the group members during the actual process of group interaction.

Although we can be confident that norms do exist, we are not always certain how and why they function in a social system. Jack P. Gibbs (1965), attempting to provide some order to the confusion about social norms, distinguishes among three definitional attributes of norms which partially clarify their functioning—collective evaluations, collective expectations, and reactions to behavior.

The attribute of collective evaluation implies the social system's evaluation of what behavior *ought* to be, and collective expectation implies what the social system expects behavior *will* be. Collective evaluations include contemporary social mores or customs, with people's evaluations often indifferent to instances of nonconformity. For example, we believe traffic laws ought to be obeyed, but we often roll through stop signs and exceed the speed limit on freeways. We know we ought to fasten our seat belts, but we often ride in automobiles unfettered by the uncomfortable webbing.

On the other hand, collective expectation implies no evaluation of nonconforming behavior of the members of the social system. For instance, we expect that Americans will drink coffee and the British will drink tea. We would even probably label "abnormal" those who do otherwise. But in no way does this expectation place an evaluation on the behavior in the sense that certain people ought to drink either coffee or tea.

The third attribute, reactions to behavior, implies the existence of rules or laws which are enforced by some authority. That is, nonconformity to the norm will result in sanctions or punishment to the nonconformist. If we rob a bank, for instance, we will be put in prison. If we wear clothes that are out of style, our friends will laugh at us. In either case, the definitive characteristic of the norm is not the expectation or evaluation of the behavior necessarily, but the sanctioning reactions to nonconforming behavior. Nor does the norm always have the collective support of the members of the social system. Many of the laws of our nation have not had the collective support of the populace. The law in the form of a constitutional amendment prohibiting the sale or use of alcoholic beverages may be the prime example, although there is strong evidence that many current laws concerning the possession and use of marijuana lack the collective support of the people. But they are norms nonetheless in that sanctions are placed on nonconforming behavior.

## Development of Group Norms

An LGD norm, however, should always be a reflection of values shared by the group members. Since the members develop their own norms of behavior, they develop only those that have collective support. On the other hand, many of the rules of social systems with little capacity for self-regulation are formulated without consideration of whether they have collective support. One example would be rules governing the operation of prisons, which are formulated despite nonsupport by the inmates. Authorities beyond their control formulate and enforce these norms. But as roles for establishing standards of behavior for members of the social system, they must be considered to be norms of that social system. The LGD, of course, is free from such extreme external authority and, thus, develops only those norms that win collective support. In fact, norms develop only because they gain collective support.

The process of developing norms in an LGD is not particularly difficult to understand. Simple repetition of behavior patterns endows those behaviors with normalcy often before we become aware of them. Think about the seating habits in your various classes. After a few weeks in most classes, you will notice the students, including yourself, seated in approximately the same seat day after day. If you come to class late and find someone else sitting in "your" seat, you probably feel slightly irritated.

Realistically, the development of norms is more complex than simple repetition when we deal with norms based on the vast range of communicative acts. Norms develop through the functioning of feedback loops. An example may clarify the influence of feedback mechanisms on communicative behavior. The members of one classroom group established a norm of argument based on personal assertions and verbally forceful dialogue. Early in the group's history, one or two members presented documented evidence to support their positions and were consistently laughed at. They then questioned the accuracy of some asserted statistics and were again shouted down. Soon they, too, adopted the norm of assertiveness and forcefulness to support their views. Once begun, they continued to assert positions and to be increasingly forceful in their assertiveness so that the group interaction became a verbal free-for-all. The feedback loops functioned through the predictable sequence of communicative acts in order to establish the norm that lasted through many hours of interaction.

Like roles, norms are also quite idiosyncratic and vary from group to group. Most cooperative groups are shocked when they first observe a particular type of encounter group with its violent and often abrasive confrontations among members. But these confrontations are the norm for such a group developed over the course of its interaction. You probably have friends with whom you exchange insults as a form of greeting but would consider that same behavior abnormal in another group in which politeness is the norm. Many people cannot appreciate the humor of comedians who rely on insults, such as Don Rickles, because they are not "normal" comedians who tell funny stories and are "gracious" to their audiences.

Williams, Martin, and Gray (1975) provide one further characteristic of norms that is important to a comprehensive understanding of the group process. We sometimes tend to believe that each member "internalizes" the group's norms. "Internalization" generally means that individual persons take on a group or cultural norm and, through some sort of psychological process, incorporate that norm within their own personalities. Williams, Martin, and Gray suggest that such a notion of internalized norms is probably quite misleading. They maintain that the formation of group norms is the process, not of any one member's learning a norm, but of an entire group's developing and learning a norm together as a group. They suggest further that norms are thus made possible through the nature of group interaction itself rather than through an individual member's internalizing processes. They conclude (p. 149): "Instead of a special psychological process, the durability of social norms seems to result from the special nature of the social group."

The variability of norms from group to group tends to support their conclusion. Norms "belong" to the group and not to the individual member. Everyone, moving from one group to another, is subject to different norms because of the differences between the groups, not because of a new internalization of a different set of norms. I shall consistently refer to group norms with the full implication that the norms do indeed "belong" to the group.

As a classroom instructor, I strive to encourage a classroom norm of argument—a free exchange of conflicting opinions and ideas. Students engage in verbal conflict with other students and with the instructor. Many students and instructors are uncomfortable with this norm and consider it inappropriate, disrespectful, and disruptive. The point is that no norm is more "correct" than another. Rather, social norms vary from one social system to another and may even conflict with one another. Therefore, a norm developed in one social system is appropriate within that social system but may be quite inappropriate in another.

### Pressures to Conform

Although deviance from norms is the subject of Chapter 8, it is important at this point to provide some discussion of conformity pressures exerted by a group on its own members. I shall take the position that not all conformity is alike. Nor is all deviation alike. The typical reaction to conformity (and, paradoxically enough, to deviance) is rather negative. That is, I feel that conformists have no minds of their own. They merely succumb to the will of some unnamed majority. Also, deviance is typically regarded as distasteful and a deviant as a criminal or an immoral person. I shall consistently argue that neither conformity nor deviance is harmful or beneficial in principle. Some element of conformity is socially healthy, as is some element of deviation from group norms. The important principle is not *whether* conformity or deviance is good or bad but, rather, *what* conformity or deviance is good or bad.

Few will disagree with the fact that groups, societies, and cultures exert enormous pressures on their members to conform to the norms established by the social system. Conformity and its counterpart, deviation from norms, are likely to be present in all groups and in all societies. Furthermore, group pressures to conform to social norms and to sanction negatively those members who deviate from them are also likely to exist in all groups, both explicitly and implicitly.

On the other hand, all norms (particularly those that develop informally through group interaction) are not consistently enforced to the letter of the law. A certain range of behaviors is expected, and a certain range of deviation from norms is expected. In this sense, members will interact and behave within a certain range of allowable behaviors without being perceived as deviants. But behaviors beyond those limits will be labeled as deviant, and group pressures toward conformity will be brought to bear on those members performing such behaviors.

Typically, informal norms are accepted by group members, so that members will generally conform to those norms. When members accept a norm, they not only acknowledge that the norm exists and that they understand it, but also that the norm applies to the behaviors of members within that group. Because norms develop as a product of the group interaction, rather than through an internalizing process of each individual member, informal norms are enforced by the group. Without enforcement of norms and punishment of deviants, the norms will cease to exist.

Certainly some of us are more likely than others to accept norms. For example, a person with a poor self-concept, a need for social acceptance, or a submissive personality trait will be more likely to conform with minimal group pressure. When conformity results from the personality characteristics of individual group members, however, the significance of those social norms to the group process decreases accordingly. More important are those norms that members accept because of the nature of the group process. That is, members who are committed to the group are engaged in active participation in the group deliberations. They feel that the group is important and are loyal to it.

In other words, conformity pressures are strongest and healthiest when they result from a healthy socioemotional dimension of the group process. Members of a cohesive group are most likely to accept the norms of that group and to conform willingly to them precisely because they perceive the norms to benefit the successful performance of the group's decision-making efforts. In the presence of low levels of cohesiveness or little groupness, the pressures on members to conform to group norms (particularly informal ones) are less likely to succeed.

Since the level of cohesiveness and members' loyalty to the group may vary considerably among groups, the pressures on members to conform to group norms are also extremely variable. One reason is undoubtedly that norms of cohesive groups are much more apparent to the group members. Members of a cohesive group know what is expected of them. They know what they ought to do and what they ought not to do in order to exhibit their commitment to the group. With little groupness, however, members are not only less willing to conform to the group norms but are even less aware of what those norms really are.

Conformity, when healthy or beneficial, is thus linked closely with the level of cohesiveness or groupness developed by a group during its interaction. Without that cohesiveness, members are unlikely to produce strong pressures for conformity on deviant members. They probably don't care whether deviant members conform to the group norms, since they are also less committed to the group process.

## The Norm of Reciprocity

Chapter 2 has discussed the phenomenon of reciprocity, specifically reciprocity of self-disclosing communication. This human phenomenon is so pervasive in groups that reciprocity has even been labeled a social "norm" (Gouldner, 1960). Humans tend to react to other humans in a manner similar to the way in which those humans behave toward them. Furthermore, humans apparently reciprocate the behaviors of others in a sense that they feel they "ought" to do so. The human value leading to reciprocal behaviors is embodied in the golden rule and even in the golden rule in reverse. When attacked we tend to fight back. The small boy will justify his aggressive behavior by saying, "He hit me first!" Apparently this norm of reciprocity justifies reciprocal fighting.

Probably no one social norm is present in all groups. But if any social norm is nearly universal among social systems, it may be the norm of reciprocity. In its state as a do-unto-others norm, reciprocity functions by a member's tendency to reciprocate similar behaviors in response to the behaviors of others. That is, if A helps B, B feels compelled to reciprocate that assistance. If A likes B (and B perceives that liking), B feels compelled to reciprocate. Consistent with previous discussions, if A confides some rather intimate self-disclosing information to B, B will tend to respond with intimate self-disclosing statements. The norm of reciprocity creates something of a snowball effect as each person's behavior reinforces the similar behaviors of the others. For this reason, perhaps, a norm embodying a pattern of communicative behaviors develops rather quickly in the continuing interaction of the group.

Perhaps the most important principle in understanding norms as they function in the group process is that group norms "belong to" the group and not to its individual members. Moreover, in the presence of high cohesiveness and high levels of member commitment to the group, those group norms become very powerful forces in shaping the behaviors of the individual members. One of the most significant indicators of the potency of group norms in shaping members' behaviors is evident in a research project performed by Lindzey and Rieken (1951). In their study of sources of human frustration, they found that they were more successful in frustrating their human subjects when they prevented them from fulfilling group expectations (that is, group goals and norms). They were less successful in their efforts to frustrate humans even when they deprived them of food.

Persons often, perhaps typically, will sacrifice their own individuality and individual needs (even physical ones, such as food) for the purpose of furthering and realizing group goals and conforming to social norms. Rather than refer to such behavior as "unselfish" (that is, contrary to self or individual needs), it is probably more reasonable to consider such behavior as "social" (conforming to group norms and goals). Therefore, the important principle remains: Social norms are group norms, rather than merely norms that are internalized by individual persons.

## SUMMARY

The two most common standards for group members' behaviors are roles and norms. A role may be defined as the set of behaviors performed by a member in light of the expectations of other group members toward those behaviors. Each person's role often varies from group to group. Role performance, however, encapsulates each set of role behaviors within the region of performance—that specific group.

Some persons may experience role strain or conflict when a role performance places too great a demand on the group member or is incongruent with role performances in other groups. Occasionally, role conflict occurs when the expected role performance is incongruent with the person's personality traits. In that case, a person typically employs one of several strategies in order to reduce the role conflict, short of leaving the group. Every group member typically performs a role which differentiates him or her from other group members. The number of available roles is very large and is typically idiosyncratic to each group, probably because of the fact that each member develops the role performance in conjunction with other group members during the process of group interaction.

Group norms provide standards for how each member "ought" to behave in the group. LGD norms nearly always reflect the values shared by group members. The members typically apply pressures on deviant members to conform. Those pressures are strongest and healthiest in a successful and cohesive group. The most common norm of group interaction is reciprocity, the tendency to behave toward other people as they behave toward you.

Chapter 7

# Leadership
# and Status

Probably the most familiar of all social phenomena is the concept of leadership. Although not studied extensively until the last three or four decades, leadership has intrigued philosophers for centuries. How and why do people come to power? Why do people so zealously follow leaders like Adolph Hitler? What do leaders do that nonleaders don't? What constitutes good or effective leadership?

It is amazing that so many people could study one phenomenon and gain such little understanding of it. The number of unanswered questions concerning leadership is staggering. The purpose of this chapter is to shed some light on leadership in a small group, specifically how leadership develops in the small decision-making group. Consistent with the perspective of communication and group process, this chapter deals with leadership as an emerging process precipitated by the interstructured communicative behaviors of all group members.

## THE STATUS HIERARCHY

One of the earmarks of any social organization is the existence of a hierarchical order of status. Although the familiar caste system of India remains the most striking example of a large-scale social status hierarchy, no one will deny that our own country is divided into social classes. Normally, memberships in a higher class involves the possession of money, but often family background and professional membership play key roles in determining one's status position. Those in the lower and middle classes strive for membership in a higher class, vicariously and realistically, by procuring symbols of a higher status—a big new automobile, a color television set, an expensive home in an exclusive section of town. We cling to the belief that any American may become President, but we know that the chances of a person who is nonwhite, poor, or female are still extremely small.

The status symbols in an LGD (a leaderless group discussion) are not quite so clear. Certainly money doesn't seem to be an important factor. Generally the social classes—that is, the status hierarchy—of the small group are an order based on the ability to influence other group members. More specifically, high-status members in an LGD are perceived by other members as having provided the greatest assistance to the group's task accomplishment. If the raison d'être of the group is to accomplish some goal, whoever helps the group make progress toward that goal is rewarded with a high-status position.

## ASCRIBED AND ACHIEVED STATUS

Status may or may not be earned by someone. This point may be obvious, but in order to avoid any misunderstanding, it must be emphasized. The person who is born with the proverbial silver spoon in the mouth or on the wrong side of the proverbial tracks acquires status through an accident of birth. Such status may be said to be "ascribed" in that the person has simply inherited the status position. On the other hand, a person may earn status by individual striving. A social group awards status on the basis of a person's past behaviors in that group. Achieved status is the major concern of the LGD, of course, since no external authority impinges upon the ability of the group to develop its own social organization.

Often two status hierarchies—one based on ascribed status and one based on achieved status—exist side by side in the same social organization. A business organization, for example, has its own status hierarchy ascribed by the organization itself. But the workers in that organization may have developed their own status hierarchy, which may not conform to that sanctioned by the organization. These two hierarchies constitute the "formal" and the "informal" structure of the organization. When the authority of the two hierarchies is in conflict, the ascribed status position of the formal structure is often second best.

The problem of ascribed and achieved status may exist in a classroom group if, for example, the instructor designates one of the members as leader. Whether the ascribed leader achieves the informal status of leader is wholly dependent on the person's behaviors during group interaction. Mortensen (1966) indicates that when the group meets for sustained interactions (more than 1 hour), assigning the leadership role exerts little influence on whether the assigned leader achieves group acceptance as leader. Apparently group members assign the highest status level to the person who they feel has provided them with the most assistance in meeting their group goals. Therefore, the functioning status hierarchy in a small group is based on the behavior patterns of the members with minimal influence from some outside authority that usually assigns status levels.

## STATUS LEVELS

Each group develops the number of levels in its status hierarchy as well as the degree to which one status level is separated from another. Of course, any hierarchy requires a minimum of two levels, although three levels often, perhaps typically, occur in the LGD. The leader may be assumed to occupy one of the roles in the top status level, with other roles ordered in relation to this role. That is, the choice of leader is generally the first step in developing the status hierarchy. Once the group members identify their leader, they compare each of the other members' roles with the leader and assign each member to a corresponding status level. Other members may share the top status level with the leader, but rarely will another member's role be judged higher than the leader's.

You will recall that status consensus is one of the dimensions of member satisfaction. Thus, a cohesive group will agree on which of its members will occupy the top status level—leadership, at least. The development of a status hierarchy should not be confused with authoritarianism or antidemocratic methods, however. Some groups, who naturally admire the ideal of a democracy, like to think that there are no status distinctions among their members. Such an attitude is not only unrealistic; it is utter nonsense! A status hierarchy is not incompatible with a democracy or with democratic methods. The fact that members of an LGD have the capacity to direct their own destiny (they have no choice but to do so) implies a minidemocracy. The group members may or may not utilize authoritarian methods. But whether they do is their own choice. More important, a status hierarchy will exist in any group regardless of the extent to which the members employ democratic methods.

One final observation about the status levels also seems necessary. The existence of two or more levels in the hierarchy does not necessarily imply that some members are perceived to be of little value to the group. Indeed, the cohesive group typically values the contributions of every one of its members. But some members' contributions are perceived to be more helpful than others. Certain members are therefore assigned a higher status. Members in the second or third status level may also enjoy high status in the eyes of their fellow group members. But relative to some other members, the second and third levels are not as high as the top level. The hierarchy of status levels, then, is a rank ordering of members' roles relative to one another, but the roles are not judged according to some absolute standard or scale ranging from good to bad.

## Leadership and Power

Several years ago I served on a committee charged with the task of selecting a chairperson for our university department. Several of our initial meetings were devoted to defining the role. We were unanimous in agreeing that we wanted a "chair" rather than a departmental "head." In other words, we agreed that we wanted leadership but that we did not want a dictator. The essential difference between "chair" and "head" was apparently the degree of power at the disposal of the leader.

The concept of extreme power in the hands of a leader is not novel. Indeed, nearly five centuries ago Machiavelli conceived of a political power so strong that rulers could use any means at their disposal to control the behavior of their followers. In fact, he believed that such power is essential for a centralized government. Machiavelli's name today refers to the unscrupulous exercise of political power. And the term "Machiavellianism" has recently been employed in reference to a person's ability or desire to dominate or control the behavior of another person during interaction.

It is important to distinguish between a "head" (for lack of a better term) and "leader." A head possesses the power to control the fate of others and thus has considerable power to coerce those under his or her leadership. A small group head would determine the goal of the group, give directions that must be obeyed willingly or unwillingly, and levy direct sanctions against nonfollowers. There would be considerable social distance between the head and the followers. In short, the relationship between head and followers is unidirectional. The head can influence followers but is less susceptible to any influence from them.

The LGD, of course, has a leader rather than a head in virtually every case. (It must be remembered that the term "leaderless" in "leaderless group discussion" indicates only that the leader, along with norms, roles, etc., is determined by the group members themselves and not imposed by an authority *outside* the group.) But a leader has power, too. The difference between headship and leadership is not the amount of power but the basis from which the power is derived. One common basis of power is the control of resources that are needed or desired by others. Saudi Arabia, for example, possesses much more power than its size warrants because the country controls a vast quantity of oil which is needed and desired by all industrialized countries of the world. And when we think of powerful countries, we immediately think of those countries with the capacity of nuclear weapons. In short, power resides in the possession of some relatively scarce resource needed or desired by others. Such a concept of power is expressed in conventional wisdom by the adage, "In a country of the blind, the one-eyed man is king."

The LGD does not typically provide such a basis of power. While intelligence, for example, might be considered a personal resource, it is not something which can be transferred from one person to another or acquired by a person in the same sense that the resources in the examples above can be acquired. Nevertheless, the leader of the LGD does have a kind of power, even though its basis is not so easily defined. Unlike the unidirectional relationship between a head and the followers, the relationship between a leader and the followers is reciprocal. Consistent with the doctrine of interdependence, a leader leads at the discretion of the followers. That is, the basis for a leader's power is "consent of the governed." A leader may be deposed at any time. When the leader fails to satisfy the followers, his or her basis of power is undermined. Hence, the leader ceases to lead. A basis of power, such as control of scarce resources, defines a leader in isolation, regardless of the will of other group members. Such a definition is contrary to the elements of process and interdependence inherent in the LGD. For our purposes, then, a leader is defined only in terms of followers. To discuss leadership is to discuss followership. One cannot exist without the other.

A leader of an LGD is, of course, recognized by group members as the leader. Their recognition takes the form of deferential behavior. That is, members accede to the leadership moves made by the leader. They accord the leader respect and, generally, liking. (We shall return later in this chapter to the subject of the leader as an object of liking.) Members perceive the leader to be aiding the group in making progress toward their group goals. Normally, such progress implies the leader's activity in aiding the group in accomplishing its task. Perhaps more important than any other definitive characteristic, the leader is the person who consistently acts like a leader by performing leadership acts.

The definition of leadership at this point is admittedly quite general, but it does provide a basic understanding of what constitutes leadership in the small decision-making group. A more precise description of why certain persons achieve leadership status is provided later in the chapter.

## PERSPECTIVES ON LEADERSHIP

The vast quantity of research and philosophical writings about leadership reveals considerable confusion. The reason for the confusion stems from the many perspectives used to view leadership. People commonly consider leadership to be embodied in a person occupying a given position in the group. Therefore, a leader is a person first and a position in a role network second. While this viewpoint is a common one, it may have hindered progress in discovering the nature of leadership. In order to provide the basis for this book's perspective on leadership and to enrich our understanding of this elusive phenomenon, an evaluative survey of the most common perspectives on leadership follows. Hollander and Julian (1969) also provide a concise summary of some recognized perspectives on group leadership.

### Traits

Letters of reference to employers, universities, and scholarship or loan agencies often ask for evaluations of the applicant on selected personality characteristics. A characteristic often included in such lists is "leadership ability." The assumption underlying this characteristic is the belief that a leader is a unique person possessing some innate ability which allows him or her to assume a leadership position in any social system. Further assumed is the belief that leaders are born and not made. Our conventional wisdom contains this same assumption in such well-worn phrases as "a natural leader" and "born to be a leader." It is not surprising, then, that the early approach to leadership searched for those individual characteristics or traits which leaders possess. Although not nearly so popular today, the traits approach still influences contemporary views on leadership.

The traits approach attempted to distinguish leaders from nonleaders on the basis of how they differ on personal characteristics. The very earliest research using the traits approach highlighted physical characteristics, consistent with the notion that the childhood leader is the biggest bully on the block. Because of consistently fruitless efforts to discover distinctive physical characteristics of leaders, this perspective soon focused on the distinctive traits of a leader's personality. The results from the traits approach have been contradictory and disappointing, however. Many personality traits have, at one time or another, been linked to leadership, including such traits as dependability, intelligence, self-confidence, enthusiasm or dynamism, originality, responsibility, verbal facility, critical thinking ability, and creativity.

A list of such traits appears consistent with common sense. One would normally think that a leader should possess all these traits. But the traits approach to observing leadership has failed to achieve consistent results. Indeed, a leader of one group does not consistently achieve leadership in other groups. In fact, the leader of one group often cannot maintain leadership even in the same group. The traits approach plainly cannot account for the change of leadership in the same group.

Virtually no one today considers the traits approach a satisfactory explanation of leadership. In addition to the fact that no trait has been consistently associated with leadership, there are other reasons for finding this approach less than satisfactory. First of all, personality is an elusive phenomenon. No one has been able to determine successfully the specific components of personality. Because no one can directly perceive personality with the senses—one cannot see, touch, hear, or taste it—one's personality cannot be reliably measured or observed. For example, it is not unusual for two people to disagree about another's personality. What one considers a pleasing personality, another finds unpleasant. In short, while personality is often used as an overall impression, it is not reliable as a specific definition or observation. Viewing leadership from the traits approach does not render leadership less abstract.

A second reason for rejecting the traits approach is that it fails to account for the apparent difference between achieving and maintaining leadership. What one needs to gain leadership in a group may be quite different from what one needs to maintain leadership after having achieved it. The successful leader of a revolutionary coup is often not successful as the leader of the newly established country. Someone who may have excelled as a revolutionary leader may be a total failure as an establishment leader.

Perhaps most important of all, the traits approach cannot differentiate between a good and a bad leader. What constitutes effective leadership as opposed to ineffective leadership? The traits approach goes only so far as to distinguish leaders from nonleaders. It is inherently incapable of distinguishing good or effective leadership or drawing any sort of distinctions among leaders. Consequently, it is not surprising that the traits approach should be discarded.

### Styles

The traits approach to leadership attempts to distinguish leaders from nonleaders and to identify those personality traits which characterize persons who rise to leadership status. The styles approach proceeds from a different perspective. Leadership styles assume an a priori identification of the leader through either ascription or achievement and a general description of how the leader leads. This approach seeks to determine which style of leadership is best or most effective in a group by comparing one predetermined style with another.

The early research utilizing the styles perspective differentiated among three general styles of leadership. Those three styles were generalized descriptions of the relationship between leader and followers based on the leader's general pattern of behavior—democratic, autocratic, and laissez faire. The laissez faire style of leadership was soon discarded because it was so difficult to define. Essentially the hands-off policy indicated by the laissez faire style implies that the leader leads through not leading at all. Even on a commonsense level a laissez faire style of leadership is an anomaly. Nonleadership is viewed as leadership. Therefore, only two leadership styles are typically recognized today—democratic and autocratic.

Numerous studies have compared democratic and autocratic styles of group leadership. Those in business management commonly refer to the two styles as "participatory" and "supervisory" management styles. Unfortunately, because the two styles are considered diametrically opposed to each other, the comparisons between them are not always realistic. Typically, an extremely democratic style is compared with an extremely autocratic style. That is, the democratic leader is totally unselfish, seeks group participation at all times, and consistently functions in the best interest of the group as a whole. The democratic leader tends to overemphasize the socioemotional dimension of the group. On the other hand, most comparisons require the autocratic leader to behave with an absolute minimum of group participation, give blatant orders, and work for highly selfish goals. The autocratic leader, then, overemphasizes the task dimension of the group. Realistically, of course, there are many leadership styles that exist between these two extremes. And a single leader may even be democratic at times and autocratic at other times.

Past comparisons, however, have discovered some differences among groups functioning under each of the two styles. For example, the group with a democratic leader typically experiences more satisfaction, and the group with an autocratic leader is more efficient and more productive—particularly when productivity is measured on the basis of efficiency (for example, fewer errors). But the differences between the groups tend to diminish over time as the group members accustom themselves to the style of their leader. Since the task and social dimensions are interdependent, the success experienced in one dimension affects success in the other. That is, because members experience greater satisfaction with a democratic leader, they will tend to work harder and increase their productivity. And because groups are highly efficient and productive under an autocratic leader, the members experience greater pride in their achievements—hence, an increase in satisfaction.

The styles approach also is not a satisfactory perspective from which to view leadership in a small decision-making group. It is intuitively obvious that no one style is most desirable or most effective for all groups and all situations. For example, a military leader in battle and an airplane pilot in a storm are autocratic leaders and undoubtedly should be. When the going is rough, neither of these two leaders can stop to take a vote. Rather, they give orders which must be followed immediately and without hesitation. Naturally, in less trying situations the pilot or the military leader often adopts a more democratic style.

Perhaps the greatest problem of the styles approach to leadership is the unduly nebulous nature of the autocratic style. Since we live in a democratic society, we would like to believe that a democratic leader is superior to an autocratic style. But certainly the autocratic leader is not inherently evil. What about the benevolent dictator? The methods may be autocratic, but this type of dictator consistently functions in the best interests of the group—a primary characteristic of the democratic leader. A benevolent dictator may consistently seek the opinions and advice of other persons while still maintaining autocratic power. Although we tend to see democratic and autocratic styles of leadership in opposition, the distinction between the two, as well as the influence of the styles on the group, is not always clear-cut.

## Situations

Because of the inability of the traits and styles approaches to provide robust explanations of group leadership, many have turned to other perspectives. Today the situational approach is by far the most popular and most common perspective used in studying group leadership. The situational perspective describes the person who rises to the leadership position with emphasis on discovering the appropriate person for the appropriate situation. Less consideration is given to what the leader does or needs to do for effective group functioning.

Utilizing the situational approach to group leadership requires a thorough description of the group situation. Although a comprehensive description is not now available, some variables have often been associated with the situational perspective. Perhaps the most common ingredient of the situation is the particular combination of personality traits of the group members, their level of interest in the task, their motivation, and so forth. Then, too, the nature of the task is often believed to be an ingredient of the situation which requires a particular kind of leader. Other less common situational variables include factors of the physical setting. For example, sitting at the head of a table has been associated with leadership in our culture, although seating arrangements have not proved to be highly successful as indicators of leadership. And the size of the group has had some bearing on leadership. Obviously, as the group increases in size, the visibility of each member becomes more of a problem. On the other hand, charismatic leadership has been closely associated with very large groups and a corresponding increase in social distance between leaders and their followers.

At first glance, the situational approach to group leadership appears to solve most of the problems associated with the traits and styles perspectives. But the situational perspective is also troublesome. There are few, if any, general principles to direct a prospective group leader on what he or she should or can do in a given situation. Of course, there are many lists of do's and don'ts to guide prospective leaders, but such lists have not proved very successful. Then, too, no comprehensive list of situational ingredients now exists. Even compiling such a list may be quite impossible. Among even those variables that have been observed to exist within the situation, there is no way of determining which ingredients provide the greatest impact on the situation.

Perhaps most important, the situational perspective provides little assistance in furthering our knowledge of group leadership. Rather than provide guidelines of how and what a group member should do or can do to exercise influence on other group members, the situational perspective instead provides general advice on adapting the person to the situation, whatever it happens to be. Rather than discover what critical behaviors are effective in leading a group as it varies from situation to situation, the situational approach can only say, "It depends on the situation." In short, the situational perspective of group leadership may be a compromise between the traits and the styles approaches, but it seems to be little more than a "cop-out" to explain the inexplicable.

**The Contingency Model of Leader Effectiveness**   One specific situational approach to group leadership is the contingency model, developed by Fiedler (1964, 1967). Central to his contingency model is the assessment of a particular leadership "trait" measured by a paper-and-pencil test. Originally Fiedler developed two such tests—one to measure the "assumed similarity of opposites" (ASo) and the other to evaluate the "least preferred co-worker" (LPC). A score on the ASo test would be high if the individual perceived himself or herself to be quite similar to the group member who was perceived to be the most different. In the LPC test, the higher the leader rated the group member whom he or she liked least, the higher would be the leader's LPC score. Fiedler discovered that the scores on these two tests were highly correlated. Therefore, the contingency model is typically based on only the LPC test.

In regard to the behavior of leaders, leaders with high LPC scores have been found to be more socially oriented. That is, they generally concern themselves with the group's social dimension. Conversely, leaders scoring low in the LPC test tend to be more task-oriented and often tend to precipitate a decline in group cohesiveness (Gruenfeld et al., 1969). The contingency model, however, does not attempt to determine how leaders behave in certain situations. Rather, the model tries to place a particular leader (that is, a high-LPC or a low-LPC leader) in a group situation in which that leader will be most effective. Thus, the contingency model provides something of a combination of the traits and situations approaches. That is, a leader with a particular trait (high-LPC or low-LPC) is thought to be most effective in a specific situation.

Fiedler determined that a leader's effectiveness would vary as a result of several characteristics of the situation. The most notable of these characteristics include the amount of structure or external demands which the task places on the group, how well the group members get along with one another (similar to cohesiveness), and the formal power given to the person occupying the leadership position (such as the power to reward and punish group members).

Numerous investigations of LPC leaders in different situations have resulted in conclusions concerning the favorability of various situations, for the leader. For example, a situation is quite favorable for leadership when it contains a highly structured task with a low level of difficulty, high commitment of group members to the task, and high formal authority of the leadership position. The more "favorable" the situation, then, the more directive the leader (that is, the leader with a low LPC score). The less favorable the situation, one might assume, the more likely it is that the socially oriented leader (one with a high LPC score) will be most effective.

Such conclusions, however, are tempered by investigations suggesting that in extreme situations (that is, those situations extremely favorable or extremely unfavorable to the leader) low-LPC leaders tend to be most effective. Such leaders apparently function with high task motivation even under arduous conditions and are able to get the task accomplished. Conversely, high-LPC leaders are apparently most effective when the situation is moderately favorable or moderately unfavorable. Evidently, their social orientation to the group's performance allows the group to function most effectively when the situation is neither extremely favorable nor extremely unfavorable.

Fiedler's contingency model appears to be a combination of traits and styles approaches to leadership, also. That is, the LPC trait, measured by the paper-and-pencil test, is associated with a particular leadership style (directive or nondirective) that is very similar to authoritative and democratic leadership styles. Consequently, the approach to determining the potential effectiveness of the leader, contingent upon situational characteristics, is an attempt to match leadership traits and styles to a particular group situation. We therefore interpret the contingency model of leader effectiveness as a specific situational approach to leadership.

Unfortunately, however, it is difficult to be assured that a situation (such as a highly structured task and high cohesiveness) remains constant. Knowledge of the group process leads one to believe that levels of cohesiveness and goal clarity, etc., will fluctuate during the process of group decision making. Thus, the styles and traits of the leader should also be capable of adapting to such fluctuations.

Moreover, the tendency to correlate the LPC score with particular leadership behaviors is generally a matter of faith. That is, it is extremely questionable whether high-LPC leaders perform specific socially oriented behaviors during the process of group decision making and whether low-LPC leaders make specific task-oriented and directive comments during group interaction. As later discussions in this chapter will illustrate, leaders, during the actual process of group discussion, will tend to adapt their behaviors to changes in the situation and to specific members of the group. To adopt a contingency model of leader effectiveness is to assume that the situation remains rather stable through time. This assumption cannot be sustained indefinitely. Moreover, the tendency to believe that a leader's behaviors during group interaction will remain rather constant is also highly suspect.

Fiedler's contingency model of leader effectiveness has been shown to be applicable in a wide range of groups engaged in a variety of tasks. But Fiedler also views leadership exclusively as a position within a network of roles. The model assumes little flexibility of either the leader's position or the task and social processes of the group. His model is a unique and creative blend of traits, styles, and situational perspectives. But it provides little insight into what a leader does or can do in specific situations. Appropriately, both high-LPC and low-LPC leaders have been observed to be successful in similar conditions (see, for example, Hill, 1969).

In short, the contingency model of leader effectiveness ignores the continuing process of group interaction. Given the perspective of communication and the group process, then, this model provides little assistance in our quest for a comprehensive understanding of group decision making.

**Group Composition**    Gilstein, Wright, and Stone (1977) also provided insight into a situational perspective of group leadership in their investigation of leaders in groups with differing compositional "mixes" of members. They attempted to determine the specific types of groups in which directive or nondirective leaders would be most effective. Among their conclusions, they state that, in their investigation, groups whose members possessed conservative sociopolitical orientations developed higher member satisfaction (that is, cohesiveness) with a directive leader. Conversely, liberal members preferred a nondirective leader. According to this and other studies cited by the authors, groups with nondirective leaders tend to generate more member-centered and task-responsive interaction. However, members of nondirectively led groups apparently perceive a greater degree of freedom to participate and, thus, a feeling of greater responsibility to participate in the group interaction. Members of groups with directive leaders, on the other hand, often turn to the leader for guidance and succeed in shifting the responsibility for interaction to the leader rather than assuming the responsibility themselves.

One should not be led to conclude that nondirective leaders will diffuse the responsibility for the group's interaction among the group members. Rather, members with particular personality traits and with specific sociopolitical orientations tend to respond differently to the perceived directiveness of their group leader. Thus, persons who are more assertive, more interpersonally sensitive, and more ideationally flexible tend to interact more and thus allow for greater group effectiveness when they are in groups led by a nondirective leader. But groups composed of less assertive, less sensitive members with more fixed ideas apparently prefer situations that are more structured. They therefore respond more favorably to a more authoritative or directive leader.

The situational approach to leadership, although highly popular and traditionally the most accepted approach to group leadership, underscores the complexity of the group situation. The number of factors which can differentiate one group situation from another is extraordinarily large. Among such factors are the personality attributes of individual members, the nature of the task, the amount and kind of external constraints on the group, the degree of cohesiveness in the group, ad infinitum. Moreover, each of these situational factors is subject to change as the group continues to interact. To account for all the factors, let alone the variation of each factor over time, is an extraordinarily challenging and probably impossible task. Even though the situational approach to leadership is conceptually attractive, it is extremely difficult if not impossible to implement.

### Dual Leadership—Task and Social

With the exception of the functions approach, all perspectives on leadership have considered leadership as a role filled by one person. Bales and Slater (1955) discovered, through the use of Bales's interaction process analysis (IPA), that leadership duties are often divided between two group members. Consistent with the IPA's separation of behaviors into task-oriented and socially oriented behaviors, the authors discovered that the leadership role is similarly divided between a task specialist and a socioemotional specialist. That is, most of the acts of the task specialist are contained in the task categories, and most of the acts of the socioemotional specialist fall into the socioemotional categories.

Bales and Slater discovered further that the task specialist was rated high by fellow members in areas instrumental to task accomplishment but was not well liked. On the other hand, the socioemotional specialist was rated high on "liking" scales. These discoveries led to the hypothesis that small groups typically have two members who divided the leadership role between task specialists and socioemotional specialties. Occasionally one person performs both task and socioemotional specialties and is well liked by other members. Bales and Slater attribute this occurrence to the presence in the group of an extraordinarily capable individual (this is sometimes called the "great man" model of leadership).

The dual presence of a task leader and a social leader is intuitively uncomfortable for those who believe the task and social dimensions of a group are inseparably interdependent. As a result, many others—for example, Verba (1961) and Turk (1961)—sought alternative explanations to Bales and Slater's duality of the leadership role. Stephen R. Wilson (1970), along with the others, argues strongly and credibly that the alleged dual leader phenomenon is a function of the members' low interest or low involvement in the group's task. That is, when members are involved or interested in what the group is trying to accomplish, no dual leadership occurs. Wilson argues that a group generally has a single leader, not because of the presence of any "great man," but because leadership is typically not divided between task and socioemotional specialties.

Wilson explains that group members, whatever their level of involvement in the group task, perceive task competence in a fellow member and will naturally consider this person to be a leader. And members will also expect this competent person to be rather directive and assertive. (Recall that assertiveness is a descriptive characteristic often associated with a leader's communicative behavior.) But group members will place a value on the leader's directiveness proportional to their level of involvement in the group task. If members are involved and find task performance desirable and even necessary, they not only expect directiveness from the competent leader but value it highly since it aids the group's progress toward their goal. If the members are uninvolved, they resent directive behavior by the leader and certainly don't value progress toward a group goal which they consider unimportant or irrelevant.

The uninvolved member feels "captive" in an unpleasant situation and wishes to lessen its unpleasantness as much as possible. Such a member certainly will not like the directive leader who is trying to urge everyone to accomplish some "unimportant" task. On the other hand, the uninvolved member will tend to like the person who is also not interested in the task but who consistently behaves in the social categories and tries to make the social experience as agreeable as possible. Hence, uninvolved members divide leadership into two specialties—the task leader whom they do not appreciate and the social leader whom they do appreciate. The group's "real" task when members are uninvolved is maintaining social pleasantness, and the social leader is their only "real" leader. When members are involved, however, the task leader is their only "real" leader.

Bales and Slater are highly susceptible to the criticism of Wilson and others, since they observed the phenomenon of dual leadership almost exclusively in research laboratory groups. Nearly all these groups were composed of "captive" members, typically university undergraduates who were fulfilling some class requirement. On the other hand, most groups in the "real world" have been formed because their members experienced some common problem or reason for joining a group effort. If members of a typical real-world group were uninvolved, they would not maintain their membership in that group. Certainly accomplishing an unimportant group goal would not be sufficient cause for their remaining in the group. Therefore, the phenomenon of dual leadership—a task specialist and a socioemotional specialist—is probably an artifact of the captive group but should not be considered typical of groups in the real world. Thus, for the purposes of this book, dual leadership is quite insignificant. Later discussions assume that a small group typically has only one leader.

### Functions

All the perspectives on group leadership—traits, styles, situations—have one element in common. Each assumes that leadership is centered in the *person* who occupies the leadership position in the group's network of roles. The functions perspective shifts the point of emphasis from the person to the communicative *behaviors* performed. Although the functions approach is certainly not new—in fact, this approach to leadership has been around for more than thirty years—no consistent search for leadership functions has developed over the years. The functions perspective has never achieved the significance or popularity enjoyed by each of the other three perspectives at one time or another. One reason for this lack of popularity may be a confusion over what is meant by "functions." While some have considered group functions to be general principles essential to group operation, others discuss functions as specific behaviors capable of being performed by one person.

The view of functions as general principles necessary for maintaining the group fails to serve our purposes and is not congruent with the perspective of communication and group process. The concept of group functions becomes diluted through overgeneralizing. Most group functions are "good advice"—principles with insufficient practicability. For example, some commonly listed group functions include: (1) to advance the purpose of the group, (2) to inspire greater activity among members, (3) to administer procedural matters, and (4) to build group cohesiveness.

Essentially, these group functions imply some sort of influence which achieves desired results, such as greater cohesiveness, increased productivity, or greater group unity. Group functions, then, are little more than desired goals achieved rather than specific communicative behaviors which help to achieve these goals.

Although there is no single acceptable list of individual functions— that is, communicative behaviors—several suggested lists indicate some individual behaviors which have been associated with leadership in the past. Cartwright and Zander (1968, p. 306), for example, distinguish between group functions and individual functions and provide such a list:

> It appears that most group objectives can be subsumed under one of two headings: (*a*) the achievement of some specific group goal and (*b*) the maintenance or strengthening of the group itself. Examples of member behaviors that serve functions of *goal achievement* are "initiates action," "keeps members' attention on the goal," "clarifies the issue," "develops a procedural plan," "evaluates the quality of work done," and "makes expert information available." Examples of behaviors that serve functions of *group maintenance* are "keeps interpersonal relations pleasant," "arbitrates disputes," "provides encouragement," "gives the minority a chance to be heard," "stimulates self-direction," and "increases the interdependence among members."

It should be apparent that not all functions included in Cartwright and Zander's list are satisfactory. Some functions are so markedly abstract as to preclude virtually any practical application. What type of behavior, for example, "increases the interdependence among members"? Perhaps more significantly, Cartwright and Zander separate functions into two categories—task functions and social functions—and consequently deny the interdependence of these two dimensions of group process. But the list does include some meaningful behaviors. For example, "initiates action," "clarifies the issue," "evaluates the quality of work done," and "provides encouragement" are some specific behavioral functions which may be practicably applied by the prospective group leader.

Mortensen (1966) devised five categories of individual behaviors which he labeled "attempted leadership." Those five categories include "introducing and formulating goals, tasks, procedures," "eliciting communication from other group members," "delegating, directing action," "showing consideration for group activity," and "integrating and summarizing group activity." These five categories are also not very practicable, but they do imply several characteristics of leadership behaviors. For example, Mortensen conceives of a leader as initiating proposals for action, asking focused questions, and summarizing group activity. These functions are also reflected in Cartwright and Zander's list.

Hugh C. Russell (1970) discovered four dimensions of a leader's communicative behaviors. Those dimensions are "goal facilitation," "emotional control," "objectivity," and "communication skill." They indicate that a leader directs the group toward the group goal, attempts to reduce tension and resolve conflicts, contributes balanced information, and possesses the qualities of a skillful speaker. Unfortunately, Russell's list of dimensions does not attempt to specify those behaviors which exercise influence or which a leader specifically uses in order to exert leadership. He does not, for example, specify a behavior that could reduce tension or resolve conflict. These dimensions are only descriptive characteristics of the totality of a leader's behavior—not types of communicative behaviors themselves.

In sum, most of these lists of leadership functions do note some specific behaviors associated with leadership. Moreover, the functions appear to emphasize those behaviors which facilitate group task accomplishment. A more specific list of behaviors comprising all the functions performed by a leader is not yet available, although a partial list is apparent and may be used as a springboard for further consideration. Certainly, the performance of appropriate leadership functions requires a social awareness of what function needs to be performed, when it needs performing, and the ability to perform it. Later chapters will provide more specific assistance in determining the appropriate times.

The functions perspective on leadership is not without its shortcomings, however. While the approach itself has vast potential, the state of knowledge about leadership functions is deplorably small. In the first place, the functions of leadership now being used are too global and not easily applied on a practical basis. Too often the list of functions reflects the perceptions of the observer or the results of the act rather than the central descriptive characteristics of the act itself. Then, too, every past effort to discover leadership functions has attempted to describe communicative behaviors or their consequences in isolation without viewing leadership acts within the interstructured sequence of group interaction. What type of act precedes and follows a leadership act? Perhaps the leadership act can be defined as a leadership function only in terms of the act that precedes and follows it. If leadership involves a reciprocal relationship of leader and follower, the behavior of the leader is probably meaningless when isolated from the behaviors of the followers. Thus, leadership functions should reflect the interdependence of the communicative behaviors performed by both leader and followers during the process of group interaction.

## ON CHOOSING THE FUNCTIONS PERSPECTIVE

It is no secret that the author of this book favors the functions perspective. Indeed, the overall perspective of communication and group process underlying the book demands the functions perspective of leadership. In other words, group leadership is a process in which communicative behaviors associated with leadership are performed by one or more group members. Those behaviors, then, develop the pattern of leadership which characterizes that decision-making group. If leadership is a process, it cannot be viewed as a personal quality possessed by some persons and not present in others. Nor can leadership be viewed simply as a structural position occupied by some person within a network of roles. Leadership develops through time as group members interact with one another. And their interaction patterns eventually reflect leader-follower relationships among members.

The problem of identifying leadership acts has not been completely solved. In fact, the "cop-out" of the situational perspective is not totally absent from the present treatment of leadership. Although the explanations should be more explicit in the later description of the leadership emergence process, the basic axiom identifying a leadership act is appropriateness within a given interaction sequence. That is, what may be a leadership act at one time during the group's interaction may be quite inappropriate at another time. If this explanation sounds similar to the situational perspective of leadership, it is at least different to the extent that it defines all ingredients of the situation exclusively within the interaction patterns of the members' communicative behaviors.

Shifting the focus of leadership from the person to his or her communicative behaviors, the functions approach no longer implies that leadership acts are necessarily performed by only one person. Typically, members of a decision-making group designate a single member as their leader in that the bulk of the leadership acts are generally performed by just one person. But it would not be extraordinary if several persons perform the leadership functions and, hence, provide the group with shared leadership. But shared leadership in no way implies that one person is a task specialist while the other is a socioemotional specialist. Rather, inherently implying the interdependence of the two dimensions, group leadership functions are shared in that several members perform these functions without partitioning their leadership responsibilities into neat pigeonholes.

The functions approach also allows for, and serves to explain, how leadership changes from one person to another within the same group or in different situations. Mortensen (1966) discovered that some leaders consistently performed leadership behaviors throughout all periods of the group's interaction and, hence, maintained their leadership positions. Others, however, noticeably declined in their attempted leadership acts, thereby indicating their fall from leadership status. As the deposed leader decreased performance of attempted leadership acts, another member or members apparently performed those acts and took over as leader.

Finally, the functions approach allows for the eventual discovery of those functions which are characteristic of a good leader or an effective leader. Conversely, it will be possible to discover the functions indicating poor or ineffective leadership. None of the other perspectives is capable of defining or characterizing the qualities of effective leadership. To do so requires evaluating what the leader actually does. Hence, the functions perspective is necessary in order to be able to evaluate leadership behaviors.

## LEADERSHIP EMERGENCE

To reiterate an earlier point, this book views group leadership as achieved, rather than ascribed status. In the event that a leader is appointed through some authority outside the group, the process of leadership emergence applies to the emergence of the informal leader. This view of leadership assumes that true small-group leadership is always achieved—not ascribed. Moreover, leadership is always achieved gradually over time and is therefore viewed as a process. Because leaders achieve their status gradually, the process bears the label "leadership emergence."

### The Process—Elimination of Contenders

A common view of leadership depicts a leader achieving status by somehow rising above all others through demonstrating superior abilities or behaviors. According to this view, leadership is a process of a leader's excelling all others in a struggle to rise to the status of leadership. Apparently, then, all members start out at the bottom of the status ladder and attempt to work their way up. Such a view, however, may be the reverse of the actual process of leadership emergence. The process apparently begins with all members contending for the leadership role. As the process continues, members drop out of contention, one by one, until only one contender remains who then achieves group recognition as leader. The process of leadership emergence is thus a process of elimination.

Geier (1967) indicates that all members typically and actively desire and seek leadership status. While he may be correct, many people would deny that they are trying to become leaders (that is, are contending for leadership). More important, whether members consciously desire to be their group's leader is really quite irrelevant to the process of leader emergence. One member of a classroom group specifically denied her intentions to be the leader of her group. In her reactions to one of her group meetings, she commented, "But I don't want to be the group's leader. Nor do I feel that anyone sees me in that position." After a group meeting later in the course, she reported, "The other members have pegged me as the leader in the group. It's kind of weird. . . . I'm really conscious of it now. But then I can really play the role up, depending on my mood. I really feel comfortable around these people, so it's OK."

This particular group member told me informally outside of class that she just wasn't the "leader type." She also said that she had too many obligations outside our class and simply did not have the time. Nor did she wish to accept the responsbility of being the group's leader. Eventually, however, she did serve in that role and accepted the fact that she was the leader, despite the fact that she never felt at any time that she was contending for the leadership role.

The important fact is that members have little choice as to whether they wish to "contend actively" for the position of leader. In the sense that every group possesses some capacity for self-regulation (i.e., is an LGD) and is thus able to establish its own informal role structure, all members are potential candidates for the role of leader. No member is able to deny being a candidate, whether he or she wants to be the leader or not. Indeed, every member "campaigns" for leadership status every time the member communicates and participates in the group's interaction. Remember that one cannot *not* communicate. Therefore, there is no way to disavow one's candidacy for group leadership—at least, the informal leadership.

### A Hypothetical Model of Leader Emergence

Leader emergence occurs over a period of time. As a process of elimination, certain members are eliminated from contention at various stages during the group's continuing interaction. The stages of the following hypothetical model, along with its variations and special problems, are adapted from the research of Geier (1967) and Charles Larson (1969), and from personal observation of classroom groups and members' diaries. The reader will note the use of a five-member group. While five members may be the optimum size for a small group, its required size is a trivial point of discussion. The model should apply to any small group regardless of its size.

Figure 7-1 depicts the presence of three stages in the group process of leader emergence. In stage 1, member E is eliminated from contention. In stage 2, members B and D are eliminated, and in stage 3 only member A remains in contention, thereby achieving the status of group leader. Geier (1967) finds that in the initial stages of group interaction, some members

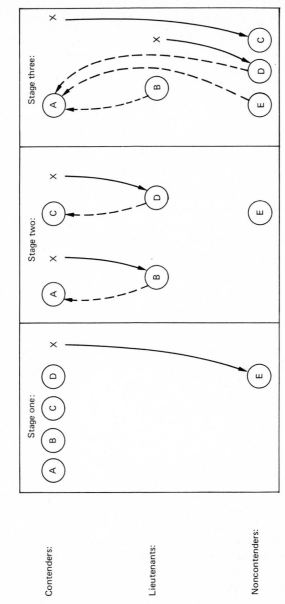

**Figure 7-1** The basic model of leader emergence.

(epitomized in Figure 7-1 by member E) reveal themselves to be uninformed or excessively rigid in their beliefs. Some members just do not contribute much to the group interaction. They may be overly shy or simply uninvolved in the group task. For whatever reason, they are significantly less active than other members and drop from leader contention because of nonparticipation. Stage 1 is usually brief. Nonparticipators are quickly recognized by other group members and just as quickly eliminated as leader contenders.

During stage 2 several members are strengthened in their bids for leadership status by gaining the assistance of other members to support their candidacies. Thus, members A and C remain contenders for group leadership while members B and D drop out of personal contention and serve as lieutenants of A and C, respectively. As a lieutenant, each becomes less an initiator of action and more a supporter of proposals initiated by one of the contenders. In stage 2, two opposing factions or coalitions develop around each of the remaining contenders. Stage 2 is typically a lengthy phase and often involves some verbal bloodletting. But as this stage comes to an end, one of the contenders loses the bid for leadership and leaves the remaining contender alone at the top. Geier (1967) indicates that the member who characteristically drops from contention during Stage 2 tends to be overly directive and uses offensive verbalization, such as stilted language or incessant talking.

Stage 3 concludes the process of leader emergence as member A remains the sole contender after the demise of member C. Member E may reenter the emergence process by supporting member A, thereby swinging the balance of power to the A-B coalition. Realistically, however, member E's support is probably not particularly significant, especially if E has continued to be a low participating member during stage 2. If, on the other hand, member E takes a more active role in group interaction, E's support is sought by members A and C during stage 2. Then E's decision to side with one or the other is a crucial factor in the final emergence of member A. Of course, member C could also drop out of contention if the support of member D as a lieutenant was lost, particularly if member C is overly directive and verbally offensive as perceived by D. Member D could easily shift the balance of power by transferring his allegiance and support to member A.

Figure 7-1 represents a basic model from which many variations might occur. For example, successful leader emergence may involve only two stages in which just one contender picks up a lieutenant, and all other members jump on the bandwagon. This variation is not at all uncommon and signifies a socially painless process of leader emergence. It evolves very quickly and allows time for the group members to develop their status hierarchy and level of cohesiveness quickly and generally satisfactorily.

Another variation involves the early emergence of a group leader who is then deposed as group leader, leaving the group once again in a leaderless situation. The process of leader emergence would then recycle back to the beginning of stage 2 and begin all over again. Unless the nonparticipating member's level of participation and involvement has abruptly increased, he or she remains out of leadership contention. The deposed group leader could even regain leadership status but would undoubtedly have more difficulty the second time around.

A third variation of successful leader emergence involves the absence of stage 3. In this case, two or more members share the leadership functions and are recognized equally as leaders. While shared leadership is not extraordinary, neither is it the typical case. One can generally expect a single person to emerge eventually as the leader of a small decision-making group.

After a contender has successfully emerged as leader, the group typically experiences an abrupt release of tension. Without a consensus among group members on the top status level, a group generally functions somewhat haphazardly and in a state of relatively high secondary tension. As soon as their doubts are dispelled concerning leadership, the members quickly release a great deal of secondary tension. The group then experiences an abrupt rise in member satisfaction—hence, greater group cohesiveness. This is not to say that the group is suddenly a highly cohesive group, but status consensus is one prerequisite for satisfaction. With that hurdle out of the way, the group is capable of developing a relatively high level of cohesiveness and, correspondingly, a high level of productivity.

With the emergence of the leader, the status levels in the group's hierarchy typically fall quickly into place. The successful group generally accords the losing contender a high-status position equal to, or slightly lower than, the status level of the leader. Thus, three status levels often appear after the completion of the three-stage model of leader emergence. The top status level is occupied by member A (and possibly member C). The second level includes members B and D (or possibly C). Member E would be in the third status level. Member E, having the capacity to shift the balance of power to Member A, however, might very well achieve higher status—perhaps in the second level. If this were the case, the group would have only two status levels. A five-member group will typically include three status levels but may possess only two. Significantly, the process of leader emergence involves not only the selection of a leader but the development of the group's entire status hierarchy.

Williams et al. (1976, p. 328) cite one additional result of effective leader emergence. They suggest that, after the leadership and status hierarchy develops, "Other group members appear to stabilize at some level of proactivity and reward seems to have little effect on them hereafter." In other words, the surge of increased cohesiveness following leader emergence provides rewards for the group members. And these rewards are apparently sufficient to sustain them through the completion of the task. The resulting increased loyalty and commitment of members to the group becomes more important than other forms of rewards or reinforcement. In other words, the collectivity of individuals has now emerged into "the group." And members' commitment to their group, however temporary, is a potent force in their perception of rewards. To a great extent, students' reactions to both the instructor and to a class in group decision making reflect their commitment to their specific classroom group. The more they like their group, the more they are apt to like the class and its instructor.

### Special Problems of Leader Emergence

The basic model of leader emergence should not, of course, be considered an unwavering rule. Some variations have already been mentioned. Each deal with successful leader emergence and a quasi-methodical process of elimination. It is not unusual, though, for the process to be less methodical and less successful. Although the following deviations from the model are not common, they are worth noting and are considered "problems" rather than minor variations. Each problem is considered a special "case" involving a particular problem which any group may encounter during its own process of leader emergence.

**The Case of the Leaderless Group**  The discussion of leader emergence has assumed up to this point that the process of leader emergence is always successful. Some groups, however, may struggle indefinitely over their status hierarchy and never satisfactorily solve their leadership problem. Usually a group which fails to develop a status hierarchy remains a collection of individuals who are unsuccessful in developing groupness. Very rarely is a group able to maintain itself without a successful process of leader emergence and a fairly well established hierarchy of social strata.

A group may continue to be leaderless if the process of leader emergence is still continuing when the group ceases to exist. It is often the case that the quarter or semester ends while the classroom group is still in the process of developing its status hierarchy. Such a group should not be considered unsuccessful. Its process of group development might be slower than desired. But one must assume that were the group to have more time for the process to continue, it would successfully develop group leadership and subsequent status hierarchy.

**The Case of the Temporary Leader**  During the struggle between the leader contenders in stage 2, a group may be unable to resolve its leadership problem by moving to stage 3. The group is in a state of limbo during this period while the leadership identity remains unresolved. This period is typically characterized by a rather high level of secondary tension. If the group cannot function at this level of tension, the members will attempt a compromise in order to release the tension. Thus, a noncontending member will be accorded leadership status so that the group can progress.

The noncontender who is granted leadership status must be considered a temporary leader. Such a person is generally accepted by the contenders as a relatively weak participator and, therefore, not a significant threat to their leadership bids. But like most compromises, the solution is typically a temporary one. Compromise leaders will find it difficult to sustain leadership status, particularly if they remain uninformed or rigid and low participators—those same behaviors which eliminated them from contention during stage 1. An abrupt change in behaviors would increase the chances for maintaining leadership status. Otherwise, the group will eventually return to stage 2 and the yet unresolved problem of leadership contention.

**The Case of the Catalytic Role**    Often a nonleader's role is crucial to a group's process of leader emergence. A particular member, whether or not a strong leader contender, may show behaviors indicating that the person fulfills a role that determines the group's development of its status hierarchy.

In the group described in Chapter 2, Tom fulfilled such a catalytic role. He was definitely a leader contender by virtue of his behaviors, but the other members of his group (all women) were acceding to his leadership moves even though they resented them as being overly directive. A second member had gained a lieutenant during stage 2 and was still in contention for leadership with Tom who, oddly enough, remained in contention without a lieutenant.

Tom's role was catalytic for his group because it was not functioning efficiently with him as a directive leader contender. When his fellow members confronted him and dropped him from contention, Tom's role was clearly decided as a top-status member but definitely not the leader. Other members valued his contributions but were unwilling to assume followership status in relation to him. When Tom's role was established, the other roles, including the leader and the remainder of the entire status hierarchy, fell quickly into place with a dramatic rise in cohesiveness and productivity.

A common catalytic role is that of the problem member—for one reason or another, the "oddball" in the group. The problem member generally is not committed to the group and consistently causes trouble for the rest of the group members by not doing his or her share of the work, consistently criticizing other members, continually arguing against decisions reached by them, and generally assigning low value to the group and the other members, "bad-mouthing" both.

One member in a classroom group completed a sociometric questionnaire at midterm and revealed herself as a true problem member. For example, in response to a question asking which member in the group she liked most, she wrote, "None of them!" Her response to a question asking which member she liked least was "All of them!" Her role was obviously a problem that the group had to control.

The member who succeeds in controlling the problem member may abruptly rise to leadership status. In this particular classroom group, one girl made an overt effort to handle the problem member both during and outside group meetings. On several occasions she talked to the problem member alone, bought her Cokes in the Union, and generally went out of her way to make her feel more a part of the group. Although the problem member never did become a high-status member wholly enthusiastic about the group's goals, she did cease to be a problem for the group. And the member who solved that problem for the group eventually became its leader.

The deviant or problem member may also serve a catalytic role. One deviant in a classroom group developed what appeared to be a personality conflict with her group's recognized leader. The leader was an older and more mature male who was quite directive in performing his leadership role. The deviant challenged the leader's authority and refused to follow his directives. The group members had been quite "comfortable" up to that point and had allowed the leader to perform most of their task efforts. In effect, the other members had served as a board of advisors and "approvers" of what the directive leader wished to do. The deviant, whom I shall call Tamara, in two consecutive meetings openly resisted the leader's ideas, argued with him, and disrupted the group's practice of allowing the leader to do its work.

Tamara remained a deviant throughout the group's history and was never perceived as a particularly valued member of the group by the other members. However, in her catalytic role, she succeeded in totally rearranging the entire hierarchy of the members' roles. As it turned out, the group had short-circuited the effective operation of the group process. The leader had assumed control and directed the group's progress from the beginning, and the other members had allowed him to retain that control. After Tamara's challenge, however, they admitted to themselves that they were less than satisfied with the obtrusiveness and the overt directiveness of their "leader." Consequently, they deposed him from the leadership role, and the entire status hierarchy of the group began its developmental process from scratch. The group then proceeded through a more familiar and traditional process of leader emergence, including the elimination of contenders.

Member E in the basic model of leader emergence may also perform a catalytic role if his or her support decides between the leadership contention of members A and C. In fact, the member who casts the deciding vote on any crucial question is invariably catalytic for the group. If one member consistently fulfills the role as ultimate decider, that member is a catalyst for the normal functioning of the group. On the other hand, a member such as E is probably less committed to the group and therefore less active in group interaction. E's record of reticent behavior diminishes the importance of his or her subsequent contributions. Group members must come to expect the deciding vote from a member if that member is to perform a catalytic role in the process of group development. Otherwise, his or her influence as a catalyst is probably short-lived.

## Behaviors of Emergent Leaders

Our present state of knowledge does not allow a thorough and specific definition of the communicative behaviors leading to successful leader emergence. But emergent leaders have been associated with certain types of communicative acts. Geier (1967), for example, pinpoints some kinds of communicative behaviors that characterize members who are eliminated from contention for leadership. Those negative behaviors include nonparticipation, uninformed contributions, and a rigidly argumentative stance in stage 1; and overly directive comments and offensive verbalization including stilted language or incessant talking during stage 2. One might appropriately infer from Geier's discoveries that the emergent leader avoids these types of communicative behaviors during each specific stage of leader emergence. But to know what the emergent leader does not communicate provides only scant assistance in discovering what this person does communicate. Hence, Geier's negative behaviors are helpful but certainly not sufficient to describe the communicative behaviors of emergent leaders.

Because it is so obvious that it might be overlooked, one absolutely requisite behavior for successful leader emergence must be emphasized. That requisite is verbal activity itself. In the LGD the member who does not "campaign" for leadership by contributing to group interaction has virtually no chance to achieve leadership status. The emergent leader, although not necessarily the member who talks the most, is among the high participators (Morris and Hackman, 1969). The emergent leader is virtually never one of the low contributors to group interaction.

In addition to mere quantity of verbal activity, the nonverbal quality of the leader's contributions appears to be important as well. The evidence that an emergent leader is a skillful communicator is indisputable. That is, emergent leaders are fluent in delivering their contributions. They express their thoughts articulately. Furthermore, leaders' participation is forceful and dynamic. Their dynamism is probably a nonverbal indication of their interest or involvement in the group task. Leadership, though, is not at all ability to win minds through glibness of vocal delivery. Quite the contrary: Communicative skill is grossly insufficient, by itself, to achieve any status and maintain it for any length of time. Nevertheless, inarticulate people are at a disadvantage regardless of the apparent value of the causes they advocate. The leader is not necessarily the most skillful communicator in the group, but apparently is among those members who are articulate and dynamic in their communicative skills.

Charles Larson (1969) discovered that the emergent leader consistently initiates more themes during group interaction than nonleaders. The leader not only initiates more total themes but consistently initiates more themes throughout every stage of group interaction. The consistency in initiating themes may be a more vital aspect of the leader's behavior than merely the quantity of themes initiated. If members come to expect the leader to be an initiator, they will look to him or her throughout their interaction to serve that function. On the other hand, an emergent leader has responsibilities to the group after having gained leadership status, too. Hence, one might infer that the leader must continue to be an initiator in order to maintain the leadership position. Otherwise, the other members might depose her or him and look elsewhere for a member to serve as their leader.

The communicative behaviors of an emergent leader also include seeking comments. That is, the emergent leader actively and overtly seeks the information and opinions of the other members. Such comments are particularly frequent and important in the early and intermediate stages of a group's task performance. The leader does not behave as though he or she has no opinions but, rather, is interested in the opinions of others and in procuring as much information as possible so that the group can reach an intelligent and informed decision. The behaviors which seek opinions and information from other members are, unlike initiating comments, not consistently employed by the emergent leader throughout the group interaction. As members of the group approach consensus, asking for additional information and opinions is unproductive and even irrelevant. Therefore, the emergent leader uses "seeking comments" frequently only when group consensus is not apparent.

Some conventional wisdom asserts that a true leader does not attempt to impress personal opinions on other members of the group. Underlying this alleged wisdom is the assumption that members resent being told what they should do and that the leader should be unselfish and overtly avoid attempting to persuade others to abandon their points of view. Nothing could be farther from the truth. The leader provides significant assistance to the group in its progress toward fulfilling its goals and cannot do so without expressing opinions and supporting them. As in the case of seeking comments, however, the leader does not take a strong stand throughout all periods of group interaction. While seeking the opinions of others initially, the leader does not express strong opinions. In fact, rigidity in stage 1 of the model of leader emergence results in eliminating members from contention. But from the intermediate stage on, the emergent leader takes stands on issues and defends them. Having strong opinions may be a negative virtue early in group interaction, but it is vitally important for successful leader emergence later.

While it is obvious that emergent leaders do express their own position on substantive matters, the position proceeds from an informed and objective basis. Recall that the emergent leader also contributes many comments which seek opinions and information from others. Thus, past behavior provides the basis for an informed and objective stance. Therefore it is imperative that emergent leaders both seek opinions from others and express their own opinions. They do not do one *or* the other but both, encouraging a spirit of free exchange of ideas among all members. Everyone has a right to an opinion and the freedom, even the responsibility, to express it. Moreover, the leader must have an opinion, too, so as not to be rejected as a wishy-washy group member.

Some recent research has suggested that the communicative functions performed by a group leader during the interactive process may vary considerably. That is, the group leader varies in his or her interactive behaviors, depending upon the specific member of the group with whom he or she is interacting. Rather than perform consistent "leadership functions" throughout the interaction, the leader will function differently with different group members.

Ellis (1976) performed an analysis of the relational interaction (e.g., symmetry and complementarity of one-up, one-across, and one-down control modes) in decision-making groups. He discovered that the perceived leader of the group performed communicative functions quite distinct from other group members, not in terms of different behaviors which function to set the leader apart, but in terms of adapting specific functions to nearly every member of the group individually. That is, the leader, when interacting with each member, differed from the interaction patterns characteristic of the group as a whole. No other members of the group consistently demonstrated variable interactive patterns with other group members. They all tended to interact with everyone else in much the same fashion.

Ellis's results suggest that the primary leadership function may not be in the form of specific communicative behaviors which differentiate a leader from nonleaders. Rather, the leadership function may be the adaptation of specific functions to specific group members. At the same time, nonleaders apparently interact with other members in the same way in which they interact throughout the entire group interaction. Ellis (p. 91) writes, "The leader does not 'do' one thing which sets him apart from other group members. Apparently, the leader takes stock of the individuals in the group and enacts behaviors which he considers appropriate for each individual."

We sometimes believe that the leader assumes the leadership role by structuring the interaction, by influencing the flow of the ideas and the relationships in the interaction. Ellis's research implies that the leader may indeed attempt to structure the interaction with some members. But in interacting with other members, the leader may defer to their structuring and may not attempt to exert any relational authority over them.

One conclusion from Ellis's research may be that there is no such thing as leadership functions which a leader performs consistently throughout the group interaction. Rather, a leader functions as a leader in adapting different communicative functions to different group members. In one case, he or she may be an authority figure and initiate the direction on which the interaction will flow. In another case, however, the leader may be a respondent to some other member's attempts to structure in interaction.

Thus, all group members perform important contributions to the group's interactions. Furthermore, these contributions may serve as "leadership functions" overall. But the leader, as an initiator, a respondent, and a reactor to those functions, is adept at knowing when to initiate and when to respond and with whom. The leader's interaction with each member is distinctive. The leader is able to adapt to every other member as a unique, contributing member of the group. Apparently nonleaders do not interact in such an adaptive manner.

The leadership function of adaptation is also the subject of an investigation performed by Wood (1977). She indicated in her report that leaders were able to adapt to situations and to past failures of the group. In terms of specific communicative behaviors, Wood's analysis is rather crude but does indicate that leaders tend to promote what she calls a "collective identity"—apparently similar to groupness. Perhaps the adaptation of specific functions to other members as unique individuals, such as Ellis depicted, is one way to weld individuals into a collective group identity.

In conclusion, then, a functions approach to group leadership is not necessarily an attempt to discover what specific behaviors or functions a leader performs and nonleaders do not perform. Rather, the functions of a group leader may be the discrimination of which functions should be performed with whom and at what times. Such an approach is consistent with this book's view of communication and the group process. We have already learned that the timing of a communicative behavior (when the behavior is performed) is often more significant than the content of that action.

It is no secret that the attempt to describe and define group leadership in terms of group functions is far from a thorough description. However, the present state of knowledge concerning leadership functions does not allow a very precise or complete explanation. Research investigations are continuing at several universities. The results of these efforts should provide more specific information concerning the process of group leadership through communicative functions. As these projects are completed, a more specific description of leadership functions and how they fit into the overall process of group decision making will become available.

### Legitimacy and Leader Emergence

Although the LGD should preclude the influence of legitimate bases of leadership, the influence of some varieties of legitimacy in the LGD should not be overlooked. The principle of legitimacy is generally defined as prescribed or ascribed approval of norms, values, roles, or other behavioral standards. Typically, an organization endows certain roles with legitimate status by prescribing a formal status hierarchy independent of the persons occupying positions in that status hierarchy. For example, a colonel in the armed forces has legitimate authority of leadership over all those of lower rank by virtue of the rank given by the organization itself and not necessarily because of any achieved informal status. A familiar theme of war movies is a story of veteran soldiers who resent the leadership of a young "90-day-wonder" second lieutenant who does not have the experience or achievements of some of the soldiers of lesser rank. But nevertheless, the veterans formally recognize the authority due to the legitimate rank of commissioned officer.

Normally, iegitimacy refers to formal recognition of approval by some external agency which has authority over the group. In a "true" LGD, no such agency exists outside the group. But a true LGD is very rare. In a university classroom, the instructor and the values of the student culture both exert an impact on the classroom LGD. Some members may have legitimate approval of their roles by virtue of the instructor's designation or campuswide status as a "big man on campus." Such quasi-legitimate recognition may endow a member with some vestige of formal leadership. But the member then must earn informal recognition of leadership status during the process of leader emergence.

Legitimacy exerts little direct influence on the LGD, but the group itself manufactures its own symbols of legitimate recognition. Certain symbols of authority are endorsed with a kind of legitimate approval, and the member who possesses one or more of these symbols takes on the aura of legitimate recognition of authority. Numerous examples of such symbols may be found in a classroom LGD. Some instructors ask classroom groups to record their interaction during each meeting on audiotape. The member who takes possession of the tape recorder, adjusts the microphone, and controls its operation possesses a symbol of authority. It is not uncommon for members who are contending for leadership to fight over the right to possess this authority symbol.

One classroom group using transistor cassette recorders encountered a problem in operating the machinery. For some reason it did not work properly, and the member who had habitually taken charge of it was unable to get the recorder working. Another member who conveniently owned a similar recorder easily spotted the trouble and fixed it. His leadership contention received a big impetus with this seemingly unrelated act. His fellow members insisted that he take charge of the group's cassette recorder in subsequent meetings. He did—and later emerged as the group's recognized leader.

Often a group sits around a rectangular table and leader contenders race to the meeting room in order to be able to sit in the chair at the head of the table. One classroom group typically held meetings in an instructor's office with the alleged seat of authority the instructor's swivel chair behind the desk. Perhaps not coincidentally, the group's emergent leader turned out to be the member who consistently occupied the swivel chair during group meetings. He admitted afterward that he initially wanted to sit in that chair because it was the most comfortable one in the room. He also expressed his surprise on several occasions when he had arrived late for a group meeting to discover that the other members had left the swivel chair vacant for him. He believed that seat was a symbol of his leadership authority apparently recognized, perhaps at a low level of awareness, by his fellow group members.

Another classroom group's emergent leader was the sole member who took notes during group discussions. As a result of his trusty legal pad, he was always an expert on what the group had decided and accomplished during past meetings and was able to organize its future activity. He often referred to his legal pad, and was consistently asked by other members what was written on it. For him and his group, that legal pad became a legitimate symbol of authority.

But a legitimate symbol of authority need not be a physical object. Often an activity by a group member receives formal recognition by the group and takes on legitimacy by itself. One group frequently met outside class hours at the apartment of one of the members. She became the hostess of the group meetings, served coffee and pop, potato chips and snacks, and enveloped herself in the legitimacy of being the authority in her own apartment. She was recognized as the emergent leader—quickly and painlessly.

A common activity which achieves legitimate recognition in the classroom group involves collecting, organizing, and typing contributions of members to form the final group document that is handed to the instructor as a class requirement. The person who types that report often acquires formal recognition for this effort and gains some legitimate recognition of this leadership bid. Rarely is such an activity unrewarded by the group.

Although there are many more examples of manufactured legitimacy in the LGD, all cases have one ingredient in common. Whether a physical object or an activity, the legitimate symbol of authority is associated with a single person who has assisted the group in making progress toward its goal. The symbol is not prescribed by some outside authority but receives formal and relatively permanent recognition by the group members themselves. While not a complete description of the process of leader emergence, instances and symbols of manufactured legitimacy do influence the process and highlight a person who is contending for leader. The combination of communicative behaviors and symbols of manufactured legitimacy allows the group or an outside observer the opportunity to perceive the process of leader emergence in operation.

## MALES AND FEMALES IN LEADERSHIP ROLES

What effect does the sex of the leader have on the group? Do males and females differ in their contributions to group interaction when they are in the leadership roles? Are leaders more likely to be male or female? Questions such as these are significant elements in group phenomena in light of the increased emphasis on the role of women in our society. Unfortunately, the answers to these questions are impossible to determine definitely. Sex-role stereotypes, although still prominent in our society, are currently in a state of flux with the increased appearance of women in nontraditional societal roles. Any attempt to answer such questions, then, is destined to be incomplete and outdated within a very few years. The following discussion, then, is not intended to be definitive but to suggest the flavor of the transition of changing stereotypes and human perceptions in the American culture.

Investigations have consistently discovered that the attitudes and perceptions of group members will significantly affect those perceptions of males and females occupying leadership roles (see, for example, Yerby, 1975). Depending upon the extent to which members hold stereotypes of men and women and whether these members are men or women, levels of group cohesiveness and attitudes toward leaders will vary considerably. On the other hand, because of the extent to which androgyny (self-concepts which include a combination of characteristics socially attributed to males or females) affects the perceptions, one is tempted to doubt whether any attempt to depict perceptions as either male or female can be successful. Furthermore, few investigators have attempted to determine whether the communicative behaviors of males and females actually differ from each other when they are performing leadership roles. Typically, the researchers have tried to learn whether group members *perceive* that male and female leaders differ in the leadership functions. One of the rare studies, designed to observe directly the interactive behaviors of male and female leaders, suggests little discernible difference in their interactive contributions.

DeStephen (1977) discovered that, overall, male and female group members in her study did not differ significantly in communicative behaviors they contributed to the group's interaction process. On the other hand, leaders differed considerably from nonleaders in that they tended more to clarify task issues and seek evaluations of task issues that nonleaders did. But in attempting to distinguish between the communicative functions of males and females in the leadership role, DeStephen found little difference. In fact, female leaders performed the same "leadership functions" as male leaders, only perhaps more so. For example, females tended to clarify even more than male leaders. But leaders, regardless of their sex, appeared to perform more clarifying functions than nonleaders did. One may conclude, then, that the distinction is greater between leaders and nonleaders than between males and females in the leadership role.

Even though it is clearly difficult to draw any conclusions about males and females during this transitional period in our culture, one might speculate as to the reasons why people tend to perceive differences between male and female leaders, even though those differences may not be apparent in the actual behaviors performed. In other words, we might speculate that people tend to behave in a manner consistent with the way we think they should respond. That is, we possess certain expectations about how males and females, leaders and nonleaders, are supposed to act. When our expectations are thwarted (for example, when males or females do not behave as we expect them to, we tend to perceive differences, but our perceptions may not be based on our actual observations.

Assuming for the moment that leaders (both male and female) behave similarly, we may perceive behavioral differences where none in fact exists. If we typically think of leadership as a male-role stereotype, we will expect males to be performing leadership behaviors. On the other hand, if we see a female performing this "male" role, we will tend to think of the female as being out of place. That is, the female leader is functioning in a manner different from the way we think subconsciously that females "ought" to behave. A male leader and a female leader may be enacting precisely the same interactive behaviors, but we *perceive* the male leader as "self-confident" and "task-oriented" and, at the same time, perceive the female leader as "pushy" or "overly aggressive."

Therefore, one might speculate that if male and female leaders really do behave similarly, our perceptions of those behaviors may still differ because of a stereotypical pattern of thinking (probably at a low level of awareness) resulting from our sex-role stereotypes. Within the next generation, we should be able to avoid such narrow-minded thought processes and respond to both males and females as individual persons, not merely as representatives of a male or female role.

## HOW TO AVOID EMERGING AS LEADER

In many ways it is difficult to know how and why certain members emerge as group leaders. The process of eliminating leader contenders, however, suggests that it may be less difficult to determine how and why certain members do *not* become group leaders. If certain people truly wish not to become leaders (as some people are quick to assert), the following list of "rules" should allow them to fulfill their goal. These principles are guidelines for assuring yourself of a low-status position in your group. Follow them faithfully, and I guarantee that you will definitely not emerge as your group's leader.

*Rule 1:* Be absent from as many group meetings as possible. You will be even better at avoiding leadership responsibilities if you provide no reasons for your absences. But with or without reasons, absence from group interaction is an effective tactic.

*Rule 2:* Contribute to the interaction as little as possible. You might also consider contributing incompetently to the group's interaction. Such a strategy, however, is more dangerous. Other members may perceive competence in what you consider to be incompetent. The safer practice is to avoid contributing and to let other members think you are incompetent or disinterested rather than to interact too much and thus to remove their doubts.

*Rule 3:* Volunteer to be the secretary or the recordkeeper of your group's discussions. The role of recorder or secretary in a group is rarely associated with the role of leader. You do risk the problem of demonstrating interest and commitment to the group by volunteering for what is indeed a valuable role. You will probably be assigned a rather high status. You should probably consider this strategy a compromise. By avoiding leadership, you may be substituting a high-status role. But if you truly wish to avoid becoming a leader, you should be willing to compromise.

*Rule 4:* Indicate that you are willing to do what you are told. This strategy is sometimes as risky as becoming a secretary. By showing your commitment to the group in your willingness to perform activities beneficial to the group's task efforts, you may be indicating too much commitment to the group. Lack of interest in the group is more effective in avoiding leadership responsibilities, but a subservient or acquiescent commitment is the next best thing.

*Rule 5:* Come on strong early in the group discussions. The timing of your verbally aggressive and directive behavior is extremely important when following this principle. If you advocate something strongly later in the group interaction, your activity may be misinterpreted as an attempt to assist the group in solving its decision-making task. It is vitally important that your advocacy be extreme and that it demonstrate an unwillingness to compromise your position, especially if another member should resist your ideas. Attempt to be unsuccessful in your early advocacy of your positions. Failure in these early stages of the group process is important. Too much success, particularly in the early stages of group decision making, is likely to lead to the undesirable effect of having other group members think you are contending for leadership. Later stages in group decision making, during which time members are advocating ideational positions, are the times to show your apathy regarding which decision proposals will achieve consensus.

*Rule 6:* Try to assume the role of joker. By telling lots of jokes early in the discussion, you will get people to like you while you are in the process of avoiding leadership. Sometimes, contenders for low-status roles tend to be uncomfortable when other members show dislike of them. If you become a joker, however, you will probably avoid such negative reactions. On the other hand, they will probably not take you very seriously. Make sure, however, that your jokes are consistently off the topic and are not combined with any opinion or information concerning it. Your funny-person role should also be consistent. Don't do anything that would indicate that you are anything but a joker.

*Rule 7:* Demonstrate your knowledge of everything, including your extensive vocabulary of big words and technical jargon. This strategy is also a bit risky in that members may misinterpret your know-it-all attitude and command of esoteric words as signs of intelligence and breadth of background. You can't afford to be timid when using this tactic. Express a comprehensive knowledge of every topic and a continuous use of words that other people probably don't understand. Consistency is the key to successful employment of this strategy.

*Rule 8:* Demonstrate a contempt for leadership. This method is rarely used but is always successful in avoiding the leadership role. One classroom group member, whom I shall call Sean, was quite successful and adept in utilizing this strategy. He verbalized frequently and vehemently his distaste for all leaders and the concept of leadership itself. He was a veteran of the war in Vietnam and had recently returned from southeast Asia. He consistently expressed his strong belief that all leaders are corrupt. One of his reactions to an early group meeting was most explicit in revealing his attitude: "I do not want to hear any fascinating facts about leadership. Leadership is for whoever wants it. If you have an average IQ and a corrupt tendency to dominate people, you can become a leader. Those who manipulate leaders are those who dominate very furtively." Sean succeeded beyond the highest expectations of all leadership avoiders. In his six-member group, he was unanimously voted the least liked member in both social and task areas. But one must be aggressive in using this strategy and must consistently resist and label every attempt at leadership contention by other members.

Of course, these "principles" for avoiding the leadership role are presented in a tongue-in-cheek manner. They are characteristic of those behaviors of persons who are eliminated from leadership contention. Rarely, if ever, does any person intend to avoid becoming a leader. Although individual group members may not intentionally attempt to be the group leader, they also do not intend to avoid leadership, at least at a very high level of awareness. During the normal functioning of the group process and group interaction, the group works out the role of each member, including the role of leader. Such functioning of the group process is quite normal and typical. Moreover, the process is functioning even though the members may not be aware of it until after the process has been completed.

The best advice to any group that is attempting to assess and understand the social and task dimensions of the group process is to become aware (at least as fully as possible) of the probable stage of group development occurring at that time. Attempting to intervene in the normal group process is likely to be successful only with such an understanding. Under no circumstances should a member attempt to counteract the normal functioning of the group process except as a desperate act of last resort. A better action would be to encourage and take advantage of your comprehensive understanding in order to manage more effectively all facets of communication and the group process, including that of leader emergence.

If your group appoints a group productivity observer, one task of that observer should be to look for the stage of development of decision making and the leader emergence (probably the same process) and the interdependent social and task dimensions of the group process. Such an observer must be highly sensitive to the group process and possess a comprehensive understanding of how communication and the group process functions. It is to be hoped that members of your group will have such a comprehensive understanding.

## SUMMARY

Perhaps the most pervasive element of social systems is the existence of leadership and a status hierarchy. In the LGD, roles fall into several hierarchical levels, typically two or three, proportional to the contribution of each member in aiding the group to achieve the group goals. In an LGD, each member achieves a status level through communicative behaviors rather than through being given status by some authority outside the group. The leader's status is based on a reciprocal influence of leader and followers—an interdepdendence among the communicating members in the LGD.

Several perspectives of viewing leadership have been popularly employed in the past. They include the traits, styles, situational, and functions approaches to group leadership. The functions perspective, unlike any of the others, focuses on the communicative behaviors of individual members and their relative contributions to the group's progress. This perspective deemphasizes leadership as defined by the person who occupies a given position in a network of roles. Because there have been so few studies of leadership utilizing the functions perspective, no comprehensive list of communicative behaviors associated with leadership yet exists. But a partial list of behaviors is available.

Employing the functions perspective, leadership is viewed as a process whereby a group leader achieves status gradually over time as a direct result of group interaction patterns. That process, termed "leader emergence," may generally be described as a process of elimination in which each member is a contender for leadership, but each is eliminated, one by one, until a single person remains and is recognized as group leader.

A basic model of leader emergence hypothesizes three stages of elimination. In stage 1, uninformed, low-participating members are eliminated. In stage 2, two or more contenders emerge by gaining lieutenants who support their leadership contention. Those contenders eliminated in stage 2 typically are overly directive and use offensive verbalization so that stage 3 includes only one remaining contender who achieves recognition as leader. Several variations from this basic model are possible in a particular small group.

Behaviors associated with emergent leaders include being verbally active, demonstrating communicative skill, consistently initiating themes, seeking opinions and information in early and intermediate stages of group development, stating opinions and attempting to persuade other members in intermediate and later stages of group development, and adopting an informed and objective argumentative stance.

The LGD also manufactures formal symbols of legitimacy in group interaction. Such symbols, which may be physical objects or member activity, are associated with a particular member and with the formal authority of leadership, although they may vary from group to group.

Although stereotyped attitudes of sex roles remain prominent, our society's attitudes are currently in a state of rapid change. Consequently, males and females who function as group leaders probably do not differ significantly from one another in terms of the communicative actions they use in leading. However, the group members or followers may perceive differences because of their previously held attitudes regarding sex-role stereotypes.

# Chapter 8

# Social Conflict
# and Deviance

The past two decades have witnessed numerous instances of social conflict and deviant behavior within our society. Many believe the recent upsurge of minority dissent is unparalleled in our history. But dissent has been present since our system was founded. Many eligible young men resisted the draft during the Vietnamese war, but draft resistance has been prevalent since the first Selective Service during the Spanish-American War. Hundreds of thousands of protesters marched on Washington, D.C., several times during the decade of the 1960s, but so did veterans of World War I some forty years before. The civil disobedience of Martin Luther King, Jr., and the Berrigan brothers led to their imprisonment just like that of Henry David Thoreau, Eugene Debs, and countless labor organizers during the early struggles of the labor movement in the United States.

Some historians have compared recent dissent to that of the colonists before the Revolutionary War. The comparison seems appropriate. Many campus and urban protests in recent years wantonly destroyed private property. But the tea thrown into the Boston harbor by pseudo-Indians was also property which those colonial protesters did not own. Soldiers fired on private citizens on the campus of Kent State as did British soldiers on the Boston Commons nearly two centuries before.

The common but erroneous belief is that protests such as those during the 1968 Democratic Party convention and on university campuses are unique to the present. Many also believe that such social conflict is detrimental and reflects some failure within our culture. Others believe that social conflict is symptomatic of a healthy society. The truth, as in most cases, undoubtedly lies somewhere between the two extreme positions. The preceding examples of social conflict are not intended to prove that current social dissent is heroic or necessary. Nor are the historical comparisons intended to degrade yesterday's heroes.

Obviously some conflict within a social system is detrimental, just as some conflict is beneficial. The point to be emphasized is that social conflict, both good and bad, is normal and a recurring phenomenon of our social system throughout its history. Moreover, social conflict has been normal in the functioning of every social system throughout the history of human civilizations.

## MUCH CONFLICT ABOUT SOCIAL CONFLICT

Many sociologists view a social system as a delicate balance of opposing forces—forces which threaten to disrupt the system and forces which maintain the system. According to this view, a social system is perpetually in a state of conflict which may at any time tip toward the disruptive forces and destroy the system.

The perspective of this book—communication and the group process, with emphasis on interdependence—is not consistent with viewing the system as a balance of opposing forces. The process viewpoint assumes that such forces, if they exist, are interdependent, so they cannot be separated or in opposition to each other. For example, "temperature" is hardly an arithmetic difference between forces of heat and forces of cold. If it were, one would be comfortable if one held a block of ice in one hand and a burning coal in the other. Temperature is a single reading and not a balance of two readings—one high and one low.

It is important to know that not all experts agree on the nature of social conflict, its effects, or its solution. Understanding social conflict from the communicative process perspective requires an understanding of the varied and often conflicting views regarding it.

### Intrapersonal—Interpersonal—Intergroup

To understand the nature of social conflict, one must first identify who or what is in conflict. Probably the most common view of social conflict is intergroup conflict, that is, conflict between opposing social systems. Intergroup conflict involves conflict between groups or societies rather than between single individuals. It embraces labor-management relations, particularly during periods of contract negotiations, as well as conflicts among nations. An individual human being, when involved in intergroup conflict, participates not as an individual entity but as a representative of an entire social system.

Although intergroup conflict is a fascinating area of concern and some examples will be drawn from it, a study of this type of social conflict does not suit the purposes of this book. Since our purpose is to understand the communicative process which characterizes group decision making, intergroup conflict is not highly pertinent.

Intrapersonal conflict, as the term implies, involves the psychological conflict that rages within the individual. The intrapersonal view alleges the existence of opposing forces within a person's mind which determine actions, beliefs, and values. Numerous balance theories attempt to explain individual behavior through intrapersonal conflict. They include cognitive dissonance theory, congruity theory, equity theory, exchange theory, and consistency theory, among others. Hawes (1969) has also explained member satisfaction within a small group through the concept of ambivalence—a balance of internal forces that attract or repel.

But an investigation of intrapersonal conflict does not serve the purposes of this book either. In the first place, internalized conflict cannot be directly observed through communicative behaviors and may or may not be indirectly reflected in group interaction. Then, too, intrapersonal conflict utilizes the psychological makeup of the individual person as the basis for understanding the small group rather than the process of interaction based on the interstructured communicative behaviors of all members.

Interpersonal conflict is most pertinent to the perspective of communication and the group process. But interpersonal conflict, for our purposes, does not necessarily imply a personality conflict between individuals. Quite the contrary, it is defined solely in terms of interact patterns. Thus, interpersonal conflict is directly observable through sequences of communicative behaviors performed by members of the group. Personalities of individual members are not considered in conflict; behaviors performed by two or more members conflict with one another.

## Affective—Substantive

A second view of social conflict considers the basis of that conflict— whether conflicting issues are affective or substantive. Typically, in reference to interpersonal conflict, affective conflict implies emotional clashes between individuals within a social system, generally over procedural or how-to-do-it problems. Such conflict does not ordinarily stem from a disagreement on opinions or beliefs but from a struggle based on selfish or personal issues. Substantive conflict, on the other hand, involves an intellectual opposition of group members on the content of ideas or issues pertinent to the group task.

Since social conflict and deviance are considered a single phenomenon in group interaction, the affective-substantive differentiation of conflict may also be called "role deviation" and "opinion deviation." While an opinion deviate disagrees with other group members on the content of ideas, a role deviate is a type of person who is not desired by other group members. One member of a student group found herself as a role deviate in her group. She received low sociometric rankings from nearly all her fellow group members. Concerned, she asked them why. Her diary immediately following that group meeting describes their reactions:

> They also said that they had projected me as being the type of person I played in class; they projected that role as being my true personality. . . . Now that they know me a little better, they could see I wasn't "Susie," a dominating woman, but "Susan"—a different individual altogether.

Role deviation and opinion deviation differ significantly in their impact on group interaction. Sampson and Brandon (1964) indicate that other group members increase their interaction with an opinion deviate and exert pressure on him or her to conform to their majority opinion. But the group virtually ignores the role deviate, apparently perceiving that type of person as a hopeless case not worthy of pressure. A social system tends to view deviance either as a behavior apart from the individual personality of the deviate or as a personality trait of the individual. As behavior, deviance affects the group process of interaction and, thus, is central to the perspective of this book. The role deviate does not significantly affect the group's interaction patterns, and is therefore considered irrelevant.

The opinion deviate is tolerated and perhaps even admired by fellow members. After all, we have been taught from childhood that rationality and independence are virtues in our society. We are urged to be masters of our own fate, to make up our own minds. "Know thyself" was the advice of Socrates. Advertising campaigns appeal to our rational independence by urging us to buy the product that gets us away from the crowd. The virtues of rationality and independence are often reflected in adolescents' rejection of their parents' ideas and beliefs. Their parents, often to their chagrin, had experienced the ultimate success in teaching two of our cardinal social virtues.

Lewis Coser (1956, pp. 48–55) distinguishes between realistic and nonrealistic conflict, which appears to be another dimension of affective-substantive conflict. According to Coser, realistic conflict is a means to an end—deviating behavior to further the group's progress toward its goal. But nonrealistic conflict is an end in itself not directly associated with any goal. For example, a worker may go out on strike to gain higher wages and better working conditions. But another worker may engage even in the same strike because of some oedipal hatred of the employer. This displaced hatred could as easily be directed against any authority figure. The point is that the person who performs deviant behavior as a means to achieve some goal is said to be engaged in realistic conflict.

The view of conflict which best serves the purposes of this book is, of course, substantive conflict—that conflict expressed as deviant behavior in intellectual opposition to ideas or issues associated with the group task or goals. Substantive conflict is realistic to the extent that it serves as a means toward accomplishing some goal.

### Destructive—Constructive

There is enormous disagreement over the effects of conflict on the social system. One school of thought seems to view conflict as inherently undesirable since it inevitably leads to disruption of the social system. An opposing view considers social conflict essential to the effective functioning of every social system. It is intuitively obvious that neither view is absolutely accurate. Some conflict and deviance disrupts the system, and other instances of conflict and deviance are beneficial to the system. Discriminating between the two kinds, however, is no simple task.

Many functions of the social system of the United States are predicated on the existence of conflict. Our economic subsystem of free enterprise assumes conflict and free competition among producers and retailers for the consumer dollar. The basis of our political system is the free and open marketplace of ideas in which societal values gain social consensus. Candidates for political office air conflicting views on the issues during the course of a political campaign. Our judicial system is based on the adversary system in which the accuser confronts the accused. Many of our recreational activities include games based on conflict—football, tennis, handball, chess, Monopoly, among others. Conflict is undoubtedly an integral part of our nation-society.

But despite the pervasive influence of social conflict in our society, most Americans are ambivalent about many of its forms. Probably the best example is the right of minority dissent, constitutionally assured in the Bill of Rights. Freedom of speech is one of our most cherished national values, epitomized in such statements as Voltaire's "I disapprove of what you say, but I will defend to the death your right to say it."

National opinion polls have reaffirmed that nearly all Americans stead-fastly uphold the freedom of speech of all Americans—majority and minority. But those same Americans, the polls tell us, would refuse to allow a professed Communist to give a public lecture. Battles over censorship laws are common in our social system. Apparently not all members of our society consider all realistic and substantive conflict or opinion deviation to be constructive. Indeed, many people consider much substantive conflict highly destructive.

A social system is too often viewed as an abstract ideal—a system of pure cooperation—so that any deviance must be unnatural. If a social system is idealized, members of the system are constrained to strive for the perfection of pure cooperation. Any deviant behavior, then, is construed as a failure of the social system and must therefore be eradicated. The typically short-sighted view of common sense would have us believe that a "perfect" social system is worth striving for. But as I hope to illustrate, the "perfect" social system free from conflict and deviance is doomed to failure because of its inherent inflexibility, its inability to cope with environmental stresses, its lack of capacity for growth and progress.

Assuming the idealized social system and the corollary that social conflict is inherently destructive leads to an incredibly naive outlook on social conflict among many members of our nation-system. Too often, realistic conflict is camouflaged and dissenting views are suppressed so that our social system masquerades as an absolutely perfect and ideal system, without fault or information to the contrary. But perfection is hardly possible in human beings or in their creations. Our nation's heroes had faults just as every other human being has had from the beginning of time. But most important, the consistent effort to "accentuate the positive and eliminate the negative" makes us naive about social conflict and more susceptible to dissenting views.

Most of our nation was shocked when some United States soldiers elected to remain with their Communist Chinese captors at the close of the Korean war rather than return to their homeland. Many people reacted by advocating stronger teaching of only the positive aspects of our society. Others advocated a greater emphasis on comparative politics—to show the realistic faults and virtues of all political systems—so that our citizens would be fully aware of all alternatives. Indeed, all of us probably believe that our system would fare well in such a comparison. At least we would no longer be naive and uninformed about social conflict and deviance.

The positive side of social conflict is represented by the functionalists—George Simmel (1955), Lewis Coser (1956), and Talcott Parsons (1951), among others. The functionalists do not deny that some social conflict disrupts the functioning of a social system and is therefore destructive. But the functionalists do emphasize the socially constructive functions of conflict and advocate an understanding of social conflict so that the social system is able to take advantage of its positive aspects. Some of the positive functions performed by social conflict are included later in this chapter.

### Reactions to Social Conflict

The typical reaction to social conflict is to search for ways to resolve it, that is, to get rid of it. At the very least, according to this view, conflict must be controlled so that it doesn't get out of hand. Naturally, some conflict must be resolved or controlled because it is potentially destructive. Destructive conflict, unchecked, would lead ultimately to dissolution of the system itself. Hence, methods of conflict resolution are essential for instances of destructive conflict. Modes of conflict resolution include such devices as compromise, bargaining, appeasement, negotiation, and mediation.

Occasionally cure-all "formula" solutions are offered as substitutes for genuine methods of conflict resolution. Such formulas are usually not realistic and stem from a grossly oversimplified view of social conflict. One such formula answer is "more cooperation." If cooperation were so simple, the conflict would not have to be resolved in the first place. A more commonly suggested formula, offered to solve virtually any social conflict, is "more communication" or "opening channels of communication." If there is no communication at all between conflicting parties, which is rarely the case, some communication is obviously called for. But communication inherently assumes specific forms, such as negotiation. "More communication" is meaningless. If present communication is ineffective, increasing the "amount" of communication does not render it suddenly more effective. More often, "more communication" is suggested as a substitute for any real effort to resolve conflicts. Such a "formula" stems from an overly naive and grossly inadequate understanding of the nature of the communication process. The nonsensical nature of such a formula solution should be apparent in ensuing chapters.

When parties in conflict cannot satisfactorily resolve their disagreement, they search for modes of controlling that conflict. One common and often effective means of controlling conflict, particularly intergroup conflict, is "encapsulation." Conflict which is encapsulated does not cease to exist. Rather, it continues under the governance of an agreed-upon set of rules. In international conflict, for example, we refer to the "cold war" between the United States, the Soviet Union, and the People's Republic of China. "Cold war" is a euphemism for international conflict that has been encapsulated within the rules of international diplomacy—

embassies in each country, exchanges of diplomatic notes, treaties limiting nuclear testing, talks and treaties on arms limitations, trade agreements involving nonstrategic materials, reciprocal visits by high-ranking dignitaries, etc. All conflicting nations agree to the rules and thereby control the conflict between their countries without attempting to resolve it.

Even wars are encapsulated, in part, by certain international "rules" of warfare, such as those of the Geneva Convention and the Geneva Accords. Thus, even armed conflict with the avowed purpose of annihilating the enemy nation is governed by rules and therefore encapsulated. Encapsulation of conflict is a common ingredient of international relations.

The belief that conflict must be resolved or controlled is consistent with the view that conflict is inherently destructive. But resolution and control are inappropriate reactions for numerous instances of social conflict—particularly the kind that serves socially positive functions. In fact, such conflict should even be encouraged and utilized to further the system's progress toward its desired goals. Utilizing social conflict in the best interests of the system requires a thorough understanding of the phenomenon itself and the ability to manage conflict in order to benefit from its positive aspects.

For the purpose of understanding the process of small group decision making, our primary interest is social conflict which is interpersonal, substantive, and constructive. Our goal is to understand social conflict and deviance as a process and to manage it constructively to the benefit of the group. This view does not deny destructive forms of conflict, but it does emphasize a view of conflict too often overlooked. While instances of destructive conflict do not typically exert significant impact on the general process of group interaction, constructive conflict plays an instrumental role in shaping the process of group interaction. Such conflict is vitally important, then, to the purposes of this book.

## FUNCTIONS OF SOCIAL CONFLICT AND DEVIANCE

According to one of the foremost functionalists, Georg Simmel (1955, p. 13), conflict is inevitably a "form of sociation." It is impossible to have social conflict without interaction among the parties in conflict, and interaction is certainly a form of sociation. Simmel says of social conflict, ". . . it is a way of achieving some kind of unity, even if it be through the annihilation of one of the conflicting parties." Although the reference to annihilation may be tongue-in-cheek, it is indisputable that social conflict cannot exist with an individual person in social isolation. Certainly conflict is a distinct type of interaction between at least two persons. And interaction is one of the basic requisites of a social system. One can only conclude that anything which encourages interaction must be a potentially positive force in the development of a social system. It is on this deceptively simple assumption that the positive social functions of conflict are based.

While we might think of conflict as some disruption in the interaction process, quite the opposite is more accurate. In fact, social conflict inevitably requires social interaction. Likert and Bowers (1972, p. 117) are quite emphatic on this point: "Every conflict, other than those internal to a particular individual, involves an interaction among persons, groups, organizations, or larger entities and occurs through an interaction-influence network." When people engage in conflict, they inevitably engage in interaction. We should not be overly concerned that conflict is present in the interaction. We should be more concerned if and when conflict functions to disrupt or discontinue the group's efforts. The important point to remember is that conflict requires interaction among parties to the conflict. Conflict is thus an active ingredient of the group process.

Furthermore, the distinction between conflict interaction and non-conflict interaction is the nature of how the actions relate to each other. According to Deutsch (1969, p. 7), "*Conflict* exists whenever *incompatible* activities occur." A conflict thus involves a sequence of activities that are incompatible with each other. For example, a statement favoring a decision proposal followed by a statement opposed to the decision proposal is an instance of a conflict interact. A one-up comment followed by another one-up comment is a symmetrical and incompatible interact, thus reflecting a relational conflict. Conflict would also be present in a one-down comment followed by another one-down comment. A statement followed by disagreement is a very common form of conflict in group decision making. In any case, social conflict requires interaction for it to take place. Furthermore, conflict is characterized by a sequence of incompatible activities performed by the parties to the conflict. Being able to distinguish social conflict is one thing, but understanding the functions it performs in group decision making is another. And those functions performed by social conflict and deviance provide the subject for discussion in this section.

### Influence on Cohesiveness

Social conflict breeds not only social interaction but also increased involvement. The member who is apathetic toward the group and toward the worth of the group task has little reason to engage in the painful process of social conflict. Moreover, the virtual absence of social conflict in group interaction is a trustworthy indication of the low involvement or commitment of group members. If the group develops even a moderate level of cohesiveness, its members will engage in rather frequent, though not extended, periods of social conflict. Thus, the natural development of group cohesiveness presupposes social conflict. In this sense, social conflict is not only desirable for the development of groupness; it is quite inevitable and should be expected as part of the *normal* sequence of group interaction.

Of course, social conflict, if it is to be beneficial to group cohesiveness, must not be perceived as threatening the group's social fabric. Substantive conflict serves to precipitate secondary tension. Therefore, the successful group develops mechanisms for managing social conflict as it arises. And a history of successful conflict management builds group cohesiveness.

Lest the term "conflict management" be misinterpreted, it is important to note that the group does not necessarily resolve the conflict or even control it through limiting its boundaries. Conflict management refers solely to the interaction sequences developed by a group to deal with social conflict and consistently used by the group when social conflict occurs. Generally, conflict management implies that social conflict will definitely occur again, although probably in slightly different form. The normal process of conflict management is part of the process of decision modification.

Social conflict also aids group cohesiveness by providing an outlet for hostility. According to Theodorson (1962), a group must discover methods for venting hostility in order to gain and maintain even a moderate degree of cohesiveness. If the group develops norms which do not permit the expression of hostility, the group members either become apathetic or drop out as their deep-rooted negative feelings become ingrained. As group members shed their inhibitions about expressing negative feelings, they develop stronger ties to their group membership. One student group member, after a particularly fruitful meeting, experienced just such a reaction. Her diary contains her sentiments about what occurred during that meeting:

> We began to function as a group. Each of the individuals in the group expressed feelings. Before really talking about our topic, we only had some "small" talk. . . . There were real differences of opinion. . . . The group became more cohesive.
>
> I began to think of myself as a member of the group. I felt more at ease with the members in my group to the extent that I felt free to disagree.

The more inhibited the group members are in expressing their feelings, the greater the frustration they experience because of their suppressed conflict. And frustration leads directly to secondary tension. Thus, social conflict may in fact serve as a form of releasing social tension.

Conflict performs a catalytic function in developing the social organization of the group. North, Koch, and Zinnes (1960) emphasize the role of conflict in increasing a group's social organization, particularly the interdependence of group members. Dentler and Erikson (1959) go further to say that groups go so far as to induce, permit, and sustain deviant behaviors of members in order to develop a social organization. Deviant behaviors allow the group members to identify and strengthen their norms and other behavioral standards. As an analogy, a law on the books that is never violated and hence never enforced soon loses its strength and visibility as a law. It becomes a "blue law" without any impact on governing the behavior of the society's members.

The deviate also allows the group to focus on a concern common to all members—the deviate himself or herself—about whom something must be done. Since the deviate is of concern to the group as a whole and not to each member individually, the group's visibility becomes greater than any individual's self.

For these reasons, then, a group induces deviant behavior from one of its members when deviance does not occur through the initiative of one of the members. In order to maintain group solidarity and organization, the successful group not only permits deviant behavior but ensures that it is evident in the group interaction. The group is in trouble when members avoid or ignore deviant behavior. Recall that the socially successful group learns to confront problems head on by recognizing deviant behavior and doing something about it. It may be said now with some certainty that the cohesive group thrives on social conflict—or, in more memorable words, "The group that fights together stays together!"

### Influence on Productivity

Since this book deals with group decision making, its major concern is substantive conflict—intellectual opposition over ideas and issues. It seems paradoxical that a group whose members continually argue over ideas and issues can be very productive. But group productivity is measured in terms of the quality of its decisions and not by its efficient use of time. Obviously a group with substantive social conflict will utilize more time making decisions than a group without any conflict. But efficient utilization of time is not a characteristic of the group process anyway.

Substantive conflict leads directly to consensus owing to increased involvement of group members with their task performance. Beisecker (1969) discovered that as conflict over issues increases, group members tend to concentrate greater effort on those issues in order to bring about solutions. Hoffman, Harburg, and Maier (1962) discovered that conflict over ideas causes groups to search for more alternatives and thereby improve the quality of their group decisions. Conflict, then, serves as a stimulus to critical thinking and stimulates members to test their ideas. It logically follows that the issues that precipitate social conflict exert the greatest influence on the decisions which eventually achieve group consensus. And, since those issues have survived the critical tests of ideational conflict, the decisions are probably of higher quality.

All members of the group benefit from the critical exchange of ideas. Committed members who engage in substantive conflict quite obviously receive the rewards of stimulated critical faculties. The undecided members, the low participants, also gain information necessary to commitment through observing the committed members "fighting it out." The principle also is present in a political campaign. Uncommitted voters apparently make their decisions after hearing the partisan voters air all sides of the issues.

One student member of a classroom group maintained that she played the role of a deviate in her group for just this reason—to stimulate the uninvolved members of her group. She analyzed her own role in the following excerpt from one of her diaries:

> I am the negative force in the group, i.e., I *can't* agree with everything that is being said. Other members in the group don't agree with decisions but are *too polite to say anything!* I voiced my opinion both for the silent majority and for myself. Also, it was a means of manipulation to get things rolling. It worked! Without this, nothing would have been accomplished. The group members agreed with me after some discussion.

One of the problems that haunts every real-life decision-making group is the possibility of superficial or false consensus. That is, members agree on the final decisions but remain uncommitted to them. Hence, the decisions are never put into effect or are implemented only halfheartedly and consequently fail. Riecken (1952) found quite the opposite with decisions reached after uninhibited social conflict. Phillips and Erickson (1970, p. 77) also assert, "Once the public conflict has been played out in a democratic group and a consensus of policy and action has been derived there is a strong personal commitment on the part of the members that motivates them to act legitimately to implement group decisions rather than to subvert them." If members are committed enough to sustain social conflict over issues, they should remain committed once consensus is achieved. Superficial or false consensus is more likely to result from suppressed conflict than from expressed conflict.

## Influence on Consensus

If consensus is the goal of group decision making, it is important to note the influence of social conflict on consensus if we are to understand fully the influence of conflict on productivity. The most commonsensical response to the relationship between conflict and consensus is probably to think of conflict as the opposite of consensus. After all, conflict indicates incompatibility of actions, and consensus should reflect compatibility. When we think of consensus as the result or outcome of group decision making, conflict is probably opposed to consensus. On the other hand, if consensus is a process, conflict interaction may perform a valuable function during that process and lead to the successful outcome of group decision making.

Torrance (1957), investigating the relationship between group decision making and disagreement, provides evidence to suggest that conflict (in the sense of interaction sequences involving disagreement) is highly valuable in achieving consensus. Among other characteristics he discovered, he found that effective decision-making groups tend to exhibit a wide divergence of judgments expressed by their members. Certain members of these groups are apparently quite willing to oppose the opinions of others and to disagree whenever they feel that the situation requires it. The conclusion of Torrance's investigations provides a strong link between consensus and conflict. In fact, greater consensus is obtained when a group experiences a greater amount of disagreement during decision-making interaction.

The four-phase model of decision emergence, discussed in Chapter 5, supports Torrance's conclusions. You will recall that the conflict phase (the second) is one element in the process of successful group decision making. This phase contains significant amounts of disagreement and the formation of coalitions of members opposed to one another on the substantive issues of the task. The evidence appears sufficient to warrant the belief that social conflict (at least, substantive or ideational conflict) is an integral part of the process of achieving consensus in group decision making.

One problem in viewing the relationship between consensus and conflict may be a mistaken belief in the notion that consensus is somehow similar to cooperation. If that were true, conflict would be quite different from either consensus or cooperation. Horowitz (1962), on the other hand, suggests that a greater similarity exists between conflict and cooperation than between cooperation and consensus. He points out three basic differences between consensus and cooperation. Consensus indicates internal agreement, but cooperation does not include such an assumption. Consensus specifies agreement on the content of behavior (the substantive ideas), but cooperation means agreement only on the form of behavior. For example, we agree to disagree and thereby cooperate. Finally, cooperation requires that cooperating persons tolerate one another's differences, but consensus requires that any substantive differences should be abolished.

Whether Horowitz's analysis of consensus, conflict, and cooperation is accurate is not really the important issue. More significant is the fact that conflict interaction requires considerable cooperation. Of course, conflict may exist as a struggle within one specific group member. That is, a member may have ambivalent feelings toward an object or idea and simply hasn't formed a firm opinion. Or conflict may be bound to the situation in the sense of a struggle over scarce resources. For example, whole nations engage in conflict in order to ensure a supply of strategic products, such as petroleum or uranium. But conflict, in terms of interaction sequences, requires a certain amount of cooperation in order for it even to occur. When people are engaged in substantive conflict over ideas, they are engaged in communication with one another. In the process of communication, they are essentially cooperating with one another.

In group decision making, the parties to the conflict are united in their quest for a common goal. Typically that goal is consensus. When the United Auto Workers and General Motors engage in collective bargaining, they are involved in conflict interaction. At the same time, they are cooperating in order to realize their common goal—agreement on a new contract. Without that common goal, the United Auto Workers and General Motors would find little reason for interacting with each other. Nor would there be any reason for their conflict. Social conflict provides a strong influence on group productivity. Not only does it influence consensus, but it also reflects cooperative interaction among persons or groups that are oriented toward a common interest.

One final note on the influence of social conflict and deviance on productivity concerns the "assembly effect"—the nonsummativity of group members which distinguishes group decision making from that of its individual members working alone. Social conflict is one of those group elements which a decision-making individual is inherently incapable of replicating. Quite assuredly, social conflict—particularly realistic substantive conflict—contributes to the assembly effect. Without it, the group decision-making effort adds nothing to a lone individual performing the same decision-making task.

### Influence on Social Growth and Change

Viewing a social system from a process focus highlights the perpetual change which every social system undergoes through time. Our nation, for example, has experienced phenomenal growth and change within the brief two centuries of its existence. As conditions within and without the system change over the years, the social system adapts to those changes if it is to continue to exist. If any system is to keep up with the times, it cannot stagnate. Progress is essential. And progress can occur only through innovation. And innovation is, by definition, deviant from the traditional norms of the past.

Social growth and change are usually explained through the principle of feedback—a concept borrowed from the field of cybernetics. Feedback, as it functions in the form of interaction sequences, has been explained and illustrated in previous chapters—especially in Chapter 4. Social growth and change in a social system occur through the amplification of deviant behavior, that is, through positive feedback cycles. Negative feedback loops serve to counteract deviant behavior. The conflict phase of group decision making (discussed in Chapter 5) exemplifies the existence of negative feedback cycles, and those cycles begin to show their strength and effects during the emergence phase. The reinforcement phase includes many positive feedback cycles as they occur to further the commitment of group members toward the decision already made.

The normal process of managing conflict and deviance in group decision making undoubtedly involves the functioning of positive and negative feedback cycles. Perhaps the most critical factor in conflict management is the element of time. Attempts by group members to resolve conflict too quickly or to control deviant behavior prematurely are unfortunately shortsighted. As Tolar (1970) states, "No matter how conducive to conflict resolution circumstances are, after a certain critical phase in the dispute has been attained [perhaps the conflict phase of group decision making], further progress must await the passage of a 'respectable' amount of time."

Patience is a virtue of members in effective decision-making groups. This volume has continually emphasized the importance of allowing the natural process of group decision making to occur. Particularly in regard to managing social conflict and deviance, premature intervention in the natural process is more likely to be disruptive than beneficial. Decision-making groups which are burdened by undue time pressure or unrealistic deadlines are destined to make decisions that are below their capabilities.

The growth and change in any social system, including a decision-making group, are products of a natural process which requires the passage of time. Central to group development in both the social and task dimensions are the presence and effective management of social conflict and deviant behavior. Successful decision-making groups develop both appropriate positive and appropriate negative feedback mechanisms in order to manage social progress for the mutual benefit of all members of the system. Effective group decision making requires effective management (not suppression or, necessarily, resolution) of social conflict and deviance.

## THE "NORM" OF CONFLICT AND DEVIANCE

To call social conflict and deviance a "norm" appears to be a contradiction in terms. Deviant behavior is by definition contrary to group norms. But the perspective of group process must not be ignored. To view conflict and deviance as either constructive or destructive is to consider only the effects of conflict and to deny the process of conflict. Our concern with substantive or realistic conflict serving a positive function in the group, along with an understanding of communication and group process, allows the startling observation that conflict and deviance are normal and observable in group interaction patterns. That is, substantive realistic conflict and deviance are inevitably present in many phases of group interaction. Since they exist in nearly all groups and constitute a significant part of the group interaction, social conflict and deviance must be considered "normal."

### Idea Testing in Decision Making

Some conventional wisdom maintains that since group decision making is a cooperative venture (which it certainly is), arguments, disagreements, and conflicts over ideas should be avoided. But even if it were possible to avoid interpersonal disagreements, a highly unlikely event, such conventional wisdom is simply bad advice. Interaction during group decision making is a curious blend of persuasion, compromise, negotiation, argumentation, flexibility, and firmness of opinions. Issues are thrown into the hopper of group interaction and provide the raw materials for the group's final consensus decisions.

During group interaction, every idea, opinion, proposal, or suggestion contributed to the group is tested under fire. Involved members focus their critical abilities on these ideas and submit them to rigorous examination. During this process of critical discussion, some ideas are accepted; others are rejected; many are modified and combined with others. The eventual outcome of idea testing includes those decisions which achieve consensus. Because the group task is to achieve consensus on decisions, the critical exchange of opinions, ideas, and information is quite normal in the process of group interaction during decision making. A more detailed description of this process is included in Chapter 5.

### Formation of Coalitions

Within every social system of any size, subgroups form around some issue or idea. Subgroups typically form and maintain themselves because of some social conflict within the larger system. These groups within groups often command greater loyalty from their members than does the larger social system of which the subgroup is a part. Criminals in our society, for example, have a legendary code of conduct which the larger society apparently has been unable to break. "Honor among thieves" and the "code of silence" are familiar terms to describe this particular subgroup's norms. A small work group in a large organization also has greater influence on its members than the large organization does. In a university, for example, students and faculty alike often identify most closely with their affiliated departments. The students generally consider themselves communication majors, education majors, physics majors, or engineering majors first and members of the larger university community second.

The formation of subgroups is neither desirable nor undesirable to the larger social system. It is inevitable and should be fully expected as a normal occurrence. Too often subgroups, particularly those representing a minority, are ignored. The larger social system would do well to recognize their existence and take advantage of their apparent group strength.

Even a small group typically contains subgroups during the normal process of group decision making. Since the subgroup is usually temporary, a more appropriate term is "coalition." As such, a coalition is a temporary alliance, among two or more members of the group, oriented toward a difference of opinion regarding the means to achieve the group goal. Specifically, a coalition unites certain group members who agree with noncoalition members on the nature and value of the group goal but who disagree on how that goal can best be achieved. Such a coalition, then, involves social conflict and deviance over means but, typically, agreement on the goal itself.

Coalition formation emphasizes the importance of having a minimum of three members in the group. With only two members, social conflict is either destructive or unmanageable. Social conflict in a dyad (a two-member group) exists without deviance. There is no minority, no prevailing opinion upon which to base a norm. Thus, dyadic conflict is resolved typically by one member dominating the other. And dominance-submission relationships thwart the group process of idea testing during decision making. Any consensus following conflict in a dyad is destined to be false or superficial consensus.

With at least three members, two-one coalitions are possible. In a four-member group, several three-one and two-two combinations are possible coalitions. The five-member group is often viewed as the optimum size for small group decision making because of the numerous possibilities for coalition formation and management. But there is no hard and fast rule governing the number of members required in a small group as long as the minimum membership is three. As long as groupness can be achieved, no maximum limit is placed on the size of a small group.

Small group coalitions based on realistic and substantive conflict are generally temporary and revolve around a specific issue or group of issues. The normal process of achieving group consensus gradually merges the coalitions into the unitary whole of the group.

## The Leadership Paradox

Leadership is a most fascinating role in a small decision-making group. As a high-status member who is committed to the group, the leader is a strong conformist. Numerous research studies have illustrated the tendency of a leader to conform closely to group norms. The conformity of a leader has even found its way into the conventional wisdom of corny jokes. You are probably familiar with the story of the rotund little gentleman during the French Revolution who was observed huffing and puffing in the wake of a riotous mob. When asked why he was chasing after the mob, he replied innocently, "I have to follow them. I am their leader."

The humor, if there is any, of this little story stems from the paradoxical nature of the leader's role as both conformist and deviate. A leader functions as an innovator who aids the group's progress toward goal achievement. In times of crisis, the leader must find new directions contrary to traditional norms in order to maintain the group and save it from impending disaster. A leader who doesn't innovate is soon deposed in favor of someone who can. Thus the leader gains and maintains that role by functioning both as a conformist and as a deviate.

Several explanations account for this self-contradictory behavior of the group leader. Hollander (1958) has suggested perhaps the most plausible explanation. He describes gaining and maintaining leadership as an economic model whose central concept is "idiosyncrasy credits." In early stages of leader emergence, the leader conforms to the group norms and accumulates credits much as one deposits money in a bank account. Later, the leader who successfully exerts influence through innovative behavior is not regarded as a deviate, having accumulated sufficient credits to allow idiosyncratic behavior. In a sense, the leader withdraws credits from a bank account and cashes them in in order to innovate. According to Hollander, strict adherence to traditional group norms during periods of crisis is fatal to the leader's position and damaging to the group. Members perceive a leader who continues to conform in a stress situation as not knowing what to do and not helping the group achieve its goals.

Hollander's economic model of idiosyncrasy credits is a credible explanation for how a leader is able to deviate as well as conform. But the model should not be construed to imply that a leader innovates only during group crises. Indeed, a leader innovates through initiating themes and performing other leadership functions throughout group interaction. In fact, the leader must be recognized as an innovator before the crisis period so that the members expect innovative behavior and look to the leader for assistance.

If there were any doubts that deviant behavior is beneficial to a group, those doubts should not be dispelled. Maintaining the social organization of a group virtually demands deviant behavior. And the group demands deviant behavior not just from low-status members but from the highest-status member of all—the leader. Moreover, the leader's deviant behavior is not only beneficial; it is normal and to be expected.

## THE PROCESS OF SOCIAL CONFLICT AND DEVIANCE

To summarize, the LGD does not control its individual members' behaviors so much as it receives its organization and its very existence from the behaviors of individual persons. If behavioral standards and conformity to them develop through the process of group interaction, then behavior which deviates from those standards must also be integral to that same process. The periods in which deviant behavior occurs in the process and how the other group members respond to deviant behavior are extraordinarily important elements within the process of group interaction.

It is important to keep in mind that the process perspective inherently defines deviance and conflict instrumental to the group process as *behaviors* performed by members and not as roles occupied by one or more of the members. While role deviation may be present in a group, it has no significant impact on the pattern of group interaction. The process view, emphasizing the principle of interdependence, also stresses the interdependence of conformity and deviance and of cooperation and conflict in forming and maintaining groupness. As interdependent elements, they are viewed not as different processes but as different dimensions of a single process. And that process embodies all the communicative behaviors of all group members.

### Flight Patterns

Several independent studies of small group interaction have discovered what appears to be a phenomenon common to many groups. When confronted with social conflict within group interaction, members typically run away from it, that is, take flight in their interaction patterns. Bennis and Shepard (1956), for example, discovered that a period of social conflict will typically be followed by a period of interaction in which members avoid discussing the task. Gouran and Baird (1972) also found that group members tend to change the theme under discussion soon after a period of social disagreement.

Why a group's interaction pattern exhibits flight from social conflict can be explained in several ways. One explanation assumes that conflict and deviance are unpleasant stimuli that group members wish to avoid. But this explanation is not very plausible in that it smacks of ignoring a problem and hoping it will go away. Sooner or later the group members must face the problem and resolve, manage, or control the conflict. Such a view also alleges that members invariably view social conflict as destructive.

Berg (1967) would probably explain flight patterns not as avoidance of anything but as merely a reflection of the short attention span of groups. A third explanation would describe flight patterns as reflecting the normal process by which groups progressively modify decisions on their way to achieving consensus. Neither of these views assumes that conflict is inherently destructive or constructive.

Whatever the explanation for apparent flight patterns in group interaction, it is obvious that disagreement spawns more disagreement, at least temporarily, in brief flurries of social conflict. It is also apparent that groups do not overtly attempt compromise as their initial response to social conflict. Groups often perceive compromise to be an unsatisfactory solution to group conflict. The group's first response to conflict among its members is apparently to fight it out in frequent, albeit brief, periods of interaction and then abruptly cease consideration of that proposal.

**Innovative Deviance**

Robert K. Merton (1957, p. 140), a sociologist, has discussed several varieties of deviant behavior in social systems. His discussion of deviance suggests four different varieties, not all of which are beneficial to the successful functioning of the social system. In fact, three of his classifications of deviance are probably disruptive and harmful to effective functioning. What we have tended to consider "blind conformity" Merton describes as a form of deviance called "ritualism." The person who "conforms" blindly to social norms solely for the sake of conformity is a ritualist. Such a person merely goes through the motions of conformity without any real understanding or realization of why the norms are being followed.

Other forms of deviance in Merton's classifications include "retreatism" (a withdrawal from society, as a hermit or another "dropout" does). "Rebellion," another disruptive form of deviance, involves a rejection of the social system's values. Rebels seek to overthrow the existing social system and replace it with a new and presumably better one.

The lone form of deviance which appears to be most conducive to providing benefits to the social system is called "innovation." Innovators in a social system are those members who are quite committed to the goals of the system or group, but they believe that the socially approved means to achieve those goals need to be revised. Innovative deviance is, perhaps, the most common type of deviant behavior in the interaction patterns of group decision making. The silent or uncommitted member may be a retreatist. The member of a classroom group who wants to get an A but is concerned only with satisfying the instructor might represent a ritualist. Sean, the veteran who hated leaders (see Chapter 7, pages 224–225) would probably represent a rebel. Innovative deviance, according to Merton, involves behavior that reflects a rather strong commitment to the group in the form of an agreement with the goals of the group. The innovator, however, disagrees with the prevailing or majority view of the acceptable means for achieving that goal.

Valentine and Fisher (1974) utilized Merton's concept of innovative deviance as the basis for a system of interaction analysis. They attempted to observe more closely the sequence of group interaction in order to determine how deviant behavior functions during the process of group decision making. The results from their interaction analysis, though not conclusive, provide some interesting speculation about how innovative deviance functions to benefit the natural process of group decision making.

Oddly enough, Valentine and Fisher discovered that innovative deviance was not associated with any particular member or members. That is, nearly all members of the group contributed some innovation to the interaction. Moreover, no one or two members appeared to contribute significantly more innovatively deviant behaviors than other members. This phenomenon may not be true of all forms or deviance, but innovative deviant behavior is apparently a phenomenon of group decision making which is not necessarily associated with one or two particular members who would then be labeled as "deviants."

Valentine and Fisher also discovered that innovatively deviant behavior accounted for a rather significant proportion of the entire group interaction. An average of 27 percent of all communicative actions performed by group members was characterized as deviant behavior. Furthermore, all but 1.75 percent of deviant behavior was innovative deviance. Innovative deviance during group interaction appeared to be most acceptable during the conflict phase and, to a lesser extent, during the emergence phase of group decision making. On the other hand, such deviant behavior is probably detrimental to the group process during the formative stage of group development, the orientation phase, and during the final stage of reinforcement as the group nears consensus.

Valentine and Fisher also suggested that during the conflict and emergence phases, innovative deviance appears to stimulate further innovative deviance. That is, during the two middle phases of group decision making, the group members appeared to interact in bursts of social conflict and deviance. Such patterns of deviant behavior precipitating further deviant behavior seems to indicate the presence of positive feedback cycles. These cycles appear to stimulate further deviance, at least innovative deviance.

What does innovative deviance look like during group decision making? According to the interaction categories utilized by Valentine and Fisher, innovative deviance is in the form of a contradiction or rejection of an assertion. Continuing a disagreement initiated by others is also classified as an innovative deviant act, as is advocating a previously attacked assertion or negatively modifying another member's assertion. A statement that supports a previous innovatively deviant statement is also classified as innovative deviance.

While the greatest proportion of innovatively deviant behavior occurs in the intermediate stages of group interaction, innovative deviance is apparently also present throughout nearly all the group discussion. The only exception to this rule may be during the final phase of reinforcement. During the latter stages of group interaction as the group is achieving final consensus, virtually no deviant behavior of any kind is evident in the interaction sequences. This conclusion from Valentine and Fisher's study appears to confirm the earlier hypotheses that any temporary coalitions which have formed around the substantive issues appear to dissipate in a spirit of unity as the group nears its final goal—consensus.

Another result consistent with the analysis reveals that most innovatively deviant behaviors appear in the interaction before the majority position of the group is clearly established. That is, most innovative behavior occurs before consensus and is apparently instrumental in formulating that consensus. This discovery seems to affirm the belief, stated earlier, that conflict leads to consensus.

While innovative deviance may generate further deviant behavior, these spurts of deviant interaction are not sustained indefinitely. That is, decision-making groups interact in bursts of deviant behavior followed by periods of interaction in which little deviant behavior is present. After a period of nondeviant interaction, the members then engage in another spurt of deviant interaction patterns. These peaks and valleys of deviant interaction suggest patterns of "flight" behavior in which members appear to avoid deviance and social conflict after brief periods of deviant interaction. But the suggestion of the fight-flight pattern in group interaction does not necessarily indicate that group members typically avoid conflict and deviance. Rather, group members may be able to withstand only so much social conflict and deviance before they abruptly change the topic under discussion. The fact that group members are apparently not avoiding conflict is even more evident when one realizes that the group members invariably return to those topics which had earlier precipitated deviant behavior and social conflict.

Many innovatively deviant behaviors involve direct disagreement with the preceding assertion. This finding is consistent with the notion that members of a decision-making group typically "test ideas under fire" during the process of group interaction. We have previously discussed the importance of disagreement in the process of effective group decision making. Valentine and Fisher's analysis of interaction confirms the observation that group members do not avoid disagreement. Moreover, disagreement is certainly part of the normal process of group decision making.

The conclusion from Valentine and Fisher's investigation regarding the identification of members as deviants is worthy of further discussion. You will recall that the results from the interaction analysis indicated that nearly all members of the decision-making groups performed innovatively deviant behaviors. This conclusion emphasizes the fact that deviance, at least innovative deviance, is probably best defined in terms of behaviors. That is, innovative deviance is a "normal" and rather substantial proportion of group interaction. Furthermore, it is apparently not a role position occupied by one or two members within a group's network of roles.

Innovative deviance, as it affects the group process, is a function of the communicative behaviors of many members, not of an individual member's personality or self-concept. Therefore, deviance should be considered as normal to the process of group decision making and not as the province of a few "oddball" members. Innovative deviance is part of the normal communication performed by all group members who are committed to the group goals.

### Phases of Conflict

An additional investigation (Ellis and Fisher, 1975) attempted to observe conflict interaction during group decision making. The purpose of this study was to provide some insight into the potential of conflict for social integration, that is, for developing groupness. This particular investigation, utilizing interaction analysis, suggests the possibility that all group decision making can be classified into three phases of conflict interaction. The first third of the group interaction involves *interpersonal* conflict. The middle third of the interaction can be characterized as *confrontation*, and the final phase involves *substantive* conflict.

Ellis and Fisher describe the interpersonal conflict phase as resulting from the individual differences among the personalities of the group members. During the early stages of group decision making, the members have not had sufficient time to generate group-centered issues. Therefore, they involve themselves in conflict which is based on their identities more as unique human beings, than as group members.

The second phase of conflict, confrontation, includes interaction which tests ideas. Present in such interaction patterns are agreement and disagreement with specific decision proposals. In the sense that confrontation involves choosing up sides and fighting out the issues, it appears to pit one coalition of members against another. The second phase of conflict interaction probably includes both the conflict and emergence phases of group decision making.

The final phase of conflict interaction is characterized by the positive functioning of information in group interaction. Nearly all contributions by members involve statements directly addressing the issues and proposals which achieve group consensus. Substantive conflict clearly indicates effective management of social conflict or, at least, the outcome or result of effective conflict management during earlier phases of group interaction.

Ellis and Fisher point out the necessity for effective decision-making groups to devise conflict management techniques that are adapted to the specific kind of conflict which is occurring in the interaction. Certainly the tactics or strategies for managing interpersonal conflict differ significantly from tactics employed to manage confrontation or substantive conflict. The problem of managing interpersonal conflict is a lack of information about task issues. Therefore, more information, generated by all group members and directed at the group task or goal, will aid in effectively managing interpersonal conflict which arises during early group decision making.

On the other hand, confrontation results from the problem of integrating voluminous amounts of information. In other words, the members have generated so much information that they are having difficulty in determining which information is most credible and which information is less worthy. Whereas managing interpersonal conflict involves *generating* additional group-related information, managing confrontation involves *integrating* existing information. Effective decision-making groups are able to discern the difference among types of social conflict and to develop strategies or techniques for managing each particular type.

Conflict management thus requires different strategies at different times (that is, in different phases) during the group process. The importance of timing is again evident. More important than the question of *how* groups manage conflict is the question of *when* to use appropriate management techniques. The proper timing of these techniques involves recognizing the type of conflict present in the interaction and being sensitive to the different phases of the group process.

## ON MANAGING SOCIAL CONFLICT AND DEVIANCE

At this point in our discussion, we should all be aware that social conflict and deviance are not so much problems to be avoided or solved as they are normal characteristics of group decision making. Of course, these characteristics need to be controlled. We have consistently discussed the control of conflict as a problem of management rather than of resolution. The key to effective conflict management is to avoid evaluating conflict prematurely. That is, group members should be careful to avoid the natural human tendency to think of social conflict and deviance as harmful, disruptive, or simply "bad."

Effective conflict management requires, then, that group members reconstruct their thinking about social conflict and deviance with the purpose of treating conflict interaction as potentially beneficial or disruptive. The problem of management thus becomes the issue of how to maximize the benefits of constructive conflict and avoid the consequences of destructive conflict.

### When in Doubt, Confront

You will recall the earlier advice, given to members of decision-making groups, to confront any social problems which may occur during group interaction. The same advice is equally appropriate for managing social conflict and deviance. Avoiding any type of conflict is the most ineffective method of management. It is always better to do something about these problems, even though it is wrong, than to do nothing. If conflict and deviance are so prevalent in group interaction (as previous investigations lead us to believe), avoidance will not make them go away. They will simply be uncontrolled.

One of the most common problems in group decision making is the presence of the deviant member. The typical member who is labeled "deviant" is probably not an innovative deviant but one who is disrupting the normal process of group decision making. In classroom decision-making groups, one of the most typically noninnovative deviants is the member who is consistently absent from group meetings. Groups soon learn to confront this problem by effectively dismissing the absent member from the group. One member's reactions, written after a group meeting, typifies this strategy: "Brenda was absent again. We have sort of unofficially dismissed her as a member. We also discovered that absence makes you have to 'prove' your membership at the next meeting." The absent member, undoubtedly a role deviant, is simply excluded as a credible member of the group. Such a member is later required to "prove" membership in the group during subsequent interaction.

The opinion deviant requires quite different management tactics. One such member of a classroom group expressed her feelings toward being an opinion deviant in her group when she wrote in her diary, "I really felt like an outsider. I argued for my suggestions only until I realized they were getting rebuffs from the others." The other group members confronted this opinion deviant in a subsequent group meeting and told her, "You have irritated some of the members with your constant criticisms." In her reactions to that same meeting, the deviant wrote, "My reaction was, 'They think *they* were annoyed. Let me tell them about annoyed!' But I said nothing. And my hostility was smoothed when they opened up and explained their feelings. We discussed our conflict, and I felt more a part of the group." Confronting the opinion deviant is not an easy task for the other group members. But the typical outcome of such a strategy is typically a more cohesive and ultimately more productive group.

One unique strategy in dealing with clearly deviant members was employed in another classroom group with extremely successful results. Apparently the deviant member was annoying the rest of the group. He would criticize the ideas of other members but could contribute no ideas of his own. The other members perceived him as being an ultranegative member but not a very constructive one. One of the members decided on her own that the best strategy for confronting the deviant with his own behavior was to role-play his deviance during an entire group meeting. She interacted as though she were the deviant throughout the entire meeting and said nothing to him about what she was doing.

In the next meeting several days later, she informed the deviant what she had done. Her written reactions to that meeting indicated her feelings: "I confronted the member I disliked with just that. I told him I had stolen his role at the last meeting to give him the feeling of despair and put him into another role which forced more responsibility on him. I like to be deviant. It's much less work to just sit back and oppose everyone's ideas then to create ideas of your own. But I will assume my regular position from now on because I put over my point."

The deviant was clearly "taken back" by this move. Nevertheless, it proved highly successful. In fact, his reactions to the meeting during which he was informed of the role-playing episode, indicated how successful the strategy really was. He wrote, "I feel closer to [the member who did the role playing] in that because of our conflict and interaction we have developed a more meaningful group relationship." And how did the other group members feel about this role-playing strategy? They wrote in their reactions to that same meeting: "I think we were able to discuss our task much better." "There is and was much tension. We accomplished a lot." "I felt very much a part of what was going on."

Confronting the deviant member by demonstrating his deviant behavior in this role-playing move should be considered only one way of dealing with noninnovative deviance. But in this particular instance, it was certainly a technique that worked. It was successful in improving the group's social and task dimensions. It was also successful in bringing the deviant into the group as an effective and committed member. And it was effective for the other group members as well. The most important element of the role-playing strategy, however, was not necessarily that it worked, but that it involved a direct confrontation of a social problem that was affecting negatively the effective functioning of the group's decision-making efforts.

### When All Else Fails (but Not Before), Compromise

This principle of effective conflict management may be stated too strongly. Compromise is not always to be avoided at all costs. Rather, compromise should be considered most effective as a last-resort measure. The problem with compromise is not that it is harmful but that we tend to think of it first as the best possible solution to social conflict. After all, compromise is somehow democratic. Even though such a belief may appear to make common sense, it does not work in practice. Remember that in a compromise, everyone loses. The typical outcome of a compromise, therefore, is some residue of dissatisfaction felt by all participants.

We tend to think of compromise as reaching agreement by each party's giving in a little bit. More often, however, compromise results in a superficial consensus—that is, an agreement with little commitment. One classroom group arrived at agreement on the basis of a compromise. The group members appeared to leave the group with a feeling of satisfaction over their decision. Their reactions to the compromise, however, reflected little satisfaction. One member wrote, "We went back and forth . . . without reaching accord. A compromise was in need. I gave in as much as possible, and she just gave in. Not a harmonious compromise, but tolerable." The other party to the compromise reacted, "I tried to get a group discussion going, . . . but they weren't really interested in what I had to say. Finally I gave up and decided to agree with them so that we could get our task accomplished. Maybe I should have persisted longer, but I don't think it would have done any good."

This compromise consisted of one member's acquiescing or giving in to the other—a one-sided compromise. The result was a superficial consensus. There was agreement, to be sure. But there was no consensus on the decision.

You probably are thinking, at this point, that this classroom group did not really compromise. The weaker member merely gave up. But a compromise generally refers to a give-and-take process involving both sides to the conflict. Another classroom group may serve to illustrate such a compromise. Each side gave in to the other. One member described his reactions to one of the group meetings in the following self-disclosing message: "I became aware of the positive aspects of compromise in the group decision-making process. Before, I resented having to be satisfied with anything except my original idea. I now realize that in order to come to any sort of group conclusion, compromise is primary. Individual pride or desire is secondary."

From this single member's reactions to the compromise, one would probably conclude that compromise was quite successful in this particular group. However, another member in that same group reacted to the compromise quite differently: "In all honesty, I thought that the other group members' ideas were unfounded. I felt that I was acquiescing to their desires in order to maintain group cohesiveness—even though I felt they were wrong." A third member felt similarly: "Since we were again running out of time, I had to consent with the compromise we reached. The thing I should have realized is that we are not really a group in the sense that we all come to decisions together. I really feel they are wrong when I say things. But now I have become more silent."

In both cases, superficial consensus was the outcome of the compromise. In the first case, superficial consensus resulted from one member's giving up and giving in to the other. In the second, superficial consensus resulted from each member's giving in a little bit. But both members were dissatisfied with the result, even though at least one member of the group felt that the compromise worked beautifully. Such dissimilarity among the members in their reactions or perceptions of the group outcome indicates a rather low level of groupness and a somewhat superficial consensus.

Is compromise always an ineffective strategy for managing social conflict? Does compromise always result in superficial consensus? Probably not. The problem is not that compromise is necessarily ineffective or undesirable, because it is neither one in all cases. Rather, the problem is the all-too-common belief that compromise is nearly always effective or desirable. It is probably more accurate to consider compromise to be an if-all-else-fails strategy for managing conflict. One should avoid thinking of compromise as the first or the most desirable means for managing social conflict.

### Some Direct Tactics

We have previously examined the role of the group productivity observer. The observer, you will recall, is a role assigned to one of the group members for the purpose of highlighting elements of the group process and bringing them to the group for explicit discussion. The observer reports his or her observations and analysis to the group on a regular basis, typically at the end of each group meeting. The group productivity observer may also be assigned the task of pointing out areas of social conflict and deviance, or the task of suggesting guidelines and recommendations to the group as to the most appropriate tactics for dealing with conflict and deviance.

Assigning such a role places extreme pressure and responsibility on a single member. The observer must be frank and honest with the other group members. Moreover, the observer, in order to function effectively, must be an extremely capable and interpersonally sensitive person with a comprehensive understanding of communication and the group process. Assigning one of the members to the observer's role requires that the members heed the advice and trust in the credibility of the observer. To assign a member such a highly responsible role and then ignore her or his advice is effectively to avoid, rather than manage, the problems of social conflict and deviance.

Another strategy that is often used as a normal part of group deliberations is to reserve a few minutes at the beginning or end of each meeting for specific discussions analyzing the group process. Spending a few moments in evaluating the group process enables the members to uncover immediately any problems that may be confronting the group (including those that may involve conflict or deviance). In one way, this strategy is tantamount to making every member of the group an observer of the group process. The purpose is to sensitize all group members to be on the lookout for any problems that may be hindering the group in performing its task effectively and efficiently.

A free and open discussion of the group process is often a preventive measure. That is, the members may be prepared to discuss a problem when it is in its formative stages. But when social problems become severe and tensions rise too high, the members often feel inhibited. Any discussion of the problem at that point is much more difficult and typically less effective.

Several elements of the group process can serve as the focus of such group discussions. For example, the group members may set aside one analytical discussion to address the issue of "hidden agendas," or issues which have been suppressed during the task interaction. The analytical discussion is thus an attempt to bring such issues into the open and confront them directly. A hidden agenda typically loses its force when it is recognized. The disruptive nature of a hidden agenda rarely lies in the severity of the issue but is typically perceived to be more serious than it actually is, precisely because it is hidden and not addressed directly.

Such a discussion also may address directly any interpersonal resentments or feelings of discomfort in individual members. Often members suppress these feelings of interpersonal discomfort when deliberating task-related issues. In addition, such analysis might include an overt discussion of the informal roles of the group members as the roles are in the process of development. In fact, your group may find it beneficial to devote an entire group meeting to such a discussion.

There are no hard and fast rules or tactics for how to manage social conflict and deviance. Effective decision-making groups develop specific strategies for specific problems. Any move that the group members feel will allow them to confront and recognize potentially disruptive elements is effective. The key is always to confront rather than to avoid, to recognize rather than to suppress any problem affecting the group process.

## Believe That It Works

Students often discuss with one another the relative value of certain instructors of classes in which they are enrolled. Instructors do the same thing regarding their students. After several years of teaching classes in group decision making, I discovered that I had fond memories of some classes but tended to forget other classes almost immediately. The classes I remember most are the "good" classes—the classes which were "fun" to teach. The one characteristic that all these classes seem to have in common is the prevalence of argument between students and instructor. Students in the "good" classes always seem to be critical, to be skeptical of what their instructor tells them. Each meeting of the class seems to be an active attempt to "get" the instructor.

I have found that most of my students appeared to exercise their greatest critically analytical powers and skepticism when they encountered anything carrying the name "Fisher." The bulk of the criticism which I recall centered on this notion that social conflict and deviance can be beneficial to the group's decision-making efforts. When I employed the slogan "The group that fights together, stays together" (and its later form, "The group that fights, unites"), the students were highly skeptical.

Nothing has been more satisfying to me, as an instructor, than the skeptical students' discovery—for themselves and as a direct result of their skepticism—that the slogans are quite appropriate. I experience this feeling of satisfaction, not because I was "right" and they were wrong," but because the students developed, through their own experience, an understanding and utilization of their knowledge of the group process. One member of a particularly "good" (i.e., skeptical and critical) class wrote in her final group member's diary, "I have enjoyed being a member of my group. I found it quite amazing that no matter how hard we tried to disprove your research, we couldn't."

It is quite painful to confront social problems, to meet social conflict and deviance head on. Without a strong conviction that your confrontation will yield a beneficial result, you will never undertake it in the first place. Moments of confrontation are socially uncomfortable. They elicit a surge of social tension, often rising to an intolerably high level. Confronting social problems frequently brings on feelings and expressions of discomfort and even hostility—feelings which are quite unpleasant, to say the least. Group members simply must develop an attitude of "We shall overcome" in order to be able to live through the uncomfortable interpersonal feelings of high social tension.

Central to that attitude is a belief in the beneficial results which will accrue. You simply must have faith that confrontation works, or you won't do it. Moreover, once you have started to confront, you must continue and carry through the confrontation. To repeat, confronting other members and social problems requires your conviction that a desirable outcome will eventually compensate for the uncomfortable period of undesirable social tension.

I have saved for years the diaries or members' written reactions to specific group meetings during the classes in group decision making I have taught. As you can tell, I have tended to quote from them rather freely throughout this book. One particular diary was really a message to the instructor. Naturally enough, this diary is one of my favorites and brings back fond memories of numerous arguments during classroom interaction. The student wrote:

> Do you like fairy-tale endings? Our group is in a state of shock, mingled pleasantly with delight and enthusiasm. . . . Conflict rode high. We clashed, resolved and emerged. . . . I have enjoyed the class and the group. Much against our wishes, we have had to admit that the conflict helped and developed us. Hot damn Fisher was right

## SUMMARY

The right of dissent in our society is one of our most cherished privileges, although conformity, inescapable and inevitable, is more often the rule. Conformity to behavioral standards of a social system implies not only uniformity of behavior but uniformity based on conflict among alternatives and avoidance of unpleasant social pressures. Pressures toward conformity in the small group are extraordinarily severe, although a deviating member gains strength to resist such pressures by having publicly committed himself or herself to a deviant position or when another member agrees with that deviant position.

Many people in our society are ambivalent about social conflict and deviance and often view the social system as functioning in a delicate balance of supportive and disruptive forces. Thus, conflict may be seen as existing within one person, between two or more persons, within the same social system, or between social systems. Social conflict is also classified as affective or substantive—emotional or intellectual.

When a perfect or ideal social system is assumed, social conflict appears as a failure of the social system and as inherently destructive. Others who adopt a functionalist approach perceive social conflict and deviance as often performing desirable, constructive, and even essential functions instrumental to the effective operation of the social system. If conflict is destructive, it must be resolved or controlled. On the other hand, constructive conflict must be understood and managed in order to achieve its social benefits. The multifaceted nature of social conflict and deviance dictates the emphasis on interpersonal, substantive conflict serving constructive functions for the small group.

Social conflict and deviance perform many functions beneficial to the group process. Conflict furthers group cohesiveness and increases productivity. Innovative deviant behavior is essential for progress as the group grows and changes through time. Groups manage deviant behavior through counteracting it with negative feedback loops or amplifying it through positive feedback cycles.

Realistically, social conflict and deviance are so common to the process of group development that they are considered normal within the group process. A decision-making group invokes social conflict as members test ideas in a critical exchange of information and opinions. Coalitions form temporarily around conflicting ideas before typically merging as the group achieves consensus. And the leader, paradoxically enough, normally conforms to and deviates from group norms in the process of gaining and maintaining leadership status.

Verbal innovative deviance, an agreement on group goals but disagreement on means to achieve them, is suggested as an insight into the ongoing process of social conflict in group interaction patterns. Verbal innovative deviance seems to account for a significant proportion of group interaction and appears in clusters or spurts of deviant behavior with normal periods of group flight behavior. Normally, only innovative deviant behaviors exert a significant impact on group interaction patterns and are generally distributed among all involved group members.

Different types of conflict occur during the process of group decision making. Social conflict may be interpersonal, confrontative, or substantive, depending upon the phase of group decision making in which it appears. Consequently, strategies for managing conflict and deviance during the group process vary considerably. Nevertheless, some general tactics for conflict management are possible. These strategies include confronting the conflict issue or deviant, avoiding compromise "solutions," and believing in the eventual positive functions of conflict.

# Chapter 9

# Improving Effectiveness
# of Communication
# and the Group Process

Some of you may have turned to this chapter and its pretentious title with the expectation that Fisher was about to give you the formula for being an effective group member. If so, you are in for a rude surprise. On the other hand, having read the previous chapters, you should have concluded that effective communication and group process rely less on the learning of techniques than on a comprehensive understanding of the dimensions of such a complex process. It is no coincidence that this chapter is one of the final chapters in the book. I assume that you have mastered the earlier discussions and can claim some understanding of communication and the group process. That understanding is absolutely prerequisite to attempting to improve your effectiveness.

Improving your effectiveness of human communication is, unusually enough, extraordinarily complex. The average human being probably spends more time engaged in communication than any other activity. One might be tempted to believe that such practice should make perfect. Therefore, the years of communicative experience behind each of us should render the adult human a highly effective communicator. Such an expectation is catastrophically false. To the contrary, people probably perform no human activity less effectively than the act of communicating with one another.

Developing effective communication within a group is no small chore. There are no sure-fire principles of effective communication, no magical formulas for maximizing cohesiveness or productivity. There are no models to follow, no lists of things to do and things not to do in order to be an effective group member. All such lists of prescriptive "good advice" do little more than give the participant the impression of doing a good job without actually increasing the effectiveness of either the individual or the group. If the truth were admitted, this entire book serves the purpose of this chapter. Knowledge and understanding of communication and the group process do more to increase one's communicative effectiveness than all the prescriptive advice now available.

Improving the effectiveness of group communication is not achieved through direct methods but indirectly through increased understanding. Personal health provides a figurative comparison of the principle of indirect methods for increasing communicative effectiveness. Health is essentially a process of living normally from day to day. Certainly health should not be defined as taking medicines when you get sick. If you know and understand the biological processes of the body, you will be guided as to what activities to perform, what foods to eat, what clothing to wear, what situations to avoid, and so forth. Such activity becomes part of your normal routine of living and is more effective than attempting to abide by some prescriptive advice allegedly leading to lifelong health.

In the same way, knowledge and understanding of communication and the group process provide a frame of reference which guides the effective member's activity as a group member. Each member analyzes what behaviors are appropriate to maximize group effectiveness and adjusts his or her behavior accordingly. In short, the healthy person is not the one who devours patent medicines and pops daily vitamin pills in order to achieve better health. Rather, the healthy person understands the principles of good physical health and lives accordingly. The same is true of the effective group member. That person knows that there are no shortcuts to effective communication other than serving a lengthy apprenticeship of learning and experience.

## SOME COMMON MISCONCEPTIONS

Dozens of textbooks and popular paperbacks expound the "ten easy steps" to just about everything, including effective communication. There are numerous "cures" suggested for ailing groups and tried-and-true "vitamin supplements" to achieve successful communicative outcomes.

Many of these lists of principles of do's and don'ts are reasonable and often quite true. But such lists are typically so general as to defy any practical application in any specific group situation. Even well-meaning lists are quite unsatisfactory; and many lists of principles are patently deceptive and based on gross misconceptions about communication and the group process. It is unfair to describe these two kinds of "good advice" as similar, but the results obtained from using either type of list to guide one's communicative behavior range from none to insignificant. Consequently, all such lists are rejected as quite unsatisfactory. I shall continue to insist that a full understanding of communication and the group process, however, requires obtaining knowledge and avoiding misconceptions. Hence, the following discussion includes a few of the popular, but nonetheless misleading, misconceptions about group communication.

### Rationality

One popular approach used in the training of participants for effective group communication has included the principles of argumentation. Many textbooks based on this approach include sections on the various types of reasoning and procedures for testing the validity of arguments. Chapters illustrate the various kinds of evidence used to support assertions, such as statistics, examples, analogies, and testimony, including the various tests of quality and quantity of evidence. Such training is, of course, extremely valuable and may be helpful indirectly to the prospective member of a decision-making group. Certainly training in argumentation develops one's ability to think critically, and critical thinking ability is an asset to idea testing—an integral part of the group's decisional process. But courses in mathematical logic also develop critical thinking abilities. Such training is simply not central to group decision making and detracts from the primary purpose of understanding communication and the group process.

The basis for most prescriptive advice for discussants, including training in principles of argumentation, is the pervasive assumption of rationality. That assumption rests on two faulty premises. The first premise asserts that whatever is rational is best. On the face of it, such an assertion seems eminently reasonable. But the assertion is not necessarily true. If we believed that the best decision making proceeds on purely rational grounds, juries would not exist. Defendants would be tried before only a judge who is trained in the law and in the doctrine of rationality. But extenuating circumstances often surround an alleged crime and require the presence of juries and nonrational means of decision making. We often speak respectfully of the "spirit" as well as the "letter" of the law.

If rationality were always the most desirable basis for making decisions, no religion or code of ethics or any moral value would be desirable. Such principles or values exist only through nonrational belief—a belief based not on reason but on faith. The philosophy of logical positivism assumed the supremacy of rationality and proved highly unsatisfactory for most people. After all, there isn't any rational basis for the confusion of people with the same names, such as Jim Smith. It would be more rational for each member of our society to be known by only an identifying and unduplicated number. (When you stop to think about it, we seem to be getting closer to that point all the time.) Democracies and representative forms of government would be replaced with governments ruled by benevolent despots. We would no longer have "hunches," and progress would virtually cease if rationality were considered the sole basis for decision making. Certainly this first premise cannot be long sustained.

A second premise assumes that humans normally behave rationally. That is, reason typically guides human actions. Such an assumption is patently absurd. Instances of wholly normal but nonrational behavior are too numerous to include more than a very few. Take the case of the necktie. There is no contemporary reason for wearing a necktie, but men do it nevertheless. Women's skirts and nylon hosiery are equally unreasonable. The desire to conform to social norms of personal appearance is certainly nonrational. Today we shudder at the unreasonable personal-appearance norms of past cultures. We are appalled at the former Chinese custom of binding young girls' feet so that they would remain small in adulthood—so small that the women could not even walk by themselves. We consider as totally unreasonable the customs of some "primitive" tribes to elongate earlobes and pierce noses to conform to their norms of personal beauty. Some future generation will probably think the same of our neckties, eye makeup, false eyelashes, long hair, and bouffant hairdos. And who can consider war, riots, hatred, poverty, pollution, prejudice, and vandalism rational? Certainly much, if not most human behavior is not rational. Sometimes it appears even irrational.

Chapter 4 indicated that even the process of information processing during group decision making is nonrational at times. Members of small groups, like members of all social systems, do not always behave in conformity to the laws or principles of reason. These behaviors do not imply that humans necessarily behave in conflict with laws of rationality, but they do suggest that one does not always have sound reasons for one's behaviors. A person who behaves on the basis of faith is not necessarily *ir*rational but is inherently *non*rational.

Proponents of rationality often admit that human behavior is not always rational, but they believe it should be. After all, they say, what harm can training in argumentation do to prospective group participants? The answer is deceptively simple. Training in argumentation obviously benefits the individual person. The ability to think critically is potentially valuable for everyone. The greater problem is the assumption of rationality underlying such training as requisite to effective group participation.

If rationality imposes demands on the group beyond the capabilities of its individual members, the members become frustrated, tensions rise uncontrollably, and the natural group process is disrupted. Relying too heavily on rationality disregards the socioemotional dimension of the group process while exalting the task dimension and thereby denies the inherent interdependence of the two dimensions. Such an assumption also assumes the existence of a "best" decision—that is, the most "rational" one.

Perhaps most important, empirical evidence indicates that the natural group process tends to persist even in the presence of such assumptions. Groups whose members have been trained in the methods of argumentation typically behave normally, that is, nonrationally, anyway.

### Agendas and Forms of Analysis

Some readers of this book will be disappointed not to find a model agenda which systematically guides the group members to consensus decisions. The agenda is generally used as a road map to follow in order to improve efficiency and quality of group decision making. The typical model agenda is an adaptation or a variation of Dewey's reflective-thinking model for problem solving.

In addition to the objections raised concerning the assumption of rationality and the corresponding deemphasis of the socioemotional dimension of group development, relying on agendas or models to guide group interaction is unsatisfactory for other reasons. The desire to improve efficiency of group decision making may be misplaced. We should probably admit that groups are inefficient as decision-making mechanisms, but the reasons for that apparent inefficiency are precisely the same reasons for group decisions being of higher quality compared to decisions made by individuals when the decision-making task is adapted to group decision making. Social testing of ideas and reinforcing group decisions make group decision making slow. But the result of group slowness is more effective implementation of group decisions.

Probably the greatest reason to dismiss the use of agendas is that they just don't work. Carl Larson (1969) found that groups instructed in some forms of analysis developed group products which were superior in some respects to those of uninstructed groups. However, the groups Larson observed were allowed to interact over a very brief period of time, highly insufficient to develop much groupness. This severe restriction of time quite obviously short-circuited the natural group process and required the members to utilize shortcut methods to arrive at decisions within the specified time.

Maier and Thurber (1969), on the other hand, discovered that when members are allowed sufficient time to establish groups, forces within the group effectively counteract the influence of external sources, which would include the use of an agenda. Thus, when the natural group process is allowed to run its full course, the influence of an agenda or prescribed form of analysis is minimal and superseded by the information-processing norms developed within the group.

Interestingly enough, Larson compared several different forms of analysis and found that Dewey's reflective-thinking model did not significantly affect the group product. On the other hand, Sharp and Milliken (1964) found that groups whose members had been trained to think reflectively did achieve superior outcomes. The results of using this particular model, then, appear to be ambiguous. Whether Dewey's model has a significant impact on group decisions remains questionable. But both these studies observed only groups who were not allowed sufficient time to establish themselves as groups. The influence of the natural group process would probably counteract the influence of any external agenda, regardless of its particular form.

Other more general comparisons of groups, such as Lanzetta and Roby's (1960), have demonstrated that prior prescriptive training of one type or another does not exert a significant impact on group effectiveness. But Hall and Williams (1970) compared groups whose members differed in the extent of their understanding of the group process and the general functioning of group decision making. Those groups whose members possessed knowledge of group dynamics were observed to be most effective. Members' understanding and experience in communication and the group process may be an indirect method of improving group effectiveness, but it does seem to work. The more direct method of using model agendas or prescribed forms of analysis to keep group members "on the track" cannot make that same claim.

## PRINCIPLES OF EFFECTIVENESS

The cardinal principle underlying effective group communication involves experience. There is no substitute for the experience of being an active participant in the process of group decision making. More experiences and a greater variety of group experiences will lead inevitably to more effective group participation. Understanding the process is a vital prerequisite to effective participation in group decision making, but the experience of participating is equally essential. Reading books on how to play chess will not make you an expert chess player. Neither will reading a book on group communication make you an effective group participant.

The adage "practice makes perfect" should be amended to specify that the practice be based on understanding. Group members who are naive about the nature of communication and the group process are able to increase their effectiveness as participants only up to a certain point, regardless of how many group experiences they have had or will have. Understanding communication and the group process heightens the value of the experience of being a group member. Conversely, group experience heightens one's understanding of communication and the group process. Experience and understanding influence each other, mutually and reciprocally, in the classic relationship of interdependence. The principles that follow are admittedly quite general. But they are intended to illustrate the extent of that interdependence, rather than merely to provide a convenient list of things to do and things to avoid doing.

## IMPROVING EFFECTIVENESS: INTRAPERSONAL FACTORS

Probably the first place to begin the search for improvement of effectiveness is with oneself—the individual group member. Because every person is, in some respects, a unique human being, it is difficult to discuss the idiosyncracies of the members of any decision-making group. On the other hand, some general principles related to the attitudes and values which are typical of members of effective groups can be isolated. Although most of these principles should be familiar and obvious at this point, I shall continue to expose the obvious rather than run the risk of overlooking it.

### Attitudes toward the Group

The psychological "set" or orientation to the group and to other group members is vitally important to the success and effectiveness of group decision making. Rarely do such attitudes exist before the formation of the group, however. Rather, members develop a certain orientation to the group and to other members during the process of group development. If a member does possess an attitude before the group is formed, an attitude which is conducive to effective group process, that orientation is probably one of open-mindedness. That is, the member enters the initial group meetings without prematurely having decided whether the group experience will be undesirable. This state of open-mindedness will also involve a considerable amount of interpersonal sensitivity in which the member is sensitive and open to the beliefs and feelings of others. Such an interpersonal sensitivity persists even though the beliefs and ideas of the others are quite dissimilar from those of the interpersonally sensitive member.

I have consistently stressed the principle of commitment in the sense of group consensus and cohesiveness. Individual members who are committed to the group experience a strong feeling of loyalty to it. That is, members believe in the potential effectiveness of the group process to the extent that they will sublimate their own goals in favor of those of the group. Commitment requires a belief that the group process will fulfill the goals of the individual and that group membership will provide benefits which are important to the individual.

An attitude of commitment, then, would be inconsistent with a desire to manipulate or control other group members or to get the other members to come around to your way of thinking. The committed group member, in a sense, sacrifices his or her own self-concept for the good of the group. In this respect, by way of analogy, the athletic coach refers to certain athletes as good "team players" and others as "gunners," "hot dogs," or "prima donnas."

With the attitude of commitment toward the group comes a feeling of responsibility. The committed group member is willing to expend time and energy for the benefit of the group. Often members of classroom groups will excuse themselves from contributing very much to the group effort by citing other considerations (for example, a part-time job, time required for other classes, not the student's major, only three credits earned in the class). But the group member, if committed, feels a sense of responsibility and will find the time and expend the effort for the group.

Without that feeling of responsibility, most group members will be content to avoid becoming heavily involved in the group effort. They are very willing to let some other member of the group assume most of the responsibility and do most of the work. The committed member goes out of his or her way to volunteer for additional responsibility and does not wait to be asked. The committed member is a responsible member. Effective decision-making groups enjoy a virtual competition among members who are actively participating in the group efforts.

### Attitudes toward Interaction

A member who is committed to the group is never a silent member. Regardless of any personality traits (such as shyness or apprehension), the committed group member simply cannot remain a low participant. Indeed, such members find that they cannot remain silent on issues which confront the group. Outside the group, however, the person may remain silent even when being negatively evaluated as an individual. Group loyalty is typically stronger in affecting the amount of interaction of individual members than other aspects of the individual's own self.

A classroom group of a few years ago exemplifies the problem of the uncommitted member whose attitude toward the group carries over into his or her participation in the group interaction. This particular group was engaged in discussing the current practice of evaluating the courses and instructors in the university. The group suffered from a woefully inadequate amount of information concerning the topic, an inadequacy which was reflected in its report of its task accomplishments. Knowing that the student association of the university was performing a lengthy and comprehensive analysis of the evaluation forms and recognizing that one of the group members was involved in the department's student advisory committee, I asked him whether he was aware of the universitywide study of course-evaluation techniques. His reply went something like this: "Of course I know about it. But this bunch of turkeys in this group wouldn't know what to do with the information, anyway. They already had their minds made up. I thought I would just let them hang themselves." Only a member with a very low level of commitment to the group would have expressed an attitude of so little responsibility and remained so inactive in the group's interaction.

A member who is committed to the group shares the responsibility for the group's decisions. The apathetic member engages in little conflict with other members. The committed member will argue vociferously. Commitment makes the member willing to challenge the ideas of others, willing to confront social problems, willing to evoke the hostility of others, in order to ensure that the group makes the best possible decision.

The willingness of committed members to express their feelings and ideas forcefully and engage in argument with other members during group interaction renders them susceptible to the risk of being proved wrong. A member with less commitment will either give up a position quickly— taking the attitude of "What difference does it make?"—or will continue to maintain a position long after it has become untenable. In either case, such a person exhibits more interest in an individualistic self-concept than in the group outcome.

Chapters 5 and 8 have discussed the tendency of successful groups to engage in considerable disagreement and social conflict over task-oriented issues. Although conflict can be considered an effective format for the critical testing of ideas, the willingness of the individual members to engage in conflict may be more important to the effectiveness of group decision making. Why would anyone engage in conflict interaction and run the risk of being wrong unless one is concerned about the group and its successful outcome? For most people, argument with friends or peers is relatively painful and socially uncomfortable. But for conflict to exist and to result in successful task performance, group members must be willing to participate in conflict. For this reason we normally think of the cohesive group as a group that is not afraid to experience conflict, to overcome conflict, and to remain cohesive despite the potentially disruptive influence of conflict.

With a social climate that is less conducive to expressing conflict, members feel inhibited. Consequently, the level of cohesiveness in that group and its ultimate effectiveness in performing its decision-making task suffer. The committed member is thus willing not only to express his or her own point of view but also to encourage the expression of other viewpoints. The result is a free and open attitude toward group interaction. Unruly? Yes. Disruptive? Potentially. But more important, such attitudes toward interaction lead to more effective communication and group decision making.

### Creativity

Although there is obviously a point of diminishing returns, the greater the volume of ideas and decision proposals which members contribute during group interaction, the higher the quality of consensus decisions. Also, leaders initiate a large number of themes during group interaction, as discussed in Chapter 7. Each of these two findings implies that one ingredient of communicative effectiveness is creativity. As a participant in group decision making, then, you would be well advised to increase your creative capacity. Let your mind go. Give your imagination a free rein. No relevant idea should be considered too irrational or too farfetched. The best advice for developing creativity is not to stifle the formation of ideas.

Certainly groups do not accept all ideas which members contribute during group interaction. In fact, the more ideas the members contribute, the more ideas the group will reject. Indeed, the period of idea testing during group interaction, particularly during the conflict phase, involves the rejection of many decision proposals. But this is the period during which members should be encouraged to contribute new ideas, too.

Members who do not fully comprehend the nature of group process will probably consider the group's rejection of their ideas a rejection of their selves, a rejection of their value as group members. Consequently, such members tend to inhibit their creative impulses, and this restraint leads to their contributing fewer ideas. Brainstorming techniques, recognizing this human tendency, do not allow brainstorming members to respond critically to any contributed idea despite its apparent irrelevance. Effective group members, on the other hand, know in advance that the other group members will reject many of their ideas, but that knowledge does not inhibit their creativity. They continue to introduce new and different proposals for group consideration. These members probably suffer psychologically from the group's rejection of their ideas, too, but their creativity does not suffer as a result.

Actually, the slowness of the group process and the inherent start-and-stop process of modifying decisions encourage creativity from group members. Each member has the time and the opportunity to mull over his or her own ideas and the ideas of others and to develop new insights. Experts in creativity consider the incubation period essential to the creative process.

The process of group decision making again suggests the importance of timing. New and different proposals benefit the group efforts most during the orientation and conflict phases. During these early stages of group interaction, the creativity of members in devising new and different ideas should be at a maximum. During the emergence phase, members should confine their creativity to reformulating and combining previously discussed proposals. Creativity in any form is definitely not an asset but a liability to the group process during the reinforcement phase of group decision making.

### Criticism

A very normal and understandable human tendency of inexperienced group members is to avoid criticism of, and conflict with, other members. Normally, no one wants to run the risk of hurting another person's feelings. Inexperienced group members tend to avoid criticism for fear of harming the developing feeling of groupness. All of us have been taught from childhood that courtesy and tact are infinitely superior to rudeness and boorishness. So we examine an atrocious painting on our neighbor's wall and call it "interesting." We may suffer through a boring party, but we will invariably tell the host and hostess as we leave that we had a great time. Certainly, effective group decision making does not require that we rid ourselves of good manners and respect for others during group decision making.

Group decision making in some respects is a unique social situation. What we would consider courtesy and tact in one situation is tantamount to ineffectiveness and avoidance of social problems during group decision making. The fear of hurting the feelings of others and suppressing realistic opinions characterize members of a group with rather low cohesiveness. Criticism and conflict are typical norms of a highly cohesive group. In fact, group decision making may not be so unique after all. For instance, we rarely if ever have arguments with acquaintances, but we argue vehemently and say whatever we feel with our very close friends. Knowing that you can be honest with one another is knowing you are in the company of good friends.

The amount of criticism is irrelevant to the group process, but the timing of criticism is again all important. Criticism in the wrong place at the wrong time is as harmful to group process as no criticism at all. Let yourself go in exercising all your critical faculties during the conflict phase. At other times, you should probably control your critical impulses and use them sparingly.

Basic to the principle of criticism during group decision making is the avoidance of neutrality. It is absolutely impossible to remain neutral and be an effective participant during group interaction. High-status members are invariably dynamic contributors who take stands and defend them. Other members consider those stands to be helpful to the group's performance of its task. A "mugwump" is destined to be a low contributor and an ineffective group member. Group interaction virtually compels members to speak out on issues and to assume an argumentative stance. (Appendix 1, Anatomy of a Decision, illustrates how language choices of individual comments often force members into taking a stand during the conflict phase of group decision making.) A neutral member is usually perceived to be wishy-washy and is generally peripheral to the action of group decision making.

One vital ingredient of group decision making and one of its principal advantages over individual decision making is the process of testing ideas. Such idea testing among multiple sources of criticism results in higher-quality decisions when high social acceptance is a key criterion of decisional quality. This process of socially testing ideas is the principle behind the "free and open marketplace of ideas" in which criticism is absolutely essential. During idea testing the group norm should encourage as much criticism as possible, both in amount and diversity of that criticism. Effective group members are not necessarily tactless but are highly critical of others' ideas as well as of their own.

### Honesty

Underlying several of these principles is the cornerstone of honesty. That is, say what you believe, and believe what you say. Candor is an essential characteristic of group communication. Without being overly dramatic or absolutely devoid of tact, the effective communicator honestly strives to benefit the group's efforts. Certainly, honesty is not always the best policy. Earlier discussions have emphasized that courtesy is sometimes best served by harmless distortions of the truth. But some distortions may not be so harmless in the long run. Conscious and consistent submersion of your true feelings creates hidden agendas which can only disrupt the effective functioning of the entire group. Again the member's judgment, based on a sensitive understanding of the nature of communication and the group process, is essential for effective group communication.

One of the superordinate goals of the many types of training groups is the development of intrapersonal and interpersonal honesty. Such groups attempt to strip away individual facades and the inhibitions of personality defense mechanisms in order to achieve the group's goal to develop greater sensitivity to and for other people. The process of group decision making is most effective when that same goal is applied to honest expressions of opinions and attitudes. Idea testing is most effective when it reflects the realistic criticism that comes from true differences of opinion. Thus decision-making groups and training groups are both committed to the principle of honesty. Training groups emphasize revelation of the member's "inner self," and decision-making groups seek honesty directed toward those decision proposals under group consideration.

## IMPROVING EFFECTIVENESS: INTERPERSONAL FACTORS

By first discussing intrapersonal factors and now interpersonal factors of communicative effectiveness, I do not imply that these factors are clearly separable. Just as a person's attitudes or psychological orientations will affect that person's participation in decision-making interaction, so also one's interaction with others will affect one's orientations and attitudes. Improving one's effectiveness in communication is plainly an intrapersonal, as well as an interpersonal, phenomenon.

### Active Verbal Participation

It should be intuitively obvious that effective group decision making is highly correlated with the active verbal participation of the members. In other words, the effective participant actively participates verbally during group interaction. Typically in much past small group research, authorities have empirically discovered the obvious (Bass, 1949; Bass et al., 1953). They have "discovered" that members who do not communicate are not effective communicators!

Earlier discussions of group cohesiveness indicated that active participation is not essential for members to experience satisfaction with their group; only the freedom to participate is necessary for group satisfaction. But if group decision making is to be effective, nearly all members must actively participate in the interaction process. And the interaction process inherently involves verbal and oral participation.

The silent member does little to benefit the process of group decision making. Moreover, contributing only infrequently to the group's interaction does not significantly benefit the individual member. Bench-warmers on a football team do not contribute much to the team's success or to the development of their own abilities. Spectating is not playing. One learns to play the game by playing it. The bench-warmer may have little choice about getting to play, but the group member is silent solely of his or her own volition.

Active verbal participation does not imply equal participation of all members. Obviously, equal participation is not only abnormal and impossible; it is also not even desirable. The contributions of some members are more valuable than those of others. The more capable members should participate more. Abilities and expertise vary among the members. Each member should seek during group interaction to participate actively but not necessarily equally with every other member.

This first principle also does not imply that any member should attempt to monopolize the discussion or control the group interaction. You will recall from the model of leader emergence that excessive verbalization results in the elimination of leader contenders during the second stage of leader emergence. Active participation implies frequent contributions but not necessarily lengthy ones. The knowledgeable and verbally active member contributes brief comments but does so without inhibition. The first general principle for increasing one's communicative effectiveness in group decision making may seem overly obvious but is nonetheless essential. The effective communicator has something to say and says it.

## Communicative Skill

There exists an old and hackneyed controversy among authorities in rhetoric and public address. The controversy dates back to ancient Greece, centuries before Christ, and is occasionally heard even today. It concerns the relative importance of "content" and "delivery" in the effectiveness of communication. Which is more important for effective communication—what is said or how it is said? Most authorities today consider the controversy irrelevant and trivial. Increased knowledge concerning the process of communication has revealed that the controversy is naive and largely incomplete. Not only is the content of a message inseparable from its delivery, but the communicative process includes additional and highly significant elements which the controversy ignores.

First of all, the value of an expressed idea is determined in part by the manner in which it is presented. A skillful presentation affects the perceived importance of the message. Only the most naive student of human communication would argue that an idea has intrinsic worth apart from its use in the communicative situation and its expression within the sequence of communicative acts. The evidence that communicative skill does affect the message content is virtually indisputable. For example, one of the dimensions of leaders' behavior in group decision making, discovered by Russell (1970), was communicative skill.

Specific characteristics of communicative skill are rather unclear. Certainly the skillful communicator is fluent, articulate, and above all dynamic in the conversational situation. Communicative skill also involves a knowledge and an understanding of the communicative process and the ability to be flexible, adapting to the demands of the social system and the situation. Without such knowledge and adaptive ability, the communicator is perceived to be not so much fluent and articulate as merely glib. The stereotyped used-car salesman, for example, is considered glib and smooth, but these are negative characteristics, while skill is generally considered a positive attribute.

Learning communicative skills is not at all similar to learning the skill of hitting a baseball or playing a trumpet. These kinds of motor skills are based on mastering techniques and performing those techniques as an individual. Communication, however, never occurs in isolation but always in a social system with the interconnected communicative behaviors of other persons. And there are no magical or even nonmagical techniques of communicative skill, no list of principles to memorize. The ability to analyze the other person and the situation and to be perceived as articulate and dynamic requires a thorough knowledge of the communicative process and a great deal of hard work. Certainly, experience and practice in many and varied communicative situations are essential for developing communicative skills. And that experience always occurs in the presence of other people—the complex social system.

### Supportive Communication

Jack Gibb (1961) has discussed two different "climates" of communication which develop because of communicative actions performed by interactants. These communication climates include "defensive" communication and "supportive" communication. While a defensive climate results from defensive communicative behaviors, a characteristic of such a climate is a reduction of effectiveness due to an erosion of interpersonal trust and groupness. Gibb strongly suggests that the most effective communication is that occurring in a supportive climate and resulting from supportive communicative actions.

Characteristic of defensive communication are behaviors which both threaten the other person and originate from a perceived threat from the other person. Such defensive behaviors include personal evaluation, attempts to control, and behaviors which appear to convey an attitude of superiority or extreme certainty of belief. Generally speaking, defensive communication tends to be perceived as judgmental, manipulative, insincere, or deceptive. Being defensive oneself tends to arouse defensiveness in the other person (reciprocity at work) and results in lowered effectiveness of group interaction.

Supportive communication generally proceeds from one person's feeling of empathy with another. Supportive communication is other-directed or problem-oriented to the extent that someone who communicates supportively is genuine, sincere, honest, and spontaneous. Supportive communication is characterized by actions that do not seek to evaluate others, although supportive communication could evaluate a problem or issue. Defensive communication results when evaluative comments appear to be directed toward the person rather than the issue.

Defensive communication typically involves little social risk, but supportive communication involves high risk. Individuals create a climate of mutual trust and respect. Although status differences will occur in the group (based on power, ability, etc.), individual members supportively communicating with one another appear to attach little importance to those distinctions. In this sense group members generate considerable cohesiveness and consider themselves unified as a group even with the presence of a status hierarchy. To recognize leadership and status in an informal group with a supportive climate is not to disrupt the sense of groupness which members feel.

Attempting to maintain a clear distinction between intrapersonal and interpersonal factors of communicative effectiveness becomes virtually impossible when discussing defensive and supportive communicative actions. Supportive acts create a climate of mutual trust and are tantamount to each person's trusting the other and perceiving that trust reciprocated by the other. Supportive communication is consistent with a feeling or attitude of mutual support on the part of each member. Conversely, that feeling of mutual trust develops as a result of the supportive communicative behaviors performed by the members. We are again faced with the dilemma of the chicken or the egg. Which came first—the *feeling* of trust or the trusting *behavior?* The supportive communicative *climate* or the supportive communicative behaviors? The answer, of course, is that they develop together. One is as much a result of the other as it is the cause.

### Responding to Others

As an undergraduate student in a class in acting, I learned that a major factor in acting is relating to other actors. I soon discovered that memorizing my lines and delivering them appropriately is only a small part of the task of the actor. In my class, most of the acting occurred when I was not delivering lines. In other words, I discovered that much of acting involves *re*acting to others.

The tendency to emphasize the pragmatic perspective of human communication in previous chapters may have led to an implication that the actions performed by individual members are the key elements in the group decision-making process. Actually, the actions of each individual person are less significant than the *inter*actions among individuals. That is, one person's action may always be characterized as a response to the action of another person. Treating each action as a response to a previous action allows for the development of some general principles on how to respond to others. These principles may be used as guidelines in determining how one should respond to others in the interactive setting of group decision making. In any case, this view of communication involves thinking of communicative acts as always directed toward another person in response to the actions of that other person.

Much of the unnecessary and disruptive varieties of social conflict involve disagreements which are based not on a critical testing of ideas but on a misunderstanding of the other person's actions. I.A. Richards (1936), more than four decades ago, suggested that the primary function of the study of communication (that is, rhetoric) is to attempt to alleviate misunderstandings. You should keep in mind, then, that your disagreement should result from a clash of issues rather than from a misunderstanding of the other person's position. One clear principle of guiding your responding to others is to ensure that you fully understand the other person's point of view.

Failure to understand can result from a number of factors. The other person may misspeak or convey an unintended impression. You may mishear or receive some information which was not intended by the other. Or the language used by the other person may need clarification. Your response in all cases is quite similar. You should always ask for clarification. The lack of a clear understanding is frustrating. Often that frustration becomes a hidden agenda when we do not ask for clarification because we do not wish to appear foolish or stupid.

One group exhibited such a misunderstanding in its interaction because of one member's use of the jargonistic term: "placebo effect." No other member responded to the term, but each continued to interact with no indication that anyone had any problem of understanding. After several moments, during which time little progress was made, one member finally asked what the speaker meant by a "placebo effect." The response was to express surprise that the other members were unfamiliar with the term. The subsequent interaction, which dealt, not only with the issues at hand, but also with the member's tendency to verbalize in a manner which was difficult to understand, undoubtedly led to increased effectiveness of that group process.

Because clarification is so significant when you are on the receiving end of the misunderstanding, you should always be prepared for the probability that other people will also misunderstand you. Consequently, you should develop the habit of checking to see whether your own expressed ideas were understood. Watch for the other person's reactions. Be prepared to restate your ideas in different ways in order to maximize mutual understanding. Realizing the fact that misunderstanding is a very common element in normal communication, you should also realize that any failure of others to understand your own communicative acts is quite normal. Their misunderstanding is not a reflection on your communicative skill. In other words, be supportive rather than defensive when someone indicates a failure to understand you.

Another general rule of thumb in guiding your responses to others is, be as specific as you can. Avoid generalizing too much, particularly in responding to the other person's comments. If you are disagreeing, you should be careful to specify clearly the point of your disagreement and the reason for your disagreement. You should make your response as concrete and precise as you can. The fact that your disagreement is with a specific issue, not with the person who raised the issue, is significant to effective group decision making. It is also highly susceptible to misunderstanding.

Recalling that evaluative judgments tend to lead to defensive reactions, you might respond to others supportively by attempting to be as descriptive as possible. Some people have suggested that communicative responses should not attempt to describe the other person or the other person's ideas. Rather, the response should try to describe your own reaction. Rather than saying, "That's the most ridiculous thing I ever heard," you might say, "My first reaction to your statement is one of bewilderment. I'm not sure I agree with you." To be descriptive rather than judgmental is not to avoid disagreement on the issues. Rather, description refers to the manner in which disagreeing responses are phrased. They are directed at the idea, not the person. They describe yourself, not the other person.

Remember that every communicative act is a response to another communicative act. This sequence of actions is an integral part of a group's interaction process. When you develop this way of thinking about group communication, you will become less concerned with what you or other members do during group discussions. Rather, you will find yourself considering such issues as how specific members relate with one another or how you deal with other persons. In adopting this manner of thinking about communication, you will be emphasizing the social and the interactive functions of communication. Moreover, you will realize that communication and the group process is a single perspective of viewing group decision making. Communication and the group process do not involve two different sets of phenomena.

## IMPROVING EFFECTIVENESS: GROUP IDENTITY FACTORS

Up to this point, we have been concerned with the individual member as related to his or her own self (intrapersonal factors) and as related to other individual members (interpersonal factors). The present discussion focuses on improving effectiveness in terms of an individual's sense of relationship with the group as a single identity. I continue to assume, however, that the intrapersonal, the interpersonal, and the group factors are not three different elements of communication and the group process. Rather, these three sets of factors are so interrelated that it is virtually impossible to determine where one stops and the other begins. The member who intrapersonally feels commitment to the group begins to refer to the group in the first person (that is, "my" or "our" group). The identity of the group stems directly from the intrapersonal and interpersonal factors of the group process.

### Sensitivity to Group Process

Because of the nature of a process, the importance of timing cannot be emphasized too much. Increasing one's communicative effectiveness is more than knowing what behaviors to perform or even how to perform them well. The most important principle of effective communication in group decision making is knowing when to communicate what.

Being sensitive to the group process enables the group member to judge fairly accurately in which phase the group is interacting. Sensitivity to the process allows the member to perceive roles and decisions as they emerge probably before other, less sensitive members of the group are aware and undoubtedly before the emergence process is completed. A group member who also possesses a modicum of communicative skills is capable of adjusting communicative behavior so as to behave appropriately in each specific phase in the process of group decision making.

Sensitivity to the group process also allows the member to pinpoint the causes of social problems and devise strategies to solve those problems. When a group is in trouble and is not functioning effectively as a group, the members generally recognize the existence of some problem. But knowing that the group is in difficulty and knowing what to do about it are two separate elements. The knowledgeable and sensitive group member becomes something of a consultant—an expert in the group process. He or she is able to discern the cause of the group's difficulties, which might, for example, be a problem member. Sensitivity to group process does not lead the sensitive person to reject the member but, rather, establishes a desire to discover the cause of the problem member's dissatisfaction with the group and to do something to alleviate that dissatisfaction.

Even sensitivity and expert knowledge do not, however, enable any member to manipulate other group members at will. Sensitivity to the group process will not necessarily allow a member to be the group leader. To the contrary, the process-sensitive member is interested not necessarily in becoming leader but, rather, in encouraging the group process to function smoothly. He or she may or may not be leader but always behaves in the best interests of the group and its performance of its decision-making task. As such, he or she will probably be a leader contender and certainly a high-status member. But there are no known techniques, principles, abilities, or behaviors which give anyone license to manipulate members of an LGD.

### Commitment to the Group

Quite clearly the effective communicator in a decision-making group is a member who is deeply committed to the group and its task. In fact, active verbal participation is highly correlated with commitment. That is, committed members tend to assume a very active verbal role in the group interaction. And in true interdependent fashion, very active participants generally possess a deep level of group commitment. If you feel strongly about something, you want to talk about it. Conversely, if you talk about something actively, you come to feel strongly about it.

One point must be emphasized. Effective communication in the group and low commitment of members are totally incompatible. If you feel you are not committed to your group, you are a liability in the process of group decision making. You have but one recourse in such an untenable situation. If you are unable to perceive value in your group membership or in the group task, quit! You will undoubtedly think you are better off without the group, but don't be deceived. The group is infinitely better off without you! Without experiencing commitment to the group and the task, you cannot be an effective group member. Without your commitment as a member, the effectiveness of the group is severely curtailed.

### Attitude toward Group Slowness

The member who understands the group process does not despair over the apparent inefficiency of the group's efforts. Particularly in the early stages of group interaction, the group mechanism seems excruciatingly slow. It is only normal to be somewhat frustrated and anxious. The inexperienced member will be distressed and eager to "get the show on the road." The effective member may be frustrated, but will not be overly anxious. He or she exercises patience and observes the process getting underway.

There is a sound rationale for not being overly eager for the group to increase its efficiency. What appears to be inefficiency at a snail's pace actually reflects one of the advantages of the group process of decision making. While the group sputters and spurts in pursuit of consensus, members are allowed time to develop new ideas and reformulate earlier proposals. Too often, time is at a premium, particularly if a group operates under pressure of a deadline. Nevertheless, the importance of "mulling time" must not be underestimated. It is a crucial step in creative and high-quality decision making. And it is an integral part of the group decision-making process.

The apparent inefficiency of the group process is also advantageous for the management of social tension in the group. Demanding greater efficiency of the group through placing tight controls on departures from the topic and requiring prolonged discussion of specific proposals probably creates more severe social problems which naturally affect the group's task efforts. The interaction process allows members some opportunities for venting their tensions and reducing the rate of their tension buildup through features inherent in the process—abrupt changes of topics and brief spurts of intensive interaction, particularly during the conflict phase.

The process of modifying decision proposals through spurts of energized interaction and reformulating proposals is apparently inherent in the process of decision making in every social system. Thus the group process inherently includes devices to manage tension—devices which are effective in the long run, even though they appear to the shortsighted and naive member to be symptoms of gross inefficiency. Effective members are patient because they know the process works.

## Formula Answers

The talented Steve Allen once remarked that you can use just one simple sentence in virtually any conversation and gain typically excellent results. That sentence is, "Well, you know the old saying" This comment is universal and explains everything while contributing nothing. Allen emphasizes the point that a cliché or an adage of conventional wisdom is available for any and every issue. Strangely enough, the cliché often commands immediate and universal acceptance, even though for every cliché, there is usually another which contradicts it. If you believe that "Two heads are better than one," do you also believe that "Too many cooks spoil the broth"? "Absence makes the heart grow fonder," but then, "Out of sight, out of mind." It is certainly true that "Haste makes waste," but everyone knows that "A stitch in time saves nine." Tidbits of conventional wisdom are more often perceived to be true than they actually are true in the sense that they reflect reality.

Some group decisions are similar to clichés in that they oversimplify at the expense of realism. Groups discussing problems confronting the society, such as poverty, crime, or discrimination, often agree that such problems are caused by the ingrained attitudes of the society's members. The group members then decide that changing the attitudes of society with a program of education will eradicate the cause and solve the problem. The solution is true, of course, but it is unmistakably naive, simplistic, and totally unrealistic. How will education change society's attitudes? Who will administer this educational program? How will they do it? Are they able to do it? Is such a program possible? How long will it take? What about the influence of peer groups and opinion leaders in the society?

In short, the formula answer does not really solve anything. It only gives the appearance of having solved it. I am reminded of my former high school football coach just before we played the conference championship team. When asked how we were going to win, he replied without the slightest trace of a smile, "Score more points" That answer solves the problem of how to win the game, all right. But its formula was not adequately detailed to be put into effect. (We lost the game, too.)

Groups formed in a classroom situation and discussing a policy problem have a penchant for devising formula answers. But classroom groups engaging in policy discussions are not typical of most decision-making groups in this respect. Classroom groups discussing such remote problems do little more than participate in intellectual exercises. After all, no classroom group has the power to legalize abortion or marijuana or abolish censorship laws or affect the national economy. The members engage in interaction as a classroom exercise and often discuss problems remote from their own capabilities as a realistic group. The real-life group, however, cannot afford shortcuts to realistic wisdom. Groups in the "real world" generally have the responsibility for implementing the decisions they make. They can then observe the success or failure of their consensus decisions in actual practice. Nor does their job end with the conclusion of an academic term. The formula answer is potentially a much more prevalent problem for the classroom group than for most decision-making groups in the society.

### Analyzing Group Episodes

Several previous chapters have included discussions recommending that groups engage in self-analysis as a means of promoting more effective decision making. Group members who engage in analyzing themselves and the group process typically do so for several reasons. One reason is to attempt to discover and confront social problems which may be inhibiting the progress of the group's task performance. A second reason is more pedagogical. Classroom groups, involved in learning about group decision-making phenomena, perform self-analysis for the purpose of furthering their understanding of communication and the group process. For whatever purpose, I cannot suggest too strongly the importance of self-analysis as a means for improving the group's communication and group process.

One focus of self-analysis is the pinpointing and analysis of "critical episodes." Typically, during the process of group development, certain events occur in the group's history which later come to exert a profound impact on the development of that group's social and task dimensions. Such events typically indicate a transition or turning point in the group's development. That is, the event serves to precipitate some subsequent interaction which either facilitates or disrupts the group's performance as a group. A group's analysis of itself may focus on those specific episodes rather than haphazardly attempt to consider the entire process of group development. Such a focus is beneficial in allowing the members to understand their own maturation as a group.

After isolating those specific historical events critical to the group development, the question remains as to how the members should proceed to analyze those events in detail. There are no hard-and-fast rules to be followed in either identifying or analyzing the critical episodes. The closest I can come to providing guidelines for analysis of episodes is to suggest some questions which members may find provocative in stimulating discussion about those episodes.

One of the most obvious questions in analyzing critical group episodes is probably, "What was going through your mind at that time?" In this case, the group member is asked to engage in some self-disclosing communication concerning those episodes. Making the self-disclosures after the fact is undoubtedly more easily accomplished by the members than discussing frankly their own feelings at the time. Therefore, a successful analysis of a critical episode requires some elapsed time between the occurrence of that historical event and the time of the analysis. Typically, critical episodes bring on periods of increased social tension which further inhibit candid discussion of the episodes. An appropriate amount of time is necessary in order to allow that tension to dissipate.

A second question which may stimulate group discussion of critical episodes is to identify the critical figure or critical role in that episode. Which member of the group played the central role in either bringing about the episode or resolving the critical episode? That is, the critical episode may have involved confronting a problem member. In this case, the problem member played a central role, but an equally significant figure may be the member who initially confronted the problem member or encouraged other group members to confront him or her. After identifying these central or catalytic roles, the group may then concentrate on the reactions of those members as potentially more important than those of the other group members whose roles may have been observers more than anything else.

Another question of a more speculative nature may involve asking what the results of the critical episode were. What happened after the event? Why did those results occur? What might have occurred differently during the episode which would have led to a different outcome, either more beneficial or more disruptive? Should any action be taken at the time of analysis as a result of the retrospective analysis of the historical event? In other words, assess the significance of the effects or results of the critical episode.

Focusing on specific events (perhaps entire meetings) in the group's history should provide some insight into the group process and the communicative functions which led to the development of the group itself. Concentrating on events, rather than on specific members or external conditions, is totally consistent with our perspective of group decision making—that is, communication and the group process.

Brown and Rothenberg (1976, p. 303) urge the use of critical episodes for group self-analysis and provide an example of their potential significance: "Although related to other components of group action—leadership, situation, the personalities of members, and social controls—the significant group episode in many ways predates all of these. The kind of person capable of coming to leadership in a group, for example, may be a function, to a greater or lesser extent, of some prior event in which another leadership style proved disastrous. . . ."

Group episodes are thus transitional events in the history of the group. They include events which led to either an acceleration or a disruption in the process of group development. Looking back on such events from the perspective of history allows the group members, not only to understand "where they came from" and how they came to be what they are at that point, but also to determine where the group is going. Analyses of group episodes provide valuable insights into a more comprehensive understanding of communication and the group process. They may also lead to significant insights into improving communicative effectiveness during later group decision making.

### POSTSCRIPT

This chapter has intended to demonstrate the hopelessness of developing cardinal rules or techniques to increase communicative effectiveness among members of decision-making groups. The process viewpoint with its inherent emphases on structure and action demands that effectively communicating members be flexible and adaptable. Timing—perceiving what behavior is most appropriate at a particular point in time during the group process—and the ability to perform the appropriate communicative behaviors demand a thorough understanding of how communication and the group process function.

Experience of group membership and understanding of the group process are inseparable dimensions of effective group communication. The general principles of communicative effectiveness included in this chapter do not lead a member to experience and understanding; rather, one's experience and understanding lead to these principles. You can't learn to swim without first getting wet. But neither does floundering in the water teach you how to swim effectively. The flailing movements motivated by a desire for survival may keep you afloat, but they are no substitute for effective swimming. Similarly, anyone can be a member of a small group and participate in a decision-making task, but that experience does not make anyone an effective contributor to the group discussion. Only a working understanding of communication and the group process, coupled with the experience of group membership, enables the member to be effective. Thus, the entire book actually serves the intended purpose of this chapter.

## SUMMARY

Developing effective communication within a group is not easy. There are no sure-fire principles for improving communication and group effectiveness. Such improvement ultimately requires a thorough understanding of communication and the group process. Misconceptions to be avoided include the naive assumption of human rationality and an overreliance on agendas.

Improving effectiveness depends on a number of interrelated intrapersonal, interpersonal, and group-identity factors. Intrapersonal factors involve each member's attitudes toward the group and toward group interaction, along with each individual member's creativity, critical ability, and honesty. Interpersonal factors include active verbal participation, communicative skill, the use of supportive communication, and sensitivity when responding to others. When identifying with the group as a whole, effective members develop a sensitivity to the group process, a commitment to the group, and a reasonable attitude toward group slowness. Most important, perhaps, effective group communication often benefits from group members' engaging in interaction that is directed specifically at self-analysis, concentrating specifically on critical episodes from the group's history of past interactions.

# Chapter 10

# Epilogue:
# Some Final Considerations

It is a sad but inescapable fact that every book on any subject is inevitably incomplete. This book is certainly no exception. Literally thousands of relevant research studies and viewpoints have been excluded from these pages. The problem of omission is compounded because this book embraces two extremely broad fields—human communication and small groups. Neither field by itself has received comprehensive treatment in the previous chapters.

Every chapter has emphasized the importance of choosing a perspective and its pervasive influence on one's observation and subsequent understanding. The perspective of the book, communication and group process, has severely restricted the range of material which can be considered relevant to the study of group decision making. Furthermore, the emphasis on decision making restricts that perspective even further by excluding some groups whose purposes are not oriented toward performing decision-making tasks.

This book, like many others, is committed to a rather narrow focus and does not attempt to cover the waterfront of group communication.

This final chapter attempts to illuminate that focus and thereby explain, at least in part, the process of selecting or omitting otherwise relevant materials and of including others. The chapter also includes some apparently random observations that are intended to round out the understanding of communication and the group process. The result is a potpourri of ideas and concepts which provide the rationale for understanding and applying the perspective of group decision making employed in earlier chapters.

## THE "NATURAL" GROUP PROCESS

A major assumption underlying the present perspective of group decision making is that a "natural" process of group development and task performance exists in nearly every group. The process is called "natural" not only because of its pervasive presence but because it continues to exist even though members may be unaware of its existence or its influence.

That members need not be conscious of the group process is important to understanding a natural process because it embodies a fundamental assumption underlying all sciences— physical, social, and behavioral. The scientific approach assumes some order in the universe—that events occur and people behave according to some set of "rules." Whether those rules are known is quite irrelevant to the fact of their existence. For example, physical laws of the universe need not be known as a prerequisite to their existence. The earth revolves around the sun and will continue to do so whether we are aware of its orbit or not. Humans existed on this planet for thousands of centuries before becoming aware of even that fact of physical science.

It takes time to develop observational tools which will uncover even the most fundamental of scientific laws. Although the study of human behavior is incredibly immature, there is indisputable evidence that humans regulate their behavior to conform to rules not unlike, in principle, the physical laws governing the universe. But because the rules governing behavior are not as apparent as laws which regulate the motion of a pendulum, for example, many people often find it difficult to believe that such rules do exist. The tools for observing human behavior are as yet too rudimentary and too unsophisticated to provide the precision to prove to everyone's satisfaction that a natural process of human behavior does indeed exist.

Although a natural process regulates the behavior of all groups, many variations from that process occur as conditions, internal and external to the group, vary. Of course, our physical laws also vary in different situations though we seldom think about such variations. Everyone knows that water boils at 212°F, but the boiling temperature of water varies according to the elevation. Anyone who has ever waited for water to boil on a camp stove in the mountains at 11,000 feet above sea level knows the effect of elevation on this "law" of 212°. Try following the usual baking instructions on a package of cake mix if you live in the mountains. Few people will come back for more of that cake.

The natural group process described in previous chapters assumes the existence of a "normal" LGD. But many groups are not normal LGDs, and they exhibit variations from the natural group process. If the natural process describes a group that develops from a primitive state, the extent to which the group varies from a primitive state at the beginning of its decision-making efforts determines the extent to which the group's development varies from the natural process. Each of these variations among groups produces variations in the group process, but in no way does a variation deny the existence of the natural process inherent in group decision making.

## Legitimacy

Earlier chapters have discussed the impact of legitimacy on the natural group process. The present discussion need not dwell on this fact. In an established social organization the status hierarchy, role system, and leadership—the entire social structure—are often prescribed by the organization itself. Many organizations also prescribe norms and procedures as well. The worker on the assembly line, for example, has a prescribed function to fulfill and is not expected to deviate from the organization's prescribed procedures for performing that function. The university student, too, must fulfill prescribed requirements, such as a minimum number of credits, minimum GPA, and specific required courses, in order to earn a degree. The armed forces also prescribe procedures for performing every function, no matter how trivial, required of a soldier. According to another cliché, "There is a right way, a wrong way, and the Army way."

The legitimate status hierarchy, norms, roles, and procedures constitute the "formal" structure of a social organization. Obviously, these legitimate forms are not subject to deviation or change through the natural group process. On the other hand, neither do they prohibit the natural process from developing a companion social structure. In virtually every social organization a nonlegitimate structure develops over a period of time consistent with the natural process. A status hierarchy, a role network, a set of procedures evolve into the "informal" structure of the organization. The inevitable development of an informal structure persists despite efforts of formalized legitimate authorities to inhibit its growth. But the wise legitimate leader recognizes both structures and attempts to function in both.

The formal structure sanctioned by legitimacy and the nonsanctioned informal structure are not always consistent with each other. Occasionally the informal structure prohibits efficient functioning of the social organizations when instructions and procedures designated by formal authorities are not followed. It has long been known that when the formal structure of a social organization clashes with the informal structure, the informal structure often demonstrates greater potency (Coch and French, 1948).

Legitimacy certainly inhibits the development of the natural group process, but it does not prohibit its development. Rather, legitimacy prescribes one structure, and the natural process allows the evolution of another structure which may or may not conform to the formal structure. But the formal structure may also thwart the natural process to the point of virtual extinction.

When the formal structure possesses sufficient power to quell any sign of a developing informal structure and when the persons in formal positions of authority choose to use that power, the informal structure has little opportunity for successful development. On a large scale, totalitarian rulers, such as the Roman Caesars, Hitler, and Stalin, ruthlessly purged even the slightest indication of an informal social structure in conflict with the formal authorities. Herman Melville also illustrated the formidable use of unrestricted power possessed by a ship's captain in *Moby Dick*.

Perhaps the most common example of a legitimate structure thwarting the natural group process in group decision making is that of the status-dominated discussion. When the legitimately sanctioned leader of a decision-making group exerts power by "pulling rank" on subordinate fellow members, the "group" consists only of a leader and "yes men." In such instances, the sole function of the group members is to wait for the leader to express an opinion and then agree with it.

The status-dominated group discussion thwarts the natural group process and inevitably degenerates into an individual's making decisions. Group members do not develop ideas through a critical exchange of opinions and information. Members are not free to develop and express their own opinions. The spiral process of decision emergence and decision modification is not present. Consequently, the status-dominated group typically develops a false or superficial consensus. Members experience no natural compulsion to work toward successful implementation of the group decision since they had no real voice in making those decisions. Hence, status-dominated discussion forfeits significant advantages and values of group decision making. In fact, the status-dominated group discussion is not group decision making at all, but an instance of individual decision making masquerading in the guise of a group effort.

Legitimacy probably results in the greatest variation from the natural group process but rarely prohibits its development. When legitimate structures exert a substantial impact on group members, the natural process undoubtedly requires more time to develop. And the extent of power at the disposal of formal authorities and their willingness to use that power restrict the extent and range of the informal structure developed through the natural process. For most social organizations in our society, those persons in positions of legitimate authority generally recognize the informal structures within their organization and their significance in affecting members' behavior. Realizing that informal structures will evolve anyway, they take advantage of them by attempting to function in an authoritative role in both formal and informal systems.

## Types of Groups

The primary concern throughout this book has involved group decision making. The natural group process has consistently been described in terms of group decision making. But many other groups exist in our society, though not for the purpose of performing decision-making tasks. The question persists as to how relevant the natural process of group decision making is to groups whose purposes do not include decision making. As usual, the answer to such a question depends on the type of group being compared with the decision-making group.

The purpose of a psychotherapy group is certainly different from that of decision making. Even the role structure is markedly different. One of the members, the group therapist, is not even a group member in terms of the purpose served by the group. Members are typically suffering from some form of mental illness and engage in abnormal or antisocial behavior. In fact, a therapy group has no real group purpose at all. The group is only a means, a context, for the cure and treatment of the illness of each individual member. If any group is significantly different from group decision making, it is the therapy group.

Talland (1955), as well as Alexander Smith et al. (1962), discovered that the interaction patterns exhibited by members of a therapy group are markedly different from those of group decision making. There is probably little reason to doubt the validity of their conclusions. While a decision-making group attempts to manage its social tension and achieve a steady state of controllable tension (in Bales's terms, to "maintain equilibrium"), the therapy group strives to achieve an unsteady state. The therapist attempts to "unsettle" patients and place them in a state of disequilibrium so that their illnesses are more susceptible to treatment. In other words, the process, as well as the purpose, of group therapy appears to be quite different from the process of group decision making.

Although there are some ingredients of small groups that characterize both decision-making and therapeutic group purposes (for example, cohesiveness and social conflict), the processes of the two types of groups are undoubtedly significantly different. The most valid conclusion is that the natural process of group decision making probably has little relevance to the process of group therapy.

One would normally think that a family group would have little in common with group decision making. But Pollay (1969) and Tallman (1970) have discovered the process of group decision making useful as an insight into the family group. Certainly the family interacts frequently enough to develop characteristic interaction patterns. And families obviously make numerous decisions as a group—decisions ranging from which color to paint the house to whether to purchase a new automobile to what time the children in the family are required to go to bed.

Research is presently underway to discover those interaction patterns which characterize the family group. Such knowledge, when it is gained, will certainly be a boon to family counselors. At any rate, there is apparently reason to believe that a natural process based on patterns of interaction does characterize the family group, although the nature of the process may differ slightly from that of group decision making. But the natural process of group decision making may be more relevant to the family group than some would normally think.

One type of group, the training group, has achieved so much popularity in recent years that it must be mentioned here. Many authorities seem to believe that a training group, whether it focuses on sensitivity training, group encounter, creativity workshop, est, or another variety of group training, is significantly different in process, purpose, scope, and structure from a task-oriented group with a decision-making purpose. The differences between the two types of groups may be much less substantial, however, than many think. Pyke and Neely (1970) indicate the process and results of both kinds of groups are really quite similar. Schein and Bennis (1965, pp. 102–104) go so far as to advocate that the training group be assigned a realistic decision-making task in order to promote the reality of the group situation.

When the pattern of interaction among training-group members focuses on decision making as Schein and Bennis suggest, there can be little difference between training groups and decision-making groups. Tuckman (1965) has also demonstrated a striking similarity in the process of group development for training groups and for decision-making groups. Although the present volume has not dealt specifically with groups whose goals emphasize the interpersonal growth of members, the natural process of group decision making is apparently clearly seen in the interaction patterns of training groups.

Although it depends on the type of group, the variation from the natural process observed in group decision making is often insignificant. Except for the therapy group whose process is apparently quite dissimilar, the natural process of group decision making is highly relevant to the interaction patterns of other types of groups with nondecision-making purposes.

### Idiosyncratic Group Structures

It is obvious that the structural characteristics of groups vary widely. Groups may be composed of all women, all men, or a heterogeneous mixture of men and women. Groups also vary greatly in other structural characteristics, such as age of members, political beliefs, personality traits, physical attributes, experience, and perceptual acuity. Thousands of studies have attempted to discover the effect, if any, of different group structures on the functioning of the group process. The results of those studies are as varied as the structures themselves.

The most significant impact of a group's structural characteristics apparently affects the outputs of the group process. That is, different combinations of structural factors often lead to different group decisions. On a commonsense level, one would expect that the decision made by a group of Northern liberals on the merits of school busing to achieve integration would differ emphatically from the decision on the same topic made by a group of Southern conservatives. A group of women liberationists would not view the *Playboy* philosophy in the same way that a group of male chauvinists would. Certainly some differences in selected structural characteristics of groups will affect group productivity both in terms of the nature of the decisions and the decisional quality.

On the other hand, there is little reason to believe that structural characteristics in a particular group exert significant influence on the process of decision making itself. Although the level of sophistication and personal biases of individual members and their comments may vary from one group to another, the *pattern* of interaction among group members remains essentially the same regardless of the structure of the particular group.

A few pieces of evidence have indicated that certain structural characteristics, such as sex (Gouran, 1969) and personality traits (Bass et al., 1953) of members, may affect the functioning of the group process, but most of the evidence seems to point to the opposite conclusion. Kent and McGrath (1969), for example, found that, compared with task characteristics, structural characteristics of a group exert only a slight impact on the group process. And Fisher (1970a) discovered the phases of decision emergence in a variety of groups discussing a variety of decision-making topics. These groups reflected great disparity of group structures, including variation in the number of members, their ages, sex, socioeconomic status, expertise, intelligence, educational achievement, and many others too numerous to mention. Differences in structural characteristics among groups may affect the nature and quality of decisions reached by that group—the group outcomes—but idiosyncratic group structures apparently exert minimal influence on the natural process of group decision making itself.

## THE "GROUP MIND"

The "group mind" is a concept that has been largely rejected by contemporary authorities on small groups and is rarely used today. Floyd H. Allport (1927), among many others, long ago laid to rest the belief that a group can feel and think as an entity separate from the feeling and thinking of its individual members. Even though the controversy over the existence of a group mind is now ancient history, many of the principles embodied in the concept of a group mind are commonly accepted today. (Gordon W. Allport, 1968, pp. 43–56, has thoroughly traced the issues of the old controversy and the problems associated with the group mind for those readers who are interested in the concept and wish to explore it further.)

It is an indisputable fact that the group does possess an identity of its own. The boundaries of group membership are clear. Members and nonmembers can be easily separated and identified with amazing regularity. Members recognize the identity of the group when they refer to it in the first person as a single entity, for example, "our group," or "we."

Obviously, no group exists apart from its individual members. Indeed, the group exists only because individual people belong to it. The social structure of the group is totally dependent on the interpersonal bonds developed between individual group members, one with another. Only individual people can behave, and the collective patterns of interaction characterizing group process are abstracted from the total sequential behaviors performed by individuals. The group exists not as any mystical force apart from the existence of its individual members, but as a whole entity directly because of its individual members.

On the other hand, the group as a social system is more than the sum of its members and their behaviors. Consistent with the principle of "wholeness," a group is "more than the sum of its parts" and cannot be adequately analyzed merely by listing its individual components, that is, its members. In analogical terms, the human body is more than the total value of the elements which comprise it. Years ago the Mills Brothers recorded a song stating that although the body is only "98 cents worth of elements," the dollar value of the chemical properties of the body do not assess the true worth of a living human being. With inflation over the years, a human body now is probably worth about $10, but this value is still meaningless in attempting to account for the value of human life. Simply stated, life is more than the sum of its chemical components. The artist's statue is much more than a block of marble. The specific arrangement of the components of the human body or the statue renders it far more valuable than the sum of the components taken separately. The same principle is true of a group—it is more than merely the total of its individual members.

One common perspective views the small group by emphasizing the properties of each individual member. Thus, a group would have no properties of its own but would be defined solely in terms of the properties of its individual members—their beliefs, opinions, expectations, motives, attitudes, perceptions. The communicative process perspective employed throughout the preceding chapters employs quite a different viewpoint. Conversely, my perspective views each of the members from the viewpoint of the group. In this respect, the individual and all the properties of her or his personality are essentially insignificant. Only that segment of the individual that participates as the group member is relevant to the group. Who each person is and what he or she does outside the group do not concern the group unless these facts affect the natural group process.

The group is an abstraction of the characteristic behaviors performed by those individual human beings who constitute the group membership. The group exists because of the interdependence of its members and the reciprocal influence which members exert on one another through their communicative acts. The group is not the members but the interdependent relationships among members—the arrangement of the components and not the components themselves. A leader is not an individual person. In fact, leadership is not a phenomenon which even exists outside the group. The leader is a characteristic of a particular group that typically identifies one of its members who has developed, with the other members, a reciprocal relationship of leadership-followership.

A group most certainly exists both because of and in spite of the individual human beings who are its members. The group assumes its identity from its individual members, and the members assume their identities from the existence of the group. To term the identity of the social system a "group mind" is a distortion of the commonly accepted existence of a "group."

## GROUP FAILURE

Earlier discussions of the group process have consistently assumed that the process of group decision making invariably leads to successful task performance. That is, the groups discussed in earlier chapters all successfully performed their decision-making tasks and always achieved consensus on their decisions. But, as Bossman (1968) has demonstrated, the value of the group process lies not in making the decisions but in the commitment of the members to work toward effective implementation of decisions once they are made. Therefore, the value of the natural group process is the effective implementation of decisions and not the assurance that the group always achieves consensus on decisions. Group decisions do not easily fail when they are implemented.

Some groups do not successfully achieve consensus on their decisions. Some groups conclude their decision-making efforts with superficial or false consensus. But false consensus is not so much a failure of the group to make decisions as a short circuit of the group process. Sometimes, though, groups cannot agree on consensus decisions even superficially. A hung jury is not uncommon in our courtrooms. Nor are nonjudicial groups that meet for hours without ever achieving consensus decisions.

What happens to groups that fail to perform their decision-making tasks? Do they give up? Do they disband? It would seem that a group which consistently fails to make consensus decisions and suffers through a prolonged string of failures will probably cease to function as a group eventually. Group members cannot endure indefinitely such consistent and prolonged instances of failure. Even a professional baseball team that loses year after year after year cannot sustain consistent failure indefinitely. The team changes managers, trades for new players, or moves to a new city. In short, the players disintegrate the group and form a new group with massive structural and environmental changes. A decision-making group cannot so easily change the structure of its group. Consistent and prolonged failures may eventually lead to its dissolution. But, amazingly enough, these instances of group self-destruction are extremely few.

Groups rarely disintegrate because of consistent failures to reach consensus decisions because they rarely experience such a continual lack of success in such frustrating proportions. The typical reaction of group members in the aftermath of group failure is that they persist. Streufert (1969) discovered that groups continue to persist when faced with failure on past decisions. After previous decisions have failed, group members persist in making decisions consistent with those past decisions. When that approach does not work, they resort to trial-and-error methods for finding new decisions. But a group does not easily give up out of frustration over consistent failures. In fact, a group with a history of past failures seldom even seeks assistance or new information from sources outside the group. The members prefer to sink or swim on their own. Thus, in the case of group failure, the members continue to function as a group until they succeed.

A primary characteristic of group decision making, then, is stick-to-itiveness. Although an individual may experience intolerable frustration rather quickly, a group is able to continue its efforts and even increase its efforts after initial failure. One useful technique employed by groups to achieve success is self-analysis. Smith and Knight (1959) indicate that the group that seeks to analyze its own group process may increase productivity in certain situations. But an understanding of the group process would tell us that self-analysis benefits the group most if its productivity is being hampered by the members' tendency to avoid some serious social problem. In that case, analyzing the process of their decision-making efforts might reveal that difficulty and encourage the members to confront their problem in a conscientious attempt to solve it. In instances of groups whose failure is attributable to other reasons, group self-analysis may be enlightening but will not necessarily lead to increased productivity.

What happens in instances of group failure to achieve consensus on decisions? Typically, group members persist and often achieve success later. The interdependence of group members apparently provides the process of group decision making with another advantage over decision making performed by an individual acting alone. Groups are more persistent and less susceptible to task failure.

## A FINAL WORD

The study of communication and the group process is certainly perplexing, confusing, and highly frustrating. At the same time, it is exciting and eminently worthy of the time and effort spent in its pursuit. After all, what aspect of human life is more worthy of understanding than how people achieve mutual understanding, how people form interpersonal ties, how people cooperate and compete in social interaction—in short, how people communicate with one another? It has been said that the human being spends more waking time in the activity of communication than any other endeavor. Certainly the quest for greater understanding of human communication is vitally important.

The formal study of communication and the group process is still very young. Compared to what remains to be discovered, the present state of our knowledge is infinitesimally small. Nevertheless, we have now a broad basis for understanding, and that understanding provides the basis for the present volume. A spirit of progress toward increased understanding of group communication is highly contagious. Progress has been so rapid even within the last ten years that virtually any book becomes obsolete by the time it sees print. This book should be no exception.

"But I," you say, "am not concerned with devoting my life to the study of group communication. I am interested in the subject only as a practicing group member. I want to know how I can be more effective and productive as a member of a decision-making small group." The response to this question is deceptively simple. The practitioner and the researcher of group decision making share one trait in common. They are both students of group communication.

Effective performance in small group decision making is absolutely dependent on being aware of the nature of human communication and the group process. The greater the members' understanding of communication and the group process, the more sensitive members are toward both their own behavior and the behavior of others. The greater the members' sensitivity to communication and the group process, the more effective they are as participating members of a decision-making group. Their sensitivity directs their behavior so that they communicate appropriately and effectively in the group process. They know that they cannot easily manipulate other members, but they also know that they can discern problems confronting the group and aid in devising strategies for the group to solve them. And they are not burdened with naive trust in clichés or conventional wisdom concerning group decision making.

One cliché seems appropriate as the final statement in this book. "The more you know, the more you know that you don't know." You have now completed one small step toward understanding group communication. For many people that first step is addictive.

# Anatomy of a Decision

Chapter 5 includes a description of the four phases involved in the process of group decision making. Those phases—orientation, conflict, emergence, and reinforcement—may appear confusing in the abstract description of the model in the same chapter. That description of the basic model of decision emergence does not include specific comments made by specific members during actual group interaction. As a result, the model may need a more concrete description. The following pages attempt to capture the "flavor" of group discussion. This section describes the communicative exchanges of specific group members as the group progresses through the four phases of decision making.

This appendix, Anatomy of a Decision, illustrates through group interact sequences, taken from audiotaped transcripts of group meetings, what the four phases of decision emergence "look like" in actual group discussion. You should probably refer to the general model of decision emergence in Chapter 5 during and after your reading of this section.

**The Situation** This six-member jury (all men) is deliberating over a verdict after observing a mock trial. The dramatized trial involved a civil suit seeking damages for alleged injuries suffered in an auto-pedestrian accident. The plaintiff, Alfred Derby, was the pedestrian who brought the suit. The defendant, Roger Adams, was the driver of the automobile which struck Derby. The jury group ultimately decided in favor of the defendant, Adams, and did not award damages in any amount to the plaintiff, Derby. Instrumental to this final verdict, the jury achieved consensus on a key decision that the plaintiff was negligent and therefore contributed to the accident.

**Orientation**   The opening excerpt of group interaction occurs during the first 5 minutes of the jury's deliberations. The six group participants are designated by the letters A through E. The ellipsis ( . . . ) signifies a pause in the interaction, not omitted materials.

   *A:* First of all, we decide whether it's a case of liability or negligence.
   *D:* Yeah . . . negligence.
   *A:* It's the same thing. In other words, you all feel that Roger Adams alone was negligent without the contributory negligence of Derby—or was it Derby's fault as much as Adams's fault—or was it either's fault—or was it just plain accident?
   *C:* Guilty or not guilty.
   *A:* It's not just those two choices, though. We've got three choices.
   *D:* What else can there be, though? I mean . . .
   *A:* It's not a criminal action like whether he robbed a store. It's just whether he is negligent, both of them are negligent, or whether . . .
   *D:* Yeah, I see. But there are still only two verdicts. Do we give the plaintiff any money or not?
   *A:* First of all, how many people here feel that just Roger Adams alone was negligent and that Alfred Derby, the person who was hit, in no way contributed to this negligence and therefore should receive compensation?

   Typical of a group's orientation phase are the members' attempts to accustom themselves to the topic and to the procedure. In this case they must accustom themselves to the procedure of the law and the legal directions they received from the judge.
   In the excerpt above, members proceed to discover what choices of final decisions are available to them. Essentially they are asking themselves. "What precisely is the task we are expected to accomplish?" With this fundamental step out of the way, the members proceed to probe one another's attitudes. Member A's final comment requests a preliminary survey of the first impressions of group members. How difficult will it be to achieve agreement? This first excerpt, then, typifies the early efforts of members to acclimatize themselves—first to the procedures, and then to one another.
   Member B responds to member A's request for his initial opinion and stimulates responses which are typical of the orientation phase. As member B provides argument for his opinions, A and C seem to experience discomfort. They

respond by invoking procedural rules formulated on the spur of the moment in order to keep B in check. In essence, they are telling B to withhold his evidence and reasons until later, at which time the group will thresh things out. For the present, A and C don't want to "rock the boat."

A more typical manner of expressing a member's initial attitude during the orientation phase is the following comment of A:

*A:* I feel that . . . I don't know about you guys, but it could have been me. I'm a reckless driver, and I can picture myself in a hurry to school. And there were a lot of mistakes brought out in the testimony . . . on both sides. First of all, I have always thought that the Banker's [parking] lot is the one next to Administration.

A is attempting to advance his opinion and includes supporting reasons. But his specific opinion is not totally clear from this comment. His manner of presenting his attitude is tentative and ambiguous. He even seems to apologize for attempting to express an opinion. He includes self-deprecation lest his attitude appear too forceful to the other members. He tempers his attitude by condemning "both sides" for having made mistakes in their testimony. He concludes by citing an innocuous error of fact—the location of a parking lot; he calculates that his remark will offend no one and even attributes it to his own misunderstanding. He delivers this comment with considerable hesitancy, with numerous pauses, and with trepidation. Such ambiguity is characteristic of nearly all substantive comments during orientation.

Another excerpt of the group interaction demonstrates a series of ambiguous responses which follow the initiation of a decision proposal of questionable relevance to the forthcoming decision:

*A:* I'm a little bit confused about this whole thing. I don't know if we can assume that what the attorneys said is true or not.

*C:* Not in summation you can't—unless it was brought out in testimony.

*D:* That one in the gray suit based his mostly on emotion, and if we were to go by that alone without regarding anything . . . I mean emotion is fine but . . .

*A:* You're right. A lot of it was based on emotion. I realize that, but still I don't know whether we should accept it or . . .

*C:* That was his job. We can't blame him for . . .

*A:* I guess not, but . . .

A originates this decision proposal by claiming he is confused and is seeking clarification. He does not appear to be looking for any argument. Only C expresses a definite attitude or opinion toward this proposal concerning the credibility of the attorneys. A and D respond to the proposal with ambiguous reluctance. The members continue to participate hesitantly. Note the number of unfinished sentences and phrases left dangling. Two members, A and D, appear to favor the decision proposal, but they are carefully tolerant of other members' opinions. A twice agrees with the attitude which he apparently disfavors, but he qualifies his agreement with a hint of disagreement—for example, "you're right . . . I realize that, but . . . ," and "I guess not, but . . . ." Including the qualifier "but" and implying both a favorable and an unfavorable opinion toward the proposal typify ambiguous attitudes toward nearly all decision proposals during the orientation phase.

The individual members each may have an opinion, but they feel inhibited in expressing it. They are neither sure of their own status in the group, nor do they know the social consequences of taking too strong a stand on any issue. Consequently they test their ideas and opinions, and the opinions of the other members first. Just as one tests the temperature of the water in the pool before taking the big plunge, the group members during the orientation phase test the group before risking their selves. They send up trial balloons and take readings of the group climate before committing themselves.

**Conflict**   Following the transition to the conflict phase, the members have completed developing their opinions. The period of testing the group atmosphere is over, and the general trend of idea development seems to be clear. Opinions and ideas in the orientation phase existed in their formative states. During the conflict phase, the process of formulation is complete. At this point, the group members proceed to choose up sides and engage in verbal battle over substantive issues. The following excerpt is typical of the interaction during the second phase of group decision making—the conflict phase:

*A:* The thing to decide is, was Roger Adams in a hurry? And did he act in such a manner that a reasonable, adult, mature person would?

*C:* You have to consider him a reasonable, prudent person. He was waved on by another person who was going to make the turn, irregardless [sic] of whether he was in a hurry or not.

*A:* I would say that if he is reasonable, he wouldn't take another person's word for it.

*C:* Oh, come on now! There is only one car on the street.

*A:* I certainly wouldn't do it.

*C:* Do you consider yourself reasonable?

*A:* I'm not reasonable. I'll admit it, too. But what does that have to do with it? I wouldn't want to use myself as an example. That doesn't say that he wasn't reasonable.

*B:* Then we're not going to get any place. You have to give some criteria. You can't just say he wasn't reasonable and let it go at that.

The tentativeness of expressed opinions, characteristic of interaction during the orientation phase, is certainly absent during interaction of the conflict phase. Member A's comment, which initiates the decision proposal concerning the possible negligence of the defendant, does not indicate his opinion toward the decision proposal. It is clearly a comment expressing an ambiguous opinion toward the proposal. But the tone of this ambiguous comment is clearly different from the tone of the typical ambiguous comment of the orientation phase. At this point, A does not hesitate, verbally or ideationally. He self-assuredly asserts, "The thing to decide is, . . . "

Tolerance for any dissenting opinion is not apparent in the language choices of any of these commitments. The comment implying "This is my opinion but I could be wrong," which was characteristic of the orientation phase, becomes, in the conflict phase, the comment indicating "This is my opinion and it is correct." C also asserts, "You *have* to consider him . . . ," and B asserts, "You *have* to give some criteria. You *can't* just say . . . ." These stylistic characteristics of the communicative acts implicitly *compel* the responding group members into a for-or-against choice. Neutral opinions are no longer acceptable. The language used during the interaction of the conflict phase virtually forces the members to express definite opinions. Essentially stylistic features of the interaction itself force members into conflict or ideas.

Member A is now clearly identified as a spokesman for the plaintiff, and B and C appear to be spokesmen for the defendant. The next excerpt from group interaction involves a discussion of the same decision proposal and illustrates more vividly the ideational division of the group members:

*C:* Most people, I think, would make sure that the other side was clear for him to go. I think it would be reasonably prudent to take a glance over there to make sure that the guy was still signaling you on.

*A:* I don't think you can trust another person. It's a fact that . . . I don't know if you've ever traveled on the highway behind a semitrailer . . . You're following, and semitrailers don't usually go as fast as you would like or necessarily the speed limit. You're back of the semitrailer. You keep swinging out to see if you can pass. You see the driver wave his arm out like this. That's illegal. You can't use this as evidence in court that it was safe to pass the truck.

*C:* We can't consider that. We judge on the testimony we heard in court today and yesterday.

*D:* That's kind of irrelevant.

*A:* But the truck driver said it was safe to pass just like this guy in court said.

*D:* It is the custom on the highway, illegal or not, for big trucks to be courteous enough to flick on and off their lights when it's safe for the guy behind him to pass.

*A:* How long has it been since you have traveled on the highway?

*D:* Last fall.

*A:* Well, most of them don't do it anymore. Besides, if this guy was a reasonable man, he would have wanted to find out for himself. Not just take another guy's word for it.

*C:* We shouldn't take in anything that we didn't hear in court.

*A:* But this pertains to what we heard in the courtroom. If he was a reasonable man, he wouldn't have taken this driver's word for it that he should go.

*C:* How many people agree with you on that statement? I don't, for one.

*D:* I don't.

*B:* I would take the driver's word for it.

*A:* No, you wouldn't

*C:* A reasonable person would.

The dissident A is fighting a losing battle to have the group consider his analogy regarding highway driving. His antagonists continue to be B and C. These three members engage in a heated verbal exchange over this issue.

During the conflict phase, group members know which members are on which side in the conflict over ideas and feel fewer inhibitions regarding the necessity for social facilitation. Disagreement is not only definite; it is vehement. Comments such as "Oh, come on now!" and "No, you wouldn't!" are quite common during the conflict phase. In fact, some comments are virtual insults and certainly not intended to win close friends. The question, "Do you consider yourself reasonable?" may be insulting; but C's final comment in the excerpt above, "A reasonable person would," is more than insulting. In the context of this interaction that comment is tantamount to character assassination.

At this point A appears to be the sole member of the group who favors the plaintiff's side in the civil case. Member D, not very active in earlier interaction during orientation, sides against A on this issue. But D's comments don't appear to be as vehement as B's and C's opposition. Note that D tones down his charge of irrelevance by saying, "That's kind of irrelevant," while C flatly asserts, "We can't consider that." Later D dispassionately appeals to A's reason about "custom," and disregards the issue of its legality. In fact, D continues to discuss the issue as though it were relevant.

Eventually D disagrees with A on this issue, but his disagreement is clearly not equivalent in tone, language, or manner to the disagreement of B and C. The next excerpt from the conflict phase casts more light on the role D plays in this second phase of decision emergence.

*A:* Do you think our Roger Adams testified truthfully on the stand?
*D:* I think he fudged a bit.
*A:* I do, too. That was my opinion. I realize that these are fixed situations, but let's pretend that it isn't. I mean, I think that he was trying to get himself out of a bad situation . . . as any normal person would, I suppose.
*C:* But the three witnesses for the defense—they all collaborated [sic] his testimony perfectly.
*A:* Which ones?
*C:* All three for the defense.
*B:* The guy that waved him on, the girl . . .
*D:* That is not strictly true, because the girl was a little off.
*A:* One person said that he stopped for one or two seconds and then shot out. Another one said he was there for half a minute. They didn't collaborate [sic] on that.
*E:* But one of them was watching him, and the other one was driving his own car and getting ready to go. They collaborated [sic] on the things that were important, though.
*A:* I can't see how you can say that. They didn't collaborate [sic] at all. Time was just one of the factors they didn't agree on.

Member A seems to have procured a lieutenant in D. Both are now identified with the plaintiff, while B and C continue to favor the defendant. One of the two most infrequent contributors to the group interaction, member E, identifies himself with the defendant in the excerpt above. Hence, two coalitions appear to be developing in this second phase of the group decision-making process. A and D form one coalition which favors the plaintiff. B, C, and probably E are members of the other coalition, which favors the defendant. Only member F remains clearly outside either coalition.

This jury is composed of six members. The sixth member, F, is still to be heard from in the excerpts taken from the group interaction. He has contributed to the group interaction sparingly, and his participation during the conflict phase is virtually nonexistent.

One can probably speculate that F's withdrawal from group participation results from a feeling of discomfort brought on by the vehement substantive conflict over ideas during this phase. He is undoubtedly aware of his low status in the group, which may or may not be of his own volition. Whether from apathy toward the group purpose or from an abiding fear of social conflict, F has chosen to withdraw from group interaction rather than take a stand and join one of the coalitions involved in social conflict over ideas.

In terms of the developing status hierarchy in the emergent group setting, leader-contenders are clearly emerging during this conflict phase. Member A is the most vehement spokesman for the "plaintiff's coalition." Member C, or possibly member B, seems to represent the strongest leader-contender from the "defendant's coalition." The conflict over substantive issues is undoubtedly relevant to the contention over the leadership roles, too. But member A, the leader-contender from the coalition opposed to the decision which ultimately achieves group consensus, will not remain in active contention for leadership much longer. As a member who has committed himself to a position opposing the consensus decision, his bid for leadership is doomed.

**Emergence**    Following the transition to the emergence phase, the substantive conflict among members begins to dissipate, as illustrated in a later excerpt taken from the group interaction:

*A:* Let me ask one more question. Do you think Derby (the plaintiff) was in the crosswalk?

*D:* I don't think so.

*C:* No, I don't. I don't think that has too much to do with it, though.

*D:* I agree.

*C:* I know there are some statutes about the crosswalk, but I mean the fact that he was in . . . I don't know. That might be kind of important.

*D:* He was on the roadway is really the issue.

*C:* I don't think it really happened exactly the way the defendant described it. I think he embellished it a little toward his side. I think it happened close enough to it, though.

*F:* As far as that goes, Derby may have his own story, too. I mean each would be looking out for himself. That's only natural.

*D:* Of course you are going to get this in any situation.

*F:* That's just it. Both of them. You can't use the two prime subjects. You have to try and go on the witnesses. Of course they are witnesses, too, and you have to consider them. And they are important, too, but . . . .

Member A has initiated another proposal for consideration, but his initiating statement expresses an ambiguous opinion toward it. He uses simple and straightforward language without argument. The communicative acts in response to his proposal emphasize the irrelevance of his proposal rather than attempting to deny its factual nature. During the conflict phase, the responses to such a proposal would probably have been an intense denial and consequently additional substantive conflict. In the emergence phase, though, the conflict over issues is muted.

In the second phase, members hammered out the issues and proposals they felt were important to getting their task accomplished. But their response to a new issue in the emergence phase is to dismiss it as irrelevant rather than to engage in additional conflict.

The level of social tension seems to be appreciably lower during the emergence phase. Member C is now much more tolerant of A's opinions and feelings, as illustrated in the last excerpt. He admits to the possibility that the issue raised by member A "might be kind of important." He even goes so far as to concede that the defendant "embellished" his testimony, an admission he would never have made in the conflict phase.

The emerging decision becomes progressively clearer during the emergence phase, and all members seem to sense the direction the group has taken. Even F joins the interaction, "jumping on the bandwagon" to offer his opinion in support of the defendant. When the other members don't wholeheartedly welcome his offer to join their side, F begins to flounder in his comments and becomes extremely ambiguous and vague in his comments. His final remark is a classic example of ambiguity. At any rate, the decision becomes increasingly evident, and even F knows it.

The overt conflict over substantive issues characterizing the conflict phase moderates during the emergence phase. Both A and D ameliorate their dissent from the decision proposals favoring the defendant. For example, while A vehemently and tenaciously expressed his dissenting view during the conflict phase, he expresses only ambiguous opinions without much tenacity during the emergence phase. The following excerpt clearly illustrates this change in A's verbal behavior.

*A:* I just wondered. Maybe this isn't really relevant, but I never really understood exactly where the point of impact was. Not in relation to the car, but in relation to the street. How far out from the curb he was. It appeared from the drawing and three or four witnesses that it was in the lane closest to the curb that Derby stepped off of. If this is the case, Adams made an illegal left turn. Of course, I might be mistaken.

*C:* Yeah, Right.

*B:* I think it was right in the middle.

*C:* Was it in the middle?

*D:* It was probably about 20 feet off. That might be closest to this curb.

*E:* He said he was about 11 feet off the curb, but he also put him closer to the middle.

*A:* If it was closer to the curb than it was to the intersection, it wasn't an illegal left turn. But it might have been 11 feet this way, and that would have been an illegal turn.

*D:* Eleven feet puts it right about the middle. No illegal left turn.

*C:* Remember he's turning, so he's got to come a little bit into the other lane on the turn.

*D:* Well, not necessarily.

*C:* It's pretty hard not to, with at least his front bumper.

*B:* It's pretty close, but he was probably all right on his turn. If he was out 11 feet, he was right there in the middle.

*D:* In that case he was only. . . . He's not negligent.

*A:* This is irrelevant, then.

*C:* I don't think it's possible to hit him in the middle. I don't think that it is physically possible.

*A:* No. He did make a wrong turn, but he wasn't completely out of his lane from where he should have been.

*C:* He was probably wrong in not watching exactly as he was turning. But I don't think it was too far away to be reasonable.


Another last-ditch effort by A to advocate the plaintiff's side in the discussion: Did the defendant make an illegal left turn? But A fails to raise many doubts concerning what is becoming increasingly apparent as the consensus decision. But the strength and tenacity of A's argumentativeness have dissipated. He initiates his proposal with reluctant ambiguity. Note his apologetic phrases, which appear throughout his contributions—"I just wondered. Maybe this isn't really relevant," "It appeared . . . ," "If this is the case . . . ," and the final "Of course, I might be mistaken."

During the ensuing discussion, A contributes another ambiguous argument indicating only the possibility—not even the probability—that the defendant was negligent in making an illegal left turn. Compared with his self-assured stance in the conflict phase, A has moderated his attitude considerably. He does not express certainty about any opinion he expresses in the emergence phase. He qualifies nearly everything with ambiguous language, such as "if" and "might." He resigns himself to losing the fight over this issue. In fact, he doesn't even try very hard to win it. He offers his resigned statement of capitulation, "This is irrelevant, then," even before the other members have completely rejected it. In fact, C again expresses amazing tolerance for A's proposal and once more appears to give it serious consideration before he rejects it. A has evidently succumbed to the apparent consensus decision. C apparently knows it and is softening the blow somewhat. C is definitely the leading contender for group leader, and he is willing to accept A as a high-status member whose opinions are worthy of consideration.

The two coalitions of the conflict phase also appear to dissipate during the emergence phase. Members of opposing coalitions responded to their "opponents" with open hostility and even contempt in the conflict phase, but they now respond with active rational consideration. The prime example of this change is illustrated by C's comments. He preferred to insult A during the conflict phase as a response to A's position favoring the plaintiff. But, during the emergence phase, C considers A's proposal, admits to its potential significance and credibility, and then rejects it.

Again, the basis for rejecting proposals favoring the plaintiff's case is irrelevance. Members argued against proposals during the conflict phase on the basis of their truth or falsity, but the basic issue on which members typically evaluate proposals in the emergence phase seems to be relevance.

**Reinforcement**  In the reinforcement phase, decisions have completed the process of emergence. Interaction during this final phase of the group process confirms decisions already made and develops the members' commitment or consensus toward those decisions. The following excerpt appears very early in the reinforcement phase:

*E:* Everybody saw the car coming.

*B:* Besides that, he said his lights were on.

*C:* His turn signal was on. It was obvious that he was coming. That would make it all the more easier [sic] to see the car coming.

*D:* Practically everybody saw that car coming. His lights turning.

*E:* That guy that was on the sidewalk. . . . He saw all this traffic, and he also saw Adams coming. That's why he didn't go. Why did Derby go? He has to be at some fault.

*C:* I feel sorry for him, and I'd like to help him out, but I just don't think I can.

*D:* I agree.

*B:* You can't base it on an emotion . . .

*D:* Of course not.

*C:* I don't think we should take into any account what they told us at the beginning, either—about Adams being a drunkard and that.

*B:* No. Don't even mention that.

*F:* No. Don't worry about it.

*C:* No.

Members B, C, D, and E all express agreement with the decision proposal that Derby, the defendant, was guilty of contributory negligence. They not only agree with one another, but they provide superfluous evidence to support their agreement. Interaction consistently includes statement after statement expressing agreement with the one before it. Member C initiates a "straw-man" proposal contrary to the decision already made. But he immediately expresses an unfavorable opinion toward it. Members B and F promptly concur, and they drop the proposal at once.

The major dissenter, A, is conspicuously absent from the previous interaction. But his former lieutenant, D, has certainly joined the other coalition. Even F is growing bolder and bolder with his comments, now that absolutely no doubt remains regarding the decision made by the group. As the group's interaction draws to a close, A leaves no doubt as to his completely modified position.

*A:* I guess I'd have to say that it was both their faults.

*C:* I say it is both their faults.

*A:* Evidently it probably is.

*B:* Derby really never should have stepped off the curb.

*D:* Right.

*E:* And there he was out 11 feet already, and he was trying to avoid another oncoming car. That's just plain stupid.

*F:* When you step off the curb, you know you are taking chances. You have to stay on your toes.

*A:* Well, he obviously didn't see him turn. But he should have.

*F:* He was right in front of him. He should have seen him turn.

*D:* Right. He must have been looking some place else.

*A:* I think Derby stepped off the curb, started walking, and was halfway through the first lane when this guy started to make his turn. It doesn't take long for all this to happen. Only a few seconds.

*C:* The plaintiff was making some kind of inference that Adams was going excessively fast across the turn. I don't think that's really possible.

*D:* No.

*B:* How fast can you take a turn without crashing into the corner or something?

*D:* Yeah. When you're accelerating, you still aren't going more than 9 or 10 miles per hour.

*C:* The average turn is about 6 miles per hour, maybe a little faster, but that isn't excessively fast.

*B:* It varies if he was trying to beat this other car.

*C:* But he couldn't have been going even 15 miles around a turn.

*D:* If you do, you're pulling out like a sports car.

*C:* If you have good cornering, you'll probably make it. If you don't, you might not.

*A:* We agree unanimously right now that it is both their faults.

(A chorus of "Yeah!")

*A:* It was both their faults. There is nothing more to do then.

*E:* I would say that it was mutual negligence—more Derby's (plaintiff's) fault.

*F:* I say it is all Derby's fault.

*A:* You say all Derby's fault?

*F:* Yes.

*A:* I think it is more Adams's fault. But both are still negligent.

*C:* Okay. Then it's unanimous.

*F:* I say that Derby was completely at fault. He shouldn't even be suing.

*C:* You mean that Adams should be suing?

*F:* Right.

*A:* There are two possibilities on this sheet. Let me read them both. "Number

1: We, the jury, find in favor of the plaintiff and against the defendant and assess damages to the sum of . . . ." In other words, we think it was Adams's fault, and Derby should pay.

*C:* Throw that one out.

*A:* Okay. We'll throw that one out. "Number 2: We, the jury, find in favor of the defendant and against . . . ." In other words, if they think it is more Derby's fault.

*D:* No. Just the plaintiff.

*C:* In favor of the defendant legally means it isn't the plaintiff. It doesn't mean that the defendant can claim damages. It just means that the suit has been dropped.

*B:* We find in favor of the defendant.

*C:* Yes.

*A:* That's how we do it then.

*B:* Write "Contributory negligence."

*D:* We are all decided.

*C:* Unanimous decision. No dissenters.

Throughout these final moments of group interaction is a pervading spirit of harmony and unity. All members agree, and everyone knows that all members agree. But they continue to discuss the decision while verbally slapping each other on the back even to the point of initiating another "straw-man" decision proposal. Three of the members join in verbally demolishing the plaintiff's argument concerning Adams's excessive speed.

Meanwhile, A firmly commits himself to the position that Derby is also at fault. His language still includes traces of reluctance. But his expression of agreement is completely understandable, given his earlier attitude of vehement opposition during the conflict phase. He closes his comments in the language of willing reluctance with such statements as "I guess I'd have to say . . . " and "Evidently it probably is." Nevertheless, he is firmly committed to the consensus decision.

The nonparticipant in the conflict phase, F, is caught up in the spirit of consensus, and he overreacts to the obvious consensus decision. He goes so far as to assess 100 percent negligence to the plaintiff. Not even members B and C want to go this far. They don't pay too much attention to F's Johnny-come-lately enthusiasm. They have made their decision, and they have reinforced it.

To avoid any doubts and probably in deference to A's rationale for making the decision unanimous, B suggests that the group explain to the court that the basis for its decision was "contributory negligence." The addition of the members' rationale is superfluous, but they do it anyway. The final comments allude to the written record which they return to officials of the mock court confirming their consensus decision.

**Summary**   The process of group decision making thus progresses through four phases of interaction—orientation, conflict, emergence, and reinforcement. The decisional process, closely allied with characteristics of the social dimension reflecting the interdependent relationship of the two dimensions, is a cumulative and cyclical process. Group members anchor their interaction to tentative decision proposals leading to, and culminating in, consensus or final group decisions.

Excerpts from an actual group's interaction reflect the "flavor" of the discussion and the importance of stylistic features of the language and changes in individual members' attitudes as their group progresses toward consensus. Although the four phases seem to be clearly separate in the excerpted interaction from each of the four phases, the transitions between phases are in reality quite gradual and not nearly as dramatic as they appear in selected excerpts. This, then, is the process of group decision making in action.

# Analysis of
# Small Group Interaction

The phenomenon of human communications is extremely complex. If there were ever any doubts as to the truth of that statement, they should be dispelled by now. Perhaps because of its highly complex nature, human communication has fascinated social scholars for centuries, dating back to Aristotle and beyond. Undoubtedly because of its complexity, communication yet evades our attempts to grasp a complete understanding of it. Simply stated, human communication is extraordinarily difficult either to analyze or to describe.

One commonly overlooked barrier to understanding communication is the tendency to conceive of it as someone's doing something to someone else. The syntactical structure inherent in our English language (subject–verb–object) encourages this unfortunate view of human communication. From our first reading of sentences, such as "The boy hits the ball," we have been encouraged to view communication as some action being perpetrated by someone on someone else. We commonly describe acts of communication in subject-verb-object language—a person persuades, informs, entertains, comforts, convinces, cajoles, dominates, leads, follows, etc., another person. The common tendency to view communication as the transmission and reception of messages also encourages a one-way linear view of action transmitted by a "source" who affects a "receiver" of that action.

This linear view of communication, highlighted perhaps by the structure of the English language, does not easily correspond to the view of communication as a process—an interdependent relationship developed among communicating people who willingly engage in a system of interstructured behaviors. The linear view of communication is also inconsistent with the view of leadership described in Chapter 7, which equated leadership with followership—again as an interdependent relationship between people's behaviors. The problem of viewing acts of human communication free from the restrictions of transmitting and receiving action is a difficult one to solve.

This section overviews some methods commonly used for the observation of human communication in the context of a small group. This overview serves as a preliminary step toward understanding why the method of interaction analysis is probably a superior method to observe communication and small groups as an interactive process. Central to the model of decision emergence discussed in Chapter 5 and Appendix 1 is a specific observational system of interaction analysis. A general description of that system is also included as an example of how interaction analysis may be applied to the observation and analysis of communication and group process in ongoing decision-making groups.

## COMMON OBSERVATIONAL METHODS

The number of different methods used to observe small group communication staggers the imagination. Nearly every method employed in the broad spectrum of social and behavioral sciences has, at one time or another, been applied to group communication. This section attempts to review only a few of these methods and does not describe any single method comprehensively. It should soon be obvious that these methods, widely used and certainly valuable for certain purposes, provide only a limited insight into communication and group process, which naturally is our primary interest.

### Self-Reports

Undoubtedly the most simple method (and one that is often overlooked for that reason) to discover what people think or feel is to ask them. The Gallup and Roper polls of public opinion, along with the almost infamous Nielsen ratings of television programs, reflect specifically this method of social observation. Members of small groups often complete self-reports in the form of oral interviews or written questionnaires. The diary, another self-report from group members, has been mentioned in several chapters. Members of classroom groups are often asked to record in such diaries their impressions and reactions immediately following each group meeting. Usually the diary does not require specific answers to specific questions but asks only what the member thinks has happened to the group and to his or her own role in that group during that specific meeting.

Members' diaries are valuable as an observational method in that people frequently record in their diaries those feelings and thoughts which they might not wish to express during interaction with fellow group members. People are generally more willing to confide in the impersonal diary those thoughts which might otherwise escape observation. They tend to be much more frank in their diaries than in actual communication with other people, particularly in a newly formed group. Self-reports thus provide important additional information to the observer of group interaction. This information is particularly valuable in order to gain insight into the group's social dimension.

Despite the obvious value of the self-reporting method of observing small groups, there are problems inherent in the method itself. In many respects, the least knowledgeable source of information on any specific person is that very person. We are often unaware of how we behave, what we do, and particularly what we are thinking or feeling. Many behaviors are performed from habit or at least without willful concentration. If it is true that people act in accordance with behavioral "rules" even though they need not be aware of those rules, then people are not necessarily aware of what they do or why they do it.

It is also extremely difficult to put thoughts and feelings into words. We just don't have the appropriate language or ability to express a feeling. Most of us find it difficult even to put our sensations into words. Try, for example, to describe the taste of an avocado or an artichoke to someone who has never tasted one. Describe the smell of some exotic cologne or perfume to someone who has never experienced that aroma. An insurmountable problem, and one that I have encountered personally, is to describe the sensation of sub-zero cold to a person who has never left the Hawaiian Islands. Our literature of song and novels is replete with attempts to put into words the common emotion of love. Such attempts have proved futile as well as amazingly contradictory. We simply don't have the language to express many of our feelings, emotions, and sensations— even those which we are aware of having experienced.

Furthermore, self-reports often distort the truth. All of us have naturally developed defense mechanisms that serve to protect our ego, our personality. When the truth is harmful to our image of self or when reporting reality would embarrass us, we typically distort our perception of our true feelings, behaviors, or motives. Perceptual distortion is not necessarily conscious prevarication. In fact, we often believe the distortion to be the truth and are not even aware of having distorted anything. Under any circumstances, self-reports from group members are to be suspect. Relying on such an unreliable method as the principal means for observing group communication can easily lead to inaccurate, as well as incomplete, information.

The members' degree of involvement in their group and their group task may also stimulate distorted self-reports. The overly involved member tends to idealize the group and evaluate the group's behavior higher than it probably merits. Conversely, the member with an extremely low level of commitment to the group tends to judge it as less effective than it is. An example may clarify this. Students routinely filling out questionnaires designed to evaluate their university classroom experience once demonstrated the effects of involvement, both high and low, on their self-reports. Responding to an item asking students to evaluate the written examinations required in the class, one student rated the exams at the maximum, "very good." Another student in the same class rated the exams at the minimum, "very poor." The response of neither the highly involved nor the relatively uninvolved student reflected reality. In fact, most students didn't respond to that item on the questionnaire—because that particular class did not include any examinations.

Finally, self-reports from group members should be suspect because they inherently rely on the individual's memory. Rather than observe group members during group interaction, self-reports consist of responses from members after the fact. The human memory is quite fallible, with incomplete and distorted information typically present. You may be familiar with the classroom exercise in which one person tells a story to a second person, who in turns relays that message to a third person, who tells it to a fourth person, and so forth. After the second or third transmission, the story bears little resemblance to its original form. The human memory is imperfect. It forgets and distorts information as a normal occurrence.

## Group Outcomes

Perhaps the method most commonly used for observing group decision making is measuring the outcome of group discussion—the quantity or quality of decisions reached by the group members. This procedure typically involves determining the structural attributes of the group as it begins its task efforts and observing the results which accrue from the members' efforts, allegedly as a result of the particular combination of structural attributes. For example, a five-man group and a five-woman group may be given the same decision-making task. The decisions reached by those two groups is then observed and compared. Any difference in the decisions reached by two groups is then attributed to the group's predominant structural characteristic of difference—the sex of its members.

Concentrating on the outcome from group discussion also possesses serious and inherent shortcomings. For example, the quantity of decisions which a group makes is typically irrelevant. Often a group has only one decision to make, such as "guilty" or "not guilty." But the quality of decisions is also difficult to measure when no objective method outside the group interaction is available to validate the group decision. When a group decision-making task is involved, there is no externally valid decision; the sole criterion of quality is the extent to which the decision achieves group consensus. How, then, can the quality of the outcome of a group decision-making task be reliably measured? No adequate answer to this question is currently available.

Because of the insurmountable difficulty involved in measuring the quality of group decisions, observers of group decision making often observe groups performing tasks more suited to individual decision making. Such tasks have a single "best" or "correct" answer, and their quality is objectively evident. But groups performing tasks intended for expert individuals are doing little more than playing pseudo-intellectual games. Such tasks severely restrict the group process and encourage expert individual members to dominate other group members. At the very least, no advantage is gained from observing groups that perform tasks unsuitable to the social context. But such observations unfortunately occur routinely.

Observing the group from the perspective of its outputs also assumes that structural conditions at the time of group formation determine what outcomes the group will eventually achieve. That is, a structural characteristic (for example, all males) or combination of structural characteristics causes the group to arrive at its decisions. Such an assumption absolutely denies the inherent interdependence of the members, their behaviors, the group dimensions, and so forth—interdependent relationships inherent in the nature of a process. In fact, the assumption that group structure determines group action is patently impossible in an open system, which is the perspective of small groups employed throughout this book.

Finally, observing only the group's outcomes is highly incomplete. At best, such an observational method answers only questions of *why* and *whether* group members achieve their outcomes. But it ignores the more important question of *how* groups achieve consensus. And only answers to the latter question can provide any insight into how we might increase the potential effectiveness of group decision making.

## Sociometry

Sociometric methods are also commonly utilized for observing small groups. Sociometry, whose pictorial representations of social relationships are often known as sociograms, concerns itself solely with selected elements of the social dimension of a system. Essentially, sociometric methods seek to discover interpersonal attractions and repulsions among various members of the group, that is, the positive and negative feelings each group member has for each other.

While valuable as an insight into a group's socioemotional dimension, sociometric methods afford at best only a partial view of the process of group development. By discovering the extent to which members are attracted to other members and are willing to work with them in other endeavors, the observer has some basis for assessing the degree of cohesiveness of that group. But in terms of any knowledge of a group's task dimension, sociometry is quite irrelevant.

Sociometric methods are also limited to the interpersonal attraction of group members at a specific point in time. That is, such methods can reveal the degree of cohesiveness only as it exists at the particular time at which the sociometric methods of observation are applied—usually as a self-report questionnaire distributed to the group members. Sociometry does not attempt to discover how the members developed their feelings, positive or negative, toward one another. In effect, sociometry's primary concern is with outcomes of group interaction in the social dimension of group development.

Not only do sociometric methods of group observation ignore totally the elements of the task dimension, but they also severely restrict the principle of interdependence inherent in a group process. Nearly every chapter in this book has emphasized the pervasive influence of interdependence, ranging from the global interdependence of the task and social dimensions to the specific interdependence of particular interacts which members perform during each successive phase of group decision making. Sociometry emphasizes the interdependence of group members only through their degree of internalized liking or attraction toward one another. That is, according to the inherent assumptions upon which sociometry is based, members of a group develop interdependent relationships only through reciprocating internalized feelings of attraction with one another. Thus, a group's interdependence is based on emotions, feelings, or other internalized phenomena rather than on the external communicative behaviors assumed by this book's perspective of communication and group process.

In summary, the three general types of observational methods used to analyze and describe small groups are generally unsatisfactory for our purposes. Certainly each of these methods provides highly valuable information about small groups, but that information is of a highly specialized and restricted scope. As far as communication and group process are concerned, these observational modes are only indirectly useful and only partially relevant.

First and foremost, all three methods—self-reports, outcome measures, and sociometry—ignore the interdependent structural and action aspects of any process. Each method is capable of observing the group at only a single instant in time and can therefore discover something about the group's structure at that time only. If the group is observed several times by using one of these methods, the observer can discover aspects of group structure as they exist at several different points in time. Comparing each observation with the others allows the observer to determine whether the group experienced any changes in its structure from one point in time to another. But how those changes occurred—the process of structural change—escapes observation. If we are committed to the perspective of communication and group process, as we are, these methods cannot be considered satisfactory for our purposes.

All three types of observational methods discussed above also ignore the actual communicative behaviors of group members in preference to observing indirectly the internalized feelings of the members. The methods seek to discover what members "feel" about something rather than to observe what they *do* about it. That is, the methods ask the group member to become introspective about his or her experiences, but not one of the methods strives to discover what those experiences actually have been. The members' communicative behaviors escape the observer's eye as the observations emphasize the effects of those behaviors. The viewpoint of this book stipulates that the interstructured behaviors of members precipitate the effects or outcomes and are therefore the most important element of all small groups to be observed.

Finally, the principle of interdependence employed by these methods is radically different from the principle as it has been discussed in preceding chapters of this book. Earlier chapters have consistently viewed interdependence as a relationship greater than the sum of its components, in which every component affects and is mutually affected by all other components. A leader leads because followers follow, which is precisely the same as saying that followers follow because leaders lead. Thus, leadership is an interdependent relationship between leader and follower and not a one-way linear influence exerted by one of the partners in the relationship. Both leader and follower interdependently form the social phenomenon of leadership.

The observational methods previously discussed, however, seek interpersonal relationships solely from the viewpoint of an individual member. Thus, the observer discovers what one group member feels or perhaps does vis-á-vis another member but forsakes the interdependent relationship which structures the behaviors of the two members and transcends the individual viewpoint of either. As these methods focus on a single component or characteristic of a group, they deny the principle of interdependence and wholeness which requires that the observational viewpoint be the gestalt of the entire group taken as a whole, single entity.

It is again important to emphasize that self-reports, group outcomes, and sociométric methods of observing small groups are important and indeed valuable as techniques to observe selected structural aspects of decision-making groups. As a fundamental observational method from the viewpoint of communication and group process, however, each of these methods is too restricted in its scope and possesses too many inherent limitations to be highly useful.

## OBSERVING COMMUNICATIVE BEHAVIOR

Obviously, any method of group observation satisfactory for our purposes directly observes the communicative behaviors of all group members. Equally obvious is the fact that observing communicative behavior is extraordinarily difficult. There are no yardsticks, no microscopes with which to observe a communicative act. Communicative acts, first of all, are not physical objects which exist principally in space, such as a molecule of water. Rather, a communicative act exists only in the dimension of time. It is fleeting and transient. It ceases to exist immediately and is not permanently available for observation. And any relatively permanent record of communicative behavior, such as film or videotape, is inherently and vitally incomplete and distorted, which further compounds the problem of observation.

Of course, not all human behavior is necessarily communicative. Although any behavior may be communicative in a given situation, some behaviors performed during group interaction are not relevant in that they do not significantly affect the group process of interaction. Thus, any observation of communicative acts must judge which behaviors are significant or relevant and which are not. No concrete guidelines are available to enable an observer to make such judgments with unquestioned validity and reliability. And authorities in communication even disagree on what communication is.

The problems involved in observing communicative behaviors are not yet solved to everyone's satisfaction. This section emphasizes only a very few of those knotty problems encountered when attempting to describe and analyze human communicative behavior.

### Verbal and Nonverbal

You may have heard Stan Freberg's rather well-known recording of "John and Marcia," now several decades old. At the time it was first released, many radio stations banned the humorist's record from being played on the air on the ground that it was too suggestive. Interestingly enough, this record includes only background organ music to male and female voices (both by Freberg) repeating just two words over and over—"John" and "Marcia." But the full impact of the record is not available by reading a verbal transcript of the spoken words. Even without the visual medium, the nonverbal aspects of the record were sufficient for many people to consider the record obscene. Admittedly, most people thought the record was just humorous.

By comparison, the observation of verbal communicative acts is relatively simple. A written transcript provides a rather permanent record of verbal communication. The language employed by communicators embodies both a syntactical structure and semantic aspect which are generally clear to users of that language. Of course, meanings of words and phrases are typically developed throughout the interaction, as McHugh (1968) has demonstrated. But, all things considered, verbal communication is quite susceptible to observation when compared with nonverbal aspects of communicative behavior.

Scheflen (1969) firmly states that a complete observation of human communication should include both verbal and nonverbal aspects. But nonverbal communication—those elements of communication which do not involve an actual language or words, those elements of communication which do not appear in a stenographic transcript—is not easily observable. Nonverbal communication possesses no accepted rules of syntactical structure and no clear-cut meanings of nonverbal symbols. A brief survey of just a few of the varieties of nonverbal communication should highlight the difficulties inherent in observing it systematically or deriving any significant conclusions from its observation.

Perhaps the most familiar form of nonverbal communication is through the use of gestures and bodily movement. Commonly known as "kinesics," this form of nonverbal communication recently achieved a modicum of national popularity with the publication of a popularized, highly incomplete, and oversimplified treatment in a book called *Body Language,* written by a free-lance writer, Julius Fast. *Body Language* was later the subject of a scathing and derisively frank book review (Huenergardt, 1971), which may be of interest to those who have read Fast's book as their only exposure to nonverbal communication.

As one might suspect, attempting to observe gestures and bodily movements as communicative acts is exceedingly difficult. What does a wave of the arm mean? How does one determine the difference between a nervous twitch and nonverbal communication? Do gestures differ in meaning and significance when used with spoken language? Attempts to answer such questions range from the unwieldy and cumbersome kinesic "alphabet" of Birdwhistell (1970, pp. 257–302) to the overly ambiguous and global analysis of Knapp (1972), discounting Fast's popularized version. The complexity of observing gestural communication is illustrated by Birdwhistell's notation system, which includes ten symbols for different movements of the neck, thirteen symbols for different eye movements, and no fewer than twenty-four different positions of the mouth. Precisely what all those movements mean in a communicative situation remains highly speculative.

Communicators also use physical space as a medium for communication. The distance between communicators, which, like kinesics, varies from one culture to another, is a variety of nonverbal communication generally known as "proxemics." The study of proxemic communication and personal space has been confounded by the discovery of territorial behavior in nonhuman species. That is, a bird or other animal tends to lay claim to a particular geographical area and to defend that area against invaders. But, despite numerous attempts to confirm territorial behavior in humans, territoriality has not been found to be a significant influence on human behavior (Weick, 1968, p. 90).

Applied to small group communication, proxemics has typically taken the form of determining whether the group leader tends to take a seat at the head of a rectangular table or whether most messages are exchanged between persons facing each other, sitting beside each other, or sitting diagonally from each other (Sommer, 1969). Such questions are probably only peripheral to a fruitful perspective of communication and small groups as a process because these questions assume a deterministic influence of the physical environment on the group's structure. Moreover, knowledge of a group process would lead us to believe that group members probably accustom themselves over a period of time to whatever spatial aspects of nonverbal communication are prevalent among the members. As group interaction progresses through time, group members tend to be less susceptible to the influence of the physical environment on their behavior.

Other nonverbal aspects of human communication appear to be significant in the observation of total communicative behavior. Williams (1970) and Lynch (1970) illustrate how stylistic features and syntactical structures of language employed by communicators may be observed, even though the observation may not be convenient or easy. Certainly vocal quality, emphasis, pitch, use of pauses, rate of speaking, pronunciation, word choice, and dialect contribute to the communicative act. Appendix 1, Anatomy of a Decision, hints at the potential significance of some of these nonverbal aspects of the language—specifically, pauses and word choice. These nonverbal aspects of verbal expression certainly are important to understanding the complete communicative situation.

Generally speaking, the methods used to observe nonverbal aspects of group communication are relatively unsophisticated at this early stage of development and unfortunately are of limited usefulness because of the narrow extent of our knowledge. Until new and more convenient methods to observe nonverbal communication are devised and related to group process, the analytical method which will be proposed for the observation of group communication must reluctantly include only verbal aspects of communication.

The omission of nonverbal communication is particularly unfortunate. Scheflen (1965) has demonstrated that nonverbal communicative behavior is potentially quite significant to a process viewpoint of interdependent behaviors in group communication. Nevertheless, the system of interaction analysis to be discussed in the next section excludes consideration of nonverbal communicative behaviors. It is hoped that such nonverbal aspects can be incorporated into an analytical system at some future date.

## Effects of the Observer on Groups

Observing all the communicative behaviors, or even just verbal behaviors, of group members during group interaction requires that an observer be present in one form or another throughout the entire period of group interaction. The observation, of course, may not require the physical presence of an observing person. But some observational device, such as a camera or a tape recorder, must be present in order to provide a semipermanent record of the group's interaction. The question inevitably arises as to whether the presence of an observer or observational device significantly affects the behavior of group members during their interaction. That is, do members of a group behave differently because they are aware that they are being watched?

Sherif and Sherif (1964, p. 10) indicate that an observer unavoidably affects the behavior of persons who are aware of being observed. On the other hand, Herrold et al. (1953) state that the effect of an observer on group interaction is not significant. But Barker and Wright (1955) are more specific in their highly plausible explanation of the extent to which an observer affects group behavior. These authors indicate that the observer exerts substantial effect on behaving persons only during a brief period when the observation begins. As they become accustomed to being observed, individuals essentially ignore the outside observer, whom they consider to be a part of the context, and behave normally.

Applied specifically to the process of small group decision making, the effect of the observer on the group process is probably negligible during most of the interaction. During the orientation phase, primary tension is at its peak, and the members are attempting to accustom themselves to the unfamilarity of the group task and the social structure of the group. At this time of self-acclimatization, the observer is just another unfamiliar phenomenon which must be considered along with all other aspects of the physical environment. It is reasonable to assume that after the members have alleviated their primary tension, the impact of an observer or observational device will be minimized.

Of course, the observer who is physically present with clipboard in hand and within sight of the "guinea pigs" may continue to develop "fish bowl" feelings among group members. Observational methods that require members to be wired to some electronic device which records their physiological responses would also hardly evoke normal behaviors from the persons being so observed. On the other hand, an unobtrusive tape recorder or camera should not reasonably evoke feelings among members that they are nothing more than guinea pigs in a laboratory. Indeed, classroom groups utilizing cassette tape recorders typically admit that they soon forget that the tape recorder is there at all. On at least one occasion, a classroom group demonstrated the minimal influence of the audiotape recorder on its interactive patterns. When the group failed to return the recorder after one of its group meetings, it was discovered that the members had concluded their meeting and left the room with the tape recorder still running. There are also numerous examples of recorded dialogue from classroom groups which, owing to the language they use and the subject matter they choose to discuss, reflect their almost total lack of inhibitions.

We can probably safely conclude that the observer of group communication may affect the communicative behavior of group members during their earliest and generally unstructured period of interaction. But the impact of the observer is probably localized within the initial period of observation and does not significantly affect the group process of decision making.

## INTERACTION ANALYSIS

The method of observation most pertinent to communication and the group process is interaction analysis. "Analysis" typically implies breaking down some whole into its component parts. For example, an analysis of the content of pure water reveals the presence of two units of hydrogen and one unit of oxygen. In this example of analysis, the content of water is analyzed into its compositional elements. The principle is the same for the first step in an analysis of interaction—reducing the whole of interaction into its compositional factors and the relative quantity of each.

"Now is the time for all good men to come to the aid of their party" is a familiar sentence used for a variety of purposes. The sentence may also be submitted to various systems of content analysis. One system might analyze the sentence into categories of "parts of speech" and use "words" as the units to be measured or counted. Such an analysis would reveal sixteen words analyzed as four nouns, two verbs, four adjectives, one pronoun, one adverb, and four prepositions. (I surely hope my English grammer is correct.)

Often this sentence is used to test the functional operation of a typewriter in much the same way that the prospective automobile buyer kicks the tires of an automobile. But a second content analysis of that same sentence using letters of the alphabet as units of measurement as well as analytical categories reveals that eight letters are not included in that sentence. Thus, the typewriter inspector would fail to observe the function of eight different keys. A better sentence used for the purpose of testing typewriters would be, "The quick brown fox jumps over the lazy dog's back." A similar content analysis of this latter sentence reveals at least one instance of every letter of the alphabet. (Go ahead and check it.)

Interaction analysis, then, is a general method for analyzing the content of communicative behaviors by breaking down the whole of interaction into its component acts. Experts in many fields of study have employed numerous varieties and methods of interaction analysis, but the remainder of this section offers only a few of those varieties. This section will further emphasize one particular method of interaction analysis exemplified by two specific systems. For a more complete description of the various methods of content analysis, many books are available which describe such procedures in much greater detail. One source book that focuses on various methods of content analysis and provides guidelines for developing new methods is Holsti's (1969).

## Characteristics

Perhaps the most important characteristic of any form of content analysis is developing the categories or "pigeonholes" to classify the units of the content which is to be analyzed. For example, the simple illustrations of content analysis, mentioned earlier, employed chemical elements, parts of speech, and letters of the alphabet as analytical categories. A postal employee is something of a content analyst, too, when sorting mail into pigeonholes or mailbags. The various destinations of mailed items are used as analytical categories.

The categories used for all methods of content analysis also possess several essential characteristics. The list of categories used to analyze the content of group interaction, for our purposes, must be exhaustive, mutually exclusive, and context-free. "Exhaustive" categories imply that every potential communicative act must be capable of being placed in one of the categories. If any communicative act does not fit into one of the categories, the categories do not exhaust all possible communicative behaviors. Hence, some known communicative behaviors are not analyzed by the system.

"Mutually exclusive" categories stipulate that any communicative act can be placed in one and only one category. In other words, no two categories overlap. However, a complete list of analytical categories of any given system may include several dimensions or subcategories. In that case, all categories within each dimension must be mutually exclusive.

Categories are "context-free" to the extent that a communicative act is the same in all groups observed. That is, acts representing any category are the same in one group as they appear in any other group. For example, a group member expresses disagreement in one group in much the same manner that another group member expresses disagreement in any other group.

Methods of interaction analysis employed in the past have varied widely in terms of the categories used for the analysis of group interaction. For example, Fisher (1970a) and Longabaugh (1963) developed categories based on the various functions performed by communicative acts. Bales (1950a, 1950b) based his categories of interaction process analysis (IPA) on task and social problems which a group encounters during interaction. Berg's (1967) and Charles Larson's (1969) categories were themes discussed by members. Other category systems might include the intent of the communicator or the act's effect on the environment. It is obvious that there are no standard categories used in the interaction analyses of small groups—no list of categories upon which all or even most experts can even begin to agree. The reason for the absence of any standard list of categories of communicative behaviors should be apparent. Experts cannot agree even on a common theory of communication. Hence, they cannot agree on specific applications (that is, concrete acts) of a single theory. Although Bales's system of interaction process analysis has enjoyed more popular usage than any other, it has probably outlived any further usefulness.

A second characteristic essential to a system of interaction analysis is the unit of measurement. In other words, what is the communicative act to be counted and placed into a category? Again there is no standardized unit of measurement. Hawes (1972a, 1972b), Berg (1967), and Amidon and Flanders (1967) counted as units of communicative behaviors time intervals ranging from 3 to 5 seconds. Bales (1950a, 1950b), along with Crowell and Scheidel (1961), preferred to use the expression of a single thought as a unit. Fisher (1970a) and Valentine and Fisher (1974) employed function units reflected in group interaction.

Interaction analysis differs from content analysis in that the former takes into account the fact that the interactional units are actions or events occurring in time. In this way, interaction analysis emphasizes, not just the content of communicative acts, but the process of how the sequences of acts are interstructured during group interaction. For the purpose of group process, it is important that sequences of acts, as well as each individual act, are treated as single units. Thus, interacts and double interacts become even more important than the nature of the individual act. Interacts (units of two contiguous acts) and double interacts (units of three contiguous acts) provide an insight into the process (both structure and action) of group communication which is missing from just a content analysis of the quantity of single acts.

Many have advocated the use of multiple units of communicative acts in interaction analysis, including Weick (1968, p. 407; 1969, p. 33), McGrath and

Altman (1966, p. 74), Fisher and Hawes (1971), Scheflen (1969), and Gouran and Baird (1972). And some people have utilized interacts (Fisher, 1970a; Amidon and Flanders, 1967) and double interacts (Barker and Wright, 1955, who used the term, "cycle") in applications of interaction analysis.

Contemporary methods of interaction analysis include two specific kinds which differ significantly in their relative emphases. In the absence of better terms, they will be differentiated as "dimensional" interaction analysis and "dynamic" interaction analysis.

The type of interaction analysis discussed thus far has been the dynamic analysis which counts a specific communicative act as a unit and pigeonholes it into a single category. Dynamic analysis further emphasizes sequential clusters of acts in the form of interacts and double interacts. This kind of analysis thus attempts to observe the process of group interaction by incorporating aspects of both the structure and action of group communication. Because this type of interaction analysis attempts to discover not only whether changes occur during group interaction but how those structural changes take place over time, it is called "dynamic analysis." The specific systems of interaction analysis which appear later in this section are specific examples of dynamic interaction analysis.

Dimensional interaction analysis, on the other hand, emphasizes specific qualitative dimensions of a single communicative act. Typically, observers judge qualitatively the degree to which certain dimensions of behavior (for example, assertiveness, objectivity, dominance, clarity) are reflected in a single communicative act. Systems of dimensional analysis, such as those developed by Leathers (1971) and, to a great extent, Borgatta and Crowther (1965), emphasize specific characteristics of single acts rather than the broader view of sequences of acts embodied in a process. By observing dimensions of selected acts at various points in the discussion, of course, dimensional analysis can discover *whether* structural changes have occurred during group interaction but not the process of *how* the structure changed.

In short, dynamic interaction analysis sacrifices an in-depth analysis of specific communicative acts in favor of an evolutionary view of process. And dimensional interaction analysis sacrifices the process view in favor of an in-depth analysis of specific acts. Of course, these two types of interaction analysis are not antagonistic to each other and can easily be combined within a single system of interaction analysis. A rather comprehensive search during the writing of this book, however, failed to reveal even one instance of such a combined approach.

Any system of interaction analysis naturally does not attempt to observe all aspects of human communicative behaviors. Rather, any analysis inherently and necessarily focuses on those communicative aspects which are relevant to the categories. Hence, the categories selected for analysis are vitally important to the outcome of the analysis itself. Aspects of any behavior or act which are not reflected in the categories are implicitly considered irrelevant or insignificant and are ignored during observation and analysis. Interaction analysis, like any form of observation, is not reality itself but an abstraction of observed reality—incomplete and selective, and perhaps even somewhat distorted.

Unlike other methods of observing small groups and the process of communication, interaction analysis emphasizes what happens during group interaction, how it happens, and how changes in communicative structure occur over a period of time. Interaction analysis inherently observes communicative behavior directly. Aspects of why members behave as they do and what influence their behaviors have on determining the specific quality of eventual consensus decisions are not central to this mode of observation. Interdependent relationships, rather than their causes or effects, are considered infinitely more important and are at the core of the specific system of interaction analysis described in the following subsection.

### A System of Interaction Analysis

Since the model of decision emergence discussed in Chapter 5 resulted from applied interaction analysis, the system which led to discovering that model of group decision making seems appropriate to illustrate how interaction analysis might function. This system is admittedly imperfect, as are all others. It includes only verbal communication and probably places undue emphasis on the task dimension of the group process. Despite its imperfections, however, the following system provides a general example of how interaction analysis might be utilized to observe group communication.

Central to this system of interaction analysis, you will recall from earlier chapters, is the concept of a decision proposal. As a member presents an issue for consideration by other group members, that issue is potentially an item which will achieve group consensus—that is, a proposed decision being considered by the group members. As each member comments on that proposal, he or she implicitly attempts to influence the group's perception of the proposal. (Naturally, a member need not be aware of attempting to influence the other members.) Thus, each comment "functions" on that proposal in some specific manner. The different functions which a member can perform on a decision proposal through an act of communication constitute the list of categories used in the analysis.

Each member's uninterrupted comment is considered a unit or an act of communication. If an uninterrupted comment contains an instance of two functions (that is, if a single comment crosses function categories before it is interrupted by a comment from another member), it is considered two units. During actual observation of groups, nearly all uninterrupted comments were found to contain but a single act or unit of communication.

These functionally defined units are quite obviously not of uniform length in either number of words or number of seconds. A single person performing a single function on the decision proposal in a single uninterrupted comment is considered to be a single act or communication unit regardless of its relative length.

The categories for this system of interaction analysis, slightly modified from their original form, are as follows:

1 Interpretation
    **f**    Favorable toward the decision proposal
    **u**    Unfavorable toward the decision proposal
    **ab**    Ambiguous toward the decision proposal containing a bivalued (both favorable and unfavorable) evaluation
    **an**    Ambiguous toward the decision proposal containing a neutral evaluation

**2** Substantiation
   **f**   Favorable toward the decision proposal
   **u**   Unfavorable toward the decision proposal
  **ab**  Ambiguous toward the decision proposal containing a bivalued (both favorable and unfavorable) evaluation
  **an**  Ambiguous toward the decision proposal containing a neutral evaluation
**3** Clarification
**4** Modification
**5** Agreement
**6** Disagreement

     Several additional symbols are employed to simplify the analysis of interaction in practice. One symbol, $O_n$, is used in addition to one of the categories above. It designates that act as the one which originates a new decision proposal (identified by a subscript number) by introducing that proposal into the group discussion for the first time. Another symbol, $D_n$, represents the act that reintroduces into group discussion a decision proposal (identified by its original subscript number) which the group members had discussed previously. These two symbols do not represent categories of acts. Rather, they are used in addition to the actual analysis of interaction in order that the observer may keep track of which decision proposal is under consideration at all times.

     A category, designated "procedural," not included in the above list, specifies acts which do not actually discuss a decision proposal and are not substantive to the process of group decision making. Such acts coded into the "Procedural" category rarely occurred during group interaction and were excluded from the final results of interaction analysis.

     Although the categories are not difficult to understand, a brief explanation of each is probably necessary. The category of "interpretation" (1) reflects a simple value judgment without evidence, reasons, or explanation offered to support the credibility of that judgment. "Substantiation" (2), on the other hand, refers to an act which does include supporting evidence or reasons to enhance the believability of the expressed value judgment. Thus, an act of "substantiation" may be considered more argumentative than one of "interpretation."

     Both "interpretation" and "substantiation" are subject to further classification in one of four subcategories or dimensions of the larger category. "Favorable" (f) and "unfavorable" (u) categories should be self-explanatory. The two varieties of "ambiguous" categories may be less clear. The comment, "That seems like a good idea, but it has some flaws," is ambiguous because it includes both a favorable and an unfavorable evaluation of the proposal—hence, a bivalued evaluation and an instance of the "ab" category. The comment, "That is a very interesting suggestion," is unclear because it evaluates the idea without expressing clear approval or disapproval of the suggestion—hence a neutral evaluation and an instance of the "an" category. Both comments, of course, reflect interpretation rather than substantiation and also both the general and the specific dimensions of the category—that is, "1 ab" and "1 an" respectively.

     The category of "clarification" (3) indicates those acts which function to render an idea pertaining to the decision proposal more readily understandable.

No evaluation is evident in such a comment. Rather, the act restates some previous act in more concrete language.

"Modification" (4) signifies an act functioning to amend the decision proposal under consideration by direct means. The section in Chapter 5 which discusses the group process of modifying decisions notes that instances of this category rarely occur during group interaction.

"Agreement" (5) and "disagreement" (6) express support or nonsupport of the immediately preceding act. A typical "5" comment, such as "Yes," "You're right," or "Okay," does not function directly on the decision proposal. But such a comment indirectly affects the members' perception of that proposal by adding weight to the act which precedes the agreement. Whatever the preceding function unit, the "5" unit assumes the functional meaning of that antecedent category and underscores it. If "5" follows a "2 f" unit, for example, it reinforces by agreement the substantiation favoring the decision proposal.

If "6" or "disagreement" follows a "2 f" act, it expresses disfavor through negatively reinforcing the favorable substantiation. The "6" unit, then, indirectly functions as a negative evaluation of the decision proposal by disfavoring the specific preceding act which favored it. An excerpt from an actual group discussion may serve to clarify how one may apply this system of interaction analysis. The following excerpt is from a management training group (all-male) discussing budget allocations for its hypothetical corporation. Decision proposal 1 might be phrased, "The corporation should seek to discover what its fixed costs will be after the proposed plant expansion has been completed." The first comment in the excerpt below initiates this proposal, and all other comments are directed toward that single proposal. The symbols which appear to the left of each communicative act indicate the classification of each unit according to the categories of the system. When in doubt, refer to the previous listing of the categories and their identifying symbols.

$1an0_1$    A: Would we want to spend $2,000 this first quarter to find out what the cost of our plant expansion is going to be?

3 (asks for) D: The cost of what?

3    A: Our fixed expenses. Would we like to know how much they are going to be?

1 u    B: No. I'm not really worried about that.

1 u    D: No. I'm not concerned about that.

2 f    A: But if we are concerned about production and profit, that's a factor. That is a fixed operating cost we are going to have to live with. We should know in advance what it is going to cost us.

6    B: No.

2 u    C: But knowing it won't influence our decision to expand or not.

2 u    D: Why pay $2,000 to get it if we are going to have to pay it anyway?

2 f    A: Until we do it the first time, we've got no idea if this is going to be another $6,000 or whether it's going to be as high as $30,000. That might influence us considerably on our long-range goals.

| 2 u | *B:* | We are going to have to expand in spite of that, though. |
| 2 u | *D:* | I don't think we are ever going to refuse to expand. So the first time that we do expand, we are going to find out the fixed operating cost. |
| 5 | *G:* | Yes. |
| 2 u | *D:* | By rights, is shouldn't be more. By normal operating procedures, it shouldn't be more than we pay right now. It should be less because our main plant has already been built. |
| 3 (asks for) | *A:* | Do you mean less than $6,000? |
| 3 (restates) | *D:* | Yes, I do. |
| 2 u | *A:* | Well, if it is anything less than $6,000, it would really be silly to spend $2,000 to find it out. |
| 2 u | *D:* | By just using common business sense, you have to say it is $6,000 or less. It can't be more unless they have to blast a hillside out of the way to get the addition to the main plant in. |
| 5 | *C:* | Yes, I think you're right. |

The above excerpt should explain by example how this system of interaction analysis may be utilized in actual practice. Note the several comments that ask for clarification. In both cases, the comment immediately following the request provides the clarification. Member D's "Yes, I do" might appear, outside the context of the interaction, to be agreement. But it is really a clarification of his preceding comment in direct response to A's request for clarification of his intended meaning. The other coded acts appear to need no further explanation.

After the group interaction has been analyzed into acts, the interaction is then divided into interacts. Figure Appendix 2-1 illustrates the interacts included in the excerpt coded above. The rows of the matrix in this figure are the categories of the interaction analysis system which include the first or "antecedent" comment of each interact. The columns across the top of the matrix are the categories of the second or "subsequent" act of each interact. Thus, each cell in the matrix represents an interact. The first act is the row across, and the second act is the column down.

The nineteen acts appearing in the excerpt above translate into eighteen interacts. The first act "1 an" is the antecedent of the second act "3." Together the two acts compose the first interact in the excerpt. The second act "3" is also the antecedent of the third act in the excerpt, also "3"; together they form the second interact in the excerpt. Thus, a sequence of three acts includes two interacts, and the entire excerpt of nineteen single acts contains a total of eighteen interacts.

Figure Appendix 2-1 shows that during even this brief excerpt, a trend develops regarding the group's treatment of decision proposal 1 in its interactive patterns. Note that the only acts expressing favor of the proposal, two "2 f" units, are immediately followed by acts which conflict with the favoring function. One of the subsequent acts is outright disagreement, "6", and the other argues the opposing side, "2 u." Once the argument started, the other members "piled it on" by positively reinforcing the seven "2 u" units with additional "2 u" units a total of three times, and twice with agreement, "5."

Scheidel and Crowell (1964) named a matrix with interacts, such as that in

Subsequent acts

| | 1f | 1u | 1ab | 1an | 2f | 2u | 2ab | 2an | 3 | 4 | 5 | 6 |
|---|---|---|---|---|---|---|---|---|---|---|---|---|
| 1f | | | | | | | | | | | | |
| 1u | | 1 | | | 1 | | | | | | | |
| 1ab | | | | | | | | | | | | |
| 1an | | | | | | | | | 1 | | | |
| 2f | | | | | | 1 | | | | | | 1 |
| 2u | | | | | | 1 | 3 | | 1 | 2 | | |
| 2ab | | | | | | | | | | | | |
| 2an | | | | | | | | | | | | |
| 3 | | 1 | | | | 1 | | | 2 | | | |
| 4 | | | | | | | | | | | | |
| 5 | | | | | | 1 | | | | | | |
| 6 | | | | | | 1 | | | | | | |

(Antecedent acts — left vertical label)

**Figure Appendix 2-1** Interacts contained in interaction analysis of decision proposals.

Figure Appendix 2-1, "contiguity analysis." Such an analysis provides the basis for analyzing possible phases of group decisions making. A single matrix can be used to summarize all the interacts during a specified time period, for example, 5 minutes, so that a 60-minute group discussion will require twelve matrices, such as that illustrated in the figure. Each matrix can then be compared with the next, and any changes in interact patterns can be easily discerned. In this way, phase progressions during group decision making were discovered.

The system of relational interaction analysis (REL/COM), described in Chapter 7 includes the following five categories:

*Dominance* ($\uparrow$+): Attempt to restrict severely the behavioral options of the other

*Structuring* ($\uparrow$−): Attempt to restrict the behavioral options of the other, but leaving a variety of options open; attempt to control the flow of interaction

*Equivalence* ($\rightarrow$): Attempt at mutual identification; interactional mode which does not seek to control or submit to control

*Deference* ($\downarrow$−): Expressed willingness to relinquish some behavioral options to the other while retaining some choice of options; "following" behavior which relinquishes control of the flow of interaction

*Submissiveness* ($\downarrow$+): Expressed willingness to relinquish behavioral options to the other while retaining little choice

Each communicative act assigned to one of the five categories of REL/COM is coded in terms of how the act relates to the immediately preceding act. Therefore, no act can be coded in isolation from the sequence of acts. The action gains its relational meaning in the manner in which it relates to the previous act.

Assume that member A makes an assertion. Member B challenges that assertion by demanding proof of documentation for that belief. Because B's response is a challenge (an "I dare you" assertion), that demand would be coded as an attempt to control the other's behavioral options—a dominant or ↑+ act. Member A may respond to that challenge by providing the information or documentation which was demanded. Relationally, A's response is a confrontation of the challenge and would, thus, be coded as another dominant or ↑+ act. If A fails to respond to the challenge, the action relationally submits to B's control and exhibits relational submissiveness. Failing to respond to a challenge is tantamount to a retreat in the face of the enemy's attack.

The interaction coded earlier into the decision-proposal system can also be coded into the five categories of REL/COM. The following sequence represents those codes:

A: (not codable; no preceding act)
D: → (equivalence)
A: → (equivalence)
B: ↑− (structuring)
D: → (equivalence)
A: ↑+ (dominance)
B: ↑− (structuring)
C: ↑− (structuring)
D: ↑+ (dominance)
A: ↑+ (dominance)
B: ↑+ (dominance)
D: ↑− (structuring)
G: ↓− (deference)
D: ↑− (structuring)
A: → (equivalence)
D: → (equivalence)
A: ↑− (structuring)
D: ↑+ (dominance)
C: ↓+ (deference)

The matrix of interacts for the five categories of REL/COM appears in Figure Appendix 2-2. The interaction analyzed in either category system may also be placed in a matrix of double interacts (sequence of three acts), triple interacts (sequence of four acts), etc. Our purposes here, however, do not include a sophisticated understanding of the various statistical manipulations employed in any observational system of interaction analysis. For information concerning such statistics, see Hawes and Foley (1976), Fisher, Glover, and Ellis (1977), and Fisher (1977a). It is sufficient that we are able to perceive how interaction analysis

Subsequent acts

|  | ↑ + | ↑ − | → | ↓ − | ↓ + |
|---|---|---|---|---|---|
| ↑ + | 2 | 2 |  | 1 |  |
| ↑ − | 2 | 1 | 2 | 1 |  |
| → | 1 | 2 | 2 |  |  |
| ↓ − |  | 1 |  |  |  |
| ↓ + |  |  |  |  |  |

(Antecedent acts)

**Figure Appendix 2-2**  Interacts contained in REL/COM analysis.

can work and how it is possible to observe an honest-to-goodness decision-making group in action.

## NOTE

These systems of interaction analysis, illustrated and explained in the preceding pages, are by no means ideal or standardized tools for analyzing interaction. But they do provide some explanation of the difficulties involved in observing the ongoing process of group communication. They should also demonstrate that, despite these difficulties, group communication can be observed reliably with just a little practice and familiarity with the categories. In fact, either category system or both of them can be employed by classroom groups to analyze their own or another group's interaction patterns. Everyone should be encouraged to try some interaction analysis, using either of the systems described above, Bales's IPA, or some other system of interaction analysis. The important point is not to determine which is the "best" method of interaction analysis, but to realize that interaction analysis does provide one method, however imperfect, for observing and under-standing group communication as a process during group decision making.

Appendix 3

# A Reader's Guide
# to Jargon

## AN INTRODUCTORY NOTE

One complaint frequently expressed by students involves the use of familiar and often incomprehensible terms peculiar to a specific area of study. Contrary to the firm convictions of most students, nearly everyone deplores the unwarranted use of jargon. Nevertheless, it sometimes appears that alleged experts speak to one another in their own specialized foreign language, familiar only to other experts within that field, just so they can "snow" those of us who are unacquainted with it.

"Jargon" has become infamous as a term commonly applied to all meaningless gibberish. In all frankness, much jargon seems to be little more than mere gibberish. But jargon, in and of itself, is not inherently evil. In fact, it is vitally important to any specialized field in order to add precision to an otherwise deplorably vague language. Distinctions in any specialized field are often so precise that no word or phrase in the common English vocabulary can adequately describe these distinctions. Hence, a new word is coined in order to describe specifically an event or phenomenon that would otherwise be inadequately described. Descriptions without jargon are, at best, awkward, lengthy, and abstract. Jargon allows specialists to make further advances in their study. Unfortunately, nonspecialists often find the jargon confusing.

Jargon is not only unavoidable and even desirable but absolutely essential to the progress of any specialized field of study. But it can also create unnecessary problems for a student who is new to that field. Problems most often arise when jargon spreads beyond the bounds of rational explanation. Unnecessarily picayune distinctions aid its proliferation in many areas. Unfortunately, the field of communication, particularly group communication, possesses more than its share of superfluous jargon. The reason for this undesirable state of affairs is probably the fact that no unifying theory exists to guide specialists in their study of communication. As a result, new "discoveries" often create new terms and new distinctions which seem uncommonly similar to other distinctions made earlier by other specialists. It is ironic but probably true that specialists in the study of communication don't communicate with each other very well. In the meantime, the jargon of communication proliferates.

This book was written by a person who possesses an intense personal dislike of superfluous jargon and who is aware of his students' even greater distaste for apparent gibberish. As a result, much of the jargon related to communication and group decision making is excluded from these pages. For example, the following jargonistic terms do not appear on any other page in this volume: synergy, syntality, comparison level of alternatives, satisficing, propinquity, parmia, propathy, dynamogenics, cyclothymia, morphostasis, entropy, and equifinality. Some of these terms, obviously jargon, do symbolize extremely important distinctions. But none of the terms was considered essential to my present purpose. Therefore, they were all omitted. Of course, some of the terms in this brief list also seem, to me personally, to be absolutely superfluous.

The following section is intended as a handy reference to the jargon used recurrently in this volume and recognized for what it is—jargon. But these distinctions are considered vital to the understanding of communication and group process. While all terms are not completely defined below, most of the key definitions are included.

One caution for the reader who uses Appendix 3: Do not be misled by simple and, in most cases, oversimplified definitions. To repeat, definitions are easy; understanding is more difficult. Do not accept a brief definition as a substitute for understanding the concept. Every definition is admittedly general and incomplete. But each definition also includes the chapter number or numbers in which the term is discussed in more detail. Memorize definitions if you must, but don't confuse your ability to define with genuine understanding and knowledge.

## THE JARGON

**Affective conflict**  Emotional clashes among members of a social system typically on procedural issues. (Chapter 8)

**Androgyny**  An aspect of one's self-concept that includes both masculine and feminine characteristics. (Chapter 5)

**ASo**  See **Contingency model.**

**Assembly effect**  The ability of a group to achieve collectively a level of productivity greater than the sum of the productivity of individuals when working by themselves. (Chapter 2)

**Barrier or Breakdown**   A cessation or blockage of communication based on the fallacious assumption that communication embodies only the structural aspects of sending and receiving messages along a channel. (Chapter 3)

**Centrality**   A characteristic of a communication network indicating the position in the network in which a member requires the fewest linkages to transmit a message to every other member of the group. (Chapter 3)

**Channel capacity**   The number of items of information which a person can effectively process at one time. (Chapter 3)

**Coalition**   A temporary alliance among two or more members of a social system; typically oriented toward a difference of opinion on the means to achieve the group goal. (Chapter 8)

**Cohesiveness**   The output of a group's socioemotional dimension; essentially, the degree to which members are attracted to one another and personally committed to the group. (Chapter 2)

**Communication distance**   See **Distance, communication.**

**Complementarity**   A form of relational interaction in which a relational behavior and its response are combined to form a complete and coherent relationship; for example, question-answer, ↑↓, or ↓↑. (Chapter 4)

**Conformity**   Uniform behaviors exhibited by members of a social system resulting from the members' choosing, from among conflicting alternatives of behavior, that alternative least subject to negative social influences. (Chapters 6 and 8)

**Consensus**   The degree of personal commitment the members feel toward the group's decision after it has been reached. (Chapter 5)

**Contingency model**   A model of group leadership, developed by Fiedler, which incorporates general predictions of leader effectiveness in selected situations. Predictions are based on scores of group leaders on ASo (assumed similarity of opposites) and LPC (least preferred co-worker) tests. (Chapter 7)

**Coorientation**   The "strain toward symmetry" in which two persons (A and B) are oriented, positively or negatively, to the same object (X). (Chapter 2)

**Decision**   In a group, a choice from among available alternatives which is validated by achieving consensus among members. (Chapter 5)

**Decision making**   As a group task, the process of choosing among alternatives for which no "best" or "correct" answer can be validated by any means other than group consensus. (Chapter 5)

**Deviance**   Behavior of members not in conformity with group norms or expectations. (Chapter 8)

**Distance, communication**   A characteristic of a communication network indicating the number of links required for one position in the network to transmit a message to another position. (Chapter 3)

**Double interact**   A sequence of three contiguous acts performed by group members. (Chapter 4)

**Emergence**   A gradual process describing how a group develops its roles, including that of leader, and its decisions in the LGD (leaderless group discussion). (Chapters 5 and 7)

**Encapsulation**   A method used for controlling social conflict through regulating conflict by a set of rules agreed upon by all parties to the conflict. (Chapter 8)

**Evolution** The characteristic of a system embodying its history, that is, the enduring changes in the system's structure and function over an extended period of time. (Chapter 1)

**Feedback** A mutually causal sequence of events or acts which, self-reflexively, exerts influence on the original act or event in the sequence. Feedback, affecting a deviant act or event, serves to counteract that deviance (negative feedback) or amplify the deviance (positive feedback). (Chapters 3 and 4)

**Flight** The behavioral tendency of a group to cease considering its task as a means of avoiding some unpleasant stimulus, commonly social conflict. (Chapters 5 and 8)

**Formal** A term used to describe the norms, status hierarchy, communication networks, etc., of a social system sanctioned or prescribed by legitimate sources of power or authority. (Chapters 6 and 7)

**Formula answer** An oversimplified and unrealistic solution to a complex problem; typically so general that it cannot be implemented. (Chapter 9)

**Function** The characteristic of a system denoted by the relationships among components in time and serving to regulate the ongoing action of the system. (Chapter 1)

**Gatekeeping** The structural function of serving as an intermediary between source and receiver in the flow of messages; receiving and selectively relaying messages from the original source to the ultimate receiver. (Chapter 3)

**Group** A collection of three or more persons whose behaviors are interstructured so that these persons exert a mutual and reciprocal influence on one another. (Chapter 1)

**Group mind** A belief, now outmoded, in the independence of a group's manner of thinking and feeling apart from its members. (Chapter 10)

**Groupthink** The phenomenon that occurs when members of a highly cohesive group disregard alternative courses of action in favor of maintaining unanimity of opinion in the group; an absence of critical idea testing and conflict typical of the natural group process. (Chapter 2)

**Idiosyncrasy credits** An economic model which explains the leader as both a deviant and a conformist and which illustrates the ability of a group leader to innovate after having conformed to the group norms for a period of time. (Chapter 7)

**Informal** A term describing the norms, status hierarchy, communication networks, etc., developed through the emergent natural group process and not necessarily sanctioned by legitimate sources of authority or power. (Chapters 6 and 7)

**Information processing** The process of using perceptions to transform data into information and then acting upon those perceptions; it may be performed by either one person or a group. (Chapter 4)

**Innovative deviance** See **Verbal innovative deviance.**

**Interact** A sequence of two contiguous acts performed by group members. (Chapters 4, 5, and 8)

**Interaction process analysis (IPA)** The system of interaction analysis developed by Robert F. Bales. (Chapters 4 and 5)

**Interdependence**   A relationship between two or more elements so that each influences, and is influenced by, the other. (Chapter 2)

**IPA**   See **Interaction process analysis.**

**Leaderless group discussion (LGD)**   A task-oriented group whose members possess the capacity to determine for themselves the group's structure, function, and behavior. (Chapter 1)

**Leadership**   A high-status position achieved in an LGD by performing leadership acts recognized by other group members as helping the group to perform its task; defined interdependently with followership. (Chapter 7)

**Legitimacy**   The principle of prescription or prior approval of norms, values, roles, or other standards imposed on a group by some person or source outside the group whose authority over it is recognized by the group members. (Chapter 7)

**LGD**   See **Leaderless group discussion.**

**LPC**   See **Contingency model.**

**Message**   A single communicative act. (Chapter 3)

**Natural process**   A process of group development, nearly universal, which is based on "rules" governing behavior. Group members need not be aware of these rules. (Chapters 5 and 10)

**Network**   The structure of channel linkages among group members which illustrates the pattern of transmitting and receiving messages. (Chapter 3)

**Nonsummativity**   A principle, inherent in any system, which stipulates that the whole is greater than, or different from, the sum of its parts because of interdependent relationships among the parts. (Chapter 1)

**Norm**   A standard which regulates the behavior of all members of a group through negative feedback directed at members whose behaviors are contrary to that standard. (Chapter 6)

**Primary tension**   The inhibitions of group members during the early period of group development; similar to the phenomenon of stage fright in an individual. (Chapter 2)

**Process**   A sequence of events or actions continuously changing over time in progress toward some goal. (Chapter 1)

**Productivity**   The output of a group's task dimension; the quality or quantity of work performed by a group. (Chapter 2)

**Punctuation**   In a system, the process of organizing the sequence of acts or events in order to discover meaning and significance in the sequence. (Chapter 4)

**Reach-testing**   The process of introducing a new idea from an anchored position of group agreement in the spiral model. Other group members test that idea through discussion and may accept it, reject it, extend it, or revise it. (Chapter 5)

**Reciprocity**   A norm typical of most social systems which encourages members to respond to the behaviors of others with similar behaviors. (Chapter 6)

**REL/COM**   A system of analyzing interaction into categories of relational control ($\uparrow$, $\downarrow$, $\rightarrow$). (Chapters 4 and 7)

**Risky shift**   The tendency of a group to make decisions involving greater risk, that is, bringing a bigger payoff but a lower probability of attainment, when compared with decisions made by individuals. (Chapter 2)

**Role**  A position occupied by a group member in an interlocking network including all group members; defined in terms of the behaviors performed by the member. (Chapter 6)

**Schismogenesis**  The escalation of either symmetrical or complementary relationships to a point that the social relationship is threatened with disruption. (Chapter 4)

**Secondary tension**  Social discomfort typified by abrupt and abnormal departures from the routine functioning of a group; induced by interpersonal conflict, environmental pressures, feeling of frustration, etc. (Chapter 2)

**Self-disclosure**  Communication which informs another person about one's private self and provides information which the other person does not know and is unlikely to acquire through other means. (Chapter 1)

**Social comparison**  The process of evaluating characteristics of one's self-concept by comparing them with those of another person or a group, typically performed by comparison with persons possessing similar characteristics. (Chapter 1)

**Spiral model**  The process of decision making involving constant backtracking and reach-testing of ideas until the idea develops during group interaction to represent the consensus of the group members. (Chapter 5)

**Status**  A social class or division rank ordered in a hierarchy from high to low. Status may be ascribed, that is, given the position by some higher authority. It may also be achieved, as in the LGD, through behaviors recognized by other group members as beneficial to the group. (Chapter 7)

**Structure**  The characteristic of a system denoted by the physical or spatial arrangement of the components at any given point in time. (Chapter 1)

**Substantive conflict**  Intellectual clashes among members of a social system on issues pertaining to the group task. (Chapter 8)

**Symmetry**  A form of relational interaction in which the response to a relational behavior is the same as the antecedent act; for example, $\uparrow\uparrow$, $\downarrow\downarrow$, or $\rightarrow\rightarrow$. (Chapter 4)

**System**  An entity which behaves as an entity because of the interdependence of its component elements. (Chapter 1)

**Theory**  The basis for explaining, describing, and understanding any set of complex phenomena, for example, communication and group process. (Chapters 1 and 4)

**Tolerance threshold**  The maximum degree of tension that will not prohibit a group from functioning normally. Social tension at a level above the threshold disrupts the ability of the group to function as a group. (Chapter 2)

**Verbal innovative deviance (VID)**  The behavior of a group member reflecting agreement with the group's goal but disagreement with the majority on the appropriate means for achieving that goal. (Chapter 8)

**VID**  See **Verbal innovative deviance.**

**Wholeness**  A principle inherent in a system which stipulates that every component of the system affects, and is affected by, every other component and that a change in any one component inherently brings change in all other components. (Chapter 1)

# References

Allen, Vernon, and J. Levine. (1969) "Consensus and Conformity," *Journal of Experimental Social Psychology,* 5:389–399.

Allport, Floyd H. (1927) *The Group Fallacy.* Minneapolis: Sociological Press.

Allport, Gordon W. (1968) "The Historical Background of Modern Social Psychology," in Gardner Lindzey and Elliot Aronson (eds.), *The Handbook of Social Psychology,* 2d ed., Vol. I. Reading, Mass.: Addison-Wesley, pp. 1–80.

Altman, Irwin, and Dalmas Taylor. (1973) *Social Penetration: The Development of Interpersonal Relationships.* New York: Holt, Rinehart and Winston.

Amidon, Edmund, and Ned Flanders. (1967) "Interaction Analysis as a Feedback System," in Edmund J. Amidon and John B. Hough (eds.), *Interaction Analysis: Theory, Research, and Application.* Reading, Mass.: Addison-Wesley, pp. 121–140.

Aries, Elizabeth. (1976) "Interaction Patterns and Themes and Male, Female, and Mixed Groups," *Small Group Behavior,* 7:7–18.

Asch, Solomon E. (1956) "Studies of Independence and Conformity: I. A Minority of One against a Unanimous Majority," *Psychological Monographs,* 70:1–70.

Asch, Solomon E. (1955) "Opinions and Social Pressure," *Scientific American,* 193:31–55.

Asch, Solomon E. (1951) "Effects of Group Pressure upon the Modification and Distortion of Judgments," in Harold Guetzkow (ed.), *Groups, Leadership, and Men.* Pittsburgh: Carnegie Press, pp. 171–190.

Baird, John E., Jr., and Sanford B. Weinberg. (1977) *Communication: The Essence of Group Synergy.* Dubuque, Iowa: Wm. C. Brown Company Publishers.

Bales, Robert Freed. (1970) *Personality and Interpersonal Behavior.* New York: Holt, Rinehart and Winston.

Bales, Robert F. (1955) "Adaptive and Integrative Changes as Sources of Strain in Social Systems," in A. Paul Hare, Edgar F. Borgatta, and Robert F. Bales, (eds.), *Small Groups: Studies in Social Interaction.* New York: Knopf, pp. 127–131.

Bales, Robert F. (1953) "The Equilibrium Problem in Small Groups," in Talcott Parsons, Robert F. Bales, and Edward A. Shils (eds.), *Working Papers in the Theory of Action.* New York: Free Press, pp. 111–161.

Bales, Robert F. (1950) *Interaction Process Analysis: A Method for the Study of Small Groups.* Cambridge, Mass.: Addison-Wesley.

Bales, Robert F., and Philip E. Slater. (1955) "Role Differentiation in Small Decision-making Groups," in Talcott Parsons et al. (eds.), *The Family, Socialization, and Interaction Process.* Glencoe, Ill.: Free Press, pp. 259–306.

Bales, Robert F., and Fred L. Strodtbeck. (1951) "Phases in Group Problem-Solving," *Journal of Abnormal and Social Psychology,* **46:**485–495.

Barker, R. G., and H. F. Wright. (1955) *Midwest and Its Children.* Evanston, Ill.: Row Peterson.

Bass, Bernard M. (1949) "An Analysis of the Leaderless Group Discussion," *Journal of Applied Psychology,* **33:**527–533.

Bass, Bernard M., C. R. McGehee, W. C. Hawkins, P. C. Young, and A. S. Gebel. (1953) "Personality Variables Related to Leaderless Group Discussion," *Journal of Abnormal and Social Psychology,* **48:**120–128.

Bateson, Gregory. (1972) *Steps to an Ecology of Mind.* San Francisco: Chandler.

Bateson, Gregory. (1935) "Culture Contact and Schismogenesis," *Man,* **35:**178–183.

Bauer, Raymond A. (1964) "The Obstinate Audience: The Influence Process from the Point of View of Social Communication," *American Psychologist,* **19:**319–328.

Bayless, Ovid L. (1967) "An Alternate Pattern for Problem-Solving Discussion," *Journal of Communication,* **17:**188–197.

Beisecker, Thomas. (1969) "Communication and Conflict in Interpersonal Negotiations." A paper presented to the Speech Communication Association, New York.

Bem, Sandra L. (1974) "The Measurement of Psychological Androgyny," *Journal of Consulting and Clinical Psychology,* **42:**155–162.

Benne, Kenneth D., and Paul Sheats. (1948) "Functional Roles of Group Members," *Journal of Social Issues,* **4:**41–49.

Bennis, Warren G., and Herbert A. Shepard. (1961) "Group Observation," in Warren G. Bennis, Kenneth D. Benne, and Robert Chin (eds), *The Planning of Change,* 1st ed. New York: Holt, Rinehart and Winston, pp. 743–756.

Bennis, Warren G., and Herbert A. Shepard. (1956) "A Theory of Group Development," *Human Relations,* **9:**415–437.

Berg, David M. (1967) "A Descriptive Analysis of the Distribution and Duration of Themes Discussed by Task-Oriented Small Groups," *Speech Monographs,* **34:**172–175.

Berger, E. (1952) "The Relationship between Expressed Acceptance of Self and Expressed Acceptance of Others," *Journal of Abnormal and Social Psychology,* **47:**778–782.

Berlo, David K. (1977) "Communication as Process, Review and Commentary," Brent D. Ruben (ed). *Communication Yearbook I.* New Brunswick, N.J.: International Communication Association/Transaction, pp. 11–27.

Berlo, David K. (1960) *The Process of Communication.* New York: Holt, Rinehart and Winston.

Berne, Eric. (1966) *Principles of Group Treatment.* New York: Grove Press.

Berne, Eric. (1963) *The Structure and Dynamics of Organizations and Groups.* New York: Lippincott.

Berne, Eric. (1961) *Transactional Analysis in Psychotherapy.* New York: Grove Press.

Birdwhistell, Ray L. (1970) *Kinesics and Context: Essays on Body Motion Communication.* Philadelphia: University of Pennsylvania Press.

Birdwhistell, Ray L. (1959) "Contribution of Linguistic-Kinesic Studies to the Understanding of Schizophrenia," in Alfred Auerback (ed.), *Schizophrenia: An Integrated Approach.* New York: Ronald Press, pp. 99–123.

Black, Edwin B. (1955) "Rhetorical Breakdown in Discussion," *Speech Monographs,* **22:**15–19.

Blau, Peter M. (1960) "A Theory of Social Integration," *American Journal of Sociology,* **65:**545–556.

Borgatta, Edgar F., and Betty Crowther. (1965) *A Workbook for the Study of Social Interaction Processes.* Chicago: Rand McNally.

Bormann, Ernest G. (1975) *Discussion and Group Methods: Theory and Practice,* 2d ed. New York: Harper & Row.

Bossman, Larry J., Jr. (1968) "An Analysis of Inter-Agent Residual-Influence Effects upon Members of Small Decision-Making Groups," *Behavioral Science,* **13:**220–233.

Brilhart, John K. (1978) *Effective Group Discussion,* 3d ed. Dubuque, Iowa: Wm. C. Brown Company Publishers.

Brown, Steven R., and Albert Rothenberg. (1976) "The Analysis of Group Episodes," *Small Group Behavior,* **7:**287–306.

Cartwright, Dorwin, and Alvin Zander. (1968) "Leadership and Performance of Group Functions: Introduction," in Dorwin Cartwright and Alvin Zander (eds.), *Group Dynamics: Research and Theory,* 3d ed. New York: Harper & Row, pp. 301–317.

Cattell, Raymond B. (1955) "Concepts and Methods in the Measurement of Group Syntality," in A. Paul Hare, Edgar F. Borgatta, and Robert F. Bales (eds.), *Small Groups: Studies in Social Interaction.* New York: Knopf, pp. 107–126.

Coch, Lester, and John R. P. French, Jr. (1948) "Overcoming Resistance to Change," *Human Relations,* **1:**512–533.

Cohen, A., W. Bennis, and G. Wolkon. (1961) "The Effects of Continued Practice on the Behavior of Problem-Solving Groups," *Sociometry,* **24**:416–431.

Collins, Barry E., and Harold Guetzkow. (1964) *A Social Psychology of Group Processes for Decision-Making.* New York: Wiley.

Coser, Lewis. (1956) *The Functions of Social Conflict.* New York: Free Press.

Crowell, Laura, and Thomas M. Scheidel. (1961) "Categories for Analysis of Idea Development in Discussion Groups," *Journal of Social Psychology,* **54**:155–268.

Culbert, S. A. (1967) *Interpersonal Process of Self Disclosure.* Washington, D.C.: N.T.L. Institute for Applied Behavioral Science.

Dance, Frank E. X. (1970) "The 'Concept' of Communication," *Journal of Communication,* **20**:201–210.

Davis, James H. (1969) *Group Performance.* Reading, Mass.: Addison-Wesley.

DeBono, Edward. (1968) *New Think.* New York: Basic Books.

Dentler, Robert A., and Kai T. Erikson. (1959) "The Functions of Deviance in Groups," *Social Problems,* **7**:98–107.

DeStephen, RoLayne S. (1977) "Leadership and Sex: Behavioral Differences in the Small Group Context." A paper presented to Western Speech Communication Association, Phoenix, Ariz.

Deutsch, Morton. (1969) "Conflicts: Productive and Destructive," *Journal of Social Issues,* **25**:7–41.

Dewey, John. (1910) *How We Think.* New York: Heath.

Drecksel, Lloyd, and B. Aubrey Fisher. (1977) "Relational Interaction Characteristics of Women's Consciousness-Raising Groups." A paper presented to Western Speech Communication Association, Phoenix, Ariz.

Dunphy, Dexter C. (1964) "Social Change in Self-Analytic Groups." Ph.D. dissertation, Harvard University.

Ellis, Donald G. (1977) "A Social-System Model of Relational Control in Two Ongoing Group Systems." A paper presented to Speech Communication Association, Washington, D.C.

Ellis, Donald G. (1976) "An Analysis of Relational Communication in Ongoing Group Systems." Ph.D. dissertation, University of Utah.

Ellis, Donald G., and B. Aubrey Fisher. (1975) "Phases of Conflict in Small Group Development," *Human Communication Research,* **1**:195–212.

Eman, Virginia A., and Benjamin W. Morse. (1977) "An Examination of the Relationship between Androgyny, Self-Esteem, Acceptance of Self and Acceptance of Others." A paper presented to Speech Communication Association, Washington, D.C.

Farace, Richard V., Peter R. Monge, and Hamish M. Russell. (1977) *Communicating and Organizing.* Reading, Mass.: Addison-Wesley.

Faules, Don F., and Dennis C. Alexander. (1977) *Communication and Social Behavior: A Symbolic Interaction Perspective.* Reading, Mass.: Addison-Wesley.

Ferullo, R. (1963) "The Self Concept in Communication," *Journal of Communication,* **13**:77–86.

Festinger, Leon. (1954) "A Theory of Social Comparison Processes," *Human Relations,* **7**:117–140.

Festinger, Leon. (1950) "Informal Social Communication," *Psychological Review*, **57**:271–282.

Fiedler, Fred E. (1967) *A Theory of Leadership Effectiveness*. New York: McGraw-Hill.

Fiedler, Fred E. (1964) "A Contingency Model of Leadership Effectiveness," in Leonard Berkowitz (ed.), *Advances in Experimental Social Psychology*, vol. I. New York: Academic Press, pp. 149–190.

Fisher, B. Aubrey. (1978) *Perspectives on Human Communication*. New York: Macmillan.

Fisher, B. Aubrey. (1977a) "Interaction Analysis: An Underutilized Methodology in Communication." A paper presented to Western Speech Communication Association, Phoenix, Ariz.

Fisher, B. Aubrey. (1977b) "Functions of Category Systems in Interaction Analysis." A paper presented to Speech Communication Association, Washington, D.C.

Fisher, B. Aubrey. (1977c) "An Interaction Analysis of Dyads." A paper presented to Speech Communication Association, Washington, D.C.

Fisher, B. Aubrey. (1976) "Relationship Rules: Still Another Step Toward Communication Theory." A paper presented to International Communication Association, Portland, Oregon.

Fisher, B. Aubrey. (1975) "Communication Study in System Perspective," in Brent D. Ruben and John Y. Kim (eds.), *General Systems Theory and Human Communication*. Rochelle Park, N.J.: Hayden, pp. 191–206.

Fisher, B. Aubrey. (1971) "Communication Research and the Task-Oriented Group," *Journal of Communication*, **21**:136–149.

Fisher, B. Aubrey. (1970a) "Decision Emergence: Phases in Group Decision Making," *Speech Monographs*, **37**:53–66.

Fisher, B. Aubrey. (1970b) "The Process of Decision Modification in Small Discussion Groups," *Journal of Communication*, **20**:51–64.

Fisher, B. Aubrey, and Wayne A. Beach. (1979) "Empirical Correlates of Content and Relationship Communication," *Western Journal of Speech Communication* (in press).

Fisher, B. Aubrey, and Wayne A. Beach. (1978) "Relational Development in Dyads: A Preliminary Report." A paper presented to International Communication Association, Chicago.

Fisher, B. Aubrey, Thomas W. Glover, and Donald G. Ellis. (1977) "The Nature of Complex Communication Systems," *Communication Monographs*, **44**:231–240.

Fisher, B. Aubrey, and Leonard C. Hawes. (1971) "An Interact System Model: Generating a Grounded Theory of Small Group Decision Making," *Quarterly Journal of Speech*, **58**:444–453.

Geier, John G. (1967) "A Trait Approach to the Study of Leadership in Small Groups," *Journal of Communication*, **17**:316–323.

Gerard, Harold B. (1964) "Conformity and Commitment to the Group," *Journal of Abnormal and Social Psychology*, **68**:209–211.

Gibb, Jack. (1961) "Defensive Communication," *Journal of Communication*, **11**:141–148.

Gibbs, Jack P. (1965) "Norms: The Problem of Definition and Classification," *American Journal of Sociology,* **70:**586–594.

Gilbert, Shirley J. (1976a) "Anxiety, Likeability, and Avoidance as Responses to Self-Disclosing Communication," *Small Group Behavior,* 7:423–432.

Gilbert, Shirley J. (1976b) "Empirical and Theoretical Extensions of Self-Disclosure," in Gerald R. Miller (ed.), *Explorations in Interpersonal Communication.* Beverly Hills, Calif.: Sage, pp. 197–216.

Gilstein, Kenneth W., E. Wayne Wright, and David R. Stone. (1977) "The Effects of Leadership Style on Group Interactions in Differing Socio-Political Subcultures," *Small Group Behavior,* **8:**313–332.

Glover, Thomas W. (1974) "Interpersonal Power in Family Groups: An Analysis of Complementary and Symmetrical Interaction." M.S. thesis, University of Utah.

Goffman, Erving. (1969) *Strategic Interaction.* Philadelphia: University of Pennsylvania Press.

Goffman, Erving. (1967) *Interaction Ritual: Essays on Face-to-Face Behavior.* Garden City, N.Y.: Doubleday.

Goffman, Erving. (1963) *Behavior in Public Places: Notes on the Social Organization of Gatherings.* New York: Free Press.

Goffman, Erving. (1961) *Encounters.* New York: Bobbs-Merrill.

Goffman, Erving. (1959) *The Presentation of Self in Everyday Life.* Garden City, N.Y.: Doubleday.

Goldberg, Alvin A., and Carl E. Larson. (1975) *Group Communication: Discussion Processes and Application.* Englewood Cliffs, N.J.: Prentice-Hall.

Gouldner, Alvin W. (1960) "The Norm of Reciprocity: A Preliminary Statement," *American Sociological Review,* **25:**161–171.

Gouran, Dennis S. (1969) "Variables Related to Consensus in Group Discussions of Questions of Policy," *Speech Monographs,* **36:**387–391.

Gouran, Dennis S., and John E. Baird, Jr. (1972) "An Analysis of Distributional and Sequential Structure in Problem-Solving and Informal Group Discussions," *Speech Monographs,* **39:**16–22.

Greenblatt, Lynda, James E. Hasenauer, and Vicki S. Freimuth. (1977) "The Effects of Sex-Typing and Androgyny on Two Communication Variables: Self-Disclosure and Communication Apprehension." A paper presented to Speech Communication Association, Washington, D.C.

Gruenfeld, Leopold W., David E. Rance, and Peter Weissenberg. (1969) "The Behavior of Task-Oriented and Socially-Oriented Leaders under Several Conditions of Social Support," *Journal of Social Psychology,* **79:**99–107.

Grunig, J. E. (1969) "Information and Decision Making in Economic Development," *Journalism Quarterly,* **46:**565–575.

Gulley, Halbert E., and Dale G. Leathers. (1977) *Communication and Group Process,* 3d ed. New York: Holt, Rinehart and Winston.

Hackman, J. Richard. (1968) "Effects of Task Characteristics on Group Products," *Journal of Experimental Social Psychology,* **4:**162–187.

Hall, Jay, and W. H. Watson. (1970) "The Effects of a Normative Intervention on Group Decision-Making Performance," *Human Relations,* **23:**299–317.

Hall, Jay, and Martha S. Williams. (1970) "Group Dynamics Training and

Improved Decision Making," *Journal of Applied Behavioral Science,* **6:**39–68.

Hancock, Brenda Robinson. (1972) "An Interaction Analysis of Self-Disclosure." A paper presented to the Western Speech Communication Association.

Hare, A. Paul. (1976) *Handbook of Small Group Research,* 2d ed. New York: Free Press.

Harnack, R. Victor, Thorrel B. Fest, and Barbara Schindler Jones. (1977) *Group Discussion: Theory and Technique,* 2d ed. Englewood Cliffs, N.J.: Prentice-Hall.

Hawes, Leonard C. (1972a) "Can A Seeker of a Process Methodology Find Happiness with a Markov Model?" Paper presented to University of Minnesota Symposium on Communication Theory and Practice, Minneapolis.

Hawes, Leonard C. (1972b) "The Effects of Interviewer Style on Patterns of Dyadic Communication," *Speech Monographs,* **39:**114–123.

Hawes, Leonard C. (1969) "Ambivalence and Productivity in Experimental Triads." A paper presented to Speech Communication Association, New York.

Hawes, Leonard C, and Joseph M. Foley. (1976) "Group Decisioning: Testing in a Finite Stochastic Model," in Gerald R. Miller (ed.), *Explorations in Interpersonal Communication.* Beverly Hills, Calif.: Sage, pp. 237–254.

Herrold, K. F., et al. (1953) "Difficulties Encountered in Group Decision-Making," *Personnel and Guidance Journal,* **31:**516–523.

Heslin, Richard, and Dexter Dunphy. (1964) "Three Dimensions of Member Satisfaction in Small Groups," *Human Relations,* **17:**99–112.

Hill, Walter. (1969) "A Situational Approach to Leadership Effectiveness," *Journal of Applied Psychology,* **53:**513–517.

Hoffman, L. Richard, Ernest Harburg, and Norman R. F. Maier. (1962) "Differences and Disagreement as Factors in Creative Group Problem-Solving," *Journal of Abnormal and Social Psychology,* **64:**206–214.

Holder, Harold, and William P. Ehling. (1967) "Construction and Simulation of an Information-Decision Model," *Journal of Communication,* **17:**302–315.

Hollander, Edwin P. (1958) "Conformity, Status, and Idiosyncrasy Credit," *Psychological Review,* **65:**117–127.

Hollander, Edwin P., and James W. Julian. (1969) "Contemporary Trends in the Analysis of Leadership Processes," *Psychological Bulletin,* **71:**387–397.

Holsti, Ole R. (1969) *Content Analysis for the Social Sciences and Humanities.* Reading, Mass.: Addison-Wesley.

Homans, George C. (1961) *Social Behavior: Its Elementary Forms.* New York: Harcourt, Brace.

Homans, George C. (1950) *The Human Group.* New York: Harcourt, Brace.

Horenstein, David, and Shirley J. Gilbert. (1976) "Anxiety, Likeability, and Avoidance as Responses to Self-Disclosing Communication," *Small Group Behavior,* **7:**423–432.

Horowitz, Irwin A. (1962) "Consensus, Conflict, and Cooporation: A Sociological Inventory," *Social Forces,* **41:**177–188.

Huenergardt, Douglas W. (1971) "Books in Review: *Body Language*," *Quarterly Journal of Speech*, 57:110.

Janis, Irving L. (1972) *Victims of Groupthink*. Boston: Houghton Mifflin.

Jenkins, David H. (1948) "Feedback and Group Self-Evaluation," *Journal of Social Issues*, 4:50–60.

Johnson, Alma. (1943) "An Experimental Study in the Analysis and Measurement of Reflective Thinking," *Speech Monographs*, 10:83–96.

Johnson, Bonnie McDaniel. (1977) *Communication: The Process of Organizing*. Boston: Allyn and Bacon.

Kelley, Harold H., and John W. Thibaut. (1954) "Experimental Studies of Group Problem Solving and Process," in Gardner Lindzey (ed.), *Handbook of Social Psychology*, Vol. II, 1st ed. Reading, Mass.: Addison-Wesley, pp. 735–785.

Kent, R. N., and Joseph E. McGrath. (1969) "Task and Group Characteristics as Factors Influencing Group Performance," *Journal of Experimental Social Psychology*, 5:429–440.

Knapp, Mark L. (1972) *Nonverbal Communication in Human Interaction*. New York: Holt, Rinehart and Winston.

Lanzetta, John T., and Thornton B. Roby. (1960) "The Relationship between Certain Group Process Variables and Group Problem-Solving Efficiency," *Journal of Social Psychology*, 7:135–148.

Lanzetta, John T., and Thornton B. Roby. (1957) "Group Learning and Communication as a Function of Task and Structure 'Demands,' " *Journal of Abnormal and Social Psychology*, 55:121–131.

Larson, Carl E. (1969) "Forms of Analysis and Small Group Problem Solving," *Speech Monographs*, 36:452–455.

Larson, Charles U. (1971) "The Verbal Responses of Groups to the Absence or Presence of Leadership," *Speech Monographs*, 38:177–181.

Larson, Charles U. (1969) "Attention Span and the Leader." A paper presented to the Central States Speech Association, St. Louis.

Leathers, Dale G. (1971) "The Feedback Rating Instrument: A New Means of Evaluating Discussion," *Central States Speech Journal*, 22:32–42.

Lewin, Kurt. (1951) *Field Theory in Social Science*. New York: Harper & Row.

Likert, Rensis, and David G. Bowers. (1972) "Conflict Strategies Related to Elliott McGinnies (eds.), *Attitudes, Conflict and Social Change*. New York: Academic Press, pp. 101–121.

Lindzey, Gardner, and Henry W. Riecken. (1951) "Inducing Frustration in Adult Subjects," *Journal of Consulting Psychology*, 15:18–23.

Longabaugh, R. (1963) "A Category System for Coding Interpersonal Behavior as Social Exchange," *Sociometry*, 26:319–344.

Lucas, Richard L., and Cabot L. Jaffee. (1969) "Effects of High-Rate Talkers on Group Voting Behavior in the Leaderless-Group Problem-Solving Situation," *Psychological Reports*, 25:471–477.

Lynch, Mervin D. (1970) "Stylistic Analysis," in Philip Emmert and William D.

Brooks (eds.), *Methods of Research in Communication.* Boston: Houghton Mifflin, pp. 315–342.

Maier, Norman R. F. (1963) *Problem-Solving Discussions and Conferences.* New York: McGraw-Hill.

Maier, Norman R. F., and James A. Thurber. (1969) "Limitations of Procedures for Improving Group Problem Solving," *Psychological Reports,* **25:**639–656.

Mann, R. D. (1959) "A Review of the Relationship between Personality and Performance in Small Groups," *Psychological Bulletin,* **56:**241–270.

Martin, Howard, and Kenneth Andersen (eds.). (1968) *Speech Communication.* Boston: Allyn and Bacon.

Maslow, Abraham. (1954) *Motivation and Personality.* New York: Harper & Row.

McDavid, J. W., Jr., and Floyd Sistrunk. (1957) "The Interpretation of Approval and Disapproval by Delinquent and Non-Delinquent Adolescents," *Journal of Personality,* **25:**420–435.

McGrath, Joseph E., and Irwin Altman. (1966) *Small Group Research: A Synthesis and Critique of the Field.* New York: Holt, Rinehart and Winston.

McHugh, Peter. (1968) *Defining the Situation: The Organization of Meaning in Social Interaction.* New York: Bobbs-Merrill.

Merton, Robert. K. (1957) *Social Theory and Social Structure.* New York: Free Press.

Millar, Frank E., and L. Edna Rogers. (1976) "A Relational Approach to Interpersonal Communication," in Gerald R. Miller (ed.), *Explorations in Interpersonal Communication.* Beverly Hills, Calif.: Sage, pp. 87–104.

Miller, George A. (1956) "The Magical Number Seven, Plus or Minus Two: Some Limits on Our Capacity for Processing Information," *Psychological Review,* **63:**81–97.

Miller, Sherod, Elam W. Nunnally, and Daniel B. Wackman. (1975) *Alive and Aware: Improving Communication in Relationships.* Minneapolis: Interpersonal Communication Programs.

Milton, G. A. (1957) "The Effects of Sex-Role Identification upon Problem-Solving Skill," *Journal of Abnormal and Social Psychology,* **55:**219–244.

Montgomery, Charles L., and Michael Burgoon. (1977a) "Androgyny as a Mediating Variable in Attitude Change and Resistance to Persuasion." A paper presented to Speech Communication Association, Washington, D.C.

Montgomery, Charles L. and Michael Burgoon. (1977b) "An Experimental Study of the Interactive Effects of Sex and Androgyny on Attitude Change," *Communication Monographs,* **44:**130–135.

Morris, Charles. (1946) *Signs, Language and Behavior.* Englewood Cliffs, N.J.: Prentice-Hall.

Morris, Charles G., and J. Richard Hackman. (1969) "Behavioral Correlates of Perceived Leadership," *Journal of Personality and Social Psychology,* **13:**350–361.

Mortensen, C. David. (1972) *Communication: The Study of Human Interaction.* New York: McGraw-Hill.

Mortensen, C. David. (1966) "Should the Discussion Group Have an Assigned Leader?" *Speech Teacher,* **15:**34–41.

Newcomb, Theodore M. (1953) "An Approach to the Study of Communicative Acts," *Psychological Review*, **60**:393–404.

Nokes, Patrick. (1961) "Feedback as an Explanatory Device in the Study of Certain Interpersonal and Institutional Processes," *Human Relations*, **14**:381–387.

North, R. C., H. E. Koch, and Dina A. Zinnes. (1960) "The Integrative Functions of Conflict," *Journal of Conflict Resolution*, **4**:355–374.

Parks, Malcolm R., Richard V. Farace, and L. Edna Rogers. (1975) "A Stochastic Description of Relational Communication Systems." A paper presented to Speech Communication Association, Houston.

Parks, Malcolm R., et al. (1976) "Markov Process Analysis of Relational Communication in Marital Dyads." A paper presented to International Communication Association, Portland, Oregon.

Parsons, Talcott. (1951) *The Social System*. New York: Free Press.

Patton, Bobby R., Mary Jasnowski, and Linda Skerchocki. (1977) "Communication Implications of Androgyny." A paper presented to Speech Communication Association, Washington, D.C.

Pearce, W. Barnett. (1976) "The Coordinated Management of Meaning: A Rules-Based Theory of Interpersonal Communication," in Gerald R. Miller (ed.), *Explorations in Interpersonal Communication*. Beverly Hills, Calif.: Sage, pp. 17–36.

Pearce, W. Barnett. (1974) "Trust in Interpersonal Communication," *Speech Monographs*, **41**:236–244.

Pearce, W. Barnett. (1973) "Self-Disclosing Communications," *Journal of Communication*, **23**:409–425.

Pearce, W. Barnett, and Stuart M. Sharp. (1973) "Self-Disclosing Communications," *Journal of Communication*, **23**:409–425.

Phillips, Gerald M. (1966) *Communication and the Small Group*, 1st ed. New York: Bobbs-Merrill.

Phillips, Gerald M., and Eugene C. Erickson. (1970) *Interpersonal Dynamics in the Small Group*. New York: Random House.

Pollay, Richard W. (1969) "Intrafamily Communication and Consensus," *Journal of Communication*, **19**:181–201.

Pruitt, Dean G. (1961) "Informational Requirements in Making Decisions," *American Journal of Psychology*, **74**:433–439.

Pyke, Sandra W., and Cathie A. Neely. (1970) "Evaluation of a Group Training Program," *Journal of Communication*, **20**:291–304.

Pyron, H. Charles. (1964) "An Experimental Study of the Role of Reflective Thinking in Business and Professional Conferences and Discussions," *Speech Monographs*, **31**:155–161.

Pyron, H. Charles, and Harry Sharp, Jr. (1963) "A Quantitative Study of Reflective Thinking and Performance in Problem-Solving Discussion," *Journal of Communication*, **13**:46–57.

Richards, I. A. (1936) *The Philosophy of Rhetoric*. New York: Oxford University Press.

Riecken, Henry W. (1952) "Some Problems of Consensus Development," *Rural Sociology*, **17**:245–252.

Roby, Thornton B., and John T. Lanzetta. (1958) "Considerations in the Analysis of Group Tasks," *Psychological Bulletin,* **55:**88–101.

Rogers, L. Edna, and Richard V. Farace. (1975) "Analysis of Relational Communication in Dyads," *Human Communication Research,* **1:**222–239.

Russell, Hugh C. (1970) "Dimensions of the Communication Behavior of Discussion Leaders." A paper presented to the Central States Speech Association, Chicago.

Sampson, Edward E., and Arlene C. Brandon. (1964) "The Effects of Role and Opinion Deviation on Small Group Behavior," *Sociometry,* **27:**261–281.

Scheflen, Albert E. (1969) "Behavioral Programs in Human Communication," in William Gray, Frederick J. Duhl, and Nicholas D. Rizzo (eds.), *General Systems Theory and Psychiatry.* Boston: Little, Brown, pp. 209–228.

Scheflen, Albert E. (1965) "Quasi-Courtship Behavior in Psychotherapy," *Psychiatry,* **28:**245–255.

Scheidel, Thomas M. (1969) "Idea Development in Problem-Solving Group Discussion." A paper presented to the Central States Speech Association, St. Louis.

Scheidel, Thomas M., and Laura Crowell. (1966) "Feedback in Small Group Communication," *Quarterly Journal of Speech,* **52:**273–278.

Scheidel, Thomas M. and Laura Crowell. (1964) "Idea Development in Small Discussion Groups," *Quarterly Journal of Speech,* **50:**140–145.

Schein, Edgar H., and Warren G. Bennis. (1965) *Personal and Organizational Change Through Group Methods: The Laboratory Approach.* New York: Wiley.

Sharp, Harry, Jr., and Joyce Milliken. (1964) "The Reflective Thinking Ability and the Product of Problem-Solving Discussion," *Speech Monographs,* **31:**124–127.

Shaw, Marvin E. (1976) *Group Dynamics: The Psychology of Small Group Behavior,* 2d ed. New York: McGraw-Hill.

Shepherd, Clovis R. (1964) *Small Groups: Some Sociological Perspectives.* San Francisco: Chandler.

Sherif, Muzafer, and Carolyn W. Sherif. (1964) *Reference Groups.* New York: Harper & Row.

Simmel, Georg. (1955) *Conflict.* New York: Free Press.

Smith, Alexander B., Alexander Bassin, and Abraham Froelich. (1962) "Interaction Process and Equilibrium in a Therapy Group of Adult Offenders," *Journal of Social Psychology,* **56:**141–147.

Smith, Dennis R. (1970) "The Fallacy of the Communication Breakdown," *Quarterly Journal of Speech,* **16:**343–346.

Smith, Ewart E., and Stanford S. Knight. (1959) "Effects of Feedback on Insight and Problem Solving Efficiency in Training Groups," *Journal of Applied Psychology,* **43:**209–211.

Sommer, Robert. (1969) *Personal Space: The Behavioral Basis of Design.* Englewood Cliffs, N.J.: Prentice-Hall.

Stock, Dorothy, and Herbert A. Thelen. (1958) *Emotional Dynamics and Group Culture: Experimental Studies of Individual and Group Behavior.* New York: New York University Press.

Streufert, Siegfried. (1969) "Increasing Failure and Response Rate in Complex Decision Making," *Journal of Experimental Social Psychology,* **5:**310–323.

Talland, George A. (1955) "Task and Interaction Process: Some Characteristics of Therapeutic Group Discussion," *Journal of Abnormal and Social Psychology,* **50:**105–109.

Tallman, Irving. (1970) "The Family as a Small Problem Solving Group," *Journal of Marriage and the Family,* **32:**94–104.

Thayer, Lee. (1968) *Communication and Communication Systems.* Homewood, Ill.: Irwin.

Theodorson, George A. (1962) "The Function of Hostility in Small Groups," *Journal of Social Psychology,* **56:**57–66.

Thibaut, John W., and Harold H. Kelley. (1959) *The Social Psychology of Groups.* New York: Wiley.

Tolar, Alexander. (1970) "The 'Natural Course' View of Conflict Resolution," *Psychological Reports,* **26:**734.

Torrance, E. Paul. (1957) "Group Decision Making and Disagreement," *Social Forces,* **35:**314–318.

Tuckman, Bruce W. (1965) "Developmental Sequence in Small Groups," *Psychological Bulletin,* **63:**384–399.

Turk, H. (1961) "Instrumental and Expressive Ratings Reconsidered," *Sociometry,* **24:**76–81.

Valentine, Kristin B., and B. Aubrey Fisher. (1974) "An Interaction Analysis of Verbal Innovative Deviance in Small Groups," *Speech Monographs,* **41:**413–420.

Verba, Sydney. (1961) *Small Groups and Political Behavior.* Princeton, N.J.: Princeton University Press.

Watson, Carol. (1977) "Sex-Typing and Androgyny: Conceptualization and Measurement." A paper presented to Speech Communication Association, Washington, D.C.

Watzlawick, Paul, Janet H. Beavin, and Don D. Jackson. (1967) *Pragmatics of Human Communication.* New York: Norton.

Weick, Karl E. (1969) *The Social Psychology of Organizing.* Reading, Mass.: Addison-Wesley.

Weick, Karl E. (1968) "Systematic Observational Methods," in Gardner Lindzey and Elliot Aronson (eds.), *The Handbook of Social Psychology,* vol. II, 2d ed. Reading, Mass.: Addison-Wesley, pp. 357–451.

Williams, Frederick. (1970) "Analysis of Verbal Behavior," in Philip Emmert and William D. Brooks (eds.), *Methods of Research in Communication.* Boston: Houghton Mifflin, pp. 237–290.

Williams, J. Sherwood, Lewis N. Gray, and Maxmilian H. von Broembsen. (1976) "Proactivity and Reinforcement: The Contingency of Social Behavior," *Small Group Behavior,* **7:**317–330.

Williams, J. Sherwood, J. David Martin, and Lewis N. Gray. (1975) "Norm Formation or Conditioning? A Study in Divergence," *Small Group Behavior,* **6:**141–150.

Wilson, Stephen R. (1970) "Some Factors Influencing Instrumental and Expressive Ratings in Task-Oriented Groups," *Pacific Sociological Review,* **13:**127–131.

Wood, Julia T. (1977) "Leading in Purposive Discussions: A Study of Adaptive Behavior," *Communication Monographs,* **44:**152–165.

Yerby, Janet. (1975) "Attitude, Task, and Sex Composition as Variables Affecting Female Leadership in Small Problem-Solving Groups," *Speech Monographs,* **42:**160–168.

Zaleznik, Abraham, and David Moment. (1964) *The Dynamics of Interpersonal Behavior.* New York: Wiley.

# Index